KV-371-306

IPv6 Mandates

DBS Library

67026

WL 004.62 Sii

This book is due for return on or before the last date shown below.

IPv6 Mandates

Choosing a Transition Strategy,
Preparing Transition Plans, and
Executing the Migration
of a Network to IPv6

Karl A. Siil

WILEY

Wiley Publishing, Inc.

IPv6 Mandates

Published by
Wiley Publishing, Inc.
10475 Crosspoint Boulevard
Indianapolis, IN 46256
www.wiley.com

Copyright © 2008 by Wiley Publishing, Inc., Indianapolis, Indiana
Published by Wiley Publishing, Inc., Indianapolis, Indiana
Published simultaneously in Canada

ISBN: 978-0-470-19119-4

Manufactured in the United States of America

10 9 8 7 6 5 4 3 2 1

No part of this publication may be reproduced, stored in a retrieval system or transmitted in any form or by any means, electronic, mechanical, photocopying, recording, scanning or otherwise, except as permitted under Sections 107 or 108 of the 1976 United States Copyright Act, without either the prior written permission of the Publisher, or authorization through payment of the appropriate per-copy fee to the Copyright Clearance Center, 222 Rosewood Drive, Danvers, MA 01923, (978) 750-8400, fax (978) 646-8600. Requests to the Publisher for permission should be addressed to the Legal Department, Wiley Publishing, Inc., 10475 Crosspoint Blvd., Indianapolis, IN 46256, (317) 572-3447, fax (317) 572-4355, or online at http://www.wiley.com/go/permissions.

Limit of Liability/Disclaimer of Warranty: The publisher and the author make no representations or warranties with respect to the accuracy or completeness of the contents of this work and specifically disclaim all warranties, including without limitation warranties of fitness for a particular purpose. No warranty may be created or extended by sales or promotional materials. The advice and strategies contained herein may not be suitable for every situation. This work is sold with the understanding that the publisher is not engaged in rendering legal, accounting, or other professional services. If professional assistance is required, the services of a competent professional person should be sought. Neither the publisher nor the author shall be liable for damages arising herefrom. The fact that an organization or Website is referred to in this work as a citation and/or a potential source of further information does not mean that the author or the publisher endorses the information the organization or Website may provide or recommendations it may make. Further, readers should be aware that Internet Websites listed in this work may have changed or disappeared between when this work was written and when it is read.

For general information on our other products and services or to obtain technical support, please contact our Customer Care Department within the U.S. at (800) 762-2974, outside the U.S. at (317) 572-3993 or fax (317) 572-4002.

Library of Congress Cataloging-in-Publication Data is available from the publisher.

Trademarks: Wiley and the Wiley logo are trademarks or registered trademarks of John Wiley & Sons, Inc. and/or its affiliates, in the United States and other countries, and may not be used without written permission. All other trademarks are the property of their respective owners. Wiley Publishing, Inc., is not associated with any product or vendor mentioned in this book.

Wiley also publishes its books in a variety of electronic formats. Some content that appears in print may not be available in electronic books.

About The Author

Karl Siil is a Senior Research Engineer, Development and Program Manager on SRI International's C4ISR team. He leads SRI's development efforts in Information Assurance for the Engineering and Systems Division. Karl has more than 25 years of experience in Information Technology and has been fortunate enough to be part of the industry's growth and change in numerous capacities, including network management, software development, and computer and network security. He is a subject matter expert both in IPv6 and the OMB-mandated federal transition and has spoken on IPv6 and the importance of well-managed transition at SecureGOV, CSI, RSA Europe, and AFCEA conferences. Karl has also participated in numerous IPv6 panels for government and industry organizations. Before joining SRI, Karl was a founding member and Chief Architect for Lumeta Corporation. Karl enjoyed a seven-year career at Lumeta during which he created and managed the company's Professional Services Organization, designed Lumeta's flagship IPsonar product, and established the IPv6 Internet Mapping Project to track IPv6 adoption worldwide. Prior to Lumeta, Karl spent more than a decade working for Bell Laboratories (now AT&T Laboratories) developing secure operating systems, consumer services, and next-generation networking platforms. Karl holds a BE in electrical engineering from The Cooper Union and an ME in electrical engineering from Manhattan College. He currently lives in Princeton, NJ with his wife and two children. Karl enjoys flying and holds a commercial pilot's license with instrument, multi-engine, and seaplane ratings.

Credits

Executive Editor
Carol Long

Development Editor
Christopher J. Rivera

Production Editor
Elizabeth Ginns Britten

Copy Editor
Kim Cofer

Editorial Manager
Mary Beth Wakefield

Production Manager
Tim Tate

**Vice President and Executive
Group Publisher**
Richard Swadley

**Vice President and Executive
Publisher**
Joseph B. Wikert

Project Coordinator, Cover
Lynsey Stanford

Compositor
Craig Thomas,
Happenstance Type-O-Rama

Proofreader
Sossity Smith

Indexer
Jack Lewis

Cover Design
Ryan Sneed

Cover Art
© Creatas Images/Jupiter Images

Contents

Preface

I discovered IPv6 in the summer of 2004. I don't recall exactly why IPv6 caught my eye, but when it did I realized it was going to be important to the company I was with at the time. We did network and asset discovery on very large enterprise intranets. What that meant was that we had tools that would find the paths through a network, producing a map of the network topology. We would then find as many assets as we could by interrogating every IP address in the network address ranges that the customer gave us. A large customer might have 18 Class 'A' networks, which amounts to more than 300 million addresses. Though a huge address space, our tools could cover it in less than a week, whereas our competition could take weeks or even months.

When I discovered IPv6, the first thing I realized was that this new protocol, with its vast address spaces and auto-configuration, would change how everybody did network management. It was something my company would have to consider sooner or later, because we couldn't brute-force test every IPv6 address like we did IPv4 addresses. I decided to take one of our tools, port it to IPv6, and experiment with whatever IPv6 networks I could find to see how they behaved compared to IPv4. This was by no means a priority in my company (or anywhere), because any mandatory IPv6 adoption was years away and nobody was interested in it in our circle of customers. That circle included many of the top financial, pharmaceutical, and other companies that are usually early adopters of technology, and not one of them cared one bit (never mind 128 bits) about IPv6. We had clients chuckle when we asked them about when they would adopt it.

Even the federal government, where we also had many customers, was not clamoring for IPv6 at that time. There was the occasional question about compatibility, but it never got to the point of affecting a sale. The government customers' concerns were more focused on our tools passing certain security accreditation criteria and supporting PKI and SNMPv3.

Still, I felt that IPv6 was something that my company shouldn't ignore only to be blindsided by it, even if that blindsiding might not come for years. I started a small pilot project, which is discussed with pilot projects in general in Chapter 13, "Using Pilot Programs to Facilitate Your IPv6 Transition." I worked part time on the project and was able to produce something workable by January 2005. The bulk of the effort occurred in late December and early January, because we had our company's annual meeting coming up and I wanted to have something ready to demo for that. I called it Project Mercury, named after the early U.S. space program. The goal of my project, as you can read in Chapter 13, was very similar to that of its 1960s namesake, in other words, prove that we and our tools could operate in alien space, in my case IPv6 address space.

Everything went great, and Mercury progressed to Gemini, which progressed to Apollo, which became the IPv6 Internet Mapping Project (I6MP), which has been surveying the IPv6 parts of the Internet autonomously since June 1, 2006. My goal was to get I6MP running unattended by that time in order to observe the 6BONE shutdown five days later. Other events that I6MP saw included the activation of China's CERNET2 network sometime in early 2005. CERNET2 was the largest IPv6 network at the time and still may be.

During all this time, I was also speaking on the inevitability of IPv6 and the "dark side" of the technology, which I termed "accidental adoption." Because so many routers, operating systems, and other network devices and software were IPv6 capable, and IPv6 was so good at auto-configuring, my concern was that pockets of IPv6 would start springing up in places where enterprise network managers didn't want them. The analogy it still brings to mind for me can be summed up in the quote from the book and movie *Jurassic Park*, "Life finds a way."

It was during one of these talks that Wiley approached me and felt that it was time for an IPv6 transition book. The June 2008 OMB mandate was starting to breathe down people's necks and there was a lot of Fear, Uncertainty, and Doubt regarding how to deploy IPv6 across the whole federal government, sanely. As you'll read shortly, that's whom this book is directed at, the CIOs and network managers of the hundreds of agencies that have to have IPv6 running (or able to be run) on their backbones pretty darn soon.

As such, this is not a book on technology as much as it is on the management of very large projects. Moreover, just like you can't write a detailed book on "How to Build a Space Program," this book doesn't try to tell you the exact steps for making the IPv6 transition of your network, because everyone reading it is running something different. What the book does try to do is teach best practices for approaching the classes of problems you will face during your IPv6 transition. There's also some tech-talk thrown in, but the heavy-duty technical topics defer to other sources, where you can find more thorough answers. There's some security stuff, too, and if you're into network security like I am, IPv6 is a gold mine.

Acknowledgments

I want to thank all of the people who helped get this book to completion, not only in its writing, but on the road to getting the opportunity to write it. Because I don't know if I'll ever get to do something like this again, I'll focus on the people who deserve the most credit. In that vein (cue the Oscar music), I would first like to thank Carol Long at Wiley for seeking me out and making all this possible. I would also like to thank Christopher Rivera and Liz Britten at Wiley for working with me to get the words and concepts just right. Going back to the start of the road that got me here, I would like to thank my grand-parents, who gave up a lot in order to raise me so that my parents could work to support us. We weren't quite Charlie Bucket's family, but it was close at times. To my dad I owe the fostering of my curiosity about technology, even the technology I shouldn't have been touching when he wasn't looking. To my mom, I would simply like to say that "I made it," because she wasn't around long enough for that outcome to be certain by any means. Finally, there's my wife, Diane, who stood by and smiled (sometimes through gritted teeth) as this project took place. To her I say, in the spirit of many other book dedications that I've seen, thanks for not freaking out (too much) at how long this took to complete and how little you saw me in 2007.

Introduction

Overview of the Book

This book is a practical guide through the process of upgrading an enterprise computer network to IPv6, a new version of one of the TCP/IP family of networking protocols used on the Internet and modern intranets. IPv6 has been mandated by the Office of Management and Budget (OMB) for the U.S. federal government to deploy, ideally by June 2008, and significant gaps in the knowledge of how to accomplish that have been discovered. This book fills the need to have a single reference source on how to undertake an IPv6 transition on an enterprise network scale.

This is not a book on technology, per se. There are numerous books and other references that get into the most minute details of IPv6 technology that make excellent companions to this book, and they are mentioned where appropriate, for working out the implementation specifics unique to each network's environment, mission, and budget. Sufficient technology is presented in this book to describe the classes of tasks to be undertaken, but the fine-grain details are outside its scope.

This is a book on how to undertake successfully a large-scale technology rollout, for which IPv6 is the chosen technology. It is about taking what appears to be a Herculean problem and reducing it to manageable parts, in some cases many parts, but all manageable ones. Possibly most important, this book is about managing a transition so that you know whether you're on track, and how to fix things if you're not.

The book guides the reader through choosing a transition strategy, preparing transition plans, and finally executing and verifying the transition of a network to IPv6. Common transition tasks, as well as risks and limitations of IPv6 and its deployment are also covered. Several checklists are provided to facilitate the reader's IPv6 transition and assure complete coverage of what must be done. A short case study documents my experiences porting a complex network management application to IPv6, mostly to show that it can be done with far fewer resources than some would have you believe. The book concludes with guidance on how to maintain your newly IPv6-capable network and keep it operational and secure.

How This Book Is Organized

The book is separated into four parts containing related chapters. The parts explain

- IPv6 basics,
- How to plan, execute, and verify an IPv6 transition,
- What you need to facilitate your transition, and,
- Managing your network after a transition has been completed.

Each part of the book builds on the preceding parts. You are expected to be knowledgeable about TCP/IP networking and large enterprise networks in general. You are not expected to know much about IPv6. The first part of the book provides a general introduction and then refers to external sources to complete your training. You'll find that the technology itself, though important, is not critical to how you adopt it. This book could have been written about one of any number of large-scale technology rollouts and much of the contents would have remained the same.

Chapter 1 introduces you to the IPv6 universe. It describes the motivations behind why IPv6 is catching people's attention after so many years of dormancy (IPv6 has been around, at least in name, since the early 1990s), part of which is the exhaustion of IPv4 addresses. The chapter also describes how IPv6 enables new application architectures and facilitates network configuration and management. The chapter introduces the federal mandates that are driving IPv6 adoption in the U.S. federal government and that drove, to some extent, the creation of this book. The chapter also introduces other motivators of IPv6 adoption, like Microsoft's IPv6 push with Vista and the plethora of IPv6 adoption-promoting organizations.

Chapter 2 presents an introduction to the mechanics of IPv6. If you are already knowledgeable about IPv6, you can probably skip most of this chapter. You should still read the section on auto-configuration. Auto-configuration comes up several more times in the book, mostly in regard to the risks that it introduces to your network, but also occasionally in how it simplifies network management. This chapter also provides a large address-space analogy or two, for example how many IPv6 addresses fit on the head of a pin. Such comparisons have become a standard part of any work on IPv6 and I'm not one to rock the boat.

Chapter 3 concludes the introduction to the basics and presents the state of the art in IPv6 including world-wide IPv6 adoption statistics. The statistics are provided to encourage those undertaking your IPv6 transition by showing that IPv6 is truly being adopted, rather than just sitting in a lab somewhere. The chapter also alerts you that the bad guys have taken notice of IPv6 and that there are already hacking tools out there to exploit the new technology. Finally, Chapter 3 provides an assessment of what IPv6 hacking tools are out there.

Chapter 4 starts Part II of the book and gets into the meat of your IPv6 transition work. The chapter starts by diffusing some of the Fear, Uncertainty, and Doubt (FUD) surrounding IPv6, especially in the federal agencies. The chapter continues by helping you select the type and rate of IPv6 transition that's right for you and your enterprise. The chapter describes the abilities and limitations of IPv6 transition mechanisms available for you to combine into solutions that fit your needs. Furthermore, it teaches you how to decide when and in what order to apply them.

Chapter 5 is about planning. It introduces project planning concepts and what has to be taken into account specifically when creating your IPv6 transition plan. For seasoned project managers, some of the chapter may be old news, but a quick refresher never hurts. Moreover, the chapter focuses far more on applying planning concepts to an IPv6 transition and the typical pitfalls of such planning, than it does on teaching planning basics.

Chapter 6 discusses how to inventory the hardware and software assets on your network and, more importantly, what services or capabilities those assets provide to your network's users. You'll learn how to decide the disposition of each asset in the post-transition network configuration. The chapter also discusses communicating the plans you're developing to everyone involved, how to schedule transition events to minimize the chance of network disruption, and how to get the approvals you'll need to start your IPv6 transition and keep it going.

Chapter 7 covers some tasks common to every IPv6 transition. You will learn that IPv6 addresses have more rules regarding their allocation and use than do IPv4 addresses. The chapter describes how to organize your IPv6 addresses into a numbering plan and how to develop network hierarchies. The chapter also discusses whether you should deploy IPsec alongside your IPv6 transition, and provides you with the means to decide if IPsec is something you need to consider. The chapter concludes with an analysis of how IPv6 affects your network bandwidth needs followed by a discussion of some of the details of advanced IPv6 features introduced earlier in the book.

Chapter 8 covers what you need to know to execute your IPv6 transition. The chapter covers organizing all the tasks you planned in the previous chapters into groups of activities containing work items and executing in maintenance windows. You'll learn how to identify and resolve dependencies between tasks and how to use the knowledge of those dependencies to put your tasks into an optimal order for execution. The chapter concludes with some final tasks you must perform before you can start your transition activities, the last task being informing everyone who needs to know that you're finally ready to get started.

Chapter 9 discusses verifying the results of your transition activities to make sure that everything turned out as planned. The chapter describes how to fit verification steps into your IPv6 transition activities. You'll also learn to identify the causes of verification failures and what steps you need to take to recover. The chapter wraps up by reminding you to clean up any loose ends from your transition activities or their verification, and to tell all the affected parties that your activities are complete and how they went.

Chapter 10 covers the risks associated with an IPv6 transition, and encourages you to seek out answers to your IPv6 security questions by directing you to venues where you can get your questions answered. The chapter also points out the potential for bugs to have been introduced into IPv6 implementations, thereby complicating the theoretical risks with vendor-specific risks. The chapter ends by analyzing some of the risks associated with Mobile IPv6, which is something you may be considering now or for future network upgrades.

While Part II of this book covers the mechanics of IPv6 transition planning, execution, and verification, Part III covers ways in which you can make your transition easier. It also covers alternative transition strategies and the use of small-scale pilot programs for you to learn more about IPv6 before committing to it wholesale within your network.

Chapter 11 focuses on one of the most important prerequisites for a successful IPv6 transition, the inventorying of your network's assets. The chapter discusses how to deploy a comprehensive asset discovery solution, including the benefits of using automated tools. The chapter describes how to integrate asset discovery tools with asset management tools. For both asset discovery and management tools, the chapter highlights specific tools on the market today. The chapter concludes with a discussion of what you need to think about if no commercial or open-source tools suit you and you want to create your own tools.

Chapter 12 looks at IPv6 transition strategies from another perspective. The chapter explores outside the bounds of the OMB mandates and discusses the benefits of isolated pockets of more comprehensive, not just network backbone, IPv6 adoption within an enterprise. The motivations for such forms of IPv6 transition are also described.

Chapter 13 describes IPv6-focused pilot projects, a form of research used to vet capabilities for your enterprise before committing to full-scale deployment of those capabilities. You'll learn how to set up and execute a successful pilot project, how to measure the pilot project's successes, and how to prepare for potential failures. After learning about pilots in general, the chapter drills down on software pilots and their particular idiosyncrasies, concluding by relating the story of a real-life software pilot that applied the principles this chapter recommends.

Part IV covers the management of your network after an IPv6 transition is complete. Chapter 14 covers the issues that were applicable to your pre-transition network and that are still applicable post-transition, for example flawed applications and how to protect them on an IPv6 network.

Chapter 15 introduces some concepts for managing your newly IPv6-capable and your pre-transition IPv4-only network segments together. The chapter explains why heterogeneous networks can work together and then discusses how to think of such networks as combinations of independent entities, rather than as one big heterogeneous infrastructure.

Chapter 16 concludes the main body of the book by discussing how to track your network's configuration and traffic with audit and logging tools. The chapter also discusses keeping your network configurations up to date based on what you learn about IPv6, including any new vulnerabilities, and your needs for IPv6 as time goes on and you get more used to running an IPv6 network.

Who Should Read this Book

This book is directed primarily at the network managers of the hundreds of U.S. federal agencies that are mandated to have IPv6 running (or able to be run) on their backbones in short order. Equally affected are the network managers of the vendors that support those agencies, because the vendors will have to adopt IPv6 equally quickly, if not faster, to support the government transitions.

In addition to the primary audience, this book serves as a valuable resource for anyone undertaking the deployment of IPv6 into their enterprise network. Though you may manage the network of a commercial company and feel that IPv6 isn't in your future, I assure you that it is, and it's probably much closer than you expect. Once the federal transitions start to complete and the large defense contractors and Internet Service Providers (ISPs) that support the government are IPv6 capable, which is already happening, IPv6 adoption will become much easier and other companies will start to deploy IPv6, if only to keep up with the (Dow) Joneses. Coupling the preceding factors with the imminent depletion of IPv4 addresses, and the aggressive deployment of IPv6 in Eastern Asia and Europe, IPv6 adoption in the rest of the world is inevitable.

The ideal reader for this book is a network manager tasked with the daunting task of planning a transition of his or her enterprise's network to IPv6 and executing that plan. The reader needs some knowledge of TCP/IP networking internals, including packet headers and protocols. Much more so, however, the reader needs a fairly solid foundation in enterprise network management. Little or no IPv6 knowledge is required for the reader on starting the book, because the book describes what IPv6 features and functionalities it needs to and refers to more detailed technical sources when necessary.

There is something in every part and chapter of this book for every reader, but there are also some shortcuts that you can take. If you're familiar with IPv6 technology and the OMB mandates, you can comfortably skip or just thumb through Part I. If you're comfortable in your skills managing large MIS/IT projects, you can give Chapter 5 a cursory glance, versus a thorough read. If you're focused purely on what OMB is requiring you to do, you can skip Chapter 12 on alternative transition strategies and Chapter 13 on IPv6 pilot projects, because they pertain to activities you probably will not undertake.

Where Do You Go from Here?

If deploying IPv6 is something you need to do, either because OMB is requiring it of you, or the trickle-down effects of government adoption have finally reached your commercial enterprise, then this book is intended to make your life easier. I recommend you browse through the whole book once, from beginning to end, to immerse yourself in the IPv6 mindset and get a strategic view of what's required for deploying IPv6 on an enterprise-wide scale. Once you have that strategic view of how your IPv6 transition should start, run, and complete, then come back to the beginning of Part II and start preparing your plans for actually doing the transition work. From there, you can progress linearly through the rest of Part II. Keep the tips you learned in Part III in mind as you put your plans together and execute them.

No matter how you choose to tackle your IPv6 transition, the main thing for you to keep in mind all the time is that you are an MIS/IT professional and rolling out IPv6 isn't much different from switching your enterprise to a new mail server application or network management tool. It's not easy, but you have done it or equally complex projects. Also, don't let all the FUD promoted in the press and by IPv6 naysayers spook you. Every technology has its warts, but the time for IPv6 has come, and it's better that you embrace it and enjoy your transition work rather than dread coming into work every day for the next few months. It's really not as bad as people make it out to be. Trust me. We run it in my enterprise and nobody notices it most of the time.

IPv6 Mandates

Starting with the Basics

What Is IPv6?

*There is only one thing in the world worse than
being talked about, and that is not being talked about.*

— Oscar Wilde

Somewhere between 1993 and 1995, the Internet started entering the everyday lives of the general public. As the number of websites grew rapidly in those early years, several different "Internet Yellow Pages" books where published to catalog the hundreds of new cyber-destinations to which to travel. These books appear to modern "surfers" more like fictional parodies than the serious reference works they were then. In today's Google/Yahoo world, the idea of going to a book to look up a website or newsgroup sounds as archaic as requiring a week to cross the Atlantic.

Nevertheless, in those bygone times of more than 10 years ago, a technology still associated with the future today was being forged. In December 1995, RFC 1883 presented one of the first introductions to a new internetworking protocol: IPv6.

Perhaps the architects of the Internet suspected a revolution was coming and the infrastructure that had served the networks of research labs and universities well for some 15 years wasn't going to be up to the task. Surprisingly IPv4, the fifth version of the defining protocol upon which the modern Internet is based, has held up an additional 10-plus years, but, change is in the air. Those interested in the predecessors of IPv4 can find a list of references for where to read about IPv0 (yes, there was a version 0) through IPv3 in RFC 762. The references are historical now, but Vint Cerf's and Jon Postel's early papers on IP are required reading for anyone curious about the how the Internet evolved.

Meet IPv6

Internet Protocol, version 6, or IPv6 for short, is the next step in the evolution of internetworking protocols. These are the packet-based network-layer core protocols responsible for moving information from one place to another on all IP-based networks, the largest and most popular such network being the Internet itself. No matter whether you are navigating a web page, sending e-mail, or downloading music, IP is the protocol that's moving the data.

From roughly 1980 to the present day, the fourth version of IP, IPv4, has been performing the heavy lifting. Conceived when there were no more than a few dozen interconnected systems, which were all cooperating with each other, IPv4 has been stretched far beyond what its designers could ever have hoped. Enter IPv6.

The next chapter seeks to demystify and explain some of the basics of IPv6 so that it can be looked at for what it is without all the Fear, Uncertainty, and Doubt (FUD), just another technology with good points and bad ones. After that, the IPv6 landscape of usage, deployment rates, and future predictions, as it exists today, is described. None of these topics is the main purpose of this book. After the modest IPv6 primer, including lists of references from which to gather the details, the rest of the book addresses one of the least understood and most feared aspects of IPv6: how to make the transition to it from the current networking technologies.

Making the Transition from IPv4 to IPv6

In 1980, it was pretty easy to upgrade from IPv4's predecessor. The total number of systems to be upgraded was less than that found nowadays in a typical small company or branch office of fewer than 100 employees. The system administrators, who often also happened to be the network programmers, all knew each other, for the most part, and the network could be upgraded in unison with minimal process or synchronization. Furthermore, if a mistake were made, the consequences were, well, inconsequential. None of these systems was critical to the world economy, national defense, or any essential communications fabrics, but, it's not 1980 any more.

Anyone in network operations or management knows that all but the most minimal of changes to mission-critical systems and infrastructure requires huge amounts of planning. A priori agreements between all stakeholders as to what to do, when to do it, and how to recover to a sane state should there be a failure along the way are par for the course. It's at worst a mild exaggeration to say that, for most large modern networks, millions (if not billions) of dollars, the defense of nations, and the abilities of first-responders to save lives are dependent on whether those networks continue to function. Getting from IPv4 to IPv6 while still keeping the lights on is what this book is all about.

IPv6 is destined to become the dominant networking protocol, but this won't happen overnight. In fact, the early days of world-wide transition, that is, right now, are fraught with peril. There will be those who leap into IPv6 with both feet, not taking the necessary precautions required with the enterprise-wide adoption of any new technology. There will be those who think they are only putting their toe in the water, only to find that they're up to their necks from a lack of planning or understanding the technology's capabilities. This book seeks to identify the risks, offer mitigation strategies for them, and generally help navigate around the pitfalls that can occur during a poorly planned or executed transition.

Looking beyond IPv6

An article published in Japan in 1996 was entitled "IPv6: The Final Frontier." Yet, for the next 10 years we barely set foot in that frontier. When we do finally become fully entrenched in IPv6, it should hardly be expected to be a final frontier by any student of the history of technology. Even so, computer networks are certainly entering a brave new world with the maturing of this latest version of IP.

We should expect to take a while to move to IPv6 and we should expect to stay on it for some time, as well. After all, IPv4 has lasted more than a quarter of a century, which is something you can be pretty sure its inventors weren't expecting in 1980. Even with its long and promising future, though, IPv6 is no more the end in networking evolution than sailing ships were in trans-Atlantic travel.

Who Should Read This Book?

This book is a practical guide through the process of upgrading complex IPv4-based networks to IPv6. The primary audience consists of network managers and the MIS/IT staff responsible for taking care of an enterprise's networks. A secondary audience includes CIOs and other senior IT managers responsible for the strategic decisions in network configuration, operations, and management.

A key group within the primary audience is the set of network managers and designers employed by or contracted to the U.S. federal government. It has been mandated that the federal government make the transition to IPv6 by June 2008, but there are significant gaps in knowledge about how to accomplish that task. This book fills the need to have a single reference source on how to upgrade networks the size of those used by even the largest of government agencies to IPv6.

The ideal reader is a network manager overwhelmed with the daunting task of planning and executing a transition of his or her network to IPv6. This book is meant for such a person to get a grasp of what needs to be done and get started doing it.

This is a book on project management. It is about taking what appears to be a Herculean problem and reducing it to manageable parts, in some cases many parts, but all manageable ones. It is about assessing the current state of your networks, defining plans for how you want them to make the transition and when and how you want them to do so. Possibly most importantly, this book is about managing a transition so that you know whether you're on track, and how to fix it if you're not.

This is not a book on technology. There are numerous books on IPv6 technology that make excellent companions to this one for working out the implementation specifics unique to each network's environment, mission, and budget. Sufficient technology is presented in this book to describe the classes of tasks to be undertaken, but the details are outside its scope. The reader should have knowledge of TCP/IP networking, including routing, tunneling, firewalls, and the troubleshooting of networking problems. At the end of this chapter, further reading on these topics is offered.

Why IPv6?

A fair question to ask is that, if IPv4 has lasted so long, why the sudden need for IPv6? The federal mandates in particular are considered by some to have been put forth by the Office of Management and Budget (OMB) from out of the blue. There are, however, several good reasons for why this is the right time to move to IPv6.

Addressing Every PC, Cell Phone, and Toaster

Demand for Internet-enabled devices is accelerating rapidly and that growth requires the use of more IP addresses. In total, there are approximately 4 billion total addresses in the IPv4 address space, that is, 32-bits worth or 2^{32} addresses. Up until fairly recently, IP addresses have been primarily used for computers, ranging from PCs to mainframes. That's changed in the past few years and will continue to do so as huge new categories of Internet-enabled devices become available.

The cellular communications industry is tying at least one IP address to each of millions of phones, pagers, and PDAs. Internet-enabled smart automobiles and appliances such as refrigerators and washing machines are being developed that can, for example, contact their manufacturer when a fault occurs. Cable television companies are looking to use IP features known as *multicast* to distribute video on demand to millions of set-top cable boxes. That requires each set-top box to have at least one IP address. Given that 82 percent of all IPv4 addresses have already been allocated (per `http://www.potaroo.net/tools/ipv4/`, as of May 9, 2007), there's not much room left for growth in all these new areas.

Further Extending the Uses of IP Addresses

The preceding are some of the nearer-term uses of the Internet, and therefore IP addresses, above and beyond the current uses by traditional computers. There are other concepts, further out, that foresee using IP addresses as identifiers to tag mass-produced items like medicine bottles, articles of clothing, supermarket shopping carts, and so on. Clearly, such concepts, even if only a few are developed to maturity, place a great load on the available IP address space.

To offer one final perspective, according to the U.S. Census Bureau's website (`http://www.census.gov/main/www/popclock.html`), there are approximately 302 million people in the United States and 6.6 billion people in the world as of May 2007. The Japan Network Information Center (JPNIC) published a report in March 2006 analyzing the IPv4 space exhaustion matter (`http://www.nic.ad.jp/en/research/IPv4exhaustion_trans-pub.pdf` offers an English translation of that report). According to JPNIC, the United States is assigned nearly 60 percent of the available IPv4 address space while the Census Bureau reports that the United States accounts for less than 5 percent of the world population. As the underdeveloped nations of the world become more connected to the Internet, it is clear there are not enough IPv4 addresses.

Predicting the Exhaustion of IPv4 Addresses

There has been a continuing debate for decades on how long the IPv4 address space will last. This debate and the ongoing fears of address-space exhaustion looming in the near future have been the primary reasons that IPv6 has endured so many years despite no significant adoption by commercial networks. Per the JPNIC report mentioned earlier, it has been generally agreed to by experts in the field that IPv4 addresses will run out some time between 2009 and 2016. When weighed against transition projects that themselves can take years to plan, fund, and execute, 2009 is right around the corner and even 2016 is starting to get uncomfortably close.

Easing Network Load

A side-effect of increased IP address space allocation is increased network load. This is beyond just increased network traffic. It also applies to the increased amount of overhead in the routing infrastructure that determines how to get IP packets from one place to another.

The world-wide allocation of IP addresses today has evolved over decades of organic growth and, therefore, huge lists representing hundreds of thousands of network routes must be maintained in all Internet routers in order for those routers to know how to forward a packet to a particular IP address. The IP address ranges in a given region, especially in Europe and Asia, are far from contiguous, requiring more route entries to represent all of the distinct non-connected blocks.

Defining a World-Wide Networking Hierarchy

In contrast to the organic deployment that IPv4 saw, the IPv6 address allocation scheme implements a more hierarchical structure that greatly reduces the size of the network route lists. Regions (for example, the Americas, Europe, Asia, Africa, and so on) are allocated IPv6 addresses in huge blocks, which is only possible due to the vast address space provided by IPv6. These huge allocations reduce the number of times each region must return to the world-wide central authority to request more addresses. They also reduce the number of network routes that each router needs to remember in order to forward traffic to another region.

Though it's a bit of an oversimplification, one can imagine the IPv6 allocation scheme as requiring a regional router to know only roughly as many network routes as there are continents or macroscopic geo-political entities. This is far different from an IPv4 regional router needing to know about what looks like every country, company, town, and hamlet.

The concepts used in the regional hierarchy are replicated at the national and, if necessary, the local level for individual countries in regions, and for Internet Service Providers (ISPs) in those countries. In this way, the complexities of underlying or far away routing infrastructures are hidden from any given router and that router needs only worry about forwarding any given packet either further down into the region/locale they service or to a peer region/locale. Routers below the regional level must also know how to forward traffic upward to the next larger level of hierarchy, but presumably there are not many of those upward routes, either. Ignoring system redundancy for a moment, one would be enough. It's more likely, however, that there will be more like two or three, still a far cry from hundreds.

Routing Each Packet Faster

By reducing the size of the network route lists, IP packets are forwarded faster. Another improvement in routing efficiency over IPv4 that IPv6 offers is the use of a constant-size packet header. Instead of combining seldom-used options as part of a single variable-length IPv4 header, IPv6's core capabilities are augmented using optional extensions providing security, custom routing features, and even vendor or application-specific options defined only at the packet's ultimate destination.

The vast majority of IPv6 packets require no extension headers and, therefore, the amount of processing to forward those packets is minimal. As an example, one computation that must be performed by every router on an IPv4 packet is determination of the IP header length. This computation is eliminated in IPv6, which is especially valuable in implementing the protocol in firmware.

Enabling the Future

A great many of the lessons learned from IPv4's shortcomings went into the design of IPv6. The increase in address space size and the extensibility of the core protocol via additional sub-headers was introduced earlier. The next chapter presents a few more details of each. More important than the implementation details, however, are the new classes of network architectures that such features enable.

Getting Rid of NAT

As IPv4 address space rarified, a scheme known as Network Address Translation (NAT) was introduced both to extend the use of the remaining address space and to introduce an additional level of security. Weighing the value of any security benefits derived from NAT versus the additional hassles of managing it is left for the next section. What is more important here is that NAT broke one of the initial principles of the IP protocol: that any device could directly address any other device.

The ability for any networked device to address and communicate with any other networked device is central to the concept of peer-to-peer (P2P) networking. True P2P distributes computing load, as well as storage and network bandwidth requirements across all the devices using an application, typically in proportion to each device's capabilities/limitations. Partly due to NAT, few true P2P applications exist, at present.

Understanding What P2P Means Today

Early P2P-like applications include the plethora of instant messaging services offered by many different providers. Because NAT makes it all but impossible for most peers to have network connections originated to them, the implementation choice has been to place central servers on the Internet, which everyone can reach. For the application to be available, these servers must be available. As such, they are built to be highly redundant and require vast amounts of processing capabilities, storage, and network bandwidth. The applications look far more like 1980's client/server, than P2P.

Implementing True P2P

Because IPv6 eliminates the address space constraints of IPv4, every device in the world can have its own unique address. In fact, each device will likely have several IP addresses. NAT can be eliminated where security is not a concern, such as in residential ISPs. In security-sensitive environments, NAT can be replaced with other IPv6 capabilities, like IPSEC, and with other emerging security architectures like Cisco's NAC and Microsoft's NAP. All of that is, however, outside the scope of this book.

Without the limitations of NAT, a true P2P instant messaging service needs only a handful of minimal directory servers with some redundancy for service availability, but nowhere near what is required now. In fact, for conversations between application users who already know about each other, the central servers need not even be involved. Eliminating that constraint alone is akin to the technological leap brought on by direct-dial telephones, versus the old days of hoping "Mable" was at the switchboard and could connect you at 2:00 a.m. The potential for business applications, not just consumer ones, is staggering.

Eliminating Configuration Hassles

Anyone who has deployed an IP network knows it's not a trivial endeavor. It's much easier than it was before the advent of the Dynamic Host Configuration Protocol (DHCP), but there's still a bit to be done.

Setting Up an IP Network Today

Assuming you already know what address space you're using, you need to configure at least one router if you're connecting to the Internet or some other network. The easiest way you can assign addresses within your network is by using DHCP. Even then, you'll have to "hardwire" the addresses of your externally facing machines, for example, your DNS, e-mail, and web server(s).

For security or logging reasons, you may want to hardwire many or all of your devices. This is often done to facilitate the administration of firewall rules and is typically achieved by binding each device's hardware MAC address with a specific IP address. For all but the smallest networks, such IP address lifecycle management, as it is commonly called, is non-trivial and there are several vendors out there that make a good living selling sophisticated products to help manage the process.

If you've been given fewer addresses than you have devices, a situation that is highly likely given the stinginess of ISPs nowadays, you'll have to use NAT if you want more devices to have access than you have IP addresses allocated to you. That's more firewall administration, plus you'll probably have to implement separate internal and external DNS services for some fraction of your devices.

Why Can't It Be Like Setting Up Switches?

Compare all of the preceding work with setting up your LAN switches. Assume that your office space occupies three floors of a building with a router in the basement that connects to the outside world. Each floor has its own dedicated interface on the router. In addition, you want to daisy-chain a number of smaller switches on each floor, rather than dedicating one big switch. Such a decision can be driven by a need for redundancy or thriftiness.

Now, assuming you're not going to use any VLANs, set up the switches. That means plugging a switch into the router interface, plugging any downstream switches into the first switch, and so on. Then, plug the end devices into the appropriate switches. That's it. You're done. The switches auto-configure, negotiating among themselves how they will move traffic between end devices and the router, and you're ready to go in a few seconds. The switches could all be from different vendors. They could be different models. It doesn't matter. Excluding running cables, racking equipment, and plugging things in, you've probably spent 1 percent of your time on configuring the switching and 99 percent on the routing. Is there a better way?

Setting Up IPv6 (Almost) as Easily as Setting Up Switches

Fast forward a few years and imagine yourself adding an IPv6 segment to your newly transitioned enterprise network. First of all, there is no NAT, because you have more than enough addresses for all your devices. As far as the security that NAT offered, that's always been questionable, because a security feature requiring complex administration is usually a wash. NAT has been replaced with more straight-forward firewall rules that forbid incoming traffic to all but a few select devices, typically your DNS, mail, and web server(s).

Your outbound firewall rules are what they would have been with NAT, except you no longer have to juggle pre-NAT and post-NAT addresses in your head while trying to assess if the rules are correct.

To hook up your router to the (IPv6) Internet or the enterprise WAN, you mostly just need to connect it and configure what networks are on what interfaces. IPv6 features like Neighbor Discovery and, by the time the protocol is as prevalent as IPv4 is today, Secure Neighbor Discovery, take care of much of the rest. Once connected and powered up, the new router will seek out its neighbors and establish connectivity automatically.

Hooking up the hosts to the router is simplified by DHCPv6, and MAC/IP address binding is accomplished by something called EUI-64, which takes a device's MAC address and automatically computes a unique and static IP address for that device. For devices with multiple interfaces, unique IP addresses are computed for each interface.

Is the preceding oversimplified? Yes, somewhat. Every network has its own requirements and limitations based on its mission, security profile, and so on. Many statically routed mission-critical networks will likely turn off much of the auto-configuration stuff, partly because of reasons recommended later in this very book. For many other networks, the administrators' lives will become far easier because of such auto-configuration features, and by the multitude of network management tools that will come about based on them as IPv6 is deployed more widely and markets for such tools are created.

Ensuring Quality of Service

The advent of streaming audio/video and Internet telephony created a demand for the ability to control Quality of Service (QoS) at the session level. Being packet based, IP networks don't implicitly support bandwidth management. IPv4's definition included an 8-bit Type of Service (ToS) field in the header to implement grades of service, but the field's original definition never came into widespread use.

The Differentiated Services (DS) model, introduced in RFC 2474, redefined the ToS field into what could be called Gold, Silver, Bronze, and best-effort grades of service for IP traffic. That definition of the bits also applies to the IPv6 Traffic Class field. In addition to Traffic Class, IPv6 was designed with the ability to define sessions or *flows* and, therefore, set quality of service parameters for them at routers along the flows' paths.

The IPv6 combination of Traffic Class and flows makes for a superior ability to manage session QoS, but only time will tell how well these models catch on. According to *The Internet Journal*, published quarterly by Cisco Systems, Inc., as of September 2006, the DS model isn't in widespread use in IPv4 or IPv6 (see *The Internet Protocol Journal*. Volume 9, Number 3, Cisco Systems, Inc., September 2006).

What Is Driving IPv6 Transition?

The federal government is the greatest driver of IPv6 transition in the United States. Leading the charge, the Defense Department is moving forward with IPv6 in a big way. Current plans are for the deployment of millions of IPv6 addresses on each individual soldier (and tank, aircraft, ship, and so on). As such, the government is demanding IPv6-compliant products and, eventually, for vendors to move to IPv6. That demand will eventually cause a trickle-down effect into the commercial sector as defense contractors and other vendors serving the government make the transition to IPv6. They will, in turn, motivate the vendors that serve them to change, and so on.

Despite the fears of IPv4 address space exhaustion and all the benefits of transition cited previously, IPv6 in the commercial sector has been slow to catch on. This is likely due to the fact that no "killer application" has come along to-date to clearly dictate a business need for transition. These applications, especially P2P ones, are starting to emerge now, especially with the recent release of Microsoft's Windows Vista product.

Those outside the U.S. have been motivated to move to IPv6 for some time, partly because emerging technological powers like China have little legacy infrastructure to preserve or change and strong government-mandated direction to implement leading-edge technologies. Also, the address space given out decades ago for IPv4 to non-U.S. interests was rather limited, so there's a stronger push overseas to expand. As other nations change, commercial businesses in the U.S., especially multi-nationals with Asian-Pacific offices, partners, vendors, or customers, may find themselves pulled into IPv6 by the need to connect to their corporate colleagues in that part of the world.

Understanding IPv6 Federal Mandates

OMB Memo M-05-22 was the document that got the IPv6 ball rolling in the federal government and what finally made IPv6 "hot" after so many years. The memorandum spells out actions required to be taken by federal agencies and when. Most of those target dates are in the past and the only remaining one in the future is the June 30, 2008 requirement that:

> "All agency infrastructures (network backbones) must be using IPv6 (meaning the network backbone is either operating a dual stack network core or it is operating in a pure IPv6 mode, i.e., IPv6-compliant and configured to carry operational IPv6 traffic) and agency networks must interface with this infrastructure."

OMB has been criticized for not being specific enough in its guidance regarding how to change to IPv6, especially as the mandate is unfunded (that is, there is no money set aside for the transition). Each agency's transition is expected to be incorporated as part of its normal technology refresh cycles. Other government bodies, including the Department of Commerce, GAO, and NIST have weighed in on the costs and risks of IPv6 transition and the Federal CIO Council continues to produce best practices and other guidance to help agencies meet the mandates.

Factoring in Microsoft Vista

Most mainstream network and end devices already support IPv6. These include the routers manufactured by all the major vendors, along with all the mainstream operating systems. Windows, Linux, Solaris, and a plethora of others have had IPv6 capabilities for some time. Windows Vista, out now, *prefers* to network using IPv6, out of the box. If a Vista system can find a router with IPv6 interfaces, it will form a network. Vista will likely be a primary driver in making IPv6 a ubiquitous and eventually dominant networking protocol.

Introducing the NAv6TF

In concert with the federal mandates and chartered by the world-wide IPv6 Forum, the North American IPv6 Task Force (NAv6TF) is an all-volunteer task force charged with promoting IPv6 in North America. NAV6TF's objectives are to:

- enhance the awareness of IPv6's capabilities
- advocate the integration of IPv6
- support the U.S. Government and its Departments and Agencies
- continue to drive and support IPv6 conferences and technical seminars in North America
- identify key application vendors and promote IPv6
- develop IPv6 deployment and readiness guides

For further information on NAv6TF, go to www.nav6tf.org.

Further Reading

Throughout the remainder of the book, further reading is recommended for topics discussed in the various chapters. For this chapter, the core RFCs defining key aspects of IPv6 are excellent sources for learning more about the capabilities of the new protocol. Some of those RFCs are:

- RFC 2460: IPv6 Specification. December, 1998.

- RFC 2463: ICMPv6 Specification. December, 1998.
- RFC 3493: Basic Socket Interface for IPv6. February, 2003.
- RFC 3542: Advanced Sockets API for IPv6. May, 2003.
- RFC 3596: DNS Extensions to Support IPv6. October, 2003.
- RFC 4213: Basic Transition Mechanisms for IPv6 Hosts and Routers. October, 2005.
- RFC 4291: IPv6 Addressing Architecture. February, 2006.
- RFC 4301: Security Architecture for the Internet Protocol. December, 2005.

The reader is encouraged to go to their favorite search engine and look for RFC and IPv6 together. An excellent source for RFC and protocol information in general is `http://www.networksorcery.com/`.

Along with the RFCs, several excellent books have been written on the technical details of IPv6 and also how to migrate to it. The most recent and therefore most accurate with respect to the still fluid nature of some aspects of IPv6 are:

- *Migrating to IPv6* by Marc Blanchet (Wiley Publishing, ISBN: 0-471-49892-0)
- *IPv6 Essentials, 2nd Edition,* by Silvia Hagen (O'Reilly Media, Inc., ISBN: 0-596-10058-2)

Both books were published in 2006.

Testing Your Knowledge

Each chapter ends with a set of review questions to allow readers to gauge their comprehension of the preceding reading. Because this chapter was, other than an introduction, a short journey down the memory lane of IP networking, the following questions are meant more as trivia than essential knowledge for IPv6 transition. As with all such sections that follow, the answers are in Appendix A.

1. What are three advantages of IPv6 over IPv4?
2. What is the biggest hurdle in the U.S. facing those planning an IPv6 transition?
3. Extra Credit: What was the dominant networking protocol prior to IP?
4. Extra Credit: If the current IP protocol is version 4 and you're making the transition to version 6, what happened to version 5?

DUBLIN BUSINESS SCHOOL

LIBRARY

Demystifying IPv6

*Any sufficiently advanced technology
is indistinguishable from magic.*
— Arthur C. Clarke

For some reason, IPv6 has taken on a mystique that can only be compared to when fire was brought to primitive cave dwellers. Some fear it. Others embrace it as the answer to all the world's problems. Still others see it as overkill and a waste of time that won't last. Across the board, it gets ranked in with technological achievements like the 1969 Moon landing. IPv6 is a really cool technology with a lot of potential (and a lot of hurdles to cross to achieve wide-scale adoption), but it should be seen for what it is: simply one of the next steps in the evolution of internetworking protocols.

What You'll Learn

This chapter presents an introduction to the mechanics of IPv6. The focus is on the packet header, its extensions, the implications of the increase in address space size, and a taste of the auto-configuration features. If you already know what IPv6 looks like on the wire, you can probably skip this chapter.

You are strongly encouraged to read the section on auto-configuration, because there can be dragons there and forewarned is forearmed. Auto-configuration comes up several more times in the book, so you should probably have a good handle on it.

Also, if you like analogies based on the huge IPv6 address space, you may want to give that section a read so you can impress people at your next IPv6 cocktail party.

Exploring the IPv6 Header

In the TCP/IP networking stack, IPv6 is a direct plug-and-play replacement for the current IPv4. In regards to unicast TCP and UDP services, the use of IPv6 changes very little.

Many of the improvements and new features in IPv6 are reflected in the packet header. The IPv6 header is defined in RFC 2460. In the universe of standards documents, the RFC is a fairly straightforward technical read. If you understand the principles of packet-switched networking, you should do fine.

A comparison to the IPv4 header lends insight into what the creators of IPv6 had in mind. To that end, the IPv4 and IPv6 packet headers are shown in Figure 2-1 and Figure 2-2, respectively. As you read this section, note the recurring trend of simplification. One of the goals of IPv6 is that, if a particular packet or class of traffic does not require a feature of the protocol, the packet or traffic should not be encumbered by that feature.

Though the IPv6 packet header is larger than the IPv4 one, you'll quickly see that it's far less complicated. In fact, if you ignore the increase in address size, the IPv6 packet header is actually the smaller of the two.

Comparing Modified Fields and Introducing New Fields

Much of the IPv4 and IPv6 header contents are based on requirements common to all packet-switched networking. From lessons learned in the quarter century of IPv4 use, IPv6 has been streamlined quite a bit, but the following field-by-field comparison shows more similarities than differences:

> **Version.** The purpose of this 4-bit field is simple: to identify the version of the protocol. The value of the field changes from 4 to 6 with IPv6.
>
> **Internet Header Length (IHL) / Total Length vs. Payload Length.** The purpose of these fields is to provide the size of the packet and the offset to the payload portion. With the IPv6 header being fixed-sized, the 4-bit IHL field can be eliminated. Because this field represented the offset to the payload in 32-bit words, not octets, its removal also eliminates the need for the packet's recipient (or an intermediary content-filtering device) to do a multiplication by four for each packet to find the start of the payload. The distinction between IPv4's Total Length and the IPv6 Payload Length is a subtle optimization. Because the IPv6 header length is a fixed value, providing the Payload Length instead of Total Length eliminates a subtraction operation for any device looking to extract the payload from a packet. Both the Total Length and Payload Length are 16-bit fields, so the total packet size has only increased trivially by 40 octets, because the header length is not included in the 16-bit length. See the header extensions section later in the chapter for packet payloads greater than 16 bits.

Version	IHL	Type of Service	Total Length		
Identification			Flags	Fragment Offset	
Time to Live		Protocol	Header Checksum		
32-bit Source Address					
32-bit Destination Address					
Options and Padding (0 to 40 octets)					

Figure 2-1: IPv4 header fields

Version	Traffic Class	Flow Label		
Payload Length		Next Header	Hop Limit	
128-bit Source Address				
128-bit Destination Address				

Figure 2-2: IPv6 header fields

Type of Service (ToS) vs. Traffic Class / Flow Label. ToS and Traffic Class are both identically specified by the Differentiated Services (DS) model defined in RFC 2474, driven by the need for Quality of Service (QoS) control in modern networking applications. The Flow Label is the only truly new field to IPv6. There is little discussion of QoS and flows in this book, because they are not as much about transition as new capabilities.

Time to Live (TTL) vs. Hop Limit. These fields, both 8 bits in length, serve identical purposes in IPv4 and IPv6, to limit the maximum lifetime of a packet and thereby prevent network overloads. The renaming is due to the original IPv4 definition in RFC 791 of TTL being far more time-based than it has become in common use. Hop Limit clearly defines in RFC 2460 that the lifetime of a packet is measured in the number of router-to-router hops it is allowed to take and has nothing to do with time.

Protocol vs. Next Header. Like TTL vs. Hop Limit, these two 8-bit fields are used the same way for the bulk of network traffic, to identify the payload type in a packet. Both versions, but more so IPv6, also use the field to string together optional capabilities, for example, authentication and privacy services or advanced routing options. IPv6 introduces the concept of extension headers (hence, the name change for the field) to implement capabilities that were IPv4 options and therefore in the variable-length IPv4 header.

Source and Destination Addresses. Probably the most straightforwardly defined fields, while at the same time the fields whose fourfold increase in size from IPv4 to IPv6 has the most impact on network infrastructures, these typically indicate the device that is sending a packet and to which device the packet is destined. Both IPv4 and IPv6 define special-purpose addresses that encode such information as types of services (for example, to find all the nodes or routers in a network) or communications channels among multiple systems, not simply interfaces on physical devices. IPv6 defines more types of addresses than IPv4, and detailed information on them is provided in RFC 4291. These special-purpose addresses are discussed later in this book, as well.

What Fields Are Gone?

In the process of streamlining IPv6, based on the decades of experience with IPv4, certain header fields were removed. As mentioned previously, the IHL field was removed because IPv6 headers are all the same length. In addition, the following fields were either eliminated or moved to IPv6 extension headers:

Identification / Flags / Fragment Offset: These fields are used for fragmenting larger packets into multiple smaller ones, so they may be passed across links that have smaller Maximum Transmission Unit (MTU) sizes. Nowadays, fragmentation is far rarer, at least in most commercial environments, than it was when IPv4 was designed. Though not entirely eliminated, the minimal need for fragmentation has caused these fields to be moved to a dedicated fragmentation extension header.

Header Checksum: The improved transmission quality in modern networks has greatly reduced the need for error detection. Still, it must be used for reliable communications. Fortunately, it is implemented in many of the protocols above and below IP, such as TCP, UDP, and Ethernet. Because IPv4 doesn't provide error detection for its payloads (the checksum pertains only to the header and any IPv4 options), the decision was made to remove the feature from that header, allowing the surrounding protocols to cover the gap. As a bonus, the removal of the checksum reduces the load on routers. This is because the IPv4 TTL field changes with every hop, forcing each router to re-compute the checksum for every packet it forwards after decrementing the packet's TTL. This computation is not required for IPv6.

Options and Padding: The packet options contained in the variable-length IPv4 header have been replaced with the IPv6 concept of extension headers. As mentioned previously, the switch to fixed-sized IPv6 headers improves performance, and the transplanting of features that the bulk of packets do not require to optional extension headers both greatly improves performance and simplifies the logic in routers, firewalls, and other network devices.

Understanding Extension Headers

The IPv6 extension header mechanism is a logical evolution from the options mechanism of IPv4. Both mechanisms implement similar capabilities, such as the ability to include additional information or use additional features of a protocol without overburdening those that don't need the information or features.

The use of IPv4 options is rarely seen for two main reasons:

1. Several of the options, such as source routing, were found to have security vulnerabilities and therefore became discouraged or forbidden. These options are turned off on most routers.

2. The space for the options was extremely limited in the IP header. A maximum of 40 octets is allowed for all options in an IPv4 header. For useful options like Record Route, which implements a capability much like the traceroute networking utility, but using far less network bandwidth, 40 octets only allows recording paths of 9 hops or fewer.

IPv6 extensions were designed to overcome the limitations of IPv4 options. Fixing security problems almost always introduces more of them and, unfortunately, IPv6 is no exception; nor should it have expected to have been. For example, the routing extension header meant partly to replicate the functions of IPv4 source routing has already been found to have its own security vulnerabilities.

On the bright side, extension headers have alleviated the space limitation problems associated with IPv4 options. Rather than having only 40 octets to play with in total, almost every extension header defined in RFC 2460 includes an 8-bit length field allowing up to 255 octets after the initial 8 octets of the extension header itself. Furthermore, the extension headers can be chained, to use multiple extensions in the same packet, with each getting far more than 40 octets.

The examples in Figure 2-3 show, from left to right:

1. a typical IPv6 packet carrying a TCP header and payload

2. a packet with a routing extension header

3. a packet with both routing and fragmentation headers

There is a required order and other limitations when combining extension headers. These are defined in RFC 2460.

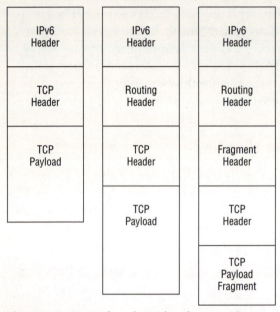

Figure 2-3: Examples of IPv6 header extension combinations

Finding a Better Home for Fragmentation

As IPv6 rolls out, the most successful extension (in terms of acceptance of and performance improvements from its new implementation) is likely to be fragmentation. It is still required for smaller-MTU network links and the removal of its overhead from the main IPv6 header is a plus for all packets. There are many well-known security issues with IP fragmentation. Though moving the fields to an extension won't make them better, it won't make them worse.

Other than moving the fields that control it, fragmentation has been redefined to be allowed only at the source nodes of network traffic. Routers do not fragment any IPv6 traffic they forward from other sources. This limitation implies that a source node needs to know the smallest MTU between itself and the desired destination of its packets. Fear not, because RFC 1981 defines a path MTU discovery protocol that a source device can use to determine the largest packets it can send before worrying about fragmentation. There is also an error message defined in the ICMPv6 protocol (see RFC 2463) that is returned if any MTU in the path to destination is too small for the packet being sent.

Finally, IPv6 requires that a minimum MTU of 1280 octets (1500 is recommended) be supported by any device supporting IPv6. Any device that wants to support IPv6, but has a lesser MTU, must handle fragmentation and reassembly at a lower layer in the protocol stack. Therefore, if a source is sending packets of 1280 octets or fewer, it doesn't have to worry about fragmentation.

What Other Extension Headers Are There?

In addition to the routing and fragmentation headers just described, IPv6 defines or incorporates (in cases where the definitions precede IPv6's) extension headers for:

- security, both authentication and privacy
- packet payloads greater than 65,535 octets, a.k.a., jumbo packets
- destination options that need only be examined by the ultimate recipient

The extension header mechanism is extensible, both by allowing new extension headers to be defined and used in the Next Header field of the IPv6 header, and by allowing new options to be defined and used within existing or new extension headers. Further discussion is beyond the scope of this book, but the reader can easily see that there is far more protocol extensibility built into IPv6 that there was in IPv4.

Grappling with the Huge IPv6 Address Space

The vastness of the IPv6 address space is the protocol's most obvious feature. An IPv6 address has four times the bits of an IPv4 address: 128 bits versus 32. To simplify using IPv6 addresses, the dot-separated 8-bit decimal fields of IPv4 have been replaced in IPv6 with colon-separated 16-bit hexadecimal fields, for example, 2112:0501:185b:0001:02e0:0000:0000:16f5.

Using Shortcuts to Represent IPv6 Addresses

There are several shortcuts defined in RFC 4291 for expressing IPv6 addresses so users are not constantly reading and writing 39-character values, with many of the digits likely being zeros.

A very useful shortcut is that any leading zeros within the 16-bit fields need not be expressed. Also, a single contiguous group of one or more 16-bit fields where each field contains only zeros can be expressed using "::". The limitation to one group is to avoid ambiguity as to how many zeros are in each group.

The "::" abbreviation is allowed anywhere in the address, including at the beginning or the end. As such, an address of all zeros in IPv6 is expressed simply as "::". The loopback address of 0:0:0:0:0:0:0:1, equivalent in function to addresses in the 127 loopback network in IPv4, can be expressed simply as "::1".

Given these two shortcuts, the preceding example address can be expressed somewhat more conveniently as 2112:501:185b:1:2e0::16f5. It's still a far cry from the simplicity of IPv4 addresses, but it's better.

Expressing IPv6 Address Spaces

IPv6 address spaces are represented using the Classless Inter-Domain Routing (CIDR) notation defined in RFC 4632. The reader should be familiar with this notation from IPv4. For example, the legacy "Class C" network whose first address is 192.168.27.0 is expressed in CIDR notation as 192.168.27.0/24, indicating there are 24 bits used to define the network portion of an address in this space and 8 bits available for hosts. In IPv4, the number of bits available for hosts is always 32 minus the number to the right of the slash, the legal range of that number being inclusively between 0 and 32.

Similarly, IPv6 address spaces are represented by the digits necessary to identify the network portion, followed by a slash and then the number of bits in that network portion. Using the shortcuts from the preceding section, the huge address space once held by the experimental 6BONE (`http://www.6bone.net/`) can be expressed as 3ffe::/16. To determine the number of bits available for hosts in an IPv6 address space, instead of subtracting the number of network bits from 32, subtract that number from 128. This means that the 6BONE had 112 bits available for hosts. That's a lot of hosts!

So, How Big Is Big?

IPv4 defines roughly four billion individual IP addresses. That's a big number, but a number we humans can grasp. For example, there were four billion people on Earth around the time of the U.S. Bicentennial (1976). Four billion seconds is about 136 years. These are not small numbers, but most "people on the street" can comprehend them.

The size of the IPv6 address space is immeasurable in any meaningful real-world terms. Two somewhat comprehendible ones are:

■ If a single IP address had a mass of one gram, the IPv4 address space would weigh about as much as 2900 cars or 1/3 the parking at the Pentagon. The IPv6 address space would be more than 50 billion times the Earth's mass. That's about double the most optimistic estimate of the number of planets in the Milky Way galaxy.

■ There are enough IPv6 addresses to allocate 2000 to every square meter of the disk of the Milky Way galaxy.

These are impressive, if not incomprehensible, numbers, and it's fairly safe to conjecture that we won't run out of IPv6 addresses for a long time. When we do run out, it won't be because there are too many devices. It will be because of poor management of address allocations or assignments. Fortunately, the world-wide, regional, and local registries are working to make sure allocations and assignments are efficient.

Managing the Address Space World-Wide

IPv4 addresses are assigned by the Internet Assigned Numbers Authority (IANA) to Regional Internet Registries (RIRs) world-wide, like the American Registry for Internet Numbers (ARIN) in North America. The RIRs are responsible for managing the further downstream allocation to National and Local Internet Registries (NIRs and LIRs, respectively) and the assignment of addresses to ISPs and end sites in their regions. Historically, allocations and assignments ranged from hundreds to millions of addresses per block, though nowadays it's tough to get more than a few dozen at a time. Hence, all the concerns about exhausting the IPv4 address space.

The numbering of IPv4 address blocks has little relation to where in the world the addresses are allocated or assigned, and can be blamed partly on the rapid organic growth of the Internet in the 1990s and early twenty-first century. A side-effect of this situation is that the representation of the world-wide address space in the Internet's routers requires hundreds of thousands of route entries, which in turn requires a lot of processing to determine where a given packet should be routed.

Easing Address-Space Management with IPv6

IPv6 addresses, also assigned by IANA to RIRs and by RIRs further downstream, are more structured. Various addressing schemes are defined in RFC 4291, with the scheme applicable to a given IPv6 address identified by the high-order bits of the address block. The most popular scheme splits addresses in half with the upper 64 bits being used for the network and the lower 64 bits used for device interfaces on the subnet.

In October 2006, each of the major RIRs (AfriNIC, APNIC, ARIN, LACNIC, and RIPE) was assigned a huge block of 2^{116} IPv6 addresses (that is, a "/12" (http://www.iana.org/assignments/ipv6-unicast-address-assignments as of May 10, 2007). Each RIR already had appreciable blocks of IPv6 addresses assigned to it, but these latest assignments dwarfed all previous assignments combined. All told, 0.12 percent of the entire IPv6 address space was doled out with those five assignments. That may not sound like much, but remember we're talking about numbers represented most efficiently using the sizes of galaxies here.

Allocating and Assigning Addresses Downstream

Each RIR has its own policies for allocating and assigning the addresses in its care downstream to NIRs, LIRs, and end sites. Using ARIN as an example, to make the bookkeeping manageable, the minimum initial allocation to a qualified ISP is a "/32" or 2^{96} addresses (`http://www.arin.net/policy/nrpm.html#six43` as of May 10, 2007). With the assignment ARIN received from IANA in October 2006, it can assign /32's to more than a million ISPs. Of course, bigger assignments are available, if the ISP qualifies.

An ISP then assigns address blocks to its end-site customers from that allocation. ARIN provides guidance to its ISPs that the minimum assignment by an ISP to an end site should be:

- a "/64" if only one subnet is needed
- a "/56" for those sites requiring only a few subnets over the next 5 years
- a "/48" for larger sites

This is from `http://www.arin.net/policy/nrpm.html#six43`, as of May 10, 2007.

Using this guidance, a residential customer of an ISP desiring static IPv6 address space at home should receive no fewer than 2^{64} addresses. A small private company should get enough to build out up to 256 separate subnets of 2^{64} addresses each over five years. The largest allocation (65,536 subnets) would be suitable perhaps for one of the larger facilities of a Fortune 500 company.

Managing Your Local Set of IPv6 Addresses

The reader can see that it's unlikely the recipients of such big address blocks as described previously need come back any time soon for more. At the same time, these assignments represent such trivial fractions of even the ISP's allocation, that it's unforeseeable how ISPs and end sites can squander them. That's, again, where this book comes into the picture. As you create your transition plan, address space management plays a big part. Sometimes having too much of something is as difficult to manage as having too little. Chapter 7, "Identifying Some Common Transition Preparation Tasks," will help you provision your IPv6 address space.

Benefiting from Auto-Configuration

One of the greatest double-edged swords IPv6 brings to the table is auto-configuration. IPv6 has robust auto-configuration that can stand up a network with no administrator participation. IPv6 end devices seek out other IPv6 end devices and routers. A concept known as scoped addresses eases sending service requests to classes of devices, like "all routers" in a network. Neighbor Discovery and Duplicate Address Detection look for other systems, the latter to assure a lack of collisions in the address space. Multicast Listener Discovery Version 2 (MLDv2) joins up groups with little or no outside help.

Auto-Configuring the Local Subnet

Even before network auto-configuration starts, device auto-configuration takes place. IPv6 defines a class of addresses known as "link-local" addresses. The addresses are called link-local because routers are expressly forbidden from forwarding traffic sourced from or destined to these addresses. In other words, the addresses stay on the local subnet or link.

Link-local addresses are useful in two ways. First, even if you don't have any "real" IPv6 address space to work with, link-local addresses are available for use much like the private address spaces defined for IPv4 in RFC 1918. A collection of devices on the same subnet can communicate with each other and benefit from all the services offered by IPv6 using purely link-local addresses. This is particularly useful when assembling a temporary ad hoc network.

The other benefit of link-local addresses is they allow devices that are not yet configured for connectivity outside the local subnet to communicate with their potential router(s) using the IPv6 protocol, rather than more primitive link-layer protocols like ARP and RARP.

What Happened to Site-Local Addresses?

Until September 2004, IPv6 addressing included a block called site-local addresses. Whereas link-local addresses are limited to the local subnet, site-local ones were allowed to be forwarded by routers, but only within the local "site." This made them more like the RFC 1918 IPv4 private addresses (which have been used with much success since 1996) than like link-local addresses.

RFC 3879 deprecated the original definition and implementation of site-local addresses for reasons of there being too much ambiguity in exactly what a "site" is. For example, is a "site" a single building? Is it the 15 buildings a company has in an office park? Is it the whole enterprise (possibly from Austria to Australia)? Those are all valid uses of RFC 1918 addresses and the onus was on the managers of the "site" to keep the local traffic contained. Even if packets did get onto the Internet, it was wired to not route them. It's hard to see the harm in the definition.

As you may have guessed, the elimination of site-local addresses was not a unanimous decision by the IPv6 community, because those familiar with IPv4 private addresses had found them very useful, despite their suffering from the same set of ambiguities.

As a replacement, RFC 4193 defines Unique Local IPv6 Unicast Addresses or ULAs. These addresses contain a 40-bit global ID field that is meant to be randomly generated, so the probability of two sites creating the same address block is highly unlikely. This way, the identity of the site is contained in the addresses. Should any traffic using them sneak out of the site, the source can be more easily found.

ULAs are fairly new and the jury is still out on them. It's probably a safe bet, though, that the random portion won't be generated as randomly by some sites as it is by others. Expect collisions of what are supposed to be unique address spaces, not that they'll matter as well-managed networks will keep ULAs contained for the most part, because they have contained RFC 1918 addresses (for example, using egress filtering to prevent their leaking out of the "site").

Limiting Auto-Configuration to Reduce Risk

With all the benefits of auto-configuration, there are, of course, downsides. One of the biggest downsides is that the side-effects of all this cool IPv6 technology are not fully understood. IPv4 has been around for a long time and, though new exploits are found every now and then, the protocol's pros and cons are well understood. Not so with IPv6.

There is a belief that one of the main reasons IPv6 transition will occur much faster than anyone expects is due to the protocol's innate ability to auto-configure, whether transitions to it are "managed" or not. This presents enormous risks to the entire enterprise, both the nascent IPv6 segments *and the existing IPv4 ones*. Furthermore, as if this comes as a surprise to anyone in computer networking, there are already attacks to exploit the flaws in IPv6, both in its native form and tunneled within IPv4.

Until IPv6 is better understood, it is best to dabble in its new features somewhere safe, like test networks and pilot projects. The last place you want to find a new IPv6 exploit personally is while upgrading your enterprise networks. IPv6 has features analogous to most of the old mundane IPv4 features. It's probably best to make the transition using those first. Then, as you (and the rest of the IT community) learn more about IPv6 in large network deployments, start using the cooler features.

The phrase "we're not running IPv6" will become the "the check is in the mail" of IP networking for the next few years, at least. Enterprises such as the federal government, that know they must adopt IPv6, have already or will soon complete their transition plans and start execution to meet their June 2008 deadlines. What they are just beginning to realize is that, no matter what dates are on those transition plans for IPv6 adoption, the transition is already well under way. IPv6, both in hardware and software, is already prevalent. To paraphrase Jack Nicholson's Joker in the context of IPv6 capabilities, organizations will find, "Well that's the gag, folks! Chances are you've [got] 'em already!"

Testing Your Knowledge

We're still not in the thick of things regarding transition planning and execution, but it's good to know the concepts in this chapter and these questions should help keep you sharp. Answers are in Appendix A.

1. Why do IPv4 packet headers require both an Internet Header Length (IHL) and Total Length field?

2. If the Payload Length of an IPv6 packet is only 16-bits, how can the maximum packet size be larger?

3. What's the difference, according to the RFCs, between Time to Live (TTL) in IPv4 and Hop Limit in IPv6? What's the practical difference?

4. List three reasons why the Header Checksum wasn't incorporated in the IPv6 header, even though it's in the IPv4 header.

5. Write the IPv6 address 2001:0000:0000:2379:01a0:0000:0000:7480 in its most-compact form.

6. Extra Credit (read, Useless Trivia): How many IPv6 addresses fit on the head of a pin? Assume the pin is made of iron (it's an old pin), the head is 1mm in diameter, 0.5mm in thickness, and has one address per atom. Hint: you'll probably need Avogadro's number.

CHAPTER 3

The Current IPv6 Landscape

Dark Helmet: When will then be now?
Colonel Sandurz: Soon.
— **Mel Brooks' Spaceballs**

When I started writing this book, I decided to leave this chapter for last so that I could present the most current information regarding IPv6 developments. For example, although I assumed that IPv6 adoption would proceed roughly linearly for the time being (and it has), I wanted to document the latest hard numbers. I also wanted to incorporate all the latest news, standards updates, and so on, so that the book would not be a historical reference before it was printed. IPv6 is moving and changing that quickly. It turns out that, other than IPv6 adoption proceeding about as quickly as expected (which is by no means a land rush), nothing much concrete has happened in the past five months. There has been some news, both positive in terms of IPv6 adoption and negative in terms of new security vulnerabilities. I'll summarize those in this chapter, and several of them are covered elsewhere in the book. I think the positives outweigh the negatives by a significant enough margin for you to feel encouraged about IPv6's destiny, unlike that of its predecessors (using the thirteenth-century meaning of that word, "those that died before it"), like GOSIP. I would like to have seen more transition progress in the past five months; this chapter would not have been too outdated had I written it five months ago, but that's a very small measurement window for something that's just started making headway and is likely to be around possibly for the next half-century. To judge IPv6 based on its middling success to date would be like judging a person based on how well he or she did in kindergarten.

What You'll Learn

This chapter, unlike the others in this book, is about informing versus teaching. The distinction is a subtle one. In general, the goal of teaching is to instruct you how to do something. Informing simply provides facts. This chapter uses facts about IPv6 adoption to encourage you that IPv6 is truly being adopted, rather than just sitting in a lab somewhere. The chapter is also meant to inform you that the bad guys have taken notice of IPv6 and that there are already hacking tools out there to exploit the new technology.

The chapter first notes that the OMB IPv6 transition mandates are being seen with clearer (and less over-reactive) eyes as June 2008 approaches. The chapter then presents the latest IPv6 adoption data, which represents global adoption, not just IPv6 adoption in the United States. The chapter concludes with an assessment of what IPv6 hacking tools are out there.

Casting Fresh Eyes on the OMB Mandate

When data networks evolved to use ATM, Frame Relay, and MPLS, there were no outcries of doom and gloom regarding what such transitions would cost or whether they were even feasible. Huge core networks were re-engineered or constructed to use MPLS and the resources were found as they always are for such projects. For some parts of MPLS adoption, a business case was formulated, a budget was drawn up, the request was made, and for simplicity in this discussion, the request was granted. Let's ignore how long it took, the back-and-forth of negotiation, and so on. The point is, the money showed up, which led to the resources, staff, and equipment showing up.

One of the sticking points of OMB's IPv6 mandate, as many are keen to point out, is that it is an unfunded mandate. What is only in the past few months becoming better understood is that OMB did not say, "Move everything to IPv6 by June 2008 and we don't care how you do it." They said, "The next time you're upgrading your equipment, at least make the core IPv6-capable." This is an oversimplification, but not by much. As a reminder, the relevant text of the June 2008 mandate is provided verbatim in Chapter 1's "Understanding IPv6 Federal Mandates" section.

The OMB mandate has been misconstrued (not by everyone, but enough people so as to cloud its true intent) to mean that every device, application, and user must speak IPv6 fluently in order to meet the mandate. As June 2008 approaches, people are re-reading the mandate and realizing that it's not as onerous as once thought, and progress is starting to be made. Perhaps it's because they are trying to tune their interpretation of the mandate in order to reduce their workload, or perhaps it's because they're seeing OMB's real goal.

Whatever the case, the transition work being performed and what was desired by OMB are starting to be one and the same.

How Quickly Is IPv6 Being Adopted?

To measure world-wide IPv6 adoption, the number of IPv6 network prefixes announced to the Internet via BGP is a popular metric, based on three properties of this measurement:

- The data are easy to collect. If you are using BGP, you can collect these data at any time by simply interrogating one of your enterprise's border routers. As seen in this section, the data are also readily available online, in case you don't have access to a router that participates in BGP. There are also a number of "looking-glass" routers scattered around the Internet that allow you to collect the data in real time, as if they were from your own router. Note that many of the looking-glass routers don't allow you to do bulk BGP dumps, so you'll have to dig a little to find one.

- The data are proportionally representative of the number of active IPv6 networks. Though BGP represents aggregated addresses, which means that a particular prefix could represent many LANs, each prefix tends to represent no more than one organization or distinct set of LANs within a larger organization. This is particularly true in IPv6, where many of the announcements are /48's, meaning that they are the minimum size assigned by some ISP to an end organization.

- The data have historical precedent. The size of the IPv4 Internet has been measured for decades by counting the number of BGP prefixes.

Looking at the Historical Data

As you can see in Figure 3-1, IPv6 adoption has been proceeding at roughly the same linear pace at least since Feb 2003, where the earliest data that are widely available start. There was a hiccup in 2006 that was partly related to the shutdown of the experimental 6BONE, but otherwise the growth has been linear.

Note that all of the data for this section came from `http://www.cidr-report.org/v6/as2.0/index.html`, which is an excellent source of IPv6 adoption data and is updated daily. The data used for this section includes what was available at that website as of October 14, 2007.

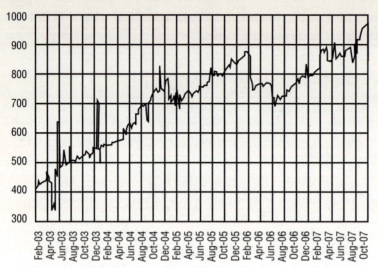

Figure 3-1: The historical data of IPv6 prefixes announced by BGP

Based on the historical data, there were 406 BGP prefixes announced for IPv6 in February 2003. The number of announced prefixes reached its latest peak on October 8, 2007 at 971 prefixes. The rate of growth from 2003 to the hiccup that started in early 2006 was slightly less than the rate of growth from mid-2006 until now, with the former being about 150 new prefixes per year and the latter being around 173 new prefixes. These latest figures give a modest indication that the adoption rate is accelerating, because the latter number represents more than a year's worth of observations.

There are two additional analyses that shed a little more light on the IPv6 adoption rates of the past 4.5 years. They are covered in the following sections.

Analyzing the Adoption Data for Annual Growth

Table 3-1 shows the annual peaks in the BGP announcements of IPv6 prefixes for the month of October from 2003 to 2007. Note the drop off in the number of announced prefixes in 2006, which is no surprise given Figure 3-1. As mentioned earlier, part of this drop off can be attributed to the 6BONE shutdown in June 2006. From February 2006 to July 2006, the number of announced IPv6 prefixes declined by 200 prefixes. The total count did not exceed the February 2006 peak value again until February a year later. Because the 6BONE represented only about 70 prefixes, something else caused the other 130 prefixes to go away. What that was is not relevant in the scope of this summary.

Table 3-1: IPv6 Prefix BGP Announcements Annually Since October 2003

MONTH/YEAR	PEAK # OF IPV6 PREFIXES	INCREASE FROM PRIOR YEAR
Oct 2003	539	N/A
Oct 2004	743	204
Oct 2005	832	89
Oct 2006	779	(53)
Oct 2007	971	192

Since July 2006, however, announced-prefix growth has continued steadily, with a few short dips, the latest of those dips still in progress right after the October 8, 2007 all-time maximum (as you can see on the right-most edge of Figure 3-1). Even with the latest dip, the recovery in 2007 from 2006's hiccup exceeded all previous years and posted the second greatest annual increase of the whole data set. Given the faster adoption rate attained after the prefix count hit bottom in July 2006, and assuming there is no further acceleration, the effects of the 2006 hiccup will be erased around 2014, because an additional 23 prefixes are being added annually, on average, and will make up for the 200 lost. Of course, every expectation is that the rate will continue to increase and the loss of 200 prefixes will be meaningless by 2014, or much sooner. As a comparison, the IPv4 prefixes that are announced by BGP fluctuate by that amount almost every day. Of course, there are nearly 240,000 IPv4 prefixes at last count, so the comparison is admittedly of apples and oranges.

Analyzing the Compounding of the Adoption Rate

The second analysis to help understand the current and historical IPv6 adoption rates is depicted in Table 3-2, which shows when the number of announced IPv6 prefixes has increased by 10 percent or greater since its previous 10 percent milestone, starting with the original 406 prefixes from February 2003. Normally such analyses use doubling as the criterion for setting milestones, so as to underscore the impressive growth rates. Given that the IPv6 prefix count started at 406 in 2003 and is getting close to 1,000 only now, using 100 percent growth would lead to there only being two lines in the table, thus the choice to track 10 percent growth.

On face value, Table 3-2 shows non-spectacular growth, again because of the 2006 hiccup, which caused the BGP announcements of IPv6 prefixes to hit rock bottom on June 23, 2006 with only 689 prefixes announced. If you look at the data (see Figure 3-1) from that low point on, however, you can see that things seem to be back on track. The last line in Table 3-2 extrapolates that the number of IPv6 prefixes announced by BGP will grow another 10 percent, since the last milestone in August 2007, by no later than March 2008. Feel free to e-mail me whether I get that right or wrong, because I'm a bit of a gambler and am pretty sure of this one, even given the most recent dip noted in the following section.

Table 3-2: Amount of Time between Periods of 10% or Greater Growth in IPv6 BGP Announcements

# OF PREFIXES	DATE ACHIEVED	# OF DAYS SINCE LAST 10% GAIN
406	Feb 10, 2003	N/A
447	Apr 2, 2003	51
633	Jun 8, 2003	67
703	Dec 23, 2003	198
826	Nov 10, 2004	323
911	Aug 17, 2007	1010
1003	Mar 4, 2008 (est.)	200 (est.)

Portending a Bumpy Road Ahead for IPv6 Adoption

A final item on the current state of IPv6 adoption concerns the ongoing hiccups resulting in reductions of greater than 10 percent in the total number of announced IPv6 prefixes. On October 13, 2007, only five days after the all-time high in IPv6 prefix announcements, the number of announced IPv6 prefixes dropped to 839, when 132 prefixes (almost 14 percent) disappeared overnight. Because the current data ends at exactly that time, it's hard to say whether this is an anomaly in data collection, a temporary "outage" of sorts (which has occurred a few times with IPv6 BGP announcements), or a permanent loss of prefixes. My feeling is that the loss is a temporary one, probably due to some configuration error somewhere, as new networks are being added all the time. Moreover, many networks are still not in their final configurations. For those networks, BGP announcements are withdrawn, the networks are reconfigured, and then re-announced as people learn how to best manage IPv6.

Announcing Two Major Transition Enablers

One of the predictions that many people, including myself, have been making for some time is that IPv6 transition by the U.S. federal government will lead to a trickle-down effect causing transitions by defense contractors and other vendors to the government. This prediction has started to come true. As mentioned later in this book, two major corporations have announced IPv6 transitions for at least parts of their world-wide networks. Both corporations have strong government and defense ties.

On September 2, 2007, Lockheed Martin announced that it would be deploying IPv6 on its Global Vision Network from California to the U.K. (see `http://www.pcworld.com/article/id,136689-pg,1/article.html`). A few days later, on September 25, 2007, Verizon Business made a similar announcement that it was deploying IPv6 on its public IP network over the next 18 months (see `http://money.cnn.com/news/newsfeeds/articles/prnewswire/NYTU05725092` `007-1.htm`). These are both positive omens for the future. If these companies are starting upgrades, then there must be money in IPv6, not just mandates.

Assessing the State of IPv6 Hacking

This section talks about IPv6 hacking. This is distinct from IPv6's vulnerabilities to exploitation in general, the risks of which are discussed in Chapter 10, "Factoring IPv6-specific Risks and Limitations into Your Plans." The distinction is that, though IPv6 has its vulnerabilities like everything else, this section covers what has been done to date to exploit those vulnerabilities.

Introducing the First IPv6 Attack Toolkit

In April 2006, The Hacker's Choice (THC) announced an IPv6 Attack Toolkit, which is billed as the first comprehensive attack toolkit for IPv6. It will surely not be the last. The toolkit comes with the following capabilities and features, to name a few:

- ICMP neighbor solicitation and advertisement spoofing
- A fake router announcer
- Man-in-the-middle sniffing with ICMPv6 redirect spoofing
- A fake announcer for multicast groups

The toolkit also includes a packet-crafting library to create new tools. Although a disclaimer that comes with the toolkit reads that it is for legal purposes only, the same site that offers you this toolkit also helps you crack GSM (cellular telephony) encryption and unlock certain types of cell phones. I'm not convinced THC is working too hard to enforce the principles of that disclaimer and maintain their good reputation. Why am I telling you about this toolkit, since one can certainly infer that it's of little use for the good guys? Because I believe the best defense comes from understanding the offense. The attackers already know about the toolkit. Now you do, too.

Dealing with Hacker Tools and Attack Kits

Now that you know that there's at least one attack toolkit out there (and surely others have been derived from the first one since 2006 or have been created independently), what do you do? In other words, how do you protect your network? First of all, if you're not officially running IPv6, make sure it's turned off.

Turning off IPv6 includes turning off IP protocol #41, in other words, the tunneling of IPv6 over IPv4, which is covered more in Chapter 4. For now, here's the scenario for the risks of protocol #41:

1. An external attacker targets your assigned IPv4 addresses.

2. A benign-looking IPv4 packet passes through your firewall headed for a legitimate target.

3. At the target, the IPv6 payload is extracted (if IPv6 is enabled).

4. The IPv6 packet is routed to the ultimate target(s), for example, an easily constructed EUI-64 address (discussed in detail in Chapter 7) based on some popular MAC addresses.

5. Should any of these secondary targets have IPv6 enabled and also have whatever bug the attacker is seeking to exploit, like buffer overflows, those targets now become "owned" systems and attack launch points *behind your security perimeter*!

The preceding address attacks were launched from the outside. What about insider attacks? Depending on who you believe, insiders constitute 75 percent to 95 percent of the threats to a network.

The following is a real-world example of a group of employees, not happy with their company's policies, who hid within the enterprise network on an independent IPv6 infrastructure. This group of people found the network operations staff a bit too overzealous about controlling user activities, with policies like no more than a very limited number of personal e-mails per day. Several users colluded to use IPv6 and stood up a covert network using link-local addresses. Nobody was monitoring IPv6 traffic, so these activities went on unnoticed.

The lesson learned from this is to monitor both IPv4 *and* IPv6 traffic. That's a tall order, considering the current state of IPv6 security products (see Chapter 16, "Managing IPv6 on the Same Network"). There are few products out there, though products with IPv6 features should start turning up as the June 2008 deadline approaches. Deadlines aside, the only thing that will drive vendors to make IPv6 products is user demand. So, network administrators, security staff, CIOs, and so on, start demanding.

Testing Your Knowledge

This chapter is more about providing facts than teaching technique or theory. Though the adoption statistics are nice, the following questions cover the two concepts you should take away from this chapter. The answers are in Appendix A.

1. What is the true goal of the U.S. federal OMB mandate?

2. Considering that hacking is at best borderline illegal (and at worst a felony), why do you need to know what the IPv6 hackers are doing?

Planning Your Transition

Choosing When to Make A Transition and How

A journey of a thousand miles must begin with a single step.
— The Tao Te Ching

I miss viewgraphs. They had lots of shortcomings compared to PowerPoint, sure, like you couldn't undetectably edit them on the fly to fix a flaw discovered just before you presented, thereby making you look like you knew what you were talking about all along, but, viewgraphs provided one great feature for audiences. Audience members could walk into a presentation and immediately get a good idea of what they were in for, depending on the thickness of the presenter's slide deck. You have no such warnings today, unless the presenter has been merciful enough to number the slides in that "Slide 1 of N" format. Only then do you know whether to get a cup of coffee or a hotel reservation before the show.

A colleague of mine is known for lengthy slide shows. Although you're expected to look at the title of the talk on the first slide, the audience is locked on the bottom corner that reads, "1 of 173." That's not an exaggeration. His claim is that some slides are simply pictures and others are tables for the audience to take home to refer to later, so they don't count. Also, because he presents to both extremes of the technologically literate scale of audiences, rarely do all the slides get used.

What You'll Learn

Getting your head wrapped around what it means to make the transition to IPv6 is like those old viewgraph decks. You walk into the transition and the first thing you see is a big bunch of books, memos, RFCs, mandates, directives, and so on, and you think, "Oh, this is going to be a long one." In truth, some of the transition stuff may not apply to you. It certainly won't apply to every single LAN you run. On the other hand, there will be those slides that look like they were written by lawyers and should be read by Joe Isuzu. You may spend more time in an area that you thought was going to be a walk in the park.

After reading this chapter, you will have the tools you need to know what your options for transition are. Computer networks come in all shapes and sizes, many with special requirements for availability, security, and so on. Nobody else can divine your specific transition steps and produce a cookbook that exactly meets your needs, but, you can be informed how to make those choices yourself. With this chapter, you will learn the abilities and limitations of the variety of IPv6 transition mechanisms that are available for you to combine into solutions that fit your needs. Furthermore, you will know how to decide when and in what order to apply them.

Taking the FUD Out of IPv6 Transition

As I discussed in Chapter 3, there are three distinct IPv6 camps. Suffering from the most FUD (Fear, Uncertainty, and Doubt) is the camp composed of U.S. federal agencies staring down the barrel of the OMB-mandated IPv6 transition gun and claiming, sometimes rightly, that insufficient guidance, best practices, and so on, have been provided by those doing the mandating. From interpretation (and misinterpretation) of the OMB mandates for June 2008, it's understandable that government IT departments may feel they have been given an edict to boil the oceans and not so much as a hot-plate with which to do so.

By examining the choices at hand for making the IPv6 transition, comparing them with the technologies they are designed to replace, and talking about them as IT solutions, rather than political mandates, I hope this chapter can melt some of the FUD away. The two things to keep reminding yourself are: 1) it won't be that bad and, 2) the alternatives are more disturbing.

In 2005, Rep. Tom Davis of Virginia held hearings, partly to learn if the United States is at competitive risk globally with respect to the Next Generation Internet, of which IPv6 is a significant component. Rep. Davis's continuing concern is that the U.S. cannot let its current success story with the Internet become a liability by relying solely on IPv4, while the rest of the world moves forward to IPv6 ("Internet Strategy: China's Next Generation Internet," www.cio.com, July 15, 2006).

Reminiscent of the "bomber gap" of the 1950s, where the U.S. Air Force was seeking funds to build more bombers to counter a perceived Soviet threat, an IPv6 gap would put the U.S. at risk, both financially and in its defensive posture. The possibility of a bomber gap was brought about by speculation and rumor regarding true Soviet capabilities, and proved to be nonexistent as U-2 spy planes brought home solid evidence of true Soviet capabilities.

Unfortunately, an "IPv6 gap," or at least a significant disparity in IPv6 deployment as a percentage of the number of networking assets in the U.S. versus overseas, can be shown to exist. Modern network survey techniques, as discussed in Chapter 3, "The Current IPv6 Landscape," clearly show where IPv6 growth is occurring and where it is not. For the time being, it appears Rep. Davis's concerns are quite realistic.

Choosing an IPv6 Transition Strategy

In this section, you learn your choices for when to move to IPv6 and at what pace to proceed. You'll become aware of the mostly non-technical aspects of the job, including introductions on planning and on coordinating the transition across the enterprise. You won't, however, have all the tools you need after reading just this section. You'll also need to know what technical mechanisms and choices you have available. Those are covered in the following sections starting with "Selecting the Transition Mechanisms." Until then, don't worry too much about terms you may not know, like dual-stack or tunneling (though, as an MIS/IT professional, you should at least know what tunneling is in the IPv4 world). Should I have to use as yet undefined terms that are explained later on, like dual-stack, I'll throw in a "discussed later" in parentheses to alert you that definitions are forthcoming.

As far as when to move to IPv6 and how fast to do so, you have four possible strategies:

1. Start now and move slowly.
2. Start later and move quickly.
3. Start later and move slowly.
4. Start now and move quickly (you'll later see why this is not a good idea).

These are listed in order from most to least favorable for a successful, timely, and orderly IPv6 transition. Whether you're part of a U.S. federal government body, a U.S. commercial entity, or a totally non-U.S. organization dictates whether you go with choice 1 versus 2 or 3. The mandate for the U.S. federal government necessitates starting now. Shortly, you'll learn why that means you should be proceeding slowly.

If you're not driven by mandates, you can put more sophisticated plans in place for a "Big Bang" change later on before touching actual equipment or network configurations. You can also run pilot projects, perhaps totally detached from your main lines of business, to understand better how IPv6 can be made to work best for you. Several such pilots, including the 6BONE and MOONv6, have already enjoyed various levels of success for educating the U.S. federal sector (though neither were purely federal efforts), but now it's time to deploy real production networks.

You'll also find out later why choice 4 is a bad idea; "fools rush in where angels fear to tread." First, let's look at the better choices.

Choosing to Start Now and Move Slowly

If you're part of the U.S. federal government, one of the few U.S. commercial organizations with the inkling, time, and resources to pursue IPv6, or you're outside the U.S. altogether, you've probably already started making your transition. At the very least, you've started to get your hands around the problem, inventorying what you have and figuring out what needs to stay and go. Most importantly, you should be figuring out what capabilities you need. IPv6-enabled hardware and software are a means to an end. Sustaining your network's mission(s) through transition means ensuring the transition of capabilities.

Moving Capabilities, Not Just Systems

When the executives and other senior officials in your organization look to your networks, they are not looking at things that offer 32-bit versus 128-bit addresses, flow labels, or improved fragmentation and reassembly of packets. They are looking for the means to achieve or obtain:

- real-time stock quotes to all your company's traders
- video on demand to your company's cable-TV subscribers
- battlefield data and tactical information from the fronts back to the Pentagon

Capabilities, like those just listed, are what your computer networks provide your organization, and these capabilities apply to many organizations' missions and transcend all of them. The two main capabilities that you need to sustain can be broadly categorized as messaging and data storage and retrieval.

Looking Back at the Good Old Days

Before computer networks, the capabilities they provide were just as necessary and achieved by other means. Couriers, including the famous Pony Express of the old American West, were used to relay messages quickly over long distances. Eventually, couriers were replaced or augmented (some messages, like legal documents, still need to be on paper) by the telegraph, stock tickers, the telephone, and so on.

Access to large quantities of information were provided by libraries, both those available to the public and those specialized and housed in law offices, hospitals, engineering firms, and other businesses. Books provided the long-term information, the knowledge about things that rarely changed, like history and physics (relatively speaking). Magazines and other periodicals were the "instant messages" of the pre-computer era, updating users on world events, scientific breakthroughs, the weather, sometimes as frequently as once or twice a day. To access all this information quickly and efficiently, the library card catalog was invented. Ironically, some of the algorithms used for quickly searching card catalogs exist in their cyber-forms to this day.

Returning to the Here and Now

The World Wide Web and e-mail have rendered the preceding section little more than a refreshing walk down memory lane for those who like a little nostalgia. Nowadays, data-retrieval and message-delivery times are measured in seconds, not hours or days. Even in the purely physical world, there was a time less than a generation ago where overnight delivery of real documents and packages was considered nice, but having no business value. Without spending more than 10 seconds, you could probably rattle off the names of at least three companies for whom overnight delivery is their bread and butter, and people couldn't live without them.

What this means to you as the person upgrading your networks to IPv6 is that those to whom you report, and who themselves report to the shareholders or the White House, don't care nearly as much about how you're going to accomplish your task. They care much more that all the services they and your network's users and customers know and love will be there throughout the process. That includes before (that's the easiest part), during (when the guts of the network are all over the floor), and after (when you're allegedly "done").

Grasping the Big Picture for Your Organization

The way to tackle the big-picture job is by breaking what looks like a Herculean effort into sets of projects distributed across business units, sites, enclaves, service offerings, or whatever other piece-parts naturally constitute the whole of your network's physical and logical infrastructure.

For example, consider your network as collections of sites, each with their own internal infrastructure. Though the physical infrastructure is probably more or less contiguous (many organizations affected by IPv6 transition have several disparate networks, for example, for mission-critical operations versus administration, or for different levels of classified information), a functional diagram of the network segments at each site would show a little of everything; however, many sites will tend to have a dominant role or two.

For this discussion, I'll use classic business roles to keep things simple. Referring to Figure 4-1, each site is tied to the collective company network via the MIS/IT network segments. The central MIS/IT backbone isn't so much a physical site as connectivity. The physical infrastructure is contained in the MIS/IT clouds located at each site, with some of the machines connecting to the backbone. The backbone cloud represents leased lines from ISPs, VPNs over the Internet, and so on, mostly things your organization doesn't own. The termination points, however, like big routers and CSU/DSU devices, you do own, and they are part of your transition responsibilities.

In Figure 4-1, you see that each site has at least a little bit of connectivity to HR & Finance; people want to check their payroll records, access the employee directory, and perhaps utilize the agency credit union online. Central HR & Finance are at the Headquarters site, coordinating the functions at the remote sites.

The rest of the functions are more site-specific. Headquarters houses aspects of all of them. A separate site serves the Research nerds, possibly with their own unique connectivity to the MIS/IT backbone. Note that these sites are more logically, but not necessarily physically, separate. The Headquarters site may be the same physical place as the Research one. You have to keep an eye on the nerds, you know.

The particular example I'm using also has a single regional office and a local branch for servicing remote clientele. It is more than likely that any large enterprise has dozens or even hundreds of such smaller sites. For the purposes of the immediate discussion, I'll focus on one of each and extrapolate out later.

Creating Site- and Function-Specific Plans

The enterprise network segments depicted in Figure 4-1 can be categorized in several different ways. Each site has its own infrastructure with a (typically) small and manageable set of physical connections to the outside world. These connections make excellent boundary points for demarcating transitions, should you choose to upgrade site by site.

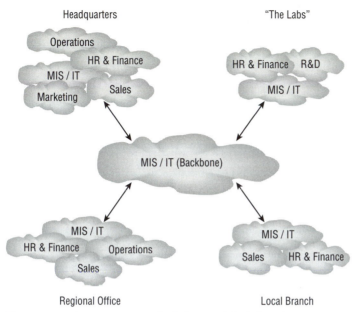

Figure 4-1: Separate networked sites and their functions throughout the enterprise

The enterprise-wide functions also provide a convenient means by which to break your IPv6 transition into smaller pieces. MIS/IT must almost certainly go first, but after that you can mix and match, staging your transition such that you don't have too many balls in the air at the same time. Once MIS/IT is moved, you can start on the HR & Finance functions, for example. One possibility is to make all the workstations IPv6-capable so they can use the new MIS/IT IPv6 infrastructure, first. Then, you can change applications one at time, re-directing the newly upgraded workstations from the legacy IPv4 servers to the shiny new IPv6 servers.

While creating your plans, remember that a device being IPv6 capable does not mean it has to be using IPv6 off the bat, either exclusively or even alongside IPv4. The HR & Finance workstations' IPv6 functionality could be left dormant until one or more applications are upgraded and are ready for use. This way, once you've checked out that the workstations still work like they did before being upgraded, you can forget about them and go focus on the applications.

Another possible twist to distribute the work of the network testing and certification efforts would be to enable IPv6 on small batches of workstations at a time to allow the users to test out the functionality for you, even before any HR & Finance applications are ready. You could direct them to simple IPv6 test applications at your site or other sites, the latter to test out the backbone. Or, you could even allow them to browse the growing set of external IPv6 websites.

Unless you're a techie or want to see the dancing KAME turtle (see Chapter 7), pickings are pretty slim out there right now. Hopefully, things will get better as others make the transition. By coupling such efforts with providing some form of incentive for users to check out the workstations' IPv6 capabilities, you'll at least shake things out and have a sounder test environment for the applications when they finally make the transition.

Coordinating Plans across the Enterprise

It's likely that there are multiple individuals or groups in your enterprise charged with planning and executing the site- and function-specific IPv6 transitions throughout the country and worldwide. Hopefully, there is one group leading and coordinating all this throughout the enterprise. If you're not in charge of overall strategic planning for your enterprise, you need to seek out that person or group and work with them to make sure your transition plans fit with those of the organization. They can also help you create your plans, because they are probably getting guidance from OMB or some other group.

Depending on how big your organization is, there may be coordinating groups within functions, and even at sites, that in turn report to the central group. You need to figure out where you fit into all this. I talk about that more in Chapter 6, "Defining the Transition Preparation Steps."

If there isn't a central group, you should work with others at your site or supporting your group's function to create one, or even become it. A benefit of being that group is that you get to call the shots and make sure everything is proceeding in an orderly fashion. The downside is that you have to clean up the messes that will inevitably occur. Only you can decide if that's the right thing for you and your team.

You must also consider the users of the networks in your care, who need to be made part of the plans so they know what's coming, can prepare accordingly, and can inform you of any constraints that must be applied while making the transition. You should both make them aware of your plans and educate them as best you can as to how the enterprise's overall transition is envisioned and is progressing.

Your users' involvement and interest will range everywhere from not caring, as long as they can get their jobs done, to wanting to kibitz about every aspect of the transition. Sticking with our fictional organization from Figure 4-1, examples of each follow.

Letting People Get Their Jobs Done

As the end of the quarter, and especially the fiscal year approaches, the HR & Finance and Sales groups will not be tolerant of disruptions, and rightfully so. You'll find a lot of resistance to change, or even to being bothered with "stuff that can wait until early next month." Sales is not as big a deal in the government sector, but every organization has some big thing, be it an annual audit, some other big project that's not MIS/IT related, or whatever that, if you know about it and work around it will be more likely to endear you to the users you serve than make you public enemy No. 1.

Engaging the Well-Intentioned Helpers Appropriately

Once hearing that IPv6 transition is coming to your organization, the R&D folks (and techies from other departments not charged with the work of MIS/IT) will seek out your team with a laundry list of well-intentioned "this would be cool" items. I've been in and near R&D my whole career and have great respect for those who are professionally seeking out the next great thing for your organization and perhaps the world, but these people's goals are different from yours. Respect them, but keep your eyes on the prize: a reliable and functioning enterprise network. Combining all those external technical folks under the umbrella of "R&D" for brevity, MIS/IT and R&D are closely related, both being technically focused groups. There are surely many collegial ties and even friendships between their members and those in your organization. To avoid disillusioning R&D while still getting your job done, don't simply shut them out because it's "none of their business."

Suggest that any ideas the R&D folks have be applied to their own subnets. They'll either agree, eagerly joining you in the good fight of IPv6 transition, or, they'll balk at touching their networks with unproven technology or concepts. Either way, you'll win and maybe in the latter case, they'll get an idea of why you're not as enthusiastic as they think you should be to throw the kitchen sink into the transition.

A side benefit of this strategy is that, should something not go to plan, other departments continue to function. Also, R&D folks are skilled resources you can use as extra pairs of hands to upgrade at least their networks, saving your people for the non-technical departments. Furthermore, should there be a glitch, you and R&D are the best minds to figure out what didn't work and fix it or improve something that's supposed to work on paper (especially the paper on which RFCs are printed). After all, that's part of both of your job descriptions.

A few words of warning though—engage the R&D staff only if both of the following conditions are met:

1. The R&D subnets must be suitably isolated from the rest of the enterprise. You don't want research experiments pouring out uncontrolled into the other business unit subnets. Look at what happened to Lilo (the one who's friends with Stitch).

2. Engaging R&D must not have the side effect of lighting up the phone lines in technical support. Not all researchers are created equal and not all are computer networking experts. If they generate questions about "how does this [sometimes irrelevant sub-feature] work" more than they add to your resource pool, don't engage them.

If either of these conditions is not met, consider instead engaging R&D in hands-off activities. Technical Advisory Boards are great ways to get honest-to-goodness useful information without too many hands touching the iron. A forum or blog of how things are going is also engaging. In either case, don't give yourself more work than you can handle. When it comes down to brass tacks, you do have the right to say "no thanks" politely to offers of help or requests for additional, but unnecessary, functionality.

Connecting IPv6 Islands

Once you're down the path of upgrading individual sites and business functions, you'll have to address how to interconnect all this stuff. Just because the R&D Labs are running IPv6 or half the HR & Finance applications are done, that doesn't mean everything will mesh smoothly across domains.

Islands of IPv6 capabilities will first come on line mostly via dual-stack implementations and tunneling (discussed later). Though a great way to get things started, your plans should include further transition steps to progress from tunnels to dual stack, and eventually native IPv6. There's no great rush on that last jump to all native IPv6, because IPv4 will almost certainly be an option for any place or any equipment that is IPv6 ready. A great incentive to get rid of IPv4, once you're satisfied that your IPv6 capabilities are sound, is that you won't have to manage two sets of address spaces, including their DHCP servers, DNS, and other infrastructure. Remember to keep IPv4 around long enough, however, until those external organizations with whom you communicate (and the Internet) are sufficiently upgraded. Remember that the more intermediate layers you remove as you connect smaller IPv6 islands together to make bigger ones, the more efficient your network will be.

IPv6 transition mechanisms are like the rigs and forms used when assembling any large structure, be it a house, a ship, an airliner, or a computer network. Up to a point, the structure can't stand on its own, so it needs temporary support. That support is as much a hindrance in the structure's final function, however, as it is an aid in its construction.

Consider the following example within one physical site, again based on Figure 4-1. You have moved some of the local HR & Finance LANs to IPv6, along with the network backbone. For efficiency's sake or perhaps security reasons, it makes more sense to connect two of the newly upgraded HR & Finance LANs through one whose transition is still in progress, rather than going into the IPv6 backbone and back out again. To do so, you have set up an IPv6 over IPv4 tunnel between the already-upgraded IPv6 LANs, using the connectivity of the IPv4 LAN. Eventually, the LAN in the middle will be upgraded. At that point, you can keep the tunnel, because the LAN will likely continue to support IPv4. Or, you can get rid of the tunnel (or retain it as an IPv6 tunnel for encryption) and simply route native IPv6 between the two original LANs in question via the third one.

Watch out for these kinds of things as you're planning and executing your transition. In the end, removing intermediate layers of complexity as they become unnecessary will make your job a lot easier.

Choosing a Quick Transition for Later

Assume that you're part of a U.S. commercial operation and have no idea what the big deal about IPv6 is, why your company would ever want to adopt it, or whether there's even a single application worth all this trouble. You're in a pretty big majority right now, but it's fair to say the times, they are changing. Without trying to hard-sell you that IPv6 transition is inevitable (face it: you must think it's a little inevitable, because you are reading this book), let's look at some reasons why you should be considering it.

Accepting that IPv6 Is in Your Network Now

Whether you like it or not, if you're managing anything resembling a modern enterprise network, you're probably running IPv6 already. Any network gear you've recently bought or upgraded from any of the major vendors is IPv6 capable. The major operating systems are likewise ready to go, especially Windows Vista, which comes out of the box looking to establish IPv6 networks.

With the exception of Vista, I've found that the IPv6 auto-configuration features need a little bit of a push to stand up an IPv6 network across a router, and even Vista will only do so if the router is likewise set up for auto-configuration. As for communicating on the same link, most IPv6 devices are ready to go, thanks to the link-local addresses discussed in Chapter 2, "Demystifying IPv6."

What Harm Can Link-Local IPv6 Do?

Remember the actual case in Chapter 3, "The Current IPv6 Landscape," of a covert IPv6 network set up under the noses of IT by a set of users smart enough to do so and dissatisfied enough with local IT policy to make the effort? You may say, "Big Deal," because the traffic won't cross your routers and, therefore, will not get out of your organization. That assumes you know where all the routers are and that they're all yours.

If the site with the users in question is somewhere in the outer rim of your network, you already have very little control over what's going on there. My experience is replete with cases of branch offices setting up DSL lines to get around slow corporate networks or "unfair" (or at least inconvenient) censorship of web content or access. These are the same types of people who would set up the ad hoc IPv6 network. With a combination of dual stacking or tunneling (discussed later), your whole network could be opened up wide to the Internet. Never mind that the RFCs say you shouldn't route link-local addresses, a rogue dual-stack system can translate the link-local addresses to legitimate IPv4 ones and route all it wants to the Internet.

Now, it's fair to say the DSL-line scenario could happen on a native-IPv4 network, and the only situations where I've actually seen such things myself are on IPv4 networks. In pure IPv4, the local site administrators stand a chance of at least accidentally seeing the oddball traffic shooting around the site and exiting the network through an unknown router, causing them to investigate. If the miscreants are using IPv6, even local administrators, never mind those back at HQ, without the proper IPv6 sniffing tools, would be unaware of what was going on under their very noses.

In addition to the unknown DSL connections issue, the rogue IPv6 link-local setup example raises two other closely related concerns. First, depending on your network's security policy, you may be required to monitor all traffic. You may have sophisticated tools to do so for IPv4. Other than raw dumps of network traffic, what do you have for IPv6? Such an ad hoc IPv6 network is a violation of that policy.

The second point is, if the users were disgruntled enough to set up the ad hoc IPv6 network to communicate secretly, who's to say they don't become further disgruntled and start hacking from this IPv6 Forbidden Zone? This is especially a threat to systems that have their own auto-configured link-local addresses enabled because that's how they came out of the box. Now, in addition to the IPv4 vulnerabilities, which you're hopefully patching, you're under attack from IPv6, and even worse, likely unaware of it.

Accounting for the Tinkering Administrator or Researcher

I mentioned previously that a little push was required to get inter-router auto-configuration going. Among the things you need is a valid address-space assignment. That's not too hard. As long as you have one valid globally routable IPv4 address, you can construct an IPv6 "/48" space of hundreds of millions of millions of addresses for your own use, via a technology known as 6to4 (see `http://en.wikipedia.org/wiki/6to4` for a layperson's description and RFC 3056 for the definitive technical details). You also need to set up that address space in a DHCP-like fashion for your router to dole out to IPv6 devices that come looking for connectivity. Regarding all this you may ask, "Why would I do that if I don't want to be running IPv6?"

The answer is that *you* may not, but somebody else in the organization with the brains and access to do so might, all in the interest of experimenting with the new technology. The good news is that they need to have administrative access to any routers they want to set up to auto-configure IPv6 or allow protocol #41 tunnels through (again, discussed later). So, to preclude this from happening at all, see the advice later for "curbing unmanaged IPv6 deployment until you're ready."

Discovering IPv6 in Your Pre-Transition Network

Pockets of IPv6 can be a little hard to see in a pure IPv4 network. The two main things to look for are IPv6-forwarding table entries on routers and IPv6 interfaces on all devices. If you are using SNMP-based network management tools, you can check out all the managed routers, servers, and so on in your whole enterprise from the comfort of your NOC. Make sure the management tools support the IPv6 MIBs; otherwise they may be blind to IPv6 configurations.

You must also make sure the end systems you are managing populate the MIBs correctly when IPv6 is in use. There are known cases, with FreeBSD for example, where IPv6 MIB elements are not fully populated, even though the systems have SNMP enabled and IPv6 configured.

Some tools will let you walk arbitrary parts of the SNMP OID tree. In that case, even if the tools don't know about the MIBs directly, you can specify the raw OIDs to see if there's data there. The SNMP MIBs you want to look at (per `http://www.networksorcery.com/enp/protocol/ipv6.htm`, May 30, 2007), in order, are:

- 1.3.6.1.2.1.48 (`iso.org.dod.internet.mgmt.mib-2.ipMIB`), defined in RFC 4293

- 1.3.6.1.2.1.55 (`iso.org.dod.internet.mgmt.mib-2.ipv6MIB`), defined in RFC 2465 (obsoleted by RFC 4293, but still in use)

If you already have some IPv6 connectivity, you should see how far it goes and make sure it's only going where you want it. If you have more than one IPv6 subnet, make sure their interconnectivity is appropriate. Basically, that means either they should show up as connected if they are supposed to be, or not connected if they're not supposed to be. This is a harder task than searching MIBs, because the unknown places your networks go are, by definition, not being managed by you. Therefore, you can't rely as much on SNMP (though it's not totally out of the picture).

For more information on discovering IPv6 in your network, see "Inventorying Existing Assets and Capabilities" in Chapter 6, "Defining the Transition Preparation Steps." You should also look at Chapter 11, "Knowing What Assets You Have," in particular, "What Discovery Tools Are Out There."

Planning the "Big-Bang"

The mechanics of planning an IPv6 transition set to occur at some later date are much the same as those for one that starts today. You will have more time to reflect on (or energetically debate over) the final big-picture view, as well as the details of what gets changed first, second, and so on Any delay brought about by such reflection is more tolerable when you're not in a mandated hurry and can slip a (likely arbitrary) transition date that's two years away by a week or two. Of course, if your organization suddenly "buys into" IPv6, where it was only a nice thing to have before, deadlines may become very real. You also won't have to worry as much about factoring the systems and networks that are already reconfigured into later stages of the plan, because the whole execution will take a relatively short time.

The difference in speed of transition is really one of perception, rather than reality. The measurement of speed that most will be using is that of how quickly the enterprise network went from 0 percent IPv6 capable to maybe 80 percent. With the slow transition mentioned previously, you ran three essentially parallel efforts of planning, pre-transition preparation work, and actual (visible) network re-deployment and configuration changes. For simplicity's sake, let's say each phase engaged ⅓ of your resources for 100 percent of the time, say a year. If you further assume the amount of work, whether you proceed "slowly" in parallel or "quickly" in series is roughly the same, a quick transition will engage 100 percent of your resources for ⅓ the time, but the final results will still take a year to achieve. If you set the expectations of those watching you correctly and tell them the transition "begins" at the start of the final ⅓ of the project, they will see the network go from 0 percent to 80 percent in four months. Wow, that was quick.

How Quick Is Quick?

Be careful about what a "quick" transition means. The transition from NCP to IPv4 all those years ago was like the flick of a switch. In actuality, it was probably the flick of fewer than 100 switches, with one person per switch. One day, the Internet was NCP and the next it was IPv4. No matter how quick you expect your transition to be, it will not be literally overnight or anywhere near that time.

A physical site, possibly representing multiple logical sites and thousands of people, much like the hypothetically collocated Headquarters and R&D sites in Figure 4-1, may switch over a long weekend or holiday break. That's about as fast as you're going to go. It's a huge effort to pull that off for such a large site, it is fraught with opportunities for disaster, there is no benefit in proceeding at that speed, and it's only one site.

Even the optimistic example earlier still managed to pull off a quick transition of the fictional enterprise in no fewer than four months. That's with eight months of planning and preparation work preceding it. Bottom line: when you're thinking quick, at least think in months, better yet quarters, for the actual network changes.

Preparing Applications before Changing Network Components

You'll see much more about this in the coming chapters, but your IPv6 transition is not just upgrading or replacing network hardware and configuring new addresses on systems. Recall, for one thing, there are all those applications to deal with that can't talk IPv6. Before you touch any network components, a later IPv6 transition allows you to purchase, prepare, or port all the applications you need beforehand. That way, there won't be any need for discussions of how to upgrade workstations, wait for the applications, convert IPv6 tunnels into native connections, and so on. You'll just upgrade the whole application and its users at once.

Still Upgrading the Backbone First

Just like with the slow transition, it's a safe bet you'll want to address the backbone first to minimize the chances that the transition will fizzle out. Isolated islands of IPv6 capability are nice for pilot programs and getting to know the technology. For upgrading the whole enterprise to IPv6, you don't want to be solving the problem of WAN connectivity over and over again each time you bring a new site up. It would be much nicer just to have long-haul IPv6 connectivity ready at the doorstep of all your sites when their transitions are ready for it. So, plan to do the backbone first when the time comes.

Waiting Means Re-Planning

You are surely aware that the network is a moving target. Though you control its configuration to some degree, other projects will come up as the IPv6 transition launch time approaches. New applications will become available that the organization "must have" to function properly. In deploying them, you will change the overall network configuration; probably enough to require re-addressing your IPv6 transition plans. This same phenomenon can occur with a slow transition, but because you're consciously aware of the transition activities from Day 1, any deviations or additional projects will factor in more naturally. On the other hand, if you create a plan today and put it on the shelf to be executed in a year, don't expect that plan to be ready to go when you are. You'll have to re-vamp it. That's another argument for proceeding at a slower pace, but starting now.

Curbing Unmanaged IPv6 Deployment until You're Ready

At the start of this section, you hopefully accepted that IPv6 is in your network already. Here you will find a set of steps to minimize unmanaged IPv6 deployment, until you are ready for it, and to reverse what unintentional or unauthorized IPv6 deployment has already occurred.

In reviewing the following steps, assume no IPv6 is allowed in your network at this time. I'll cover limited authorized IPv6 capabilities next. The steps you need to perform to check the unmanaged spread of IPv6 in your network, until you are ready to make the transition, are:

1. Check and lock down your managed infrastructure. That's easiest, because you have SNMP and your network management tools to help you. Verify that protocol #41, and in the rare case that IPv6 routing is actually going on, is turned off in your managed routers and end systems. Make sure that there are no IPv6 addresses configured, not even link-local ones. That's easiest by not allowing any IPv6 interfaces to be configured, active or not. The border routers are most important here, because they are exposed to the outside world.

2. Verify that you're not the cause of unintentional IPv6 deployments. Check the master images and configurations from which you build new servers, workstations, and so on. As with the managed gear, turn off protocol #41 and IPv6 routing, if applicable. Disable all IPv6 interfaces, if possible. Un-install (or don't install) any IPv6 feature packs if they are separate modules.

3. Using the techniques and tools from the this section, Chapter 6, "Defining the Transition Preparation Steps," and Chapter 11, "Knowing What Assets You Have," give your whole enterprise a periodic once over to make sure IPv6 hasn't crept in by accident or from tinkering or hacking.

4. Continually educate your staff and anyone else with privileged access to routing equipment, servers, and so on, that your organization is not ready for IPv6, plans are being formulated, and any "research" into its operation should not be conducted on the enterprise's networks. For those who want to experiment, Chapter 13, "Using Pilot Programs to Facilitate Your IPv6 Transition," offers information on how to set up pilot programs without disrupting the day to day business of the network.

Accounting for Existing Authorized IPv6 Infrastructure

Several organizations that are not ready to bite the bullet on full-blown IPv6 transition nevertheless have, in some cases significant, IPv6 infrastructures already in place. The obvious caveat to the preceding steps for preventing unintentional IPv6 deployment is to make an exception of authorized infra-structure. That doesn't mean you don't perform the steps. It means, in the case of step 1, all routers not involved in the authorized IPv6 infrastructure should be configured with no IPv6 capabilities enabled. This means drawing clear lines of demarcation as to where the IPv6 infrastructure is legitimately allowed to go, but that's planning you should do anyway.

For step 2, master images and configurations not going to build systems in the authorized IPv6 infrastructure should still be managed as described previously. If you have the resources and budget, it would be best to keep at least two types of sets of images: one type for the IPv6-capable stuff and one for everything else.

Scanning the network is still a good idea, as is educating your administrators and power users. The education step is especially necessary in this case, because with limited authorized IPv6 infrastructure the line of what's legitimately allowed on the enterprise network and what isn't is far blurrier than when all IPv6 functionality is outright forbidden. You need to point people at the IPv6 sandboxes and keep them there.

Rejecting the "Quick and Now" Transition Choice

A strong temptation, when facing an upcoming deadline, is just to get the project started and tackle problems as they come along. Whereas this may work for painting a room (or writing a book), it is a very bad idea to start tearing up your enterprise's network with no plan at all. In projects of the magnitude of an IPv6 transition, it's safe to remember the mantra "planning then doing beats planning when doing."

No matter what your end goal is for transition, you need to know from where you're starting. There are very few organizations that have comprehensive inventories of their equipment and application assets, and generating such inventories is not an overnight job. You learn more about how best to inventory assets and capabilities in Chapter 6, "Defining the Transition Preparation Steps." For now, rest assured, it's hard to create the inventories and even harder to keep them current.

In addition to understanding where you are currently, you need to know the "destination" of your transition and the path. What is the right combination of IPv6 transition mechanisms for your enterprise? If there are a lot of legacy IPv4 applications, you'll likely have to think more about dual stack (discussed later). If your applications are fairly new, some of them may already support IPv6. It's more than likely that there will be areas of your network that can make a 100 percent transition to IPv6 with minimal changes and others that need to cling to IPv4 until your vendors or in-house development teams catch up.

What is absolutely certain is that, without putting a fair amount of thought into it, a knee-jerk reaction will lead to wrong choices, a lot of re-work, and upset managers and accountants. So, whether you're executing now or later, do the planning methodically. With that said, understand that planning methodically doesn't implicitly mean planning slowly or to the nth degree. Check out the section in Chapter 5, "Creating Your Transition Plans," about planning enough, but not too much.

Selecting the Transition Mechanisms

At this point, I'll examine your choices of IPv6 transition mechanisms. Referring to Figure 4-2 through Figure 4-7, I'll get you acquainted with the various types and combinations of IPv6 and IPv4 stacks and tunnels. I'll discuss the highlights and lowlights of each and where each is most appropriate.

For those who may notice their pet IPv6 technology or concept missing, understand this book is not a compendium and comparison of every RFC, best practice, and bright idea for IPv6 transition. There are so many conflicting ideas and ideas with personal or corporate agendas behind them that picking the best from all the choices would be like picking the best car by test-driving all makes and models.

This book tries to make a hard problem tractable by applying project-management processes and providing a decent set of tools to guide you, the one who's supposed to make the transition happen yet who's still not sure (while sitting in your office at 10 p.m., probably near downtown Washington DC) how the heck you're going to get 10,000 IPv4 routers able to speak IPv6 to each other by June 2008.

Describing the Playing Field of Different Device Types

Before I get into the thick of things, let's define a few terms so you know what I mean when I talk about a device's capabilities. The devices I'm going to be discussing for the rest of this book fall into three classifications of capabilities:

- **IPv4-only devices:** These devices can only communicate using IPv4. That also means they can't tunnel IPv6 over IPv4, either. They are completely unaware that IPv6 exists.

- **IPv6-only devices:** The same as the IPv4-only devices, except they only know IPv6. Unless IPv4 has been administratively turned off, there are not likely to be such devices. The potential of having devices with IPv4 administratively disabled, for security reasons or whatever, must be considered, so I include these types of devices.

- ▪ **Dual IPv4/IPv6 devices:** These devices support both protocols. Unless specified otherwise, I'll assume they support all aspects of both protocols, including tunneling, IPsec, and so on.

If a device is mentioned as an IPv4 device (or an IPv6 device) with no other caveats, the assumption is that it has both sets of capabilities, but I only care about the IPv4 (IPv6) devices for the discussion at hand.

Here's one last note on IPv6-only devices. IPv4 may be systematically turned off on such devices as time goes on to allow reclamation of the enterprise's IPv4 address space for transfer to parts of the network that can't upgrade to IPv6 as quickly. Nice organizations might even give the IPv4 addresses back to their ISPs or LIRs. The latter is unlikely, however, until IPv6 is more solidly deployed, because organizations wouldn't want to take the risk that, once they've given back the addresses, they would be unable to reacquire the same amount of address space.

The types of transition devices are described more fully in RFC 4213.

Understanding What Enables Your Transition Choices

At the most basic level, your choices range from running IPv6 natively everywhere to running IPv6 in a tunneled mode in a prominently IPv4 environment. For the 2008 OMB mandates, the amount of IPv4 you use, especially in your backbone, limits your choices to a smaller set than those available to organizations not part of the U.S. federal government.

Reviewing Network Stacks

Figure 4-2 is the first of several network stack diagrams I'll be discussing. The network stack concept has been around even longer than IPv4 has. The exact origin of the concept goes back much further, but I don't need to dive deep into that here.

Network stacks are composed of layers, placed one on top of the other. Each layer relies on the services of the layer beneath it and provides services to the layer above.

The implementation of a particular layer is typically called a protocol. Protocols are not always explicitly called such. Sometimes they are referred to simply by the name of the layer at which they are implemented or by a new layer inserted between two existing ones. The latter can occur when a new protocol introduces functionality not envisioned by the definers of the stack, at least not at the layer where the new protocol is implemented. Such a protocol usually becomes the driver for a new layer in future stack definitions.

For example, the Secure Sockets Layer (SSL) is a protocol implemented at approximately the sockets layer of the stack. It is not a layer unto itself. Some would argue, and they wouldn't be particularly incorrect, that because SSL implementations themselves use sockets, they are more accurately placed at the application layer. There are other examples, but suffice it to say, I'm going to be using the term "protocols" for the things that are used to implement the layers of network stacks.

Note that I am not discussing the pure OSI model network stack in this book. For one thing, the OSI stack does not have a Sockets layer. Secondly, with the overwhelming adoption of TCP/IP, the OSI model is more an academic one than one of actual implementation. I'll be using stacks like the one in Figure 4-2.

Defining the Layers of our Stacks

The stacks I'll be talking about mostly have six layers. When I talk about tunneling, I'll add a seventh layer to represent the protocol being tunneled, but more on that later. From bottom to top, the layers are:

1. **Physical:** This layer encompasses the wiring, plugs, connectors, radio spectra for wireless networking, and other real-world items that make up the network. I won't spend much time here, because the wires that can carry IPv4 will carry IPv6, too. Any transition issues relating to the physical layer will be accounted for when I talk about equipment upgrades you'll need to get IPv6 functionality.

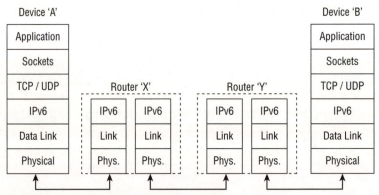

Figure 4-2: End-to-end native IPv6 stacks

2. **Data Link:** The first logical layer of the stack, the data link layer (or just, the link layer) addresses the formatting, transmission, reception, and oftentimes error-detection/correction of data going over the wires or radio waves from link to link. Its goal is to get a frame (as opposed to a packet) from one physical device to another directly linked device. With the proliferation of link-layer switching, this strict definition is now

rarely true, because practically every frame first travels to a switch before reaching its actual link-layer destination. If you think of all those switches as nothing more than "smart wires," the definition is good enough for our needs. There are changes in some link-layer protocols for IPv6; for example, in Ethernet there is a new EtherType for IPv6. These changes will be of little more concern than those at the physical layer and I will treat them the same way; by encompassing them in discussions about IPv6-capable equipment.

3. **Network:** Enables data to get from any device on the network to any other device. The network layer is responsible for enabling communications between devices, be they co-located in the same data center rack or half-way around the world from each other. These mechanisms include the addressing of network devices and the determination of the fastest, most reliable, or most cost-effective paths by which to allow devices to communicate. This is where both the IPv4 and IPv6 protocol are implemented and where the bulk of the transition discussions are centered. The stack diagrams you see in this book have either IPv4 or IPv6 written in the network-layer box, because I won't be talking about anything else.

4. **Transport:** This is where the concept of a connection-oriented network data stream is introduced in the stack, though not all transport-layer protocols are connection-oriented. The Transmission Control Protocol (TCP) and User Datagram Protocol (UDP) are the predominant members of this layer in the TCP/IP universe, and I will focus on little else in the transport layer. TCP and UDP enable network-based services via an abstraction known as a port number. TCP and UDP ports allow a single device to offer typically tens, but theoretically up to tens of thousands, of distinct services selectable by doing nothing more than having the requestor connect to the appropriate port(s) for a given service. For IPv6 transition, there is very little to do here. The protocols that run on the old favorite ports like DNS, HTTP, IMAP, POP3, SMTP, SNMP, SSH, and SSL operate no differently from a transport-layer point of view. New IPv6 protocols, like DHCPv6, define new TCP and UDP ports for their use, but legacy applications don't need to know about them. Firewall rules may have to be changed to pass the traffic, but that's a different matter. The stack diagrams in this book show TCP, UDP, or both at the transport layer.

5. **Sockets:** A pseudo-layer separating the application using network services and the TCP connections and UDP datagrams that communicate the data. The TCP/IP model blurs the lines between the OSI model's presentation, session, and transport layers. Rather than try to sort it all out,

I'll offer a pragmatic compromise and sweep the whole thing under the rug with what I'll call the sockets layer. Sockets offer a set of APIs with which application developers can open and use TCP connections and send or receive UDP datagrams. The nicest thing about sockets is that the complexity of programming them is roughly proportional to the complexity of what you have to get done. Put another way, you don't have to know the details of the four layers beneath you to send a simple "Hello, world" message to a server on another system. For all their blurry simplicity, sockets are included here, because the IPv6 transition of applications relies heavily on changes to how sockets are used. This is where the rubber meets the road for software vendors porting their applications to IPv6. It's also where in-house development groups will get their biggest exposure to what IPv6 transition really means. I talk more about porting applications in the coming pages, with some real-life experiences in Chapter 13, "Using Pilot Programs to Facilitate Your IPv6 Transition."

6. **Application:** The implementations of specific, sometimes complex, capabilities, composed of one or more network services, and accessed via sockets and ports in the TCP/IP universe. For example, though the TCP port number for the Simple Mail Transfer Protocol (SMTP) is defined at the transport layer (port #25), the guts of the SMTP payloads that travel up and down the TCP connections are created at the application layer. The same holds true for HTTP web transactions, FTP file transfer, virtual terminals like Telnet and SSH, and a host of others. There are other application layer protocols that implement inter-machine services, like BGP, DNS, NFS, and OSPF, which users rarely see. The goal of IPv6 transition is to minimize the impact on application-specific payloads.

You can see from this list that the epicenter of the IPv6 earthquake is in the network layer, radiating a little downward, but mostly upward to the sockets and application layers. The transport layer is barely scathed, as the shock waves travel through it heading upward, so perhaps IPv6 is more like a tornado that inexplicably leaves some homes standing while leveling those next door.

In Chapter 13, "Using Pilot Programs to Facilitate Your IPv6 Transition," I discuss what kinds of network applications are least affected by IPv6 transition and which are most affected. Without giving too much away, those that encode information from other layers in their data (for example, IP addresses in application-protocol payloads) will likely have a tougher time transitioning.

Leveraging the Benefits of Network Stacks for IPv6 Transition

The two properties of network stacks most germane to IPv6 transition are:

1. A protocol at a given layer of the stack only need know how to communicate with the protocol above it and the one below it.

2. Whatever protocol is implemented at a certain layer in the stack on one device must be the same as or compatible with the protocol at the same level in the stack on a device with which communications are desired.

Let's look at these properties one at a time. First, how does a protocol communicate with those above it and below it? Implementations vary from the straightforward, that have interchangeable modules for all the protocol layers, to those that use hardware acceleration to collapse several layers or the whole stack together into one module or chip (while still presenting a logical view of all the layers). In all cases that subscribe to modern programming practices, an Application Programming Interface (API) is employed to define a set of services offered by a protocol to those who use it.

Using APIs to Isolate Stack Layers

If you've programmed sockets, you've used the sockets API. Like sockets, each protocol layer presents an API to the one above it. An API is not required to be presented by upper protocols to those below them. Instead, the lower-level API is used by the upper protocol. Data and control information travel up the stack via the lower protocol populating buffers provided via its API by the upper-level one or as exceptions/interrupts out of band with regular control flow, but still defined by the API.

Lower-layer APIs can be as simple as sockets to use, at least in theory. Because APIs below sockets are usually very specific to the platform in question, rarely used or changed except by the creators of the platform, and can also be proprietary, documentation may be scarce. It's safe to say, however, that for any two different protocols that implement the same layer in the stack, there are far more similarities in the APIs of the two than there are differences.

Let's take the example of a simple UDP datagram and how it would be passed to the API of IPv4 versus IPv6. By the time the data to be sent reaches UDP from sockets, the UDP source and destination ports have been specified and that's about all you need for UDP. To construct the datagram header, UDP fills in the port numbers, computes and adds the fields for length and checksum, and appends the payload. The resulting datagram is passed down to the network layer as a single buffer. There is likely a helper data structure defining network-layer and perhaps even lower-layer parameters that UDP receives from the sockets layer and passes down with the datagram, but this data structure is opaque to UDP. As such, the IPv4 and IPv6 APIs probably look identical from the UDP point of view. One difference in UDP with IPv6 is that the checksum, which is optional with IPv4, must be populated correctly in the UDP datagram. This is almost certainly because of the removal of the checksum from the IPv6 header.

It is this property of layer isolation via APIs that limits the effects of IPv6 transition mostly to the network layer. I talk about the implications of what's in the helper data structure mentioned previously in Chapter 13, "Using Pilot Programs to Facilitate Your IPv6 Transition."

Pairing Compatible Protocols at Each Layer of the Stack

The second property of network stacks that greatly reduces the headaches of IPv6 transition is that, as long as you have available compatible protocols on two devices that desire to communicate, the odds are that they will be able to do so.

Protocol pairing is enabled by the API-based isolation I just discussed. As data get moved down one stack, protocol headers are added at each layer, protocol trailers may be appended, and the data themselves may be modified in some reversible way, for example, encrypted. On arrival at the destination device, the overhead added and the transformations applied on the way down are stripped off in such a way that whatever data structures and payload a protocol sees coming up the stack at a certain layer look a lot like the ones that its peer protocol on the sending device sent down.

For the same UDP datagram in the preceding section, as it travels down the stack an IP header is added. If IPsec is in use, additional headers and trailers may be applied, as well as encryption of the datagram itself. The whole thing is put in an Ethernet frame and transmitted as electrical impulses down a wire or over radio waves.

On arrival at the receiving device, the Ethernet frame is processed and discarded, because its only purpose was to get the IP packet contained within it to this particular device's link layer. The IP packet is passed up to the network layer, any IPsec encryption is reversed, and the IP header is stripped away and discarded, having served its purpose of getting the UDP datagram to this specific device's network layer. The UDP datagram is then passed to the transport layer's implementation of UDP. This is the same exact datagram that left the sending device in the first place.

Mixing and Matching Paired Protocols

A subtle nuance of pairing protocols is that the protocol pairs do not all have to be the same in a given network. If a device implements multiple protocols (for example, at the network layer), then it can act as a translator between two devices that do not have compatible protocols at that layer. If you're savvy, you'll realize I'm going to get a lot of mileage out of this when I start talking about dual stacks, that is, IPv4 and IPv6 in the same device.

Of course, it can't be that easy. A dual-stack device, as described earlier needs to know several things before it can relay traffic between native IPv4 and IPv6 systems. For one thing, each end device lives in a different address space. You can argue that this shouldn't be too much of a problem because the IPv4 address space is mapped to a proper subset of the IPv6 one (see RFC 4038 and RFC 4291). Well, what about the other way around? Can an IPv4-only client initiate a communication to an IPv6-only server? Yes, but only with a little help from the translating device. The translating device needs to advertise IPv4 addresses for the IPv6 server that the translator then re-maps itself into IPv6 addresses. There are several techniques for this and I talk about them more when I focus on deploying dual stacks for IPv6 transition.

Reviewing the Basics of DNS

Ask yourself whether the car you drive uses English or metric parts. If you're mechanically inclined, the question's probably pretty easy. Knowing who manufactured the car can lead you to an educated guess, though many foreign cars are made in the U.S. nowadays and vice versa. The correct answer: Who cares?

As the driver, you don't interact at the nuts and bolts level with the parts that make the car go. You interact with abstractions: the steering wheel, pedals, turn signals, gauges, and so on. A similar role is fulfilled in IP networking by the Domain Name System (DNS).

Making the Web Friendlier via Domain Names

DNS adds human-friendly context to IP addresses. What's your favorite search engine? Mine is `64.233.161.99`. Where do you like to shop online? I buy a lot of stuff from `72.21.203.1`. And, where do you go for a good laugh? Two of my favorite spots are `204.78.53.196` and `65.61.134.200`. If this were how the Internet worked, it wouldn't have gone anywhere. As a technical person, it was a minor pain to do the DNS lookups for those addresses. As a layperson, Alice or Bob Consumer, I would have walked into the Internet and walked right out and Amazon would have just been a river in South America.

While the Internet was still quite tiny in the early 1980s, a group of clever people came up with idea for DNS. Up until then, they had been using local "hosts" files or even raw IP addresses at the user-interface level to communicate between devices. Whether they foresaw the Internet's impressive future is debatable; though they may have hoped or dreamed it. What is more certain is that enough systems were being connected that sharing "hosts" files was no longer practical.

Understanding that DNS Is More Than a Phone Book

Some have referred to DNS as a phone book for the Internet. Although I suppose that's a pretty good analogy, here's where it breaks down for me. If I need to talk to someone I've never met before or call infrequently, sure I have to look up their number, but, I also know at least a dozen phone numbers of friends, colleagues, and favorite restaurants, right off the top of my head. No phone book is required. It's not that amazing and many other people are the same way. As far as the IP addresses of websites and so forth that I use regularly go, I don't know a single one. That's partly because IP addresses are complicated and partly because DNS does so much more than provide lookup services.

Of course DNS told me that 64.233.161.99 is Google, 72.21.203.1 is Amazon, and 204.78.53.196 and 65.61.134.200 get me to Dilbert and The Onion, respectively. Here's the even cooler part. I bet if you look up those domain names as you're reading this, some or all of them are not the same as what I got. Some lookups may return several values, and others may return different values each time you do the DNS lookup. Other than the services possibly having moved, what you're experiencing is DNS load balancing, virtual hosting, or some other advanced DNS-based service. Well, DNS is taking that load balancing capability in particular and adding a new twist with IPv6.

Giving DNS a New Job

The neat trick DNS learned for IPv6 is the ability to influence domain name lookups toward the IP protocol version the owners of the website want you to use. This is extraordinarily powerful, and a little dangerous.

Refer to the example I gave earlier for the organization whose network is represented by Figure 4-1. Let's say you upgraded the backbone and the HR & Finance workstations, and the workstations can now use IPv4 or IPv6 to access web services. Of course, the desired services must be running on the protocols being requested. An in-house application, let's simply call it Payroll, is located at https://www.hq.my.org/payroll, and until recently only available via IPv4. To get at the application, the user's web browser requests a DNS resolution of the IP address referred to as www.hq.my.org. Up until today, DNS has been returning an IPv4 address. That's about to change.

Controlling Which Version of an Application Is Preferred

Last night, in our example, an IPv6 version of Payroll was brought on line and seems to be working OK. So, the IT staff changed the DNS records to include the IPv6 Payroll server as the preferred address behind the domain name. In case something goes wrong, the old IPv4 address is still there. You can do that, because IPv4 addresses use what are called "A" records in DNS, whereas IPv6 addresses use "AAAA" records. They're four times the size, get it? Bottom line, www.hq.my.org can refer to IPv4 and IPv6 addresses at the same time. So, which one gets returned when queried?

For the technical details of how DNS has been augmented for IPv6, refer to the DNS-specific RFCs, particularly RFC 3484, and other references listed in "Further Reading" at the end of the chapter. For now, here's the 50,000-foot view.

The set of addresses, both IPv4 and IPv6 that DNS knows for a particular domain name can be ordered by preference. When DNS receives a query to resolve a domain name into an IP address, and the query simply asks for one address or any address, DNS returns the most-preferred one. This is independent of the underlying IP protocol version used to send the query. So, a DNS query made over IPv4 might return an IPv6 address and vice versa, unless the query is more constrained. If the query is for all addresses belonging to the domain name, DNS must respond (per RFC) with all the IP addresses. It is then up to the querying browser to decide which address to use. Or, the browser could try all the ones it's able to—all the IPv4 addresses if the browser is IPv4 only, all the IPv6 addresses if the browser only supports IPv6, or both if the browser supports both. This is the most robust solution and, if the application server is listening on even one of the addresses returned, the browser is most likely to make contact this way.

Using DNS as a Transition Tool

You can see how the preceding DNS features can be used during your IPv6 transition. The first thing you need to do is upgrade to a DNS that supports the IPv6 features. That's mostly a backbone thing, and I've already assumed you're doing that. Once it's in place, you can use DNS to act as a sort of railway switch, steering client workstations to the correct servers.

Before transition and during its early stages, DNS will be pointing at your legacy IPv4 servers. If you add any totally new IPv6-only servers, they'll get added to DNS, too. The interesting stuff starts as IPv4 applications on servers start to make the transition. When you get the first IPv6 versions running, you can change the DNS records to point to them as first choice. Should problems be encountered with the applications, you can reverse the rollout quickly and keep things running in the organization. If the application has a client side that's more than just a web browser, you can program the smarts into it to gather all the IP addresses for the application's domain name and then try the IPv6 ones and fallback to the IPv4 ones if no IPv6 connection can be made. This way, you don't have to change DNS except to add the IPv6 records in the first place.

Recalling That DNS Has Its Problems

You should be aware (and you are now) that DNS has its security flaws including cache poisoning, server spoofing (though that's not purely a DNS problem), and others. Relying on DNS to ease your life during transition is a double-edged sword and the more security conscious among you may want to scrutinize and apply your own security policies on what DNS returns, always asking for all IP-address records for a given domain name and picking the best one yourself. There are networks, several in the U.S. federal government, that don't use DNS at all. The security risks of DNS are too much to swallow for some highly secure networks or for those with missions with great operational criticality. For them, DNS as a transition tool is not an option.

Talking Realistically About Upgrading Applications

The choices in application upgrading can be boiled down into whether you want to:

1. write a new application from the ground up that cleanly handles IPv4 and IPv6

2. translate the IPv4 version of the application to use only IPv6 constructs, discarding the IPv4 ones and requiring both applications to be available and maintained for full functionality in both environments (for example, `telnet` and `telnet6`)

3. add IPv6 functionality to the old IPv4 version of the application, making one application that does it all, but maybe not as cleanly as the first option, because it's kind of a patch job

Few have the time for the first choice, plus you're introducing tons of new bugs with a totally new application; bugs that are distributed throughout every module and function. Now you're not just debugging networking code any more. The third choice is often the best from a usability perspective (you don't have to pick your application based on the IP version you want), but can also be pretty hard. Getting up and running quicker than choice 3 and with code that's sounder than with the first choice is best handled by choice 2.

When I get to Chapter 13, "Using Pilot Programs to Facilitate Your IPv6 Transition," you'll see that translating a networking-intensive application to IPv6 does roughly double the amount of code to maintain, but the translation is only about half as hard as adding IPv6 and retaining the IPv4 functionality in one application. Having the separate code base also allows you to experiment with the IPv6 version without messing up the, presumably deployed and relied upon, IPv4 one.

RFC 4038 is chock full of useful guidelines for upgrading applications. Its credibility is diminished a little in that it offers the ideal (and somewhat optimistic) advice that applications should have been written modularly in the first place with the networking code isolated and therefore easily replaceable or augmentable with IPv6 code. That's all very nice motherhood and apple pie talk, but hardly anybody does that, or, if they had set out to do it originally, adding more software developers into the mix over the course of the application's natural lifecycle slowly deteriorates modularity due to either pressures to hit release schedules or a lack of understanding of the intent of the initial functionalities, the overall software architecture, or the application's problem domain. Moreover, it's likely the key applications in your organization started life the same time you started grade school (or high school, if you're over 40) and modularity was even rarer then than it is now.

What you want is some way to get your devices and applications on IPv6 quickly and reliably. At the very least, you want to know clearly whether something is *not* going to work, so you can take the extra steps to fix it or replace it. Even if you do control the source code to your legacy applications, it's probably easier for you, at least initially, to surround the running application with an IPv4 environment and do the messy code changes at a saner pace later on when the IPv6 backbone settles down. RFC 2767 comes in very useful for that.

Addressing Security Issues

My work has orbited around security for my whole career. I've gotten as close to it as building pure security products (and e-policing the campus computer center) and as far from it as having to "consider" security when building products peripheral to it, like websites for purchasing consumer goods. Security permeates every aspect of the Internet, perhaps invisibly to the users at times, but it's always there (or should be). And, oftentimes, even when new capabilities or technologies come out, the basic security problems and solutions remain fundamentally the same. IPv6 is no different.

For example, in all the IPv6 transition mechanisms described next, essentially the same concepts apply as in IPv4. For example, IPv6 firewalls are a little different from IPv4 in the sizes of addresses and the description of network ranges. The TCP and UDP ports on top of IPv6 are the same for the purposes of setting up firewall rules. Stateful inspection is the same, as well.

IPv6 does introduce some new security issues of its own. I've talked about and will continue to discuss the need to be cautious with auto-configuration. The IPv6 community will tackle these new issues as they come along and protection mechanisms and best practices will develop over time.

Though there are the security issues inherent in the IPv6 mechanisms, what you really need to determine is whether the domain-specific or mission-specific security mechanisms, software, and procedures you use in your enterprise and day-to-day life will upgrade satisfactorily to IPv6. No IPv6 security working group is going to solve those for you, because they are unaware of (and possibly not cleared to know) them.

These issues include any requirements placed on you for authentication, access control, audit, and whatever other security concerns your organization has. For example, if you have any surveillance equipment, badge readers, or automated door locks that log to a central server the entry and exit of people to or from your facility, you need to know whether these devices can be configured with an IPv6 address or if a little piece of IPv4 infrastructure has to remain in place for them. This isn't the book to address that level of enterprise-specific detail. You need to talk with your security officer, CSO, or corporate security folks, if you aren't doing so already as part of your transition preparations and planning. You'll also need to talk to the vendors of such devices.

Considering Advanced IPv6 Capabilities during Transitions

In Chapter 7, "Identifying Some Common Transition Preparation Tasks," I'll be touching on new sets of features introduced with IPv6. At the same time, I will continue to favor the use of the more vanilla mechanisms that replicate existing IPv4 functionality. Part of the reason is that many of the new features are still in flux, and I don't want to muddy the transition waters by having to deal with standards built on shifting sands.

One exception, as I've noted, is auto-configuration. Because it's such a key component of IPv6, both as a transition easer and as a potential security nightmare, I can't gloss over it. Flow labels, advanced multicasting, and mobile IPv6 can all be deployed later, after the main transition has had a chance to take root and prove itself.

You are encouraged to research these advanced features, and Blanchet's book, listed in the "Further Reading" section of Chapter 1, "What Is IPv6?," is an excellent source. Heck, since you're tearing up everything anyway, like with IPsec, while you have the engine out of the car, you might as well think about changing the head gaskets. Perhaps mobile-IPv6 or multicast can solve some problem in transition better than anything else.

Deploying Native IPv6

The best choice for IPv6 networking, and the one we'll all likely be running by 2038 or so, is to deploy a pure IPv6 backbone, followed by the applications, servers, and user workstations. Looking at the top-right and bottom-left parts of Figure 4-8 and how they have nothing between them but the native IPv6 backbone, it's clear the native mechanisms have the fewest and least-complicated parts. It is, in the IPv6 universe, the equivalent of the native IPv4 environment you see everywhere today.

A fully native deployment has the downside of providing no safe backup, should a glaring flaw be found in IPv6. There have already been minor to moderate flaws found, but they mostly mimic similar flaws in IPv4. As such, features such as source routing are not relied upon in IPv4 and the fact that IPv6's equivalent to source routing is also flawed doesn't mean much. In fact, it sounds a little naïve in hindsight to assume an IPv6 feature that looked so much like a flawed IPv4 one wouldn't have similar flaws of its own.

So far, there have been no glaring flaws in the basic IPv6 packet header. Being that it's quite a bit simpler than the IPv4 one, this is not surprising. Traffic class and flow label are the most complicated things in there and the most rarely used. To go out on a limb, let's say that there are no inherent flaws likely to be found in the basic IPv6 header; at least not any that aren't also present, and well-understood, in the equivalent fields of the IPv4 header.

Running Dual Stacks

It's a simple conclusion to draw that, if you could quickly and transparently replace IPv4 at the network layer in all your routers, servers, PCs, laptops, and so on, with IPv6, this whole transition brouhaha would be that much hot air.

The practical matter is that, even if it were a transparent change, the only way you could do it and retain full network functionality throughout the whole transition would be if you did it everywhere all at once. In addition, all the applications would have to upgrade at once, which means you would have to wait until each and every last application was IPv6 capable or was retired or replaced by an IPv6-capable one. In some cases, especially in the federal government, that could take decades before you could even contemplate a transition.

Although a pure native IPv6 network is the best long-term choice, the reality of things is that there are many applications (and some devices) that are just not ready for such a big leap. You've probably already drawn the logical conclusion that for any pragmatic IPv6 transition, you have to run both IPv4 and IPv6 stacks, a.k.a., dual-stacks, on much of the equipment; certainly in the network backbone and likely in the LAN routing equipment, as well. This is actually less complicated than it might sound. It's not like you have to have two of everything, the way you would if you needed natural gas and electric utilities in your home.

Because you're upgrading to IPv6, it's obvious you'll be buying IPv6-capable equipment. Well, the good news is, as I hinted earlier, that I'm not aware of a single IPv6-capable device out there that isn't also IPv4 capable. The relationship between the IPv4 and IPv6 capabilities of a particular piece of network hardware, or application software for that matter, is much more like that of HDTV versus regular old-fashioned TV than it is gas and electric appliances. If it runs the more modern one, it is almost certainly compatible with the older one. Another good example is pulse versus touch-tone telephones. Have you ever seen a touch-tone only (non-cellular) telephone?

Having the Best of Both Worlds

When you think about dual-stack networks, you probably think about configurations like the one depicted in Figure 4-3. The figure shows two routers and two end devices connected to an IPv6 backbone that also supports IPv4. This way, two legacy IPv4 devices can connect to each other and communicate with no knowledge of the IPv6 capabilities along the path between them. Similarly, IPv6-capable end devices can communicate in a native mode with no tunneling or translation in between.

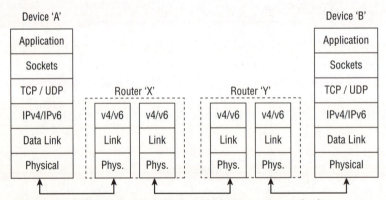

Figure 4-3: Connecting two dual-stack devices using a dual stack backbone

Mapping IPv4 Addresses to IPv6 Addresses

I mentioned earlier that there are IPv4-mapped IPv6 addresses (see RFC 4291). The nice thing about increasing the address-space size, especially by the amount IPv6 did, is that you can set aside a chunk of addresses to support the old space. So, in many cases, if an IPv6 device wishes to communicate with an IPv4 device, from its point of view it need only enter the IPv4-mapped IPv6 address. It's not that easy of course in the grand scheme of things, because the purely native IPv6 device will emit an IPv6 packet that will not be understood by the IPv4 destination, if the packet even gets anywhere near that destination.

What also needs to happen is that someone, perhaps the originating device or perhaps a router along the way, needs to translate that IPv6 packet into an IPv4 packet *and* provide an IPv4 source address so the destination can respond in a way that it understands. On the way back, the IPv4 packet needs to be transformed to an IPv6 packet and the original IPv6 source address (now used as the destination for the response) needs to be inserted in it. The source address of the responder, however, need only be encoded in the IPv4-mapped IPv6 format.

The preceding is an example of the "Bump in the Stack" (BIS) mechanism outlined in RFC 2767. With such a mechanism, a dual-stack workstation can use IPv4-mapped addresses to allow a local IPv4-only client application to communicate transparently with remote IPv6-only servers. A reverse mechanism would allow IPv6-only clients to talk to IPv4-only servers, as long as there was BIS functionality in a device in the path between client and server. The eventual goal is to create an application that supports both native IPv6 and IPv4 addresses, but IPv4-mapped IPv6 addresses are a good way to get started fast.

Figure 4-4 shows an extension of the concept with the BIS mechanism implemented in Router 'X' to allow the legacy client 'A' to talk with upgraded server 'B'. The original RFC implementation would collapse 'A' and 'X' into one device. For this to work, another mechanism from RFC 2767 must be used: a DNS resolver extension to provide 'A' with an IPv4 address for 'B' that would route through 'X'. 'X' also needs to be able to gather from DNS the association between the IPv4 address sent to 'A' and the real IPv6 address of 'B'.

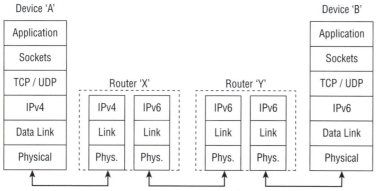

Figure 4-4: Connecting an IPv4 device to an IPv6 one using dual stacks

Going Through Tunnels

When driving in the mountains, there are times when the only way to get from one point to another is by going through a tunnel. The same was true for IPv6 in its early days. With no wide-area native connectivity, tunnels were where IPv6 got its start and did a lot of growing up.

Some of the first tests of IPv6 occurred on a test-bed network called the 6BONE, a short form for IPv6 backbone. I won't be going into the 6BONE much here, but you can read up on its history from the "Further Reading" section references and by visiting `http://www.6bone.net/`.

One final lesson to be learned from the 6BONE is that, once something is part of the infrastructure, it takes a truly long time to go away. Though phased out in June 2006 by RFC 3701, as of May 2007 there were still at least 18 active routers on the Internet with 6BONE addresses. In fact, according to data from Lumeta's IPv6 Internet Mapping Project (see `www.lumeta.com`), from April 1st (no joke) through May 25, 2007, the number of routers with 6BONE addresses has steadily oscillated between a minimum of 16 and a maximum of 21.

Adding a Layer to the Stack

Several pages back, I talked about the six-layer stack I was going to use for describing transition mechanisms. You were warned that a seventh layer was going to be introduced, and here it comes.

There are a few ways I could have described tunneling. Technically, both the IPv4 and IPv6 protocols are in the network layer, and tunneling is just one protocol using the services of the other, so, it's not really a new layer. To simplify explanations of concepts like protocol pairing and the use of APIs to isolate stack layers, the extra-layer description seemed the best for what is not meant to be an overly technical book.

Figure 4-5 shows the network stacks for how IPv6 started out life. In a totally IPv4 environment, researchers wanted to test IPv6 on a grander scale than just a few labs, so the resources of the existing Internet were brought into play. That demanded IPv6 be wrapped in IPv4.

Recall the example of a simple UDP datagram passed to a network-layer API for transmission. When tunneling IPv6 over IPv4, UDP sits on top of IPv6. The datagram is passed down along with the helper data structure I mentioned, and the IPv6 header is constructed. The resulting packet would normally be passed to a link-layer protocol, like Ethernet. Instead, the packet is passed to IPv4, but, there's a catch. It's no longer a UDP packet, so you can't put in the protocol number for UDP. Fortunately, IPv4 is extensible enough to deal with this.

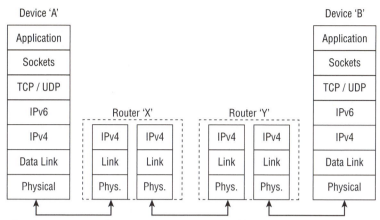

Figure 4-5: Tunneling IPv6 over an IPv4 backbone

Introducing Protocol #41

The network stack concept is one of the most wonderful things about modern computer networking. You can mix and match protocols with quite a bit of abandon and be pretty darned sure in the end that what you've built will work. Think of all the "over" protocols you know. For the purposes of IPv6 transition, there's IPv6 over IPv4 and vice versa. In a broader scope, there's also:

- **PPP over Ethernet:** First defined in RFC 2516, PPPoE is a modification of the Point-To-Point protocol used initially with serial dial-up lines. With the advent of Digital Subscriber Line (DSL) technologies, PPP adapted to broadband.

- **Protocols over HTTP:** At the opposite end of the stack, many protocols have been implemented to run over HTTP, due to the ubiquitous nature of the web and the porousness of firewalls to it.

- **IP over Carrier Pigeon:** RFC 1149, one of the great "April Fool's" RFCs, presented the concept of carrying IP datagrams by carrier pigeon. Though meant as a gag, the concept was certainly feasible, if not practical, thanks to the network stack concept. In fact, in April 2001, an implementation of the protocol was successfully tested. You can read the details at `http://www.blug.linux.no/rfc1149/`.

Protocol #41 is designated for encapsulation of IPv6 packets within IPv4 packets (see RFCs 3056 and 4213). The encapsulation is entirely opaque, as it should be, meaning IPv4 has no special information about the payload it is carrying other than that it is using protocol #41.

Recalling the property of protocol pairing mentioned earlier, the IPv6 payload is transported by IPv4 to the destination IPv4 address. This requires additional information in the helper data structure, both the IPv4 and IPv6 addresses of the destination device. The IPv6 address is provided via the application using sockets, because the application thinks it's only using IPv6. The IPv4 address is either permanently set or brokered between the sending device and the device terminating the tunnel.

Figure 4-5 shows the termination point of the tunnel being the same as the destination of the IPv6 packet. This is by no means a requirement. Figure 4-6 shows the more-typical case for tunneling where the tunnel is terminated at Router 'Y'. I'll cover that shortly.

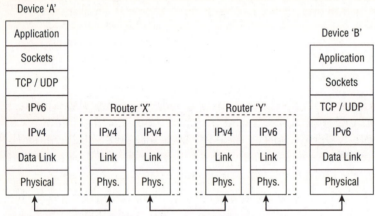

Figure 4-6: Combining tunneling with dual stacks

Understanding the Routing of Tunneled Packets

Another nice property of network stacks is that data in transit need only go far enough up the stack of an intermediate device, a router at the network layer or a bridge at the link-layer, to determine the next place it has to go.

For routing, a packet comes in one interface of a device, because that's where the link-layer frame is addressed, and is pushed to the network layer. The network layer protocol determines that the packet is not destined for any of the IP addresses the device is using, so it has to decide what to do with the packet. In the purely sunny-day case, the router consults its routing table and determines the interface out of which the packet must be sent to continue its journey. The router transmits the packet out of that interface and that relationship between packet and router comes to an end. That's why the Internet is so efficient: no long-term commitments to packets. For a comprehensive discussion on routing, see, for example, *Network Routing Basics: Understanding IP Routing in Cisco Systems* (Macfarlane, Wiley, 2006).

Because you are tunneling IPv6 over IPv4, you don't need to push the packet up to the IPv6 protocol. You don't even have to dismantle the IPv4 encapsulation packet en route. Referring again to Figure 4-5, the intermediate devices 'X' and 'Y' need only push the data up to IPv4, which then determines that packet has farther to go. On reaching device 'B', IPv4 determines that the packet is in fact destined for the local device and, therefore, strips off the IPv4 header and pushes the payload (the IPv6 packet) up the stack. The local IPv6 implementation is none the wiser that this has occurred and treats the packet just as if it had been passed up by Ethernet or any other link-layer protocol.

Terminating Tunnels at a Common Point

The preceding example describes an end-to-end tunnel. In other words, the tunnel starts at the device that wishes to communicate and terminates at the destination device. This simple example is not how tunnels typically are implemented, unless end-to-end security is required. IPsec and other security protocols focus more on end-to-end tunnels, because the overarching goal is security versus just connectivity. As end-device hardware continues to get more powerful and less expensive, end-to-end tunnels may become more the norm. For now, VPN concentrators and tunnel peering points are still the way to go for plain old connectivity.

Let's go back to the example of driving through the mountains from way back at the beginning of our tunneling discussion. The purpose of a tunnel is to allow traffic to get through something that the native transportation method can't negotiate (for example, a car can't drive through solid rock). Furthermore, tunnels are more expensive to build than roads, so you want to reuse them whenever you can.

If the mountain through which I want to get our tunneled traffic has on the other side of it a hotel, gas station, and restaurant, I'm not going to build three tunnels terminating in the parking lots of each establishment. I'm going to build one tunnel to some convenient common point and then run less-expensive roads the rest of the way. This is how tunneling is done in IP networks, too.

Understanding Tunneling to a Common Point

Comparing Figure 4-5 and Figure 4-6, you see two distinct differences. In Figure 4-6, Router 'Y' has both an IPv4 and an IPv6 stack. Device 'B' has no IPv4 protocol implementation in the network layer. Router 'Y' has taken on the characteristics of a common termination point for IPv4 tunnels to a native IPv6 network. So, how does this change what happens to the traffic en route?

Upon reaching Router 'Y', the IPv4 packet containing the IPv6 packet is pushed, as before, to the IPv4 implementation at the network layer. The packet is different, however, from the one in the preceding example. Instead of the IPv4 destination address being on Device 'B' (which is good, because 'B' doesn't have an IPv4 stack), the IPv4 destination address is on Router 'Y'. The router, therefore, determines that the packet is for one of its local IPv4-addressed interfaces.

What happens next is that the router strips off the IPv4 header, because the packet has reached its final (IPv4) destination. For normal end devices, the payload would then be pushed up to the transport layer and ultimately an application using the stack to communicate. The router serving as a tunneling end point has enough smarts to realize that the payload is an IPv6 packet, and takes that packet and passes it to the IPv6 protocol, to let it decide what to do next.

The IPv6 protocol examines the packet passed from IPv4, though the packet could just as easily have come from Ethernet. IPv6 performs routing processing just like IPv4 does, in this case determining that the destination address is not local to the router. The protocol implementation consults the IPv6 routing table at that point and determines from which interface to transmit only the IPv6 packet (remember, the IPv4 packet is long gone) so that the packet may continue its journey to the destination.

The IPv6 packet is transmitted, arrives at Device 'B', is processed the same way as described before, and gets pushed up to the transport layer and ultimately the application.

As you might expect, the response from Device 'B' to 'A' follows the reverse path. Upon the IPv6 packet's reaching Router 'Y', the router realizes the only way to get to Device 'A' is through a tunnel. The router constructs the appropriate IPv4 header, appends the IPv6 packet as the payload, and sends the whole thing out the appropriate interface so that the packet can make its way to 'A'.

Without too much muss or fuss, the two devices are communicating over IPv6 and only Device 'A' and Router 'Y' are even aware that tunneling is going on. As for Router 'X', it's just forwarding IPv4 traffic and is also totally unaware (or at least uncaring) that tunneling is going on.

One last thing to take away is that there is no reason in the world why Router 'X' can't be similarly equipped as Router 'Y' with a dual stack and the ability to tunnel. In that case, you can remove the IPv4 implementation from Device 'A', and both end devices will obliviously believe they are on a native IPv6 network with no clue that IPv4 is anywhere to be found.

What about Tunneling IPv4 inside IPv6?

To cover all the bases, if I'm going to talk about tunneling IPv6 inside IPv4, what about the opposite case? For one thing, someday the tables will be turned and IPv6 will be the dominant protocol. Just as there are still some stragglers on the "phased-out" 6BONE, there will be IPv4 stragglers in the IPv6 world.

What are the options for tunneling IPv4 over IPv6? Fortunately, as is often the case when a new thing replaces an old one, the new thing is aware of the old thing and can take it into account.

RFC 2473 is all about tunneling in IPv6. It covers both IPv4 and IPV6 tunneled through IPv6. Why would you want the second type? Three letters: V-P-N.

Referring to Figure 4-7, you see tunneling IPv4 inside IPv6 is pretty much the mirror image of IPv6 inside IPv4. In fact, you can understand how IPv4 tunnels inside IPv6 simply by re-reading the section "Understanding the Routing of Tunneled Packets," while substituting the term IPv4 for IPv6 and vice versa. The same holds true for switching IPv4 and IPv6 in the discussion about "Terminating Tunnels at a Common Point."

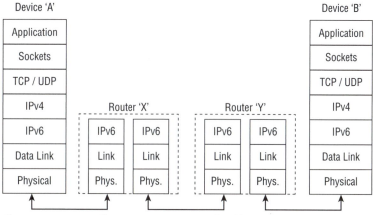

Figure 4-7: Tunneling IPv4 over an IPv6 backbone

Factoring MTU Issues into Tunneling

IPv6 introduces new Maximum Transmission Unit (MTU) minimums that are greater than those of IPv4. Basically, MTU is the maximum packet size a link will allow before requiring fragmentation. In IPv4, any packet of 576 octets or fewer was guaranteed not to have to be fragmented, at least at the network layer. IPv6 raises that value to 1280 octets. Any packet that size or smaller, if it cannot fit through the link in one piece, must be fragmented and reassembled transparently below IPv6 (for example, at the link layer).

In tunneling one protocol over another, there are two minimum MTU sizes to consider. For IPv6 over IPv4, potential fragmentation needs to be accounted for, because IPv6 could ask for packets larger than 576 octets to be tunneled and the tunnel may have to fragment. Such an IPv6 packet could require two or more IPv4 packets to transmit it through the tunnel. This means any configurations you had in place that limited tunnels to less than 1280 octets need to be reviewed to make sure fragmentation is supported and works correctly. For typical connections, the MTU is set to 1500 octets, so this shouldn't be too much of a problem.

In the inverse case of tunneling IPv4 over IPv6, fragmentation isn't as big a deal, because the IPv6 packet is guaranteed to carry at least 1280 octets, less the size of the IPv6 header and any extension headers. Still, a large IPv4 MTU (even 1500 octets) and a small IPv6 one could still cause problems. Remember, IPv6 only fragments at the source of the packet. So, the IPv6 packet has to be small enough when transmitted from the source to fit through the tiniest MTU en route to its destination.

You can read more about fragmentation issues and tunneling in RFC 4213. All the gory details are too technical for this book, but things you'll have to think about in your IPv6 transition planning. In this book, I'll cover the MTU topic by making it one of the criteria for upgrading or replacing equipment, cabling, other connectivity should MTU values not be acceptable.

Assessing the Security Requirements of Your Tunnels

I've been implicitly assuming the tunnels you'll be using are as secure as you need them to be. That means, if you just need basic tunneling and have no concerns about privacy or authentication (perhaps you're using link-layer mechanisms), then simple encapsulation is fine. Otherwise, IPsec and other such protocols may come into play. In that case, RFC 4891 provides you with what you need to use IPsec for secure IPv6 over IPv4 tunnels.

Considering IPsec

IP Security, or IPsec, has been around in RFC form at least since 1995. It is a suite of protocols designed to provide strong authentication, privacy, integrity, and other security services, mostly through the use of strong cryptography.

IPsec support is optional for IPv4 implementations, but mandatory for IPv6. What that means is not that IPv6 networks must use IPsec. Rather, it means that they must *be able to* use it. This is different from IPv4 where a particular piece of network gear may not support IPsec. Note that this also adds to the cost of IPv6 equipment. Because you're going through an IPv6 transition, you have the equipment and the equipment has the features, perhaps you should be using IPsec.

Benefiting from Strong Authentication and Encryption

There are many benefits to strong authentication and encryption. The basic services offered with IPsec at the IP layer enable very useful features higher up the networking stack and in applications. Privacy and integrity services, available via higher-level protocols like the Secure Sockets Layer (SSL) for e-mail and web transactions would be possible for all legacy protocols considered impossible, or at least financially infeasible, to secure.

Three very useful services, whose greatest weaknesses are in their security (or lack of it), are SNMP, Telnet, and FTP. Security services have been grafted onto these protocols in later versions, or replacement protocols have come into favor, but the insecure versions are still very popular and security-conscious users or administrators are sometimes forced to look the other way, because the business need for a protocol outweighs its security flaws. IPsec could help these people breathe easier.

Combining Two Big Changes to Ease the Pains of Both

You already know that your IPv6 transition will not be an easy job. The addition of enabling IPsec won't make the job easier. What it may do, however, is reduce the total workload associated with doing both projects. By assessing if IPsec is something you should be using now or fairly soon, you can decide whether to have one transition or several.

Making the transition of your networks to IPv6 requires you to address the fate of nearly every piece of network and end-device hardware, along with every application in your environment. The purpose of this book is to guide you through the complexities of such a huge endeavor. Because you are doing all that work, and because there are so many benefits to IPsec, this would be a great time to see if you can manage to incorporate IPsec into your IPv6 transition.

You can use IPsec to protect your new IPv6 networks and choose to leave IPsec off in IPv4. This way, as you are upgrading, you can be even more comfortable that the two different networking infrastructures are interacting only in ways that you desire.

Being Comfortable the Workload Is Manageable

A critical factor for deciding whether to include IPsec in your IPv6 transition is whether the resulting workload is manageable. If you were lucky enough to have resources or budget dedicated for IPv6 transition, those who dedicated the amount will likely not have thought about IPsec. This is sort of an academic question because the people who decided how much to dedicate to IPv6 should be working closely with you and should be informed of what work and capital outlays are required, but, perhaps you presented your staffing and budget requests before thinking about IPsec. Before continuing, be sure that what was received will be enough, should you decide to go with IPsec.

For those of you who received the unfunded mandate to make a transition to IPv6, the reasoning is that IPv6 comes along for the ride with regular technology refresh cycles. Though debating the validity of that reasoning is left to other sections of this book, here I'll note that the enabling of IPsec being included in the mandate is unlikely. It is more likely that the technology refresh argument was focused more on renumbering assets and replacing equipment and applications as necessary to enable IPv6.

Though I just discussed the potential for overloading your resources by doing a combined IPv6 transition and IPsec deployment, this section applies to every aspect of your transition effort. Don't lie to yourself. More importantly, don't over-commit when setting the expectations of others.

Realizing a Hybrid Approach Is the Best

As with all things in life, one solution does not solve all problems. Your IPv6 transition will almost certainly end up deploying a combination of native IPv6, dual stacks, and tunneling. You'll also upgrade your applications every conceivable way I discussed, because there are far more applications than transition mechanisms and each application fits best with only one or two of the mechanisms.

Each of the mechanisms described earlier is a tool in your IPv6-transition toolbox and each has its pros and cons. Deploying IPv6 using a combination of mechanisms, emphasizing their strengths and accounting for their weaknesses, is no different from selecting a hammer to hang a picture and a wrench to tighten a bolt. It could be done the other way, but the results wouldn't be as good.

Assembling the Jigsaw Puzzle

I find concrete examples, even fictional ones, work wonders to get ideas across. So, let's take a look at a fictional pure IPv4 enterprise network and how it might use the mechanisms described previously to make the transition to IPv6.

Like one of those cooking shows that first presents you a sample of the finished meal, Figure 4-8 shows the intermediate results of a transition that used all of the mechanisms to one degree or another. Understand, I say intermediate because the final product is not the hodge-podge of native IPv6, dual stacks, and tunnels. The ideal steady-state that will eventually come of all these changes to your network is a fully native IPv6 network with no reliance on whatever vestigial IPv4 is left over. That's what you're working toward, right?

Checking Reality on Future Pure IPv6 Networks

Before you get your stomach all in knots that you've got to get everything in your network to IPv6 for the transition to be complete, take a moment to recognize that this will never happen.

Just like NCP gave way to TCP/IP on what the Internet was in January 1983, IPv4 is expected eventually to bow out, leaving the world to the mainstream (at some future date) IPv6 protocol. One difference between NCP and IPv4 is that, when it was time to get rid of NCP, everybody (and I do mean everybody) using the Internet at that time agreed to do so at the same time and together flipped a switch to turn NCP off and engage TCP/IP.

That's not how IPv4 will go. Just like the 6BONE is lingering, don't expect IPv4 to go quietly into the night just because somebody (or a lot of somebodies) said it was time to go. To quote Stuart Smalley, "...and that's...okay." In fact, I'm willing to bet that when IPv6 is firmly ensconced, there will be some upstart group of researchers with their new protocol, call it IPv186K, gaining acceptance because IPv6 was so poorly designed for handling the inevitable faster-than-light communications that the future world so clearly needs. That's the way things go in evolution. There's never a clean break.

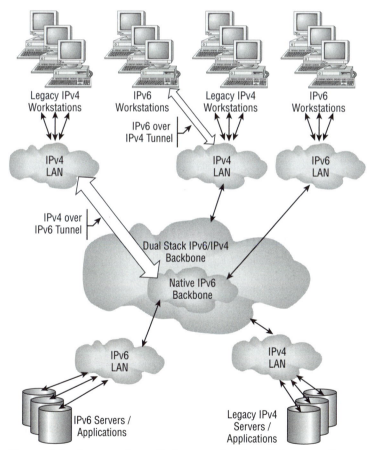

Figure 4-8: A composite realistic network using all the preceding mechanisms

Returning to the Example IPv6 Transition in Progress

In the example shown in Figure 4-8, you see a network that's well along in its IPv6 transition. This network started from the "before" state of a bunch of IPv4 LANs connected by an IPv4 WAN. There was probably tunneling being done, for remote access by VPN, for example, but, it was likely IPv4 over IPv4 tunneling, so I can lump that into the pre-transition state.

The figure does imply that there may have been at least little snippets of IPv6 tunneling on IPv4. This is hinted by the IPv6 workstations you see still using tunneling to an IPv4 LAN to connect to the network. They could use one of the IPv6 LANs natively without tunneling, but the purpose of the example is to show what odd configurations rise up during organic network growth and have to be taken into account. Perhaps the workstations can only access the IPv4 LAN shown for reasons of geography or cost. Whatever the case, things like that are there and you will have to deal with them.

Meeting the Mandates as the First Order of Business

If you're part of the U.S. federal target audience of this book, you know the first thing that you have to work toward is enabling your network backbone to support IPv6, either natively or with the use of dual stacks. Figure 4-8 shows that you've gotten that done. A native IPv6 backbone is in place that can carry IPv6 traffic for those who need it and can take advantage of it. Moreover, you've implemented the inevitable dual-stack portion of the backbone, as well.

In Chapter 6, "Defining the Transition Preparation Steps," and again in Chapter 14, "Understanding That Your Network Isn't New," you'll discover that the hardware constituting the backbone in the figure that looks all brand new and shiny is probably mostly in place right now. Along with the (probable) minority of systems that you will have to replace or upgrade, the biggest components of this phase of the transition will likely be the deployment of IPv6-compliant software and the assigning of IPv6 addresses to everything in a manageable way.

Keeping the Old Stuff Running

The prime directive while getting your backbone upgraded is to continue providing the services your network was built for in the first place. That is why you're using dual stacks and tunneling. Figure 4-8 shows IPv4 servers running legacy applications. These applications, whose IPv4 LANs are now connected to the dual-stack backbone, are either in the process of being replaced by IPv6-compliant programs or are being ported to IPv6, by the vendor that sold them to you or your in-house development team.

You need to understand that some of these applications, especially those which are home-grown and highly specialized, may be around for a long time. Their source code may have been lost in the sands of time, or they are so mission critical that lives would be in danger if they went out of service for any significant length of time. Given the current list of organizations most focused on IPv6 transitions in the U.S., which includes the Department of Defense, Department of Energy, and Federal Aviation Administration, this is not just hyperbole. As a pilot, I would like to see the FAA's air-traffic control systems remain running, please. Visually blind in the clouds on an instrument approach down to 200 feet, I don't care if the equipment is using IPv4 or IPv6. In any case, replacing applications on networks such as these simply may not be an option for the foreseeable future.

There are also legacy IPv4 workstations in Figure 4-8. Some of them may be in remote parts of the world or literally embedded in some larger custom-built system. Ripping them out and replacing them also may not be an option right now. Because the level of redundancy in connectivity to the backbone is proportional to the criticality of the given servers and workstations, and because you have to factor in that you will lose at least some connectivity some time (that's why you have redundant independent connections), the legacy IPv4 LANs can be systematically upgraded from the existing IPv4 backbone to the dual-stack backbone as part of regular maintenance downtimes or special maintenance events that you have to do from time to time for other reasons. I cover that in more detail in Chapter 6, "Defining the Transition Preparation Steps."

Adding in the New Native Stuff

While you're upgrading the legacy IPv4 LANs to use the dual-stack backbone, you're also upgrading other existing LANs to native IPv6, so they may enjoy connecting directly to the native IPv6 backbone. You can change any LAN to 100 percent IPv6 if all of the end devices on the LAN (and the applications running on those devices) can handle the protocol natively or by tunneling IPv4 in IPv6 over the upgraded LAN. You may also be deploying entirely new LANs, possibly collocated with the old IPv4 networks, in the name of upgrading while keeping the old stuff running. Possibly, the LANs are totally new as part of network growth, and hopefully you'll soon reach the point where any such new infrastructure will be plugged into the native IPv6 backbone.

Wrapping It Up with Some Tunnels

I've almost covered everything in Figure 4-8. There are two classes of things left. You'll see the legacy IPv4 LAN in the upper-left of the figure is not connected to the dual-stack portion of the backbone. Instead, it is tunneling directly into the native IPv6 portion. It is using the most common form of tunneling mentioned earlier, where the tunnel is not between end devices, but rather between common termination points on routers that serve entire LANs of devices. Both the dual-stack router(s) on the legacy IPv4 LAN and their peers in the native IPv6 backbone provide a path for IPv4 traffic to get from the workstations to the legacy IPv4 servers in the lower-right of the figure.

From what you have learned about network stacks and tunneling, you may have already guessed that the tunnel does not necessarily terminate upon arriving in the native IPv6 backbone where the thick white arrow does. The tunnel could terminate there, implying that the terminating router has a dual stack, and that it is one of the border routers between the native IPv6 backbone and the dual-stack network. In that case, the next place a packet coming out the tunnel goes is into the dual-stack backbone. From there it is routed in the outer cloud to the legacy IPv4 servers. Depending on factors not considered in this example, that architectural choice may be more practical than connecting the legacy IPv4 LAN to the dual-stack backbone directly.

Tunneling Through the Backbone

A more likely case is that the tunnel does not terminate in the upper-left of the native IPv6 backbone cloud. Instead, the termination point is closer to the lower-right portion of the cloud, at the legacy IPv4 server LAN. The efficiency of this choice is more obvious: if you have to tunnel the legacy IPv4 traffic to the native IPv6 backbone anyway, for whatever reason, allow the IPv4 packets to remain encapsulated in IPv6 for as long as you can. The packets will still have to travel through some part of the dual-stack backbone to get to the legacy IPv4 server LAN, but this option makes sense if staying in the native IPv6 backbone makes the total path shorter, faster, or cheaper than terminating the tunnel sooner.

Adding New IPv6 Workstations with Tunnels

The last set of equipment I'll connect to finish Figure 4-8 is some IPv6 workstations with no IPv6 LAN nearby. The closest LAN to the workstations is an IPv4 LAN, so you'll have to tunnel the IPv6 to the native IPv6 backbone. The IPv6 workstations each may be terminating one end of a per-workstation tunnel, with the other ends terminating at a common point in the native IPv6 backbone, or, maybe the workstations' traffic is being routed through a common tunneling system installed deliberately to support them, and it's the only piece of dual-stack equipment in the LAN.

Choosing Your Options

I've covered quite a lot of mechanisms, strategies, and options in this chapter. Don't worry. I will go on in later chapters to drill down into the gory details of the creation of your IPv6 transition plans, preparation for transition, and then execution. At this point, you should be armed enough to know what factors will influence your planning. That makes this a good time to catalog those.

The checklist that follows summarizes the transition choices discussed previously and the factors driving them. I suggest you gather as many answers as possible to the checklist items from all the decision makers in application development and support, network infrastructure, corporate security, user communities, and so on, that are part of your IPv6 transition. Review the answers against this chapter and the reference materials cited later for how to proceed with each issue.

Checking Out Checklists

Starting with this chapter, I'll be providing convenient checklists for you to make sure you've covered all the things you need to do during a particular phase of transition planning, preparation, or execution. Checklists are a good tool for executing well-defined work. They work best if they are comprehensive and if they account for anomalies, as well as the sunny-day cases. They are also good for boiling down complex technical topics into simple steps that someone not totally skilled in the underlying reasoning, but who is skilled in executing the work, can follow.

Checklists also allow you to execute tasks under duress with assurance that you've accounted for everything and haven't missed a crucial step. Hopefully, most of your move to IPv6 will not constitute an emergency, but when I talk about reverting from a failed upgrade of part of your infrastructure, especially at 2:45 a.m., which is when those things fail, you may feel some comfort in having a checklist to back things out.

CHECKLIST: Custom Needs Assessment

Apply this set of tests to the infrastructure, applications, devices, and so on, that you are upgrading to IPv6. The answers will provide you the foundation for creating your transition plans:

❑ Can you take advantage of the IPv6 auto-configuration features? Are you disallowed from using them for security or other reasons?

❑ Do you have any special security concerns, like the handling of multiple levels of classified information, necessitating several disjoint network infrastructures?

❑ Are there any special network-based auditing requirements placed on you, for example, needing to be able to collect and analyze all traffic on the network?

❑ Are your networks mission-critical to a degree that you need to treat them with kid gloves, thus making the transition require more planning up front before execution?

❑ Are there any availability or operations issues? Do the networks that you run have certain uptime requirements that they provide to their users? Then you have to plan for backup-network strategies or possibly building dark network infrastructure to be switched over in one clean break or to start as an offloading spare, eventually picking up the whole load.

❑ Are there any times of year (for example, tax time for the IRS) when you cannot upgrade your systems? Are there limitations to the amount of time a particular set of infrastructures can be out of operation? You may have to break up the job of upgrading those systems into smaller chunks.

❑ Are there any very distant sites that are hard to access or modify?

❑ Do you have any archaic sites that are basically going to need to be torn down and rebuilt because upgrading them is impossible? Is the continuation of their functionalities beyond IPv4 required?

❑ Do you have any non-standard equipment, either home-built or where the vendor's out of business?

❑ Are you running any special or home-built protocols on top of the network layer that may not be able to upgrade to IPv6?

❑ Are there any applications that you can't live without that you must upgrade? How old are they? How complex are they? Are they written by your organization or provided by a vendor?

❑ Is your infrastructure outsourced? Is the provider capable of planning, preparing for, and executing the IPv6 upgrade of the outsourced infrastructure or applications? If not, you may have to engage a third party.

❑ Are you or your organization rolled up into somebody else's IPv6 transition? You have to work with them.

❑ Do your networks have issues with MTU sizes and fragmentation?

❑ Is there any infrastructure in your network that is IPv6 unfriendly, for example, low-bandwidth cables or radio or satellite links? This is related to the preceding minimum MTU question.

❑ Do you have any multicasting in use already with IPv4?

❑ Do you have transitory assets where mobile IPv6 might be helpful?

❑ Do you have any applications or equipment not capable of computing checksums for UDP packets? IPv6 requires UDP checksums. They are optional in IPv4.

Further Reading

I feel a certain sense of comfort that this chapter is a comprehensive look at your transition choices, after having written most of it while referring to the RFCs purely for information like the IPv6 MIB OIDs, and then double-checking my facts against the RFCs more thoroughly to find I covered the topics fairly well. This holds especially for RFC 4213. Time and the critics will tell how well I did.

To gather your own information (or check mine), the following will help guide you in choosing how to make the transition to IPv6. For your convenience, relevant references from Chapter 1, "What Is IPv6?", have been repeated here, as well:

- RFC 2767: Dual Stack Hosts using the "Bump-In-the-Stack" Technique (BIS). February 2000.
- RFC 3056: Connection of IPv6 Domains via IPv4 Clouds. February 2001.
- RFC 3142: An IPv6-to-IPv4 Transport Relay Translator. June 2001.
- RFC 3484: Default Address Selection for Internet Protocol version 6 (IPv6). February 2003.
- RFC 3493: Basic Socket Interface Extensions for IPv6. February 2003.
- RFC 3542: Advanced Sockets Application Program Interface (API) for IPv6. May 2003.
- RFC 3596: DNS Extensions to Support IP Version 6. October 2003.
- RFC 3901: DNS IPv6 Transport Operational Guidelines. September 2004.
- RFC 4038: Application Aspects of IPv6 Transition. March 2005.
- RFC 4213: Basic Transition Mechanisms for IPv6 Hosts and Routers. October 2005.
- RFC 4291: IPv6 Addressing Architecture. February 2006.
- RFC 4293: Management Information Base for the Internet Protocol (IP). April 2006.
- RFC 4472: Operational Considerations and Issues with IPv6 DNS. April 2006.
- RFC 4891: Using IPsec to Secure IPv6-in-IPv4 Tunnels. May 2007.

The following Internet draft, though expired, is worth reading for guidance and to be aware of, for example, security concerns with IPv6 transition:

- `draft-ietf-v6ops-security-overview-06.txt`: IPv6 Transition/ Co-existence Security Considerations. October 22, 2006 (Expired April 25, 2007).

For the 6BONE history buff or to learn a little about how the very first IPv6 "transition" was handled, the following RFCs may also be of interest:

- RFC 1897: IPv6 Testing Address Allocation. January 1996.
- RFC 2471: IPv6 Testing Address Allocation. December 1998.
- RFC 2473: Generic Packet Tunneling in IPv6 Specification. December 1998.
- RFC 2772: 6Bone Backbone Routing Guidelines. February 2000.
- RFC 3701: 6bone (IPv6 Testing Address Allocation) Phaseout. March 2004.

Understand that the IPv6 community has learned a lot since the 6BONE was established in 1996 (and hopefully a little more since it was phased out). The preceding 6BONE RFCs represent early knowledge and experimental strategies for using IPv6. They are advisory guidelines on what to do (and what not to do) for your upgrade, but don't implicitly take them as best practices.

Testing Your Knowledge

Each chapter ends with a set of review questions to allow the readers to gauge their comprehension of the preceding chapter. Answers are in Appendix A.

1. What are the three main IPv6 transition mechanisms?

2. What is the most important set of things to migrate to IPv6: network infrastructure, applications, capabilities, or users?

3. You've decided to start your IPv6 transition now and proceed slowly. Magically, you've come up with a total estimate of 21 months to get the job done. What's a good back-of-the-envelope estimate for how long it will take you to upgrade "quickly" to IPv6, by planning everything first and then executing all the plans at a more rapid pace? Include the planning and pre-transition preparation work in the estimate, not just the network changes.

4. When using IPv4-mapped IPv6 addresses, what additional mechanism(s) do you need to complete a communications path between an IPv4-only application and an IPv6-only server?

5. What is the minimum MTU for IPv6 links and how did it change from the IPv4 one?

6. Silly Trivia: What were the round-trip times of the successful IP over carrier pigeon implementation in April 2001?

Creating Your Transition Plans

A good plan today is better than a perfect plan tomorrow.
— George S. Patton

When entering into any new endeavor, your satisfaction with the outcome will be greatly influenced by the expectations you had at the start. If you expect everything to come up roses, any minor disappointment can appear like a catastrophe and be overly disheartening. Similarly, if you expect the worst, problems that are surmountable may cause you to quit prematurely. With that in mind, let's set your primary expectation for creating your IPv6 transition plan: No matter what you do, you will never have perfect information for planning. There will always be unknowns. Therefore, your plan will never be perfect and you will inevitably have to make corrections during the plan's execution. If you accept this, you will be much happier during the transition. That said, there is no reason that you can't account for the unforeseen by creating a plan that is comprehensive (allowing you to get as many of the unknowns addressed ASAP) and flexible (allowing you to roll with the changes). Those two attributes are common to all good plans.

What You'll Learn

A whole book can be devoted to project planning alone, and many have been. In this chapter, you will find enough of an introduction to project planning concepts and what has to be taken into account when creating a plan to allow you to create your IPv6 transition plan. For seasoned project managers, some of this may seem like old hat, but a refresher in planning never hurts. Plus, the chapter focuses far more on the typical pitfalls of planning and plan execution, all of which I have encountered in real life at one time or another.

In addition to the planning basics that span all projects, you will learn an approach that is specific to IPv6 transition planning. How to attack a problem is often the key to solving it the best and most efficient way. Because we are talking primarily about a network transition, though the applications are equally important, we decompose the IPv6 transition planning problem into a layered approach, much like the layers of the network stack. Though this isn't the only way to address the planning work, it has many positive points. You are welcome to come up with your own approach, and hopefully, this chapter will allow you to cover all your bases in doing so.

Approaching Your Planning Work

In creating this chapter I documented an approach that I realized I've been using for a long time, but that I've never formalized. It's nothing earth-shattering or new, but it's what I use to come up with the best plan I can. It has the following three parts:

1. Preparation: Collecting what you need to create the plan.
2. Creation: The actual writing of the plan, sub-plans, tasks, and so on.
3. Tracking: Considerations to assure the plan can be followed.

The following sections look at these in detail.

Planning to Plan

Before you can get too far in any planning exercise, there are some prerequisites you must have in place. Some of these things you may have readily available. Others may take a little work to find, but these are all things that, realistically, you can't produce a plan without.

The planning prerequisites shouldn't be thought of as all the things you'll need to start planning. For example, if you have everything you need to plan the IPv6 transition of a particular department or a specific application or sub-net, by all means plan away. This section represents those things without which you cannot finish the plan. In project-management lingo, the plan creation cannot finish any sooner than the gathering of planning prerequisites does. That doesn't mean you can't get the last prerequisite and then finish the plan an hour later.

Determining Your Plan's Objectives

A rather obvious prerequisite is figuring out what you're looking to accomplish in the first place. Be it the construction of a house, the authoring of a chapter in a book, or the transition of a network to IPv6, you need to have some idea of what the finished product should look like or what it should do.

For some projects you'll be able to say, "I want my house to look just like [insert famous celebrity name here]'s house." If there's a pre-existing example of the target objective that you wish to achieve, that makes things a lot easier. It's sure easier than saying, "I want to create the next killer application for the Internet." This is a well-defined objective in some ways, too, but one with no clear process of how to obtain it.

With the IPv6 transition, you're kind of in the middle of the two extremes. One of your main objectives (or at least of many of the enterprises moving to IPv6) will likely be, "I want my network and applications to provide all the services they did in IPv4 with at least the same amount of reliability, security, and so on." That's the easier part. The harder part is figuring whether and how all those cool new IPv6 capabilities can be applied to your particular circumstances, making the transition meaningful not just from the perspective of being mandated, but also by virtue of adding functionality to your network and applications.

Because we're talking about changing a lot of things during the IPv6 transition, the recommendations throughout this book tend toward replicating the functionality you have in your pre-transitioned network, rather than turning your transition into a research project. For some people, there will be clear cases where an IPv6 capability (for example, mobility, improved multicasting, sounder IPsec) will be an obvious choice, rather than trying to upgrade some dinosaur implementation. While that may be, for the most part we'll focus on the safer path, seeing as many people during this transition rely on their networks to do some pretty important stuff.

Once you're on solid ground after the transition is well under way or complete, you can experiment. You can, of course, also experiment in parallel if you have the resources. This is encouraged as long as it doesn't hurt your primary goals. I cover the value of pilot projects to test out IPv6 capabilities in Chapters 13, "Using Pilot Programs to Facilitate Your IPv6 Transition," and 14, "Understanding that Your Network Isn't New."

Covering All the Bases in Your Planning

Perhaps you will find, as I have, that certain mental triggers help you explore every facet of the planning process and create a plan with the most comprehensive coverage. I'm most comfortable expressing them in checklists. By checking off items on a checklist or asking yourself a set of standard questions, you bring to light aspects of a particular project that, on closer examination, may require more effort than a cursory glance indicates.

I'm sure you've had those moments where somebody says, "What about X?" and you suddenly realize you've failed to account for some implicit piece of work that's obvious to the person who suggested it. In cases where you don't have access to all the subject matter experts you may need (or you're in a new realm of endeavor where there are few, if any, such experts), the mental exercise of listing tasks you had to do in the past to see if you need to do them for this project can work wonders.

Taking a Tip from Journalism

Everybody thinks a little differently and what works for me may not work for you. For good or bad, the ability to produce a realistic and workable plan is something that comes much from experience, rather than just book learning.

As an alternative to checklists, the formula used to create a newspaper article may work better for you. When writing a newspaper article, common guidance is to cover the five W's: "Who, When, What, Where, and Why?" By getting yourself into the habit of asking these five questions, every aspect of your planning should get at least some coverage.

Some of the answers to the five W's will have straightforward answers at a high level, for example, "When and Why?" Your first answer may be, "By June 2008, and because the OMB is making me do it." What you really want are answers to more significant or focused questions, so you should ask them not just once for the whole project, but instead for all the sub-projects, and in some cases tasks, that compose the project.

You may ask, "Why are we moving Version Q of that application?" The application in question may be 20 years old or soon to be replaced by the vendor with a later version with IPv6 capabilities already in it. You may choose, instead of force-fitting the old version into an IPv6 network, to wait for the new version, or you may choose the path where you fill the gap before the new version comes out with a dual-stack implementation or tunneling (see Chapter 4, "Choosing When to Make a Transition and How"), either of which can act as a suitable interim solution to maintain access to the old version while you're waiting. The choice is, of course, specific to the application and your circumstances, but the point is that you should ask the question.

Following the journalistic approach a bit further, I'll address those five W's and see what needs to be accounted for in planning for each.

Who Will Work on the Project?

It's an old saw, and sometimes a cliché that is paid only lip service, but all projects begin and end with people. How else will the project get done other than if *somebody* does it? The robots aren't quite there yet.

You can put together the tasks you have to execute in the plan without knowing who's going to do the work, but you can't estimate how long it will take to do those tasks until you know who's doing them. To get started or if you're drawing from a large or anonymous resource pool, you can choose some average performance numbers to convert effort into time; for example, it takes an engineer two days to install a router.

You can personalize the plan more and assign the exact people who will do the work. This doesn't scale well to large organizations, but it can lead to better accuracy. For example, whereas it takes Alice two days, it takes Bob three days (or one day) to do the same job. Everybody gets things done at a different speed (and to a different level of quality, but that's another matter). Oftentimes the variance is so small in respect to the total time the work will take that there's more effort in getting exact estimates customized to individuals than there is in simply using averages.

Once you know how long each piece of the work will take to be performed, you will almost be able to produce a timeline and estimate how long your whole plan will take to execute. You still need to account for dependencies between pieces of the project, but we'll get to that shortly.

Where Are the People Coming From?

To figure out who is going to work on the project, you need to know what resources you have available on your staff of regular employees and consultants. You may also have vendors under contract who offer professional services or product support, either rolled up into the products' purchase price or as additional service or training items for which you pay additional fees. You also have the option of outsourcing the work, either to a project-specific vendor (like one specializing in IPv6 transitions) or to a general contractor or "body shop." These are the biggies. Other choices may exist for your particular case, but the point to take away is that this is one of the questions you have to ponder to address your specific situation.

Combining Resources to Do a Better/Faster Job

Depending on how your enterprise's people are organized or what their capabilities are, you may have to be creative with how you deploy them to undertake your IPv6 transition. For example, instead of having the one network engineer who works in your particular department do your whole transition single-handedly and take a long time to do so, a group could be formed by pooling people from several departments. The group could learn to specialize in doing transitions and then perform them one department at a time in the set of departments from which they came. The overall set of work may not get done any faster (though I would argue it will), but any given department will be "in transition" for a lesser amount of time. Also, should your network engineer be ill or want to take a vacation, the work won't stop during the absence.

Accounting for Your People's Availability

One of the prerequisites you'll need, once you've determined who's doing the work, is when they are available to do it. For employees and individual consultants, you'll need people's vacation schedules. This is something you should already have for the near term depending on how far ahead your people are required to file their vacation requests.

For longer-term projects, like your IPv6 transition, it's hard to get exact dates for when an employee is planning to take a vacation a year from now. In those cases, allotting a reasonable amount for time off to be used some time during the overall project makes more sense. When it comes down to picking the exact time when a particular person's allotment will be used, the time should be taken such that critical dependencies or deadlines can still be met despite the person's absence.

Should your people have other assignments than just the IPv6 transition, you need to account for any time that is devoted to work on higher priority projects. Such projects may or may not exist, but if they do they need to be taken into account when planning the time that people can work.

Assuring the Availability of External Resources

Many external resources, like professional service organizations, provide you essentially continuous service committed to a definitive result, rather than just a number of hours worked. In those cases, the external organization (not you) has to worry about when its people are on vacation and how those people's client engagements get done on time. You do, however, have to schedule service engagements, sometimes far in advance depending on the size of the engagement. Make sure you identify in the course of your project planning the types of external organizations you need and start the contracting process early.

For external organizations you utilize on a retainer-like basis (and plan to use for your IPv6 transition) to augment your work force, rather than just for one-off projects, make sure any long-term contracts you have in place cover the time you need their resources. If not, a good time to renegotiate those contracts may be during the planning phases of the transition, rather than two weeks before the contracts expire, half-way through the project. It's happened. Be forewarned.

Dedicating Resources to Planning

Your IPv6 transition is a rather large project, so you will almost certainly have to have somebody dedicated to doing the planning. You can't just have somebody whose job it is to run the network day to day take an hour every now and then and put together an IPv6 transition plan for the entire enterprise. You can start that way and put some frameworks together with which to start your more serious planning exercises, but at some time some amount of resources proportional to your organization's size need to be set aside to organize the plan. Most likely, these people will become the people who maintain, track, and even execute the plan.

When Do You Need to Finish the Transition?

Unless you're in the U.S. federal government, your transition date is entirely up to you and based on many factors including:

- your perceived rewards for going to IPv6 (or penalties for not going)
- the priority of the transition versus the priorities of other projects
- the size and complexity of your networks
- legacy applications that would be difficult to upgrade
- the need for interoperability with customers, partners, vendors, and so on
- your available resources, both human and financial

The mood in the commercial U.S. markets has been lukewarm at best regarding IPv6 transition. That may change if government agencies ask their direct (and eventually indirect) vendors to switch over. It may also change if multi-national corporations with interests in IPv6 "rich" countries like Japan and China see it as a good thing to make a transition company-wide. Rather than speculate about future trends, it's best to leave it to you to determine the best transition time. For those in the U.S. federal space that have a mandated deadline, we'll focus further on what those deadlines really mean and how best to work with them.

Working with the OMB-Mandated Deadlines

As with any project, your IPv6 transition does not exist in the vacuum of a deadline and no other requirements. Though some of you appear to have before you the immutable date of June 2008, it is not truly immutable. Y2K was immutable. January 19th, 2038 is immutable. Even President Kennedy's 1961 commitment/challenge to land a man on the Moon within the decade represented more immutability than the IPv6 mandate. Though the mandated IPv6 transition deadline is mutable, it should be equally well understood that the end results meant to be accelerated by the mandate are inevitable.

Others have compared the IPv6 mandates to some unsuccessful government mandates of the past with the goal of showing just how unlikely IPv6 transition (at least on the mandated timeline) is, and therefore that all this transition hype is pointless and a huge waste of resources. Although I don't believe every U.S. federal network will be upgraded by June 2008, that doesn't mean I buy into the mandate comparisons. To motivate you that your plans are not pointless or a waste of resources, let's compare the IPv6 transition mandates to those mandates of the past.

Understanding How IPv6 Differs from Past Mandates

To get an idea of why the IPv6 mandate won't "just go away" like many of its predecessors have, a quick comparison should cement why all your planning efforts will eventually yield valuable fruit.

I've seen several government mandates come and go. Three that come to mind are:

- The Ada programming language in the 1980s
- The "C2 by [19]92" trusted systems initiative
- GOSIP for computer networking in the late '80s and early '90s

Each of these mandates had strong indicators of why they would not succeed that were visible from the start.

Avoiding Wholesale Change in High-Risk Environments

I worked in a company building airborne Radar Warning Receivers (RWRs) when Ada started making the rounds. Ada was advertised as the new and improved way to create software for real-time mission-critical applications, like our RWRs. Being what is called a high-level language, you could more readily express in Ada the concepts and structures of your application (for example, transmitters, receivers, and signals in the case of radar). Our environment before Ada involved low-level "assembler" programming, which focused much more on manipulating data within the CPU, memory, and I/O devices of the computer doing the work, instead of the real application. It was not easy and something like Ada was very attractive.

Despite the potential improvements, our company's strategy was to seek a waiver from the mandate; something I consider even now as having been the totally appropriate and correct choice. At the time, Ada was seen (at least from where I was sitting) as an inefficient language for real-time applications, despite all the assertions to the contrary by its creators and pundits. How could it possibly be fast enough to allow us to meet our performance requirements for detection and effective deterrence (for example, the jamming of an enemy aircraft or missile emplacement)? Once they started throwing around talk about dead pilots all for the sake of a software mandate, the waivers came pretty fast. Ada may have been up to the task — my bet was that it wasn't — but determining that in live combat was just a dumb idea. On a slightly related topic, the maiden flight loss of a European Space Agency Ariane 5 launcher in 1996 was due to an Ada programming error. This suggests we were right to be skeptical in 1986. See `http://sunnyday.mit.edu/accidents/Ariane5accidentreport.html` for details on the Ariane accident.

Avoiding Security That Doesn't Help You

I don't recall much talk about waivers for the C2-by-92 mandate. Perhaps it's because I wasn't a customer, but a vendor, by that time. We were selling a secure operating system that easily met the government's "Orange Book" requirements for a C2 level of security. We thought we had it made. Of course, neither we nor any of our competitors offered any compelling features, new applications, or capabilities, except making everyone's job harder with more security. Put simply, there was no business incentive, even for the most paranoid of government agencies, to raise *every* desktop to some low-water mark of trust (and C2 wasn't all that great in the first place). The systems that had to be secured already were, granted either with proprietary home-grown means that had their own maintenance and support problems, or via policies and procedures that seemed like they were created to prevent work rather than secure it. So, much like by endangering pilots for no apparent worthwhile gain, risking national security for similar rewards didn't catch on as we and our government supporters had hoped.

Avoiding Standards for Standards' Sake

The GOSIP mandate was a different beast altogether. Ada was a superior, but unproven, technology with some very useful features and capabilities. C2-by-92 attempted to propagate enhanced security features to every system in the enterprise, but with downside risks of host, application, and network disruption and little perceived increase in true security. GOSIP, again from the point of view of someone in computer networking at the time, had no obvious benefits, not even ones that were offset by more important business drivers like in the cases of Ada and C2-by-92.

GOSIP addressed the network stack and is, therefore, the best choice for comparison with the current IPv6 mandates. GOSIP was the government's attempt to procure and eventually make a transition to products that used the OSI 7-layer networking model, which had been around since 1977. For contemporary information on the GOSIP mandates, see RFC 1169. It's a bit of a scary read with all the similarities to IPv6 transition terminology and goals. Without debating whether the OSI protocols were good or bad, the point of why GOSIP was a tough pill to swallow was that nearly everyone was using TCP/IP by the time GOSIP came around. The GOSIP mandates felt like we were all being asked to start driving on the other side of the road, because that's what a bunch of academics and standards people said was a better idea. GOSIP passed away quietly in 1994, coincidentally just as consumers and non-technical users were discovering the nascent Internet.

Planning for a Transition That's Coming Anyway

Contrary to the failed transition mandates of the past, the IPv6 transition is more realistic. It represents the U.S. government's realization that the rate of inevitable adoption of IPv6 in the United States is too slow and that lack of urgency is based partly on complacency that the current IPv4 technology is "good enough." Though current technology may be acceptable for now, as IPv6 takes hold in the rest of the world there will come a time where the U.S. says, "Gee, we would like all that cool stuff, too." That will be followed by, "Wow! We should have done this much sooner." By that time, it will take years to catch up and another technology with its roots in the U.S. will migrate abroad.

That an IPv6 transition is going to happen is certain, so best to start planning now, while there is significant interest to help you coming from many directions. The government has mandated a certain date. Whether or not the date is realistic is a different matter. That the date exists is simply impetus to get the job done. Other organizations, especially including the Asia Pacific area are well under way with their transitions, as we've pointed out many times. They weren't doing C2-by-92 transitions and they certainly weren't doing GOSIP before we put those unrealistic mandates in place. Obviously they see value in IPv6, so maybe we should, too.

Setting Deadlines in the Real World

As mentioned earlier, a project's initial deadline (let's be more positive and call it a target date) does not exist in a vacuum. Excluding the few hard and fast exceptions listed previously, all target dates are controlled by more than the desire of those who set them to be on time.

For one thing, the quality and completeness of your IPv6 transition obviously cannot go to zero or you'll have more things to fix than you had to upgrade in the first place. It's difficult to say in generalities what the appropriate amount of quality is. Each organization has its tolerances, but everyone has some low-water mark that they cannot go below.

Furthermore, those covered by the IPv6 mandate know it is unfunded. That means the organizations making transitions will get no more people or other resources to do the job. People can work only so fast, so given a set number of people and a minimum requirement for quality, the deadline almost sets itself; certainly the earliest possible date does. I cover the concepts underneath these conclusions shortly in the section about the project triangle.

Using Waivers to Set Achievable Goals

The same document (OMB Memorandum M-05-22) that created the IPv6 transition mandates also created mechanisms (some would say loopholes) for getting waivers to those mandates. Waivers are not a new thing, as seen by the Ada example, and they have a rightful place in broad programs like IPv6 transition.

The OMB memorandum provides a checklist for agencies to inventory their assets and identify those that are not IPv6 compliant. For those non-compliant assets, each agency must state what they are going to do about making them compliant. The choices that require IPv6 transition work to deal with the non-compliant assets are either to upgrade them or modify them. Another choice that doesn't require IPv6 transition work specifically is to declare the asset a "legacy." Such an asset will be gone by June 2008, so it doesn't need to be upgraded. The fourth choice for how a non-compliant asset will meet the IPv6 mandates is that it will not. The agency declaring so must submit its reasoning why a waiver should be issued for such assets.

There are many sound reasons for requesting waivers. Because OMB expected you to do your transition within your normal technology refresh cycles and with no additional budget beyond that, perhaps you weren't planning on replacing a particular non-compliant asset until after June 2008. You could apply for a waiver to allow the asset to stay until its originally scheduled refresh time. Or, perhaps there's some piece of ancient software that's critical to your organization's mission, but changing it is non-trivial without introducing undue risk. Fortunately, as you saw in Chapter 4, "Choosing When to Make a Transition and How," you can probably build an IPv4 world around it that talks to the new IPv6 world and it can live out its life until someone comes up with a better solution. Heck, that kind of waiver may even be permanent, versus just a delay.

Now, we all know there are darker sides to things like waivers. How you choose to use them is between your conscience and you. The point of mentioning them is not to give you a way out of something because you don't want to do it. It's to give you a way to do it right, but maybe a little late or with one or two parts not meeting the original ideal mandate.

Isn't it Too Late for Waivers?

Some of you may wonder why we're even talking about waivers, because the OMB memo mentioned specifically says that the last of the inventories was due June 30, 2006. Though that is true, the wording of the mandate's last milestone, the one for June 2008, includes what is appropriate for all initiatives of such vast scope. The mandate requires that agencies "will include progress reports on meeting this target date as part of their EA transition strategy."

A legitimate message of any progress report (and one could argue the only reason for having them in the first place) is that you're not on track; more exactly, that you're behind. Well, if you're not on track, what can you do? You can work harder. That, as I've made a recurring theme, has its limits. You can get more resources, which also is reasonable, but limited. Or, you can do less or get it done later. The last two items are what waivers address, and even though you may not have filed for the waiver you would like now back in June 2006, that doesn't necessarily mean it's off limits.

Getting a waiver that you hadn't accounted for earlier during the actual transition is something between you and the people granting the waivers, and the chances of success depend greatly on the magnitude of the waiver(s) desired and the impact to the overall organization or particular units depending on you stemming from the delay or lost functionality. Although there are no guarantees a particular waiver will be granted, it's fair to say it's never too late to ask for one.

Focusing on the Ultimate Goal

All the preceding talk regarding the fluidity of end dates is not meant to make you feel better about playing fast and loose with the project schedule. What I'm trying to convey is that, in the end, you want to have an enterprise network that has been upgraded to IPv6 in a timely manner, but also to an acceptable level of quality or better, and with the resources you have at hand or can afford to add. In the long run, a slip of a day or two, or a week, or even a month may be acceptable and nobody will remember five years from now that you made the transition in July (or September) versus June. The point is, do the job right, which partly means picking dates that are at least realistic when you create the plan (and maybe for a couple of weeks into it, too).

Getting and Using Appropriate Planning Tools

Included in the set of resources you need to prepare a proper plan are the appropriate project management tools. For those following along with the journalism approach, consider these the answer to the "what" that you will need. Everybody has their favorites. I prefer Microsoft Project, mostly because it comes with their Office suite and has the same general look and feel as programs I am comfortable with and use every day.

Whether it is MS Project or anything else, you have to know the tool's strengths and weaknesses. For example, with MS Project, I can get what I consider a well-organized plan together using less than 50 percent of the tool's capabilities. On the other side of the coin, I feel that unless you're working on the Space Shuttle program, there are a lot of features you won't need. Using them just because they are there is often a bad idea, because you may find yourself out of your league, frustrated, or behind on your planning work because you're spending too much time getting to know the tool. There are also interactions or built-in assumptions in most tools about how projects should be organized or tracked that sometimes butt heads with how I want to do it. I can usually work around them, but if they're really a pain, I try another tool.

You may consider improving your skills with a tool by trying one new feature per new project or some other such method for ramping up. Before using a tool effectively, though, you will need some basic familiarity with it. To get that familiarity, invest in some training, even if that means reading the manual, one of those fantastic *For Dummies* books, or attending an online or classroom course or two. You'll be happier that you did. I find that the hardest part of picking up a new software tool is figuring out what paradigm the designers had in mind. Once I know how they want me to do it, and that comes with training, I can decide whether that's for me and, if it is, I can work within their model.

Understanding the Costs of Rolling Your Own Tools

Most people with decent project management skills and a good understanding of office automation software can perform simple project management tasks with general-purpose tools like spreadsheet software. If you can program, especially in a GUI environment, you might actually consider developing specific project management tools. Though this gives you the freedom to impart your particular project management style into a tool, consider your primary mission. Is your job to write software tools or to upgrade a network to IPv6?

Whether it's simple (and oftentimes not so simple) spreadsheets or more complicated software or paperwork manifestations of your ideal project management strategy, there is a cost of creating them and maintaining them.

Consider the following example: A project management tool costs $500 per user. The typical user of the tool makes $50,000/year or about $25/hour. If it takes them 15 minutes to update their project status every week and they work 50 weeks a year, that's an annual cost of $812.50/user to buy and use the tool. Note that we haven't counted the cost of populating the tool with the project plan, but that's OK.

Now let's take that same typical user and give them a home-grown tool. Assume over the course of the year, the average time to update project status is 30 minutes. The user will get better at it as time goes on, but those first few times will be tough. Remember, because it's home grown, odds are there are no manuals, training classes, user groups, web searches for help, or any other things to aid the user. There's only their interaction with the tool's author, who by the way probably has another full time job. Each user's status updates will cost the company $312.50 more for the year, but we save the $500 of purchasing the mainstream tool, so the total annual cost is $625/user. As with the other case we don't count the cost of populating the tool in the first place here, but for similar reasons as to why day-to-day updates are more expensive, the initial setup will be higher than with the case of a mainstream tool.

What we also don't count is the cost of constructing the tool. Considering we're saving less than $200/user with the homegrown tool, exactly what kind of tool can we realistically construct? Even if there are 10 users, that's $2000 saved in a year. Assuming the person that built the tool is paid the same as those who use it, any more than 80 hours work on the tool during that year results in a net loss. That time includes development costs plus any "support" the developer has to provide to the user community.

As noted earlier, the learning curve for a new tool is as important as the initial cost of constructing it. This is especially true for those users who have done project management before, because they have to learn not just how your tool works, but also your project management paradigm, if it's not standard project management speak. Also, you'll have to train everyone who walks in the door, because though you can find tons of people with skills in MS Office and Project, how many people can you find that know "Terry's Project Strategy" (TPS)?

Determining Where the Transition Will Happen

The first place that should come to mind when talking about where your IPv6 transition will happen is, of course, in the network itself. Before you can complete, and in many cases, start your planning, you'll need network diagrams for connectivity and equipment locations. Your network's schematics and asset inventories will also help you determine if anything can be consolidated or eliminated. You don't necessarily need to have the detailed wiring diagrams for every building, but you do need to know where the main lines of demarcation are, so you can see where well-defined instances of IPv6 transition can occur and where networks marked for later transition can be cordoned off until you are ready to address them.

Surveying the Application Space

The other venue where your IPv6 transition takes place is within the myriad of applications running on your servers and workstations. These are not just the distributed network-centric applications like e-mail and web services. They are also the desktop applications like word processors, spreadsheets, and so on, that are traditionally seen as stand-alone, but really aren't. Most modern-day applications support online help functions, as well as updates from their vendors. Although these functionalities may not be critical to you and you can get around them not being IPv6 compliant (perhaps with a waiver), you should at least be aware they exist.

Getting a Count of What's Affected

Part of your planning exercise may be to execute an inventory of the equipment on your network, or your network inventory may already exist and be an input to the plan. In either case, the inventory is required for your transition to get past the point of planning. Similar to a network inventory, you'll need an application inventory with information like the applications' capabilities (for example, IPv6 capable or not) and from where each application is acquired and who supports them (for example, vendor or in-house).

Specific kinds of assets are more important to the inventory than others. Gateway firewalls, for example, which provide your security protection (and often translate your private IPv4 addresses to/from public ones), will likely have to provide IPv4/IPv6 header translation, tunneling, or additional protection against external IPv6 networks once you've transitioned. I talk more about both of these inventories in Chapter 6, "Defining the Transition Preparation Steps."

For those in the U.S. federal government, both the network and application inventories should have been completed by June 2006. For completeness, however, they are included in this list of required planning inputs.

Determining the Sources for New Equipment and Software

It's highly likely you'll be upgrading, and probably replacing, some portion of your equipment and software. As you inventory your hard and soft assets, you should also start to line up all the vendors for equipment and software procurement. If you don't know where all that new stuff is coming from, part of the plan is figuring out where.

Another soft asset you'll need to get is your brand new IPv6 address space. In order to figure out how you'll be numbering your systems, you'll need to know how much space you'll need, what you can get, and from where you can get it. This is a pretty complex topic and Chapter 7, "Identifying Common Transition Preparation Tasks," discusses it in detail.

Obtaining Service-Level Minima and Best Practices

How you make the transition to your IPv6 network depends a lot on how well you have to do it. As we'll discuss shortly, the required quality of the work directly affects how many people you need and how long it will take. To factor quality into your planning, you'll need to know your service-level commitments to external organizations, plus your own internal standards. These standards include metrics like Mean Time Between Failures (MTBF) and the percentage of network or application availability in a given period of time (usually a sequence of two or more 9's, as in 99.999 percent). Service-level agreements to external departments will also help you decide when you can upgrade things. In short, go and find what other people expect of you and make sure your IPv6 transition plans meet those expectations.

CHECKLIST: Planning Resources Inventory

Let's summarize what we discussed, also adding some specific items you should address in creating your IPv6 transition plan, into a tool to make sure you have everything you need to get started creating your plan.

❑ Do you have the set of capabilities or services currently offered by your organization? Include things like applications for which you own the servers or data repositories, network connectivity services where you act as the transport or a gateway, and so on.

❑ Do you have the service-level and quality minima that others expect of you for your services? This includes required up time and MTBF, for example. For software development teams, this includes the best practices to be followed for developing quality software.

❑ Are there any additional capabilities or services required of your organization that must be implemented along with your IPv6 transition? For example, do you need to transition by a given date *and* have a new database application running, as well?

❑ Are there any capabilities, services, or applications that will be discontinued during the IPv6 transition?

❑ Are there any IPv6 advanced capabilities, for example, mobility, multi-casting, or IPsec, that you would like to include or investigate in your transition? Will the extra work required to plan and implement them warrant the additional functionality in the end or are these capabilities that are better off being experimented with after the successful transition or in a parallel, but not mainstream research or pilot project?

❑ Have you gathered the list of employees, consultants, and external organizations that you plan to engage for your transition? Are the consultants' and external organizations' contracts appropriate for the level of effort and duration of the IPv6 transition project?

❑ Do you have metrics for planning the rate at which either the average person or specific individuals will perform the tasks to which they are assigned?

❑ Do you have all the types of human resources, for example, network engineers, application developers, and so on, you will need for the transition or will you need to team up with other organizations or hire external vendors to complete your required skill sets?

❑ Do you have the availability information for those people you directly manage, for example, vacation schedules or allowances, committed times to other higher-priority projects?

❑ Do you have dedicated project planning and management resources or sound reasons why your IPv6 transition is not a full-time planning job?

❑ If applicable to your organization, have you already filed for waivers from the IPv6 mandates? Since then, have any other issues arisen that may require waivers before your transition completes? If you haven't filed any waivers, do you know how to and with whom, should you have to do so?

❑ Do you have the project management tools you will use for planning and managing your IPv6 transition, and does everyone who needs to know how to use them know how? Have those that don't know how been scheduled to be trained?

❑ Do you have the network and application inventories of everything affected by the IPv6 transition, including if possible the disposition of each asset relative to the transition? If not, have you scheduled or planned the inventory exercise and acquired the required tools or software or engaged an external vendor to perform the inventory?

❑ For those assets that will need to be replaced or upgraded, have you identified the vendors or other sources that will provide the replacements or upgrades? Have you engaged them or in some other way determined that they will have what you need when you need it?

❑ Are there any additional or different electrical requirements? You may be adding, and not just replacing, equipment. Is there enough power, including UPS backup? Will the replacement or new equipment use the same type of plugs? Will it need the same quality of backup power?

❑ Have you identified the sources for your IPv6 address space assignment(s)? For multi-national organizations covering multiple RIRs, you may have to get assignments from several sources. Have you contacted those sources and started the application process for assignments?

Creating a Comprehensive Plan

One goal of your IPv6 transition planning exercise is to be as comprehensive as possible. The more you can account for up front, the fewer surprises you are likely to face during the transition itself. Recall, however, that I opened the chapter by saying that you will never have all the information you need. The purpose of this section is to work with what you know to produce the best plan for entering the transition. Later I'll cover how to handle the surprises that inevitably show up.

Understanding the Project Triangle

Project managers often refer to the Project Triangle, which illustrates the opposing goals of doing a project well, doing it quickly, and doing it inexpensively. The triangle's three corners represent quality, time, and resources and the concept it expresses is often glibly stated as, "Good, Fast, and Cheap: Pick any two."

To change your project's requirements regarding any corner of the triangle, you must alter at least one other corner. To illustrate, here are a few quick examples:

▪ If a project requires the utmost quality of work, that project will take a long time or be expensive. Should you also require the project be completed as quickly as possible, then cost likely will go through the roof. Such projects were the U.S./Soviet space programs in the space race of the 1960s.

▪ Projects that must execute with the greatest of urgency need to sacrifice either quality or cost savings. Your first thought, if you're in the U.S. government, may be that your IPv6 transition falls into this category, because the project is facing a tight deadline. As the OMB mandate is unfunded, you will be forced to be cost conscious, too, but some of you can't sacrifice quality.

■ When budgets are tight, you can reduce the number of people on a pro-ject or you can spread the work out over several budget cycles. Either way, you will increase the amount of time required to complete the work. Alternatively, you could cut corners or eliminate capabilities, thereby reducing quality (or at least completeness). This too smacks of the decisions to be made in planning your IPv6 transition.

The dilemmas in the last two examples should be obvious. They are what project managers and engineering teams wrestle with all the time. As sug-gested, in most cases you decide which two corners of the triangle are most important to you. You optimize those two, not necessarily equally, while keep-ing an eye on just how sub-optimal you're willing to allow the third corner to go. There are upper and lower bounds for each corner, beyond which you can-not optimize.

Knowing When More Resources Won't Help

A project cannot be distributed efficiently over more than some maximum number of resources. Put another way, there are aspects of many projects that will simply take some amount of time that cannot be further minimized by parallelization.

Because the space race has already come up once or twice, it seems appro-priate to mention an expression famous in project management circles and which is attributed to Wernher von Braun, director of the Saturn rocket pro-gram. His original quote was, "crash programs fail because they are based on theory that, with nine women pregnant, you can get a baby in a month."

The obvious point is, of course, whatever your project, at some point adding more resources will not make it go faster (nor come out any better). A more subtle message in the quote is that, whether you're talking about having babies, curing concrete, or traveling at the speed of light, a certain amount of time *and no less* must be allotted to reach certain goals.

Documenting Your Assumptions

As you make plans, you typically find yourself making assumptions. Some are explicit like the number of people available to do the work. A more implicit assumption that may escape you is that those people will stay on throughout the whole project. Depending on the length of the project, either attrition or other priorities may take them off your list of resources.

To help track the explicit and implicit assumptions, keep a running list of them as they come up. Also, try to scrutinize your planning decisions by ask-ing yourself what you are assuming when you make them. This typically works best when planning in teams or when reviewing your plans with your team or management.

Defining Where Plans Come Together with Dependencies

Closely related to assumptions are dependencies. Tracking dependencies, meaning what you expect from other groups, specific applications, or some part of the network infrastructure, is also important. Automatic allocation of IPv6 address space using DHCPv6 is a good example of where one organization may depend on another. Toward this example, each plan should call out which address spaces they plan to use and whom they depend on, if not themselves, to serve up the addresses on the network. Note that this may be different from who is going to contact the appropriate network authorities to actually get the IPv6 address space assignments. I cover address space management in Chapter 7, "Identifying Some Common Transition Preparation Tasks."

Avoiding Scheduling Traps and Pitfalls

When you're creating a schedule, especially one where you feel you're already under the gun to deliver on the project, there are several seductive shortcuts you can take that will likely lead to a lot of frustration, a decline in team morale, and eventually missed deadlines. By realizing these shortcuts almost never work in shortening the calendar time spent from the start to finish of the project, you can avoid them altogether.

Keeping Planned Overtime out of the Schedule

If you've already got an idea of how many hours a particular project will take, and from that you have concluded the ideal deadline isn't going to happen, the temptation to build the schedule with more than the standard number of hours per day or per week becomes difficult to reject. Even if you aren't driving to hit a particular date, basing your schedule on getting done ASAP, come whatever may, will also raise the temptation to allocate more than the standard work week to the project. Understand that, if you do plan overtime into the schedule and your estimates for the time required to do the work turn out to be too low, there's no place left to allocate extra time to stay or get back on track.

Projects that are planned based on the imperative, "we're going to work seven days a week and get this thing done!" are almost certain to run out of time because there's no safety margin of any kind to account for miscalculation. Moreover, people are not machines. Bursts of overtime to overcome a slip are manageable and with the right morale (or financial) boost, people will commit to pull a week or two or three of OT, but planning an entire project that may take months with almost every waking moment devoted to the job will burn people out and the project will eventually fizzle. At that point, you aren't looking only at missing a schedule. You've probably damaged overall quality of the work, too. That will soon be followed by an exodus of disgruntled people looking for a place to work where they can see their friends and families and have lives.

Giving People a Break

Akin to and extending the above concept of not planning in overtime from the get-go is planning so your people can take time off without affecting the schedule. It is sometimes insignificant compared to project length, but from the point of view of morale, people appreciate it. There are very few things that can throw a wet blanket onto a project like the statement, "there will be no vacation until the job is done." People in general are honest and hardworking and want to get a project done, especially one to which they have committed, either to you, your organization, or even just to themselves, but at a certain point you can work people too hard. You have to remember that most technical people are working more at their option than yours. The worst part is that if they're among the more talented people, they are even more likely eventually to be gone.

In addition to time off, you have to assume that people will get sick. This is particularly true during the winter months, but applies in general all year long. Account for your people to be able to take a certain amount of sick time. It can be represented in the plan as part of the same allowance that's there for vacation, though you should allow for both, not just one or the other. Remember, the reason for the sick-time allowance isn't just to keep the schedule on track due to one person's being out. It's also there to incent the sick person to stay home and not get everyone else on the project sick, too. If a person believes they are giving up a vacation to stay home and be sick, they'll be more likely to drag themselves to work and expose everyone to their germs.

Accounting for Maintenance and Other "Side" Projects

We've already discussed that the people performing your IPv6 transition may have other higher-priority projects, as well. That discussion only covered the known projects. You can account for those in your planning by allocating only a portion of such people's total time at work to your transition project. In addition to other planned projects, however, most technical workers have several to dozens of little (often interrupt-driven) jobs that they do now and again and that may be ill-defined or variable in scope or duration depending on external stimuli. Such jobs may divert them for a few minutes, for a few days, or even longer.

One diversion that reduces the likelihood of being able to commit someone to a project 100 percent comes about if your organization performs regular application or network maintenance. In that case, you should plan an allowance for such maintenance activities. Hopefully, you have kept enough data on prior maintenance activities to know what kind of time and staffing factors are involved in a particular case, ranging from simple periodic tasks, to a major overhaul operation. Assuming no unusual circumstances, the historical utilization of time and resources for the particular forecast maintenance should suffice.

For example, if you just installed a new major release of an application, it is fair to assume that the application has bugs. Whether your team created the application or simply procured and deployed it, if you're maintaining it you should expect the same number of technical support calls as you did on the last major release. There may be fewer, there may be more, but there's little point in trying to predict any further than historical trends unless you have additional data to work from, for example, that this particular release carries additional risks because the application was acquired from a new and unproven vendor.

The longer a given person's role in your transition, the less likely it is that getting them for the full time you planned will be realistic. About the only thing you can do, apart from pushing back on any unexpected increase in diversionary work, is to allow for such diversions in your planning as suggested earlier by the application maintenance example. The allowances you provide for diversion should be a function of the total schedule length, not some fixed up-front time, to account for the fact that the longer the schedule is the greater the chance for diversions. That way, if the schedule's length should increase by 10 percent for some reason, you would budget an additional 10 percent of allowance for diversion, not retain the fixed value from the original estimate.

Compensating for Those Imprecise Estimates

The preceding allowances we've discussed are all concrete to one degree or another. You have a pretty good idea of the range of vacation allowance to give to staff. You often have the data you need to budget for maintenance activities that divert your team from the project at hand. Even after accounting for all that, there are still the unknowns mentioned all through the chapter.

Though it's unpopular (or at least inconvenient) in engineering and other detail-oriented disciplines, the truth is that you won't be 100 percent correct on everything in your plan, so you'll need to work with various additional allowances for mistakes, re-work, re-definition of work, and so on. These types of allowances stem more from personal experience and gut feeling than any other analysis and are typically called fudge factors. For many people, including myself, the major deficiency to overcome is an optimistic view of the time it takes to accomplish a project. Closely related to that is over-optimism regarding the true level of effort involved.

What your gut feeling is on either of these aspects of the project versus what reality is can sometimes be radically different. Learning what your gut feeling really means only comes from the planning, execution, and subsequent analysis of the outcomes of several projects, possibly over several years or more. This will eventually lead to you saying things to yourself (or your staff) like, "well, I think it's going to take about three weeks to do this and the last time I thought that it took five weeks, so I'd better give myself five or even six." Doing this kind of analysis in the open with your team can work out for everyone involved, but consider how much you want to share and how. If you present information about why you should take longer on a particular aspect of a project the wrong way or to the wrong people, you could be seen as overly conservative, incompetent, or worst of all, lazy. My recommendation is to strive to make the process become an inner dialog. Then, you simply look from the outside like a terrific project planner.

Explaining Why Easy Things May Not Be So Easy

Related to gut feelings and fudge factors is how you handle aspects of the project that might look "easy" to the casual observer. If you know (or at least feel) differently, you have to back that up to get buy-in (from your team) or approval (from your management) that you're simply not padding the schedule. Historical information here is best. Some will dismiss your new project's historic risks as being unrealistic because this project is different from the past ones, and therefore easier. "We've done this kind of thing before" or "we're much smarter now" are arguments that may be true. Convince yourself if they are or are not, and then endeavor to convince others the same way to your line of reasoning.

Walking the Narrow Line between Over- and Underestimation

You need to be careful on your project estimates for two obvious reasons. If you underestimate, you either are going to be working a lot of overtime, missing your deadlines, or both and you're not going to be happy. If you overestimate, you might possibly get the work done on time, but you may be viewed, as noted earlier, as overly conservative or even lazy.

For projects that are built up from sub-plans upon higher-level plans leading to an overall project plan, assume that fudge factors derived from gut feelings will be applied at every layer, typically because those at a lower tier tend to assume you will overestimate their capabilities or available time for your project; or that you will simply cut their estimates by some percentage to account for what you believe is their overzealous fudging. This can lead to an overall plan that forecasts a much longer total time to completion to the point of looking absurd. The surprising thing is that, even if this absurd plan is accepted, Parkinson's Law states that "work expands so as to fill the time available for its completion." So, you won't finish early even if you are allowed twice the time of your worst-case estimates.

I can attest to that because I have personally never been on a project, no matter how overestimated, that I've had time to sit around and "relax" while waiting for the project deadline to arrive. Therefore, it behooves you to estimate more on the side of optimism. That said, the estimates you give should be within the realm of realism certainly to a casual observer; but also (or more so) to somebody who has technical knowledge of the project you're estimating, especially if they're a peer or somebody who has influence on the management and the project's outcome.

Planning Enough, but Not Too Much

Though it is important to plan projects to sufficient granularity to allow you to assess, during the project, how far you've come and whether you're on track, trying to play it safe or make things more certain or measurable by over planning has its flaws, too. Plans take time to create and the more moving parts they have, the harder the planning work gets and the harder it is to increase the level of detail across the board.

The IPv6 transition you are planning involves lots of people and numerous interwoven dependencies. You have to account for all these things, but understand that arbitrarily deciding that you want a certain level of absurd granularity in the name of better tracking will cost you in the time it takes to estimate the plan and its schedules and will even make the plan *harder* to track once it's in motion. The latter apparently contradictory result comes from the increased level of effort needed to update tons of metrics day in and day out just to see how on track or off you are. To help you set a balance for your planning granularity, let's look at the concepts of precision versus accuracy.

Understanding Precision Versus Accuracy

If you have two numbers, say 3.5 and 4.5, added together they make 8. If you're instead talking about the measurement of two values that are accurate to plus or minus 0.5, then for planning (or engineering or scientific) purposes, their sum must be expected to be anywhere between 7 and 9. In shorthand, this can be written as, 8±1. You could also write, 8.00±1.00, but there's little point, because the numbers that make up the sum are not that accurate.

Knowing how accurately you can measure your plan's execution goes directly to how you should put that plan together in the first place. You won't be able to depict accurately below a certain level how long a particular activity will take. You can represent it to an arbitrary amount of precision, but that can be misleading or just plain wrong.

Determining the Right Granularity for Your Plans

A basic set of guidelines for the units of measure to employ in your planning follows in Table 5-1. These are by no means rock solid and you should determine your own comfort level when planning. Avoid straying too far from the guidelines, however, because you will wander into places where the granularity will be too small to use accurately or too large to provide enough planning milestones for the project.

You should strive not to put together monolithic project plans or ones greater than a year or so in length. Instead, as soon discussed in this chapter, you should decompose long projects into smaller chunks with intermediate deadlines that are easier to calculate and to react to, should the plan stray. Too much can happen in a year to create a meaningful project plan. Such spans of time are best suited for planning using constructs like roadmaps, strategic visions, and so on. This way, you can communicate where you want to go without wasting time (or setting false expectations) on details that will invariably change. Think of it like planning a drive from New York to San Francisco. You know you'll be on Interstate 80 for about 2500 miles, but it's hard to say exactly when you'll hit Omaha.

After you've put the plan together with one set of units, if the total project length happens to extend into the next range (or further) on Table 5-1, don't waste time resetting all the units. Each project carries with it a sort of "memory" or implicit accuracy that the participants share. In some cases, when talking about days in the project plan, everyone knows you're really talking about that value plus or minus some measure of accuracy.

Table 5-1: Suggested Values for the Granularity of Project Time Planning

PROJECT SPAN	MINIMUM UNIT OF TIME	RECOMMENDED UNIT
Up to a month	1-2 hours	¼ to ½ days
1-3 months	days	days
4 to 6 months	days	weeks
7 to 12 months	weeks	weeks

Developing Plans within Plans

As alluded to earlier, you are not going to have one master plan that's 5000 pages long and covers the entire enterprise. Much like a computer program, a flowchart, or a building schematic (or any other surveying results), the overall "plan" is composed of sections or sub-plans. Each individual sub-plan goes into great detail about local features and refers to other sub-plans or a more master plan for context, indicating how everything interacts.

If you were managing a building, the layout of that building is broken up into floor plans showing rooms, common spaces, the building's structural elements, and so on. Also included are spaces for stairwells and elevator shafts to show the locations and means in and out of a floor, but with little or no further information about adjacent floors.

Your floor plan may or may not include the furniture layouts to be placed in each room. To reduce the amount of detail in each sub-plan, there may be further sub-plans parallel to the one simply showing the layout of walls, and so on. Those parallel plans might show the furnishings in each room, plumbing and heating, electrical connectivity, computer and telephone network access, and so on.

In addition to keeping the clutter down in your plan, another important reason to create parallel sub-plans addressing the same floor of the building is that the work associated with those plans is often done by completely different organizations. One team of workers might need to know how many square feet of wall to paint or carpet to put down. A drawing with furnishings, electrical connections, and so on, would not only be confusing, but also overly complex to create while maintaining clarity for all the different disciplines that need it.

Laying Out Your IPv6 Building

Your IPv6 transition plan will be similar to the example floor plans, except you won't only be talking about physical space. There will be sub-plans for network routing, application deployment, server and workstation software inventories, and a host of other items. You may also have to put together business-unit or department-level sub-plans, some of which may be sharing the exact same physical space, routers, or disk drives on a server.

Creating your IPv6 transition plans also requires finding all the organizations in your enterprise that run network infrastructure or applications and making sure they're tied into your plans appropriately (and you into theirs). This will be easier for you the further up you are toward the CIO's office, because you'll have more insight into overall enterprise operations the further up you are. If you're not that high up, you'll need to figure out a way to get in contact upwards and laterally, at least with neighboring organizations that provide you with or to whom you provide services. You probably have satisfactory communications channels in place for day-to-day network operations. In addition, you may want to set up internal IPv6 conferences or work groups.

During your discovery process for others with whom you need to work in order to make the transition, be aware that you may not be the first person or organization in your enterprise to decide it's time to upgrade to IPv6. You may not even have been the one to have created the first plan. There may be plans in place for changing out departments, laboratories, and specific buildings even, depending on the size of the organization. For example, the R&D group may already have their "How we want to transition R&D to IPv6" plan put together. Business-facing groups, such as Finance and Sales, will not likely have transition plans because they're focused on their particular goals, which are not network or technology centric in most cases. In working with all these groups remember that it's about compromise and cooperation. Make sure everyone's needs are met, not that your plan is the one that gets done, no matter how hard you worked on it.

Planning at Each Layer of the Network Stack

Part of the effort of putting together a plan that takes your whole enterprise into account is figuring out how you can most comfortably think about the big picture while making sure you are covering all the little details. Just like it is easiest to represent buildings as sets of floors, one approach that may work for you is to address your IPv6 transition from the point of view of each layer of the network stack. Recall the network stack layers defined in Chapter 4, "Choosing When to Make a Transition and How." They were:

1. Physical
2. Data Link
3. Network
4. Transport
5. Sockets
6. Application

The layers will not all be equally affected by IPv6 transition and some of them can collapse further into groups of layers. To get you thinking, let's take the transition issues we need to address and the capabilities we have available and assign them to network stack layers. While doing so, to stimulate your thinking about what needs to be covered by transition plans, I'll also raise the questions you need to answer at each layer.

Making the Transition at the Physical Layer

This is where the wiring, cabling, and bandwidth issues are addressed. CSU/DSU and inter-campus transmission of IPv6 versus IPv4 are almost irrelevant at this level, as are packet header fields and formats. You may have to account for the larger IPv6 headers, what extension headers you will use, and how they affect the network. In Chapter 7, "Identifying Common Transition Preparation Tasks," I discuss such bandwidth issues.

You also have to account for growth of non-IPv6 transition specific demand, that is, your network is growing and changing outside the scope of the transition. If you have to put in new equipment to be IPv6 capable, make sure that equipment is of appropriate capacity to account for growth in user population, traffic in general, and so on, until the next time you are able to upgrade or do a technology refresh cycle.

We'll choose to put at the physical layer, though it transcends all layers, the needs of remotely managed equipment and whether it should be IPv6 capable. Link-layer switches and other lower-layer devices that aren't necessarily impacted by the IPv6 traffic that passes through them may be affected in as much as how they are remotely managed. For example, a link-layer switch with an Ethernet-based management console port is probably listening on HTTP, telnet, or some other protocol. Can that management port be assigned an IPv6 address? If not, then you may need to keep IPv4-based network management infrastructure around or replace the equipment.

We'll also cover inter-campus physical connectivity at this layer. If your campuses are connected by dedicated T-1 lines, there is little to worry about with IPv6 transition, outside of bandwidth issues. Any endpoint equipment, if managed by the T-1 provider, will likely not fall in your realm. ISPs, on the other hand, will be covered at the network layer, because with them IPv4 versus IPv6 connectivity matters.

Upgrading the Link Layer

Switching, unlike routing in the next section, is largely unaffected by IPv6. The link layer relies on automated configuration of switching topology, which makes things easier. Plus, the link-layer addressing scheme is not changing with IPv6. For Ethernet, there is an IPv6 EtherType that is placed in the frame in lieu of the IPv4 one. This is only applicable to native IPv6 or IPv4 tunneled over IPv6. The EtherType depends on the protocol directly above Ethernet, so tunneling IPv6 over IPv4 is not affected.

Larger minimum MTU values with IPv6, discussed in Chapter 4, "Choosing When to Make a Transition and How," and fragmentation associated with the larger MTUs, need to be addressed at this level, partly because of the elimination of en route fragmentation of IPv6 packets. Only source devices can create fragment packets, so if fragmentation needs to occur en route, it will either have to occur at the link layer or the packet must be dropped and an alternate path between the two devices discovered or created.

To give you an idea of where to look for MTU troubles, Table 5-2 shows the default MTU sizes of some popular link-layer protocols. Except for the IPv6 minimum, defined in RFC 2460, these are defaults and not minimums. This means smaller MTU values can be configured, so watch out for them.

Table 5-2: Some Default IPv6 MTU Sizes

TECHNOLOGY	DEFAULT IPV6 MTU (OCTETS)	SOURCE
Minimum Allowed	1280	RFC 2460
ATM	9180	RFC 2492 / 2225
Ethernet	1500	RFC 2464
FDDI	4352	RFC 2467
Fibre Channel	65280	RFC 2467
Frame Relay	1592	RFC 2590
IEEE 1394	1500	RFC 3146
PPP	1280	RFC 2472
Token Ring	1500	RFC 2470

VLANs deserve a minor mention; if for some reason your MTUs are close to the IPv6 or media limits, VLAN tagging may take things over the edge. Otherwise, VLANs shouldn't care whether they contain IPv6 or IPv4 traffic.

Upgrading the Network Layer

At the network layer, there will of course be lots of change. Oddly enough, the physical and application layers cover a lot of the transition issues, at least the way we divided them up. The sockets layer takes some of the burden, too.

IPv6 addressing comes in here. Where are you going to get them? In many cases, they will come from your ISP. Can you get them directly from an RIR or multiple RIRs, if your enterprise covers many regions? How many IPv6 address blocks are you going to get? Addressing plan construction and maintenance, including tools to do so, comes in at this layer. Use of link-local and Unique Local IPv6 Unicast Addresses (ULAs) is covered here, as well. These topics are all discussed in Chapter 7, "Identifying Some Common Transition Preparation Tasks."

IPsec resides in this layer, being that it's an extension header for IPv6. You need to create plans for IPsec, if you're going to use it. You can find more on this in Chapter 7, as well.

Routing is addressed at this layer of the plan. You need new versions of protocols like:

- BGPv4 (RFC 4271)
- OSPFv3 (RFC 2740)
- RIPng (RFC 2080)

Those are the biggies as far as routing protocols go. You may also be using IS-IS, for which there is an old Internet draft on how IS-IS will work with IPv6. Or, you may be using IGRP or EIGRP. See Chapter 7 for details on BGPv4, OSPFv3, and RIPng. See your Cisco representative for information on IGRP and EIGRP, because they are proprietary Cisco protocols.

Multicasting is addressed at this layer, too. Are you using it now? How will it change? Do you plan to use it? We'll cover this and other advanced IPv6 features in Chapter 7, too.

Network Address Translation (NAT) is supposed to disappear, at least in its current form. SIIT (RFC 2765) and NAT-PT (RFC 2766) will allow IPv6 and IPv4 devices to communicate, but that's a little different. Still, I'll conjecture that, for security and not address-space savings some will continue to want and some vendor will eventually offer IPv6 NAT similar to IPv4. Or, it's easy enough to roll your own. Assuming NAT does go away, you have to plan on how you will provide what NAT is giving you after it is gone.

Firewalls come into play at the network layer, though they also exist at the link layer. The latter, however, other than having to be able to handle IPv6, have no additional issues. At the network layer, you'll have to draw up plans to change your firewall rules commensurate with address changes, new devices, replaced devices, and so on.

Upgrading the Transport Layer

The traditional transport-layer protocols, for example, TCP, UDP, ICMP (ICMPv6 for IPv6), and so on, should see little or no impact from IPv6 transition. Because the next layer up in our stack model is sockets, we have to include more than pure transport protocols here. Protocols like FTP, telnet, SNMP, and the like, for planning purposes we'll note here. Any protocols that embed IP address information will be affected by IPv6 transition. Make sure you have implementations that handle that.

Port-level firewall rules shouldn't change too much, once you've got the IP addresses translated, but firewalls are as much (or more) about controlling access to transport-layer ports as network-layer addresses, so we'll mention them here, too.

Upgrading the Sockets Layer

As another somewhat arbitrary line of demarcation (remember, this network stack methodology/example is to help remember all the aspects of IPv6 transition that you have to plan, not necessarily exactly where the technologies live in the stack or what layers are literally changing), we'll address your home-grown applications in this layer, because they use the sockets interface. Third-party applications we'll leave for the application layer. RFC 3493 and RFC 3542 address the basic and advanced sockets APIs, respectively.

Things you have to watch out for in sockets programming with IPv6 include the fact that raw sockets are not nearly as raw as they used to be with IPv4. They are more "parboiled." For example, there is no socket-layer control of fragmentation, at least not in the RFCs, nor in the FreeBSD implementation. Windows or other flavors of UNIX may differ.

There are data structure changes in the sockets APIs. The RFCs defining the IPv6 sockets APIs and RFC 4038, which addresses how to port applications to IPv6, will help you with those changes. In short, you can either use the IPv6 data structures in lieu of those in IPv4, or you can use a new class of data structures that accommodate both address types.

Upgrading the Application Layer

This uppermost layer covers the applications you purchased, as opposed to those you wrote yourself. One of the primary criteria as to which applications are in this section is whether you have direct access to the source code and whether it is your people who are modifying it.

The section covers everything from the most trivial to the most complex of network applications and includes simple web browsers all the way through to complex network-centric applications. The applications don't only need to change in that they can communicate on an IPv6 network. Much like the protocols beneath them at the transport layer, those applications that manipulate IP addresses need to be able to handle IPv6 ones. Most notable in this set of applications are the network management ones that focus primarily on network infrastructure. They will require the greatest changes of all. See Chapter 13, "Using Pilot Programs to Facilitate Your IPv6 Transition," for some real-world information on just how hard (or not) it was to upgrade such an application to IPv6.

As a simpler example, web browsers and other applications that manipulate or use URLs need to account for the new URL format used with hard-coded IPv6 addresses. Because IPv6 addresses use colons as field separators, an ambiguity arises with the colon separator used to distinguish the IP address from the transport layer TCP port being accessed. To resolve this ambiguity, when URLs contain hard-coded IPv6 addresses, the addresses are delimited by square brackets (for example, `http://[1912:4:15:1140::1]:8080/`). In this example, the URL points to a server at IPv6 address `1912:4:15:1140::1`, running on port `8080`.

This section also includes the applications that are not primarily networking ones, but that are enabled to use the network. The word processors and spreadsheet programs mentioned earlier that allow searches of remote knowledge bases are one example of a non-networking program, per se, that still may need to be upgraded.

Scoping the Boundaries between Plans

As you put your plans together, it's important to define the boundaries between your plans and those of neighbors. You will have neighbors in many respects, not just physically adjacent departments, offices, or network links. Organizationally or functionally above you might be a plan that ties your plan in with many others. Below you may be many sub-plans that your plan ties together. In more abstract realms, your network plan may border on the application transition plan in regard to where dual stacks, versus tunneling, versus native IPv6 will be used. As you can see, it can get pretty complex.

In creating the plans, negotiating agreements as to what you will provide your neighbors and what you expect of them will take you a long way toward a smoother transition. These agreements become part of the assumptions you were advised to document earlier. Regarding the form the agreements take, in some cases, a verbal agreement and a handshake are satisfactory. In other cases, formal documentation may be required.

Understand the enforceability of your agreements. For the riskier agreements that a neighbor may renege on, you should have a contingency plan in place or understand the impact of going on without that particular agreement being met. In some cases, you might be able to work around the broken agreement. In other cases, the loss will be so critical to your operations that you will have to communicate that and work to seek an alternate solution or relief on what the violation of the agreement cost you.

One alternative is to be prepared to pick up that work if it's within your particular skill sets, because at the macroscopic level the enterprise is less likely to care about a particular failure, compared to getting the entire project done. Although this may seem "unfair" to you, it's how business works.

Minimizing Overlaps in Plans

Along with defining the boundaries between your plans, you want to minimize any overlaps. For example, there may be two networking groups in your enterprise. One is organized by physical facilities, the other by functionality. Planning independently, both may lay claim to a particular LAN, for example, because it is at Site X, but it is also part of HR & Finance. Obviously, that LAN doesn't need to be upgraded twice. You need to figure out a way to decide who will do which overlapping functions.

In minimizing overlaps between plans, there are two tools you can bring to bear. One is to have access to all the plans, analyze them, and therefore be able to see the overlaps. This is a huge amount of work to compare what could be hundreds of plans.

The second tool to minimize overlaps is to set up rules of engagement or turf for each of the organizations involved in the IPv6 transition in an open forum attended by representatives from all those organizations, so everybody knows their bounds. Potential solutions to the scenario of two overlapping networking groups include giving all the transition work to one of them. Or you could temporarily assign the responsibility over all the HR & Finance network assets, independent of their geographic location, to one group and do the same with another department and the other networking group later. The example is a little contrived, but you get the point.

Tracking and Adjusting the Plan

The quality of your planning will become evident as soon as you set your plans into motion and how soon the first anomaly appears. As we've discussed, the theme of this chapter is that you will never get your plans 100 percent correct at the start. To this point, we have striven to create a comprehensive plan that accounts for everything you have to upgrade, where it is, who will do the work, and so on. Now, let's look at what we need in the plan, both before the project's start and during its execution, to keep things on track.

Keeping the Original Plan in Sight

Once your IPv6 transition plan (or any plan) is in place and the ship is underway, that plan becomes your baseline so as to document your original assumptions and estimates. The importance of tracking your plan's execution to the original baseline cannot be overstated. You may hit a bump in the road that pushes things a day or two out, but you feel that you compensate and get back on track. The baseline is that track. If you don't keep a baseline and compare the present-day situation to it regularly, you don't know whether you're on track, behind, or, in that rare case, ahead of schedule.

Limiting Changes to the Baseline

Keep your baselines intact so as to preserve their intended use; compare them to how you thought things were going to go. This is valuable for tracking, but it's also valuable for analysis after the project is complete. By doing a post-mortem (or the more positive, "lessons learned") exercise after the work is done, you can tune your planning to do better next time.

A temptation that often comes up in projects that are not fairing well is to reset the baseline for some reason that sounds like it makes sense, but really doesn't. Do not reset baselines for arbitrary events or project changes. If you do reset, make sure that everybody understands why it's being done and that it's an anomalous event (like the scope of the work has doubled or half the staff quit); not simply because the deviation from the original plan is getting too uncomfortable and re-synchronizing would be nice to make people feel better about the future. Most importantly, understand why you're making the changes, what assumptions failed, what impact they have on other aspects of the project, and whether what caused you to change the baseline also causes other dates to change.

Keeping an Eye on the Time You're Spending

Determining whether you're on plan includes measuring whether you're consuming time at the rate you expected. For example, if you're hitting all your deadlines (or worse, if you're not), but everyone's working 20 hours of overtime a week, then you're not on the original plan; you're applying additional resources.

If, in the back of your mind, your personal fudge factor is to plan for normal days while knowing deep down that there are going to be *a few* 60+ hour weeks, then perhaps that's just the way you work best. As long as you hit the deadlines that others are expecting outside your organization and you (and those working with or for you) can tolerate the occasional overtime, then this is not a terrible planning technique.

If you initially believed your plan would require no overtime and you've been burning the midnight oil for some time (months in some cases I've seen), you should review the plan and make sure it's truly achievable in the calendar time required. This is because, as mentioned earlier, sustained overtime cannot be maintained and, if you've grossly underestimated your resource needs, it's best to reassess and correct before you're too close to that deadline iceberg and have room to maneuver by adding additional people versus time. You may also be able to renegotiate your deliverables, provided you give sufficient advanced warning so as not to surprise anyone too much.

Being Honest about Project Tracking and Reporting

At the very least, in the preceding example, you should not lie to *yourself* that everything's fine if you're spending undue amounts of additional time on the project and barely keeping up, or worse yet, you're still slipping. If others are charged with planning and tracking your project's overall progress or the progress of a larger group, you should inform them of your troubles. This is not only so that they know how much time you're consuming or how much you intend to consume. Informing others also lets them try to work with you possibly to help by eliminating or limiting the assignment to you and your people of those additional interrupt-based work items that pop up now and again.

Building in Safeguards with Intermediate Checkpoints

Set personal, group, or project-wide checkpoints. If you do not achieve or maintain these, you should consider yourself uncomfortably off track. For example, if

- you're too far behind schedule
- the work is of too poor quality
- too much money has been spent
- more than a certain number of resources have been removed from (or have left) the project, either by attrition, reassignment, termination, or a host of other reasons

If any of these check conditions are reached, the project truly is in jeopardy and action must be taken.

Tracking Slips without Picking Nits

Tracking to the plan is important and any significant or sustained slips should be taken seriously. As with most things, there is a happy medium point, rather than one extreme versus another in what you track and adjust for, too. This follows from the earlier discussion of precision versus accuracy. No matter what numbers and units are on your plan's schedule, understand that you cannot track a six-month plan down to plus or minus one day of accuracy.

If you or someone else on the project needs a half a day to do something else, be it work-related or personal, don't immediately update all project plans by that amount, unless the amount represents a significant chunk of the remaining time or a key dependency will need to move. If such things do come up, limit the slip to near where (when?) it's happening. Don't just blindly propagate it to the next month's worth of tasks as a math exercise.

As personal advice to anyone involved in executing the plan, except for extraordinary unexpected changes in the amount of time that you can contribute to a project or if unforeseen and extensive difficulties in the work come up, try to suck up that minor slip with a little overtime, as long as you're not killing yourself. This way, when you do have a slip that requires a schedule to be changed you won't have already been labeled as someone who can't hit a milestone.

Assessing How Much of a Slip Is Recoverable

You may have already been in the situation of being several weeks behind schedule and simultaneously within a few weeks of a deadline. You say to yourself, and maybe even your team, "We've still got the weekends," or some other inspiring saying implying that 10–20 days of slippage can be recouped in 2–4, for some strange reason because those catch-up days are Saturdays and Sundays.

I don't know why some people think that they can work 10 times faster on the weekends. True, the common office interruptions are not as prevalent as they are Monday through Friday (because oddly those doing the interrupting never work the weekends), but you still have only 16–20 hours of true additional work time and even with a 25 percent improvement in efficiency (assuming two hours of your regular day are consumed by "administrivia"), that's barely half a regular week. If you're several weeks behind, the only way you're going to catch up working weekends is if the deadline is at least a month out. Even then, with holidays, family commitments, and other non-work items, you can't expect everyone to be available 24x7.

To play it safe, I would suggest assuming four weekends for every week you need to recover to get back on schedule. You can substitute an equivalent amount of evening hours, but understand that will take more calendar time, because you only have four or five evening hours at most per day and the same things that (rightfully) compete for your weekends compete for your weeknights, too.

Finding Resources to Help with the Transition

Everything I've been talking about in this chapter can get pretty daunting. Fortunately, especially for the IPv6 transition, you're not in this alone. There's nothing wrong with seeking help, particularly if that help can be had for free. I'll wrap up creating your transition plan with a few suggestions on where you can get assistance in creating it.

Seeking Guidance from OMB

For those of you in the U.S. federal government, you may think that the OMB has done you no favors by forcing these IPv6 mandates on you. We've discussed why the mandates are a good idea already, so let's not belabor that here. It might interest you to know that, in addition to mandating IPv6, OMB has stepped up to the plate and produced guidelines, best practices, and advice for IPv6 transition for those coming to grips with the task. And, OMB continues to work with other agencies and private-sector organizations to refine those guidelines and put bodies in place to help agencies make the transition. This is far better than C2-by-92 or GOSIP ever was.

Even if you're not with the government, the documents posted at the OMB website (`http://www.whitehouse.gov/omb`) are available for you to use, as well. By going to the site and searching for IPv6, dozens of documents on enterprise frameworks and transition strategies pop up. For what it's worth, I'm as big a skeptic of large bureaucratic organizations trying to "help" as the next person, but I've been reading the OMB documents and memoranda since 2005 and I've caught myself thinking that their methods are exactly how I would go about the transition. Now you just have to decide if I really know what I'm talking about.

Engaging Professional Help

Companies, like Command Information (www.commandinformation.com) and Lumeta (www.lumeta.com), and others that specialize in IPv6 transition are also there to help you. Of course, unlike OMB their advice and help is not all free. Alex Lightman's IPv6 Summit organization (www.usipv6.com/index.shtml) can also get you in touch with people that can help you or they can help you themselves. Last, but not least, the North American v6 Task Force (NAv6TF) (www.nav6tf.org) and its sister organizations world-wide mentioned in Chapter 1 are an excellent source of guidance and pointers to others who can help.

Another source of professional help is, of course, actually hiring individual contributors: much like you would hire web developers or people with any other skill set. That said, the global pool of IPv6-savvy network administrators, developers, and project managers is probably still a little too shallow to contemplate this alternative too seriously, especially in the United States. You could hire resources from the areas that are developing these capabilities, like Europe and the Asia-Pacific region. For U.S. federal transitions, depending on clearance requirements, this may not be an option for you.

Further Reading

The following list of RFCs is provided as a reference for you to look up the technical details upon which to base your planning. Specifically, the RFCs listed provide information to help decide what is affected and how to go about addressing it in a way compatible with the larger Internet community.

- RFC 2080: RIPng for IPv6. January 1997.
- RFC 2225: Classical IP and ARP over ATM. April 1998.
- RFC 2460: Internet Protocol, Version 6 (IPv6) Specification. December 1998.
- RFC 2464: Transmission of IPv6 Packets over Ethernet Networks. December 1998.
- RFC 2467: Transmission of IPv6 Packets over FDDI Networks. December 1998.

- RFC 2470: Transmission of IPv6 Packets over Token Ring Networks. December 1998.

- RFC 2472: IP Version 6 over PPP. December 1998.

- RFC 2492: IPv6 over ATM Networks. January 1999.

- RFC 2590: Transmission of IPv6 Packets over Frame Relay Networks Specification. May 1999.

- RFC 2740: OSPF for IPv6. December 1999.

- RFC 2765: Stateless IP/ICMP Translation Algorithm (SIIT). February 2000.

- RFC 2766: Network Address Translation - Protocol Translation (NAT-PT). February 2000.

- RFC 3146: Transmission of IPv6 Packets over IEEE 1394 Networks. October 2001.

- RFC 3493: Basic Socket Interface Extensions for IPv6. February 2003.

- RFC 3542: Advanced Sockets Application Program Interface (API) for IPv6. May 2003.

- RFC 4038: Application Aspects of IPv6 Transition. March 2005.

- RFC 4271: A Border Gateway Protocol 4 (BGP-4). Address Resolution Protocol (ARP) Packets over Fibre Channel. January 2006.

Part of project management and planning can be learned from books. The rest has to be learned on the job. Though they are a bit dated, two good books on project management that I've used are:

- DeMarco, Tom, and Timothy Lister. *Peopleware: Productive Projects and Teams* (Dorset House Publishing Co., 1987; ISBN: 0-932-63343-9)

- Rosenau, Milton D., Jr. *Project Management for Engineers* (Van Nostrand Reinhold Co., 1984; ISBN: 0-534-03383-0)

Testing Your Knowledge

Here are your questions for creating IPv6 transition plans. Answers are in Appendix A.

1. What are the three corners of the project triangle?

2. What are the interfaces between various transition plans called and why are they important?

3. List some of the things you need before you can start your transition planning (or at least before you can finish it)?

4. What factors do you have to take into account when scheduling people's time on the transition plan?

5. Why are project baseline schedules important?

6. Where can you find help for your transition planning?

7. Extra Credit: What makes the IPv6 transition different from Ada, C2-by-92, and GOSIP?

8. Silly Trivia: What happens January 19th, 2038? At what time (to the second, please)?

Defining the Transition Preparation Steps

Before anything else, preparation is the key to success.
— Alexander Graham Bell

While searching for quotes to open this chapter, I found many different ones on the importance of good preparation. Then, while writing this preamble to close out the chapter, I suddenly thought of one expression that I had completely missed and that has implicitly been with me most of my life. That's the motto of the Boy Scouts of America, "Be Prepared." Those two words advise (or command) a person to think ahead of the here and now and put the necessary pieces into place beforehand to handle life's little (and big) emergencies. You'll spend the next fifty or so pages or so reading about how to prepare for your IPv6 transition. As you read the chapter, think about how your particular network's idiosyncrasies apply to the preparation steps described here. For cases that are not covered, make the effort to figure out the right thing to do ahead of time, perhaps based on analogies to or extensions of recommendations that the chapter does discuss. When determining what it is you should do, run the scenarios of what could go wrong in your head and decide how you'll mitigate their impact to the network. Decide how, no matter what the circumstances, you can "Be Prepared."

What You'll Learn

This chapter will help you with figuring out what hardware and software are on your network and, more importantly, what services those assets provide to your network's users. Once the assets and capabilities are all accounted for, you will learn how to decide the disposition of each asset in the post-transition network configuration. Some assets will remain unchanged, excluding the activation and configuration of IPv6 capabilities, which is covered in later chapters. Other assets will need to be upgraded before being configured and those that cannot be upgraded will be replaced. You will read about consolidating assets both to reduce network complexity and to free assets (possibly even IPv6-capable ones) for use elsewhere in your network. Before concluding the chapter, you'll learn about the importance of communicating the plans you're developing, how to schedule transition events to minimize the chance of network disruption, and how to get the approvals you'll need to start your IPv6 transition and keep it going.

This chapter is written to be helpful in preparing for IPv6 transitions ranging in scope and complexity from some select network and software functionalities all the way up to the transition of your entire network. As has been mentioned in earlier chapters, if you're part of the U.S. federal government, your mandated transition for June 2008 is to upgrade your network backbone to support IPv6. This mandated transition is meant to be the first step in a journey toward the upgrade of your entire network. For the parts of the chapter that are not applicable to your current transition activities (for example, software applications), it is safe to ignore them and focus on network assets only. You should at least consider the following advice. Though you have no mandated worries regarding end workstations, client or server applications, and so on, one could argue that the effort of putting IPv4 over IPv6 tunneling in place rather than simply upgrading at least some of your end systems to IPv6 capabilities is a wash, and you should go with the latter choice because you'll have to do it eventually anyway.

Inventorying Your Assets and Capabilities

It should come as no surprise that to know what you need to upgrade or replace for your IPv6 transition, first you'll need to inventory what you have. This inventory includes network elements like routers and switches. You'll also need to inventory applications like databases, e-mail and web servers, and you'll need to inventory individual workstations and other systems at the edges of your network to determine what operating systems, web browsers, productivity software, and other applications need to be upgraded or replaced. Before you panic about having to go out and count what no doubt amounts to tens or hundreds of thousands of hardware assets and who knows how many different applications and versions of applications, read on and see how creating an inventory can be easy.

There are many ways to inventory your assets. Because an IPv6 transition is a network-centric thing, a good starting point might be to count your networking assets, starting with the broadest collections of assets and working your way down to the smallest individual ones. As you go through this process, you can inventory what software is running on each asset, from the big routers all the way down to the workstations and laptops.

There are, of course, other methods, each with their own advantages and disadvantages. For example, you can start from the bottom up and count workstations, then see what routers they connect to, and then what joins those routers together. Alternatively, you can count your software assets first and then find out where they're deployed, piecing the inventory together in that way. Rather than going through all the possible methods in detail, I'll attack the problem from the top and break it into pieces as needed.

Defining Your Inventory Goals

As mentioned, you can conduct your inventory in a number of ways. Common to all the possible approaches are three overarching goals.

1. Validate your hardware and software assets and their capabilities as reflected, preferably in some form of Configuration Management Database (CMDB), or in combinations of electronic and paper spreadsheets, documents, and so on, which also constitute a CMDB of sorts.

2. Discover any assets of which you were unaware and that were not in your CMDB. Add them, including their capabilities. Such capabilities may be additional instances of those found in other assets or unique to the new assets found.

3. Eliminate any assets from your CMDB that you find are no longer present in your network. Also eliminate any reference to their capabilities. If the eliminated assets are the last with a given set of capabilities, note that your network no longer has those capabilities. Later, you'll need to decide if you still need those capabilities, but that's not part of an inventory exercise.

In regard to the inventory you need for IPv6 transition, the set of capabilities you need to track particularly well are, of course, those for IPv6. For example, does a router support IPv6 routing? Can a web server be configured to serve its content on an IPv6 address? Are the additional capabilities for IPv6 in DNS, OSPF, BGP, and other protocols supported where they are needed? This is a small set of the capabilities you need to track. You can find a more comprehensive analysis in Chapter 4, "Choosing When to Make the Transition and How."

Distinguishing Your Assets

Before getting too far into how to create your inventory, you should decide how you're going to identify and locate the assets in it. You probably already have an asset inventory of some kind in place that predates the one you need for your IPv6 transition, in which case you've addressed this matter. If not, or if your inventory isn't all you would like it to be, let's make sure you've got the basics.

Identifying Network Assets

How you identify your assets is not as important as the requirement that you identify them uniquely and in a way that you can easily find them within your enterprise. For network hardware assets, many enterprises use the link-layer MAC address, which is supposed to be unique to every piece of network hardware in the world. Though that's not always the case nor is it in any way enforceable, all MAC addresses are likely to be unique in your enterprise (unless somebody is attempting to circumvent MAC-address based security, which is a different problem). If a duplicate is found, you will likely detect it if you have a thorough inventory. How you handle the duplicate is outside the scope of this book.

The advantage to using MAC addresses is that a large portion of them are readily discoverable by automatic means on your network. That reduces your overall inventory workload, but MAC addresses are not the only unique identifiers you can assign your hardware assets. Other enterprises use everything from the manufacturers' serial numbers to enterprise-specific ID codes assigned when the assets are procured and enter the hardware inventory. The point to take away is not what's the best way for you to identify your network assets, but rather that the assets should be readily able to be uniquely identified.

Finding Your Inventoried Assets

Besides needing to be uniquely identifiable, your network assets must be able to be found. Your network asset inventory needs to record the physical location of each asset and track the asset if it is moved. Again, every enterprise does things a little differently, but the common goal is to enable an administrator or technician to walk over to the asset so he or she can fix, upgrade, or replace it.

As elaborated in Chapter 11, "Knowing What Assets You Have," there are several applications available for asset management and tracking. Their capabilities will only be touched on lightly here. The key capabilities for locating assets are that the assets can be assigned some form of physical or street address to locate the building housing them. If the assets are in a large mono-lithic campus, a building number is also likely needed. Once the building is identified, the floor and room number need to be tracked. Because most assets are stored in standard racks, the rack number also needs to be recorded. If a particular asset resides in a building devoted entirely to being a data center, it's possible the rack number provides enough information to locate the asset within the building. Some asset inventories also include shelf numbers within the rack to further ease the location job. Whatever system and parameters you choose, remember that uniqueness is what counts for locating assets, just as it does for identifying them.

When you're deciding how to specify the location of a network asset, you'll need to balance how much information you need to store to be able to find the asset against how often that information can change. The more exactly you record the asset's location, the more likely you are going to need to change it. In some cases, it may be sufficient to say that an asset is on the third floor of the building at 123 Main Street. If that's a small building, finding the asset by matching the unique identifiers of all the assets on the third floor against the one you're looking for may be an easier job than tracking the exact room in which the asset resides in your inventory. This is especially true if the asset is a more mobile one, like a piece of test equipment that may move from room to room in the course of its normal use.

You also don't need to track the asset as closely if it's readily identifiable by its appearance. As with the example of a piece of test equipment, it may be the only such device at 123 Main Street, whereas there may be hundreds of rack-mounted network servers, which would require more accurate location tracking. Like-wise, if the asset is a large one, saying it's on the third floor may be enough. In the early days of computers, the third floor may have been the computer.

Identifying Software Assets

Because of the nature of software and how easily it can be replicated, identify-ing software assets differs from identifying hardware ones. The uniqueness and location goals you have for network hardware assets remain the same, however, because you need to know how many unique copies of the software you have and where they are.

Regarding how many copies you have, for the purposes of IPv6 transition, you're concerned about the number of installed copies and not the total num-ber of copies you own. This is because the software application as a whole either meets your IPv6 capability requirements or it does not. Simplistically speaking, if the application is IPv6 capable, you don't have to worry about it and the installed instances can remain unchanged. If it is not IPv6 capable, you have to know how many installed instances there are in order to upgrade or replace them. You don't need to care how many copies of non-IPv6-capable media are around, because you don't have to upgrade those. You simply don't install from that media again.

As far as locating your software assets, specifically your installed instances, you'll read more about that in the section about inventorying software assets. The basic answer is that installed software can be found by virtue of associating it with the hardware on which it is installed.

Identifying License-Key Based Software Assets

Much of the distinction between hardware and software assets has disappeared in many software products with the promulgation of the use of license keys to manage software sales and distribution. Typically, each key is a unique identifier to allow the use of one copy of the software. Many manufacturers enforce this 1:1 ratio by requiring you to activate the software, usually by connecting to the manufacturer's website and submitting the license key. You are then provided some form of identifier (for example, a software serial number) in return that you either manually enter into the software application or that is automatically installed. For computer systems that cannot connect to the Internet (for example, for security reasons), telephone-based methods are also available where you exchange a set of alphanumeric values with the manufacturer's customer support site and then enter the value they provide you into the software application to activate it.

If your application's license keys each allow you to use only one instance of the software legally, you can use that key's value as the software asset's unique identifier. In some cases, however, a license key may allow installation and use of the software on more than one computer system legally. Such multi-instance keys are insufficient to use as unique identifiers. The identifiers or software serial numbers just described that are returned during the activation process would make good substitutes.

If the activation process does not return a unique identifier or there is no activation process at all, the software may track its own installation via recordable media, like a floppy disk. In that case, it is likely you can query the installed application for some form of software serial number and use that for the software asset's unique identifier. Because many applications compute such serial numbers partly from the host computer's MAC address, the unique identifier would be tied to the hardware. That's not too bad, as is discussed later, because you want to tie software assets to hardware ones anyway. If you uninstall the software asset and install a new licensed copy on another computer system, it's highly likely the serial number will be different. The best thing to do in that case would be to delete the old software asset and add a new one, tied to the new hardware asset on which it is installed.

If none of the preceding applies to your license-key based software asset, for example if the license key is for an enterprise-wide license and no serial numbers are available for each instance of the installed software, you will have to treat the asset as a "bulk" software asset, which is described in the next section.

As mentioned earlier, for purposes of upgrading or replacing software assets while performing your IPv6 transition, you only need worry about the keys actually used in running copies of the software. The keys you have not installed do not require any additional attention because you will simply not use them if the application is not IPv6 capable. Of course, because you probably paid for those unused and now worthless keys, you may want to negotiate some form of refund with the manufacturer. That, however, is beyond the scope of this book.

Identifying "Bulk" Software Assets

For this section, the term "bulk" software asset refers to a software application that offers no way to identify its individual installed instances uniquely. This includes enterprise-wide licenses of software where (usually for a princely sum) a customer is licensed to install as many copies as they desire. Such licenses are economical when purchased for applications requiring hundreds, if not thousands, of installed instances. Operating systems and office automation products are good examples of software applications that are sold with enterprise licenses.

The kinds of software sold at an enterprise scale may come with an enterprise license key that allows an unlimited number of activations, or it may have no licensing mechanism other than the manufacturer taking the word of the customer that no more than the licensed number of copies will be installed, which for an unlimited enterprise license is certainly sufficient.

In addition to enterprise licenses, other software that falls into the "bulk" category is the huge variety of shareware and freeware applications available online. Many of them have no licensing mechanisms nor serial numbers and, therefore, no explicit unique identifiers. Also, software developed by your own enterprise internally may or may not have any unique identifiers.

In all these cases, the solution to identifying the software assets uniquely falls back, as has been mentioned, to the hardware asset on which it is installed. Fortunately, at least as far as your IPv6 transition goes, every instance of software asset you care about can be tied to a hardware asset. If your asset management system requires a unique identifier, you can either leave it blank or use the MAC address of the host computer system.

Distributing Your Inventory Work

Much like you read in Chapter 5, "Creating Your Transition Plans," about distributing planning across your enterprise, rather than having a grand-unified IPv6 transition plan, performing an inventory for IPv6 transition can also be distributed. This is a far better path to take than creating some enterprise-wide master list of everything you have. In fact, by the time you were even halfway finished compiling such a list, it would be incorrect simply due to natural changes that occur in your network all the time. What you need to come up with is more of a list of lists and the owners of those lists need to take care of what's in their domain.

Defining a Piece of the Inventory

Let's say you have a branch office in Wheeling, WV, with 50 employees, each having a desktop PC. Each PC has an operating system and office automation software like word processors, spreadsheets, and presentation preparation tools. There are about 10 servers for network support services like DHCP and DNS, e-mail, collaboration like scheduling and calendar management, and other typical office applications. There's a router, separate firewall, and three switches implementing the network infrastructure in the office and providing connectivity both to the rest of the enterprise and to the Internet. One of the above mentioned servers also acts as a VPN gateway for secure connectivity to headquarters. In total, the branch office's inventory is around 65 pieces of hardware and, depending on how much you've standardized your software procurement and deployment, a dozen or two software applications.

The preceding level of detail is necessary for the Wheeling office's own transition planning, preparation, and execution. At the enterprise or perhaps regional office level, it's likely, and better from a project-management point of view, that there is little more than a line item or two representing the Wheeling office. Within those line items is a reference to the Wheeling office's latest inventory and, more importantly for the summary plan, the associated budget request/allocation for the IPv6 transition. No more need be said about Wheeling at a higher level.

Automating Your Distributed Inventory

One synergistically positive outcome of performing your inventories for IPv6 transition is that you'll know, at least for some given moment in each branch, regional office, and so on, what you have and where it is. With modern web-page authoring technology, this would be a great time to institute a side project, at least informally, to make those inventories known to those further up the network management food chain. Creating a collection of web pages that documents each office's assets would be a good start. Consider it while counting everything you have. The web pages don't have to be fancy. They could even be little more than links to spreadsheets that you post online. That solution alone would put you ahead of the asset inventory management practices of many enterprises out there now.

There are also several asset management tools available and you are encouraged to investigate and deploy the one(s) that are right for you. If your time or budget don't allow purchasing yet more software, the previously recommended simple approach can be quite useful when you need to review what you have six months from now.

Distributing Inventory Work Organizationally

As an additional or alternative approach to distributing your inventory work by physical location or network topology, you may choose to distribute it organizationally, for example from the CIO down. This is a good choice because each manager, starting at the CIO, knows who their direct reports are and each of these reports can be delegated the inventory work for the assets they own. The reports can then delegate further to their people. Assuming every asset has a human owner, you're guaranteed to get a complete inventory. Of course, there are assets that nobody will claim to own (or perhaps even know about) and others that will be double-counted, due to misunderstandings of organizational lines of asset demarcation or turf battles. That's why this approach isn't as perfect as it might appear, but it's still a good choice.

The key component of an organizationally distributed inventory approach that makes it very useful is based on how a human manager differs from a backbone router in a network infrastructure. The manager knows all of his or her direct subordinates. In a network infrastructure, a router may have an interface on a LAN thought to have only one other router on it. Instead, somebody may have installed a third router on that LAN and added a whole new and possibly significant chunk of network infrastructure of which the first router is totally unaware. If a manager in a human organization suddenly found himself with an additional direct report he had been previously unaware of, you could argue that he is not doing a very good job managing.

That little bit of facetiousness aside, although you're aware of everybody who reports to you and they are in turn aware of everybody who reports to them and so on down the chain of command, you still may not have a complete list of everybody running network infrastructure in your enterprise. There are numerous cases where employees run down to the local consumer-electronics store and purchase a small home-office router so they can hang the three computers in their office off it, many times in the name of getting their jobs done better. Because it may be against corporate policy to add such equipment to the network, such an employee may choose not to file an expense report for the router, either. This scenario is worrisome from more than an inventory perspective, because some of those computers may not be in the CMDB and therefore are not likely being patched or protected from viruses.

Purely from the point of view of taking an inventory of IPv6 capabilities and gaps in those capabilities, and assuming that the employee's three computers are all doing required work for the enterprise, you now have a router that MIS/IT is unaware of and that is required for some facet of the enterprise's functions. This little router likely doesn't support IPv6, either, because at the time of this writing, none of the small home-office routers does nor probably will any time in the near future, except one that you have to flash with firmware you customize yourself.

Will the employee add this router to the inventory, assuming he or she is even asked about it? That's hard to say, especially because its existence in the network may be against corporate policy and, because the employee wasn't reimbursed for it, it's his or her private property. If it's truly performing some type of crucial function, this is the kind of thing you're not going to find out about until you're further down the road on your transition.

This example is somewhat simplistic, but realistic. More complex and equally realistic cases exist where infrastructure, including external connectivity over cable-modem and DSL lines, that MIS/IT should be aware of goes below the inventory radar. The point is that no inventory system is perfect and that's why Chapter 11, "Knowing What Assets You Have," is devoted to further helping you discover all your assets.

Inventorying Your Networks and Their Assets

From the network-centric top-down point of view, the first assets you need to count are your networks themselves, followed by more granular inventories of groups of network assets, individual assets, and so on. The following short physical-world example should clarify this inventory approach.

When drawing up or updating a set of maps and regional demographics regarding population, for example, you first survey the land. You survey the roads, starting with the highways and other major roads. Then you survey the minor roads and houses, which gets you to the point where you can do a census of each house's occupants. During the census phase, you go to each individual house and ask how many people live there and maybe ask what they do. As you find all the accountants and architects and computer administrators and all the other professions, you can develop a set of demographics that says there are this many of that and that many of the other thing.

This example relates directly to a network inventory or survey and a census of applications and their capabilities, (for example, accounting software, network management applications, and so on).

Bearing the land survey and census physical analogy in mind and returning to your network inventory, from the top down you start with the easiest thing to discover, your IP or network-layer infrastructure. It covers your entire enterprise. It is accessible from your entire enterprise if you have sufficient administrative privileges, which if you're part of the group performing the

IPv6 transition you probably do. In Chapter 11, you'll see how existing software tools allow you to do much of your inventory work from the convenience of your Network Operations Center (NOC). The remainder of this chapter pertaining to inventorying describes how to view your network as composites of logical pieces all using the same physical infrastructure. By introducing these perspectives for viewing and describing the network, you should get a better understanding on how to perform your inventory work.

Distinguishing the Logical Networks within the Physical One

Most enterprises think of themselves as having one big ubiquitous network, at least at the IP (network) layer and above. You may have legacy networks or proprietary ones that don't use IP at the network layer, but it's likely IPv6 transition is not applicable to them or implementing IPv6 on them is not so much a transition as building a whole new network. We'll focus on the IP networks only. Also, some enterprises have a couple of distinct networks with very limited interconnectivity, for example to separate mission-critical operations from more routine administrative needs. There are also different networks at some enterprises to separate levels of classified information. That said, let's focus on any one of those physical enterprise-wide networks, be it your only one or one of several, and view it from the perspective of the different logical networks that it represents.

To grasp something as huge as an enterprise network, you need to break it down into smaller logical pieces. For any one of the enterprise networks mentioned in the preceding section, there are several logical networks contained in it. You can argue that the network itself is a logical entity and not a purely physical one, because it's not necessarily one contiguous physical thing. This is especially true today with all the wireless and satellite-based connectivity. That said, let's lump all the things you can actually point your finger at, even if they are microwave antennas or satellite dishes with no physical ties to the antennas at the other end, and call that your physical network. If you ignore for a moment the definition of the physical layer of the network from Chapter 4, "Choosing When to Make a Transition and How," this shouldn't be too hard to visualize.

The logical networks within the previous loosely defined physical one are those that serve different functional purposes or are views of the physical network from different perspectives. At a minimum, most enterprises have three or four classes of logical networks or perspectives (see Figure 6-1), which are the:

- **Outward-facing, internal, or "inside" network:** This is the physical network or some subset of its segments as seen by users within your enterprise. The line of demarcation between inside and outside is defined as the network perimeter and is elaborated on further in this list and the following few sections. The perspective of inside versus outside networks is facilitated by using something called split DNS, for example, which resolves domain names one way for inside users and another way (or not at all) for outside users. This allows `mail.tla.gov` to point to different mail servers, depending on whether you work for the TLA agency. It also allows for resolution of an internal web server's domain name, for example, `www.inside.tla.gov`, to an internal IP address, while not resolving that name at all to the outside world. Of course, split DNS is not enough. You also need appropriate network addressing, routing, and firewalls to direct and limit incoming and outgoing network traffic.

▪ **Inward-facing, external, or "outside" network:** This is the physical network or its usually peripheral segments as seen by users external to the enterprise. The perspective of being outside is implemented with the same mechanisms as the inside network, including split DNS. The outside network is minimally composed of the perimeter systems as seen from the outside, but depending on the enterprise, the outside network may be quite significant beyond just the perimeter systems' external interfaces. For example, Amazon, Google, Yahoo, and all the other web-based merchants or services have extensive production infrastructures entirely external to their perimeters and composed of hundreds of systems or more.

▪ **De-Militarized Zone or "DMZ" network:** Not required, but almost certainly present in all enterprises, this piece of the overall physical network can often be viewed as spanning (and implementing) the perimeter between the inside and outside networks. It is assumed to have some level of trust beyond the purely outside network, though not as much as the inside one. In the real world, most systems you would think are on the outside network (for example, external web and mail servers) are usually on some form of DMZ where the connections to the outside world have some minimal set of filtering to keep out the types of traffic nobody wants. Because this is not a book on designing secure networks, let's leave it at that. Just remember your DMZ(s) when it's time to inventory your networks.

▪ **Management network:** An often forgotten perspective for most users, this is the physical network as seen by those who run the network infrastructure, monitoring and controlling devices and applications. More than just a perspective, it often includes network segments devoted solely to the management of your infrastructure. It is usually more trusted than even the inside network and is accessible from only a few places, for example the NOC.

You may have additional logical networks. For example, there may be two logical management networks in your enterprise, one run by network operations and the other by the corporate security or information assurance people. There may also be distinct logical networks for applications management versus network infrastructure management. You may also have different external networks for trusted remote users versus the general public. The list of possibilities and combinations is practically endless, but the point is that the network provides different things to different people, groups, and other entities, and it is a lot easier to view it that way rather than as one big monolithic infrastructure.

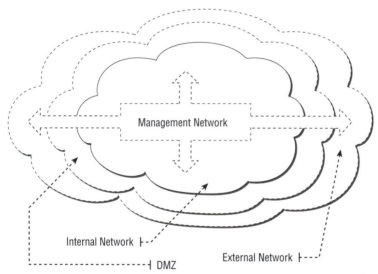

Figure 6-1: An example of the different logical networks in your physical one

Differentiating Logical Networks and Sub-Networks

While reading the last few sections you may have been thinking to yourself that the things being described as logical networks are simply sub-networks or subnets. Though logical networks and subnets are closely related, to call a logical network a subnet is too limiting, given the typical definition of a subnet.

The term "subnet" is typically used to represent a contiguous collection of IP addresses, for example, the 10.5.22.0/24 subnet, which is the CIDR notation for the IPv4 addresses from 10.5.22.0 through 10.5.22.255. These addresses are part of a private address space defined in RFC 1918 and often called the "10-net." It is there for every enterprise to use internally as it desires and is not routed by the Internet. Assume this subnet is part of your internal (behind the firewall) network. There may be hundreds of such private subnets within your enterprise and you can aggregate them together into a huge chunk (by IPv4 standards) of address space and represent it by `10.0.0.0/8`, which is the total 10-net address block defined by RFC 1918 and is itself a subnet. Your enterprise's whole internal logical network may be within the `10.0.0.0/8` subnet, in which case you could say that your internal logical network and the 10-net subnet are identical.

What if for a multitude of possible reasons you decided to use other private address spaces internally, as well? RFC 1918 also allows you to use `172.16.0.0/12` and `192.168.0.0/16`, both respectably large chunks of IPv4 address space in their own right. Also, there's no reason that you can't use any public address space you own, for example `192.0.0.0/17` (which, as of this writing, nobody owns) inside your network. In the IPv6 world, you are strongly encouraged to do so to allow any internal device to be readily accessible from the outside, should the need arise in the future.

Technically, you can even assign addresses from space owned by someone else, as long as traffic that uses those addresses stays within your network. This is frowned upon for various reasons by the Internet community at large and is commonly called IP "squatting." Squatting is an artifact from the pre-Internet revolution days of TCP/IP networking where enterprises deployed IP networks internally and assigned addresses willy-nilly because they would "never be on the Internet." It is a pain to renumber 50,000 or more machines, so squatting still persists in some enterprises. Obviously, none of these systems can communicate directly on the Internet and must go through a NAT proxy. Otherwise, all the responses to their packets would go to the legitimate owners of the squatted-on addresses who would in turn be very confused by the unsolicited responses.

If you are using addresses from all corners of the IPv4 space, it's hard to say you have a single internal subnet. Throw IPv6 addresses into the mix and the term subnet becomes almost meaningless when referring to your internal network, because IPv4 and IPv6 addresses can never be in the same subnet. So, that's why the term "logical network" is more accurate.

From here on, the logical network terminology, which is admittedly cumbersome, will be implied except where it is explicitly needed for clarity. Logical parts of your network will instead be referred to using terms like the internal or external segments or LANs, leaving the "logical" part unstated. The point is to remember that a logical network can be composed of many not necessarily contiguous segments of your overall network with more functional, security, and other properties in common than different.

Finding Your Physical Networks

To count and catalog all the assets you'll need for your network inventory, you'll have to know where to go to count them. You'll have to know where all your offices, data centers, and outsourced inventory are located. It was taken for granted earlier in this chapter that you knew the extent of your physical network(s). You likely know about the one that you plug your desktop computer into and the one whose routers and switches you manage. They may well be one and the same. For the network(s) you manage in particular, you probably know a lot about them, but do you know enough?

Whether you're only responsible for some small network segment or for the whole enterprise, the questions you need to answer to determine if you know enough about what you own to prepare for an IPv6 transition are essentially the same. To answer these questions, let's divide the network into two concepts, its contents and its perimeter. The contents are everything you know about via your network management tools, asset databases, and so on. The perimeter is where your knowledge ends. Beyond the perimeter lies what you assume to be there. Those assumptions may be correct or they may be outdated representations of a network that was documented a long time ago.

Shooting Fish in a Barrel

Let's return to the Wheeling, WV branch office example. The contents of your network are all the things listed in the example, like the router, switches, and workstations. The perimeter is where the single router in the example connects to the outside world. In an office the size of your Wheeling branch, that connection is likely via an ISP. The ISP is not part of your trusted enterprise network, so any connectivity back to headquarters or a regional office is going to be by some sort of VPN. You could, of course, have a dedicated line that wouldn't require a VPN, but that changes the scenario only slightly. In any case, at the network layer in the stack where IP lives, let's assume you have trusted connectivity to the rest of your enterprise. If that's all there is to it, then you have all you need as far as knowing about your physical networks for your IPv6 transition, but it's hardly ever that simple.

Going Fishing for Real

Let's scale things up (no pun intended) and make the Wheeling office a 5,000-employee campus with a dozen buildings, 100 times the workstations and 20 times the routers and switches of the former branch office. You no longer manage a branch network. You manage the network of a very large regional office. Though you're not likely to miss something while inventorying a 50-person branch, you can miss quite a bit if enough infrastructure to support 5,000 people is involved.

Now, let's say you're in the final stages of adding a new building to the complex. Whether you built it from scratch or simply leased another building in an existing office park is immaterial. In either case, it's going to have network infrastructure and that means something new for you to manage. The physical network connectivity has all been run, including external ties into the rest of the enterprise. In this case, you probably are using dedicated lines. The configurations for routing protocols like OSPF (and perhaps even BGP) have been modified so IP traffic can flow into and out of the new building. Everything is functioning fine, so there appears to be nothing left to do. In other words, everybody feels the job is done.

Coincidentally, during the time the building was being completed, turnover in the MIS/IT department was particularly high. The exiting staff didn't bother updating the asset management system and the new employees didn't know it needed to be updated or thought their predecessors had done it. Enough is listed in the asset management system to suggest the new building has been accounted for, so there are no immediate red flags that something is amiss. Unfortunately, the new building's network asset inventory is not complete and, *most importantly*, nobody's aware there are gaps.

Learning from the Fish Story

The events described in the preceding example happen all the time. They are sometimes caused by MIS/IT turnovers, as in the example. They are also caused by corporate mergers, reorganizations, natural disasters, and a host of other disruptions where inventory information is simply lost in the shuffle. The best you can do is to account for what you believe is your known inventory, or what we've defined as the contents of your network, and strive to define a perimeter that clearly demarks your assets from somebody else's. Not surprisingly, just like you may have more things than you think you have, you may also not have some of the things you think you did. For a more detailed discussion and help discovering things both within and on the perimeter of your network, refer to Chapter 11, "Knowing What Assets You Have."

What About Your Stuff on Other People's Networks?

An interesting question comes up in how you upgrade infrastructure at co-location or "co-lo" facilities, in other words, things that are being hosted outside your facilities. If the managers of the co-lo facility are not planning to upgrade to IPv6 any time soon, perhaps you should coax them, because you are a customer. If that doesn't work, for example if you're not a big enough customer, one thing to do is consider another co-lo facility. If that's not an option or at least not one you can exercise immediately, you'll need to use dual stacks or tunneling to get to your assets on external networks. The world-wide Internet will, of course, have access to those assets' external or DMZ interfaces over IPv4, because IPv6 just isn't there yet for people to be using it as their Internet preferred protocol. You'll need to get to the assets' internal or management interfaces by IPv4, too, which means you have to retain some IPv4 capabilities.

Checking Back with Reality Regarding the World after IPv6 Transition

Many people are still viewing IPv6 transition, particularly the one mandated for the U.S. federal government, as a type of light-switch event. The presumption is that when IPv6 is turned on at an enterprise level, IPv4 will be turned off. As you're thinking about accessing assets in external facilities after you've gone to IPv6, it is important to remember that you will still have IPv4 capabilities. You will still need to get to the IPv4-based Internet, which is not mandated to change any time soon and too valuable for you to simply drop off. You will also need to interoperate with those customers, vendors, and business partners of yours who have yet to make the jump to IPv6. This will all be possible using the inherent dual-stack capabilities of every piece of IPv6-capable hardware and software you have.

Clarifying the Definition of Dual-Stack Devices

The term "dual-stack" was introduced into the IPv6 transition vernacular primarily to describe routers and other devices that can speak both IPv4 and IPv6 and offer some form of translation capabilities between the two protocols. For example, as seen in Chapter 4, a router with IPv6 and IPv4 interfaces could tie two IPv4 subnets together over a native IPv6 backbone. This capability allows systems that cannot communicate using IPv6 themselves to communicate with each other using IPv4 even after IPv6 has become the wide-area transport for your enterprise after transition.

Neither the translation capabilities just described nor the dual-stack concept in general are meant to suggest that there are any purely IPv6 devices that do not know how to communicate in IPv4. The light-switch analogy presented earlier is unrealistic. As mentioned elsewhere in this book, the analogy is much more like HDTV versus "old-style" analog TV, touchtone versus rotary dial, or digital versus analog cellular telephony. Every device that uses the new technology does and will support the old one, as well, for the foreseeable future.

There is one exception to this rule. It is possible that a device's IPv4 functionality can be turned off by virtue of, for example, being administratively prohibited on the network. Though it is true that most devices out there allow IPv4 to be disabled (or, similarly, left unconfigured), to be able to access devices on external networks, IPv4 simply will have to be turned on within the devices requiring such access.

Inventorying Your Software Assets

Your software assets inventory is complementary to the inventory of your network assets. You can choose to perform the software inventory in parallel with the hardware one, that is if all the assets, hardware and software, fall under your jurisdiction. Many enterprises have separate groups for different types of assets, for example network hardware, application servers, and application software. Each group procures, manages, and maintains all instances of each type of distinct asset. Of course, as suggested in Chapter 5, "Creating Your Transition Plans," representatives of each of these groups could form a de facto inventory team, thereby reducing the number of total visits by distinct inventory teams to each branch, regional office, and so on.

Another benefit of performing all your inventory work at once is for consistency. Let's say you perform a network asset inventory that takes a month or two and then go back to do a software asset inventory. You'll likely find that there are new network assets as well as network assets that have been removed from service. Figuratively speaking, you could bring your network inventory with you and adjust it as you find discrepancies, but if your enterprise is divided into separate management groups based on classes of assets, this may not be as easy as it sounds.

Tying Software Assets to Hardware

No matter how you choose to coordinate your network assets and software inventories, you'll not find too many network assets, be they routers, switches, desktops, or laptops, that don't have some form of software asset closely tied to them. Of course, you won't find a single software asset that isn't tied to a hardware one.

Software assets are sometimes indistinguishable and effectively inseparable from the hardware they run on, for example in the case of devices whose firmware cannot be upgraded apart from at their home factory. It's simply easier not to count such software in your inventory, and instead associate the hardware and software functionality with the hardware asset itself.

Cataloging Your Distinct Types of Software

Just as there are many types of network or hardware assets, there are many types of software. You'll likely find so many different types of software that you won't be able to create a single comprehensible inventory to cover all of them. This is where you should, as with other aspects of your IPv6 transition, decompose the problem into smaller pieces. If you haven't figured it out yet, this is a key tactic in problem solving and one of which I am very fond. There is a saying, "How do you eat an elephant?" and the answer is, "One bite at a time." Remember this and apply it whenever you can. It will make your transition much easier.

To decompose your software inventory, you need to know what classes of software you have. There are some that every enterprise has. These include operating systems for their PCs and other hardware, word processing applications, spreadsheets, contact-management applications, and other office automation software. You will also likely have one or more of the popular general-purpose databases, web servers, e-mail servers, as well as more techie things like DNS servers, SNMP-based network management systems, firewalls, proxy servers, and so on.

There are also industry-specific applications that not all enterprises have, but that all the ones in a specific industry do. For example, many engineering firms use Computer-Aided Design (CAD) applications. There are several popular applications of which you may own copies of one or more, if you're in that industry. There are industry-standard publishing applications, as well as applications standard to the legal profession, financial and investment services, and even nuclear waste management.

It would be very hard to create a single inventory spreadsheet for all your different types of applications. It is a good idea, however, to create a single comprehensive and succinct document describing all the different types of software you have, and then create separate inventories of each type and refer to those inventories in the catalog.

Creating an Inventory for Each Software Type

As mentioned, you want to decompose your overall software asset inventory into inventories of the different types of software. One way to do so would be to create a spreadsheet for each software asset type with columns, for example, representing all of the operating systems used throughout your enterprise. Another column would list your hardware assets and the intersections of the columns and rows (that is, the cells of the spreadsheet) would indicate which operating systems are on which hardware. An example of such a spreadsheet in tabular form is shown in Table 6-1.

Table 6-1: An Example of an Operating System Inventory

ASSET	OS 'A'	OS 'B'	OS 'C'
Server #1	X		
Server #2	X		
Server #3		X	
Desktop #1			X
Desktop #2			X
Laptop #1			X
Laptop #2		X	X

Note that Laptop #2 has two operating systems indicating that it is either a system that "dual boots" into either one or the other at a given time or that it is running some form of virtualization software, which means both operating systems could be active at once.

Tracking Software Asset Versions

There are subtle differences between versions of software and different software types. Between updates, patches, and service packs, a software asset type that looks identical to another one may not be. For instance, Windows XP with Service Pack 2 (SP2) could arguably be called the same asset type as Windows XP with SP1 or even plain-old vanilla Windows XP with no service packs installed. On the other hand, few would argue that Windows 2000 and Windows XP are two different software asset types, because they are different products. Oddly, considering all the changes introduced in Windows XP SP2, it's probably as different from vanilla Windows XP as Windows XP is from Windows 2000.

As with other aspects of your software asset inventory, it's up to you to decide how you want to distinguish different software asset types. A recommended rule of thumb is to consider all the different flavors of the base software product (even with upgrades, service packs, and so on applied) as one software asset type. This is because, from the point of view of an IPv6 transition, IPv6 capabilities are more likely a property of the product overall, not a property of a specific service pack. With that said, SP2 did introduce IPv6 to Windows XP and, though one could argue it is not fully IPv6 capable (by virtue of how it does DNS), it is more capable than vanilla Windows XP. IPv6 capability, because that's what this inventory is about, may therefore be a consideration when deciding how to classify software asset types.

Inventorying In-House Developed Software

A possibly special class of software asset types is the one that covers all the software written by your own development teams. If you think about it, however, home-grown software, at least from an inventory point of view, is not too different from that which you purchase or download as shareware. The only real difference is that the vendor is you. In some ways, that can be quite positive.

All the discussion about distinguishing software assets with unique identifiers and tracking their locations so that you can upgrade or replace them applies to home-grown software. Depending on how sophisticated your development teams are, your software may even be using license keys, online activation, and software serial numbers. The real discussion then, in regard to IPv6 transition, is whether the "vendor" (you) will be making the software

IPv6 capable, whether they'll be doing it on a timeline that meets your deployment goals, and whether the upgrade or replacement process will be an easy one. From the point of view of inventorying what has to change, there is no difference between software created in-house or that which is purchased or downloaded from outside.

Documenting What Exists Now

Implicit in this discussion is that you are expected to be writing down all this inventory information so that you can refer to it when the time comes to upgrade or replace all those network and software assets that are not IPv6 capable. Also, if you're part of the U.S. federal government and you haven't done so already, you'll have to submit it to OMB as part of the IPv6 transition mandates.

A comprehensive hardware and software inventory of a typical enterprise is a difficult thing to collect accurately, but it can be as difficult to document in an organized, concise, and legible manner. It is even more difficult to maintain, because a given inventory is obsolete before the ink is dry. Fortunately, there are tons of tools available for creating and tracking asset inventories. Depending on the size of your enterprise, their purchase prices and ongoing maintenance costs might seem daunting, but the saved time and improved efficiency of your MIS/IT organization is oftentimes worth it. These tools are listed and their capabilities discussed in Chapter 11, "Knowing What Assets You Have."

As mentioned in the section regarding automating your distributed inventory, anything is better than nothing when it comes to documenting it and making it available to all those who need it. If you can't afford the tools described in Chapter 11, then perhaps you can afford to hire consultants to come in and set up an inventory for you with inexpensive open-source tools. You could be trained to use it and update the data in it. The consultants could periodically be called in to update your inventory throughout your IPv6 transition or this might be a task that is within the limits of your resources and budget. In any case, you should strive to maintain as comprehensive and up-to-date an asset inventory as you can. It will pay you back in savings of time and effort many times over.

Knowing Your Inventory Is Correct

Correctness of your inventory is, of course, what the inventory is all about. Based on the goals asserted in the beginning of this chapter, it means that everything in the inventory is actually somewhere out on your network or, in the case of software, running on some network asset. It means there is nothing in the inventory that isn't actually deployed and there is nothing deployed that isn't in the inventory. That's a mighty tall order and a moving target. You might as well face it now that your inventory will never be "correct." At its best, it will be accurate enough to get your job done and the jobs of the other people in your enterprise done.

If you were looking for closely held asset tracking secrets of the IT community in this section, I'm sorry but there aren't any, other than persistence, good planning, and lots of elbow grease. To steal and twist a quote from Thomas Jefferson, the price of a correct inventory is eternal updates.

Many products have come (and gone) that claim to ease your asset inventory pains. Most work to some degree or another and address different aspects of the inventory job. I cover some of the better ones in Chapter 11. Some products are good at finding your network assets all over the world from the comfort of your NOC. Others are good at cataloging software, but are limited to the local LAN or a few LANs, requiring multiple instances of them to be deployed. Still others are good for organizing all that inventory data, but don't do anything to collect it. The best bet for you probably is a combination of these products, along with training and professional help to put the products together into a solution that fits your needs.

Assessing Your Network's Capabilities

From all the talk of inventories, you might think they are the most important measure of your network and its assets. This time taking a page from Capt. Jack Sparrow of *The Pirates of the Caribbean*, you might say that your network is not its inventory. The routers, switches, workstations, operating systems, and other assets are not what your network is. They are what your network "needs." What your network "is" is the collection of its capabilities.

The purpose of inventorying your enterprise as part of your IPv6 transition preparation is twofold. It provides you with the list of network and software assets you need to upgrade or replace as part of your IPv6 transition. Performing the inventory also allows you to catalog your assets' capabilities. This doesn't mean just the IPv6 capabilities. It covers all the capabilities your network provides from mundane things like e-mail and calendar management all the way through to mission-critical capabilities like real-time data on troop and weapons deployments for the military and air-traffic control for agencies like the FAA.

Reviewing What Your Enterprise Does and How It Does It

A review of your business processes including the associated paperwork and forms you use, interactive and real-time software programs that are employed in doing business, and so on, will give you some insight into what your capabilities are. For example, the FBI likely has a process for another agency or law-enforcement organization to get data on a suspected felon. There is probably a form that has to be submitted and verified, which causes an information retrieval request to be generated against some database(s). The results are then returned to the requestor. Nowadays this process may be more web-based so, if you're the FBI, assessing which of your network and software assets are used to populate and verify that form and fulfill the information retrieval request will tell you what capabilities and associated assets are required to remain functional after the IPv6 transition is complete.

In addition to determining the capabilities your network has for providing services to others, you need to review your business processes for network capabilities you use as a consumer of other people's services. For example, when issuing requisition forms or purchase orders to your vendors, are there any special network or software assets used to provide special connectivity to those vendors or their intermediaries? These assets may be provided by your vendors, but because they are on your network and providing services for you, you have to include them in your assessment of the capabilities your enterprise needs to perform its functions.

There can be hundreds or even more such processes in your enterprise. Some are simple request/retrieval processes as shown in the FBI example. Others are far more complex and real-time, for instance how the FAA's air traffic control services manage an airline flight from New York to San Francisco. Determining all your enterprise's business processes and through that your network's capabilities sounds quite daunting. The first thought that should pop into your head when presented with such a Herculean task is to distribute the task across your enterprise to reduce the load on any one person or department and to get a more accurate answer. Each department surely knows what it does best and what network and software assets it needs to do it.

Creating Use Cases to Describe Your Business Processes

Assume each department will review its business processes and assess what capabilities it needs from the network now and after the IPv6 transition. One good way to do so is with a concept known as "use cases." Use cases allow you to create scenarios describing what you do in day-to-day business, be it accounting, sales, or support of other departments. Basically, use cases are a way of describing the things that you do regularly in the form of examples. Use cases are also good to describe how you would like to do things and are a popular way of creating requirements to specify what you want a new thing to do that does not yet exist. If you are planning on changing some of your business processes along with performing your IPv6 transition, use cases can help assess the capabilities you will need after the transition. For more information about use cases, see `http://en.wikipedia.org/wiki/Use_case` and the external links referred to there.

Completing Your Capabilities List with Application Specifications

Although use cases are a fine requirements management tool, thousands of them would surely be required to depict accurately all of the functions of something as complex as an air-traffic control system. Undertaking the exercise to create all those use cases, especially for something as peripheral to the application context as IPv6 transition, is not reasonable. The good news is that, when you bought the air-traffic control system and had it installed (which likely means dozens or hundreds of systems nationwide), the vendor surely provided a specification that was approved by you. The vendor also provided a pile of quality-assurance data in the form of test plans, procedures, and individual test cases along with passing test results to assure that the system met the specification. You can incorporate those specifications into your capabilities assessment instead of creating thousands of use cases. You can also use the vendor's test plans and test cases as the basis for how you'll know that the system works after the IPv6 transition.

Verifying that Your Required Capabilities Work

As with your asset inventories, your capabilities list should be vetted by execution, simulation, or at least inspection. You should not just write down processes or capabilities the way you believe they exist. You should spend the time to check that your business processes are in place the way they are documented and that they work.

Try to exercise all your documented processes and all the capabilities they require. You may have emergency processes that you do not wish to exercise or that would be expensive to exercise or that would alarm other organizations, agencies, or departments. In that case, a simulated exercise on a lesser scale may be the way to go. Bear in mind these do not have to be complicated exercises, but they do have to be at least somewhat realistic. The more steps you gloss over or perform "and then step X happens" hand waving on, the more you are going to miss things. You should get as close to the actual steps as possible.

CHECKLIST: Asset and Capabilities Inventories

Use the following checklist to help organize and cover all the different types of assets and capabilities within your network so as to get the most out of your inventory efforts.

❑ Collect as much of the inventory and capabilities documentation as you can find for your network as it exists today. Pay particular attention to finding documentation on existing IPv6 capabilities and which assets have them.

❑ Familiarize yourself with your asset and capabilities categorization taxonomy. If you don't have one, create one. It doesn't have to be comprehensive at first, but should be designed to be extensible as new asset and capabilities types are added or found.

❑ Determine what unique identifiers you use for network and software assets. Also determine how you handle assets without explicit unique identifiers provided by the manufacturer or vendor.

❑ Determine what location identifiers you use to locate a network or software asset quickly within your enterprise.

❑ Investigate and implement as many automated inventory processes as possible to facilitate the repeated inventory functions associated with your IPv6 transition.

❑ Determine how you will distribute your inventory functions across the enterprise for the most efficient process possible. Choose an effective combination of organizational, regional, perimeter-based, and network-function based methods.

❑ Inventory all your network infrastructure assets including routers, switches, firewalls and other security systems, and other network hardware.

❑ Inventory all the different types of servers, workstations, laptops, and other hardware that resides on the edges of your network.

❑ Make a special effort to identify and inventory any special hardware types unique to your enterprise, for example network-enabled manufacturing machinery, medical devices, process-control systems, and so on.

❑ If you create and use your own network-enabled hardware devices, identify the different types, and inventory them.

❑ Inventory all the types of field-upgradeable device firmware and operating systems.

❑ Inventory all your network infrastructure applications like DNS, DHCP, e-mail, web, and other servers.

❑ Inventory all the applications that enable your business processes like configuration control, sales, vendor, and customer contact management, and trouble-ticketing.

❑ Inventory all general-purpose, custom, and proprietary database software that is not considered part of some other application.

❑ Inventory the software on all user-facing devices including office-automation applications like word processors, spreadsheet programs, e-mail and calendar-management software, and web browsers.

❑ Identify and inventory all the custom client and server applications unique to your enterprise.

❑ Make sure that all your software assets are tied to specific hardware running the software and to installation media.

❑ Make sure to include version information as required in your software asset inventory.

❑ Make sure that all your network and software assets in co-location facilities are included in your inventories.

❑ Update your CMDB and other inventory documentation based on the results of your inventory activities. Make sure that everything that exists in your network, and only what exists, is in the CMDB.

❑ Develop use cases and tests to validate your network's capabilities to be used during the pre-transition inventory and afterwards to assess that required capabilities have survived the transition.

Defining the Post-Transition Configuration

Your transition plans and tasks should build on each other utilizing the results of earlier work to facilitate later steps in the project. By taking your asset inventory and capabilities assessment and working with your vendors and internal development teams, you will be able to figure out which assets can be left in place as is, which require upgrades, and which must be replaced entirely. This collection of existing infrastructure, upgrades, and replacements will become your post-transition configuration.

For your IPv6 transition to be considered successful, your post-transition configuration needs to meet certain goals. These goals include:

1. Keeping your transition costs minimal, in other words limiting how many new assets are acquired to accomplish your transition. Closely related to limiting the number of new assets is maximizing the reuse of as many pre-transition assets as possible.

2. Retaining all the required capabilities of the pre-transition configuration. You will likely have more capabilities after your IPv6 transition and you may even be able to get rid of some you realize during the transition you no longer need. In any case, those capabilities that you needed before transition had better be there afterwards.

3. Optimizing the configuration wherever possible to have an even better network when your IPv6 transition is complete. This ties closely to the first goal of minimizing cost, because it includes eliminating spares and

consolidating functions into fewer network assets. If you find yourself already taxed by the other transition goals, this goal is also well suited for a later refresh cycle or new project.

4. Documenting the post-transition configuration. The new configuration will probably not match exactly to the plan you had in mind when you started. Ideally, you will adjust your asset inventory, capabilities assessment, and CMDB as you perform your IPv6 transition. If not or if you feel some things may have slipped through the cracks, you should perform another asset inventory and capabilities assessment after the transition is complete or close to it.

Note the references to the "completion" of your IPv6 transition in the preceding goals. This is a good time to remind you that the completion being discussed is not the ultimate conversion of every network and software asset into an IPv6-capable one. Rather, the completion being referred to is that of any given phase of your overall IPv6 transition program.

For many of you, especially those in the U.S. federal government, the definition of IPv6 transition means upgrading the network backbone and little more, if anything. Though this admittedly large effort has been equated to encompass the full meaning of the term "IPv6 transition" by many, it is but the first major milestone in a far more ubiquitous (and as yet, ill-defined) IPv6 transition mandate. OMB themselves acknowledge that this first transition is part of a journey and not the end goal.

Therefore, to make this book easier to apply to your first IPv6 transition phase and all the to-be-defined phases that follow (for example, applications, workstations, vendor connectivity, mobility, multicasting, and so on), it is better to consider each phase as its own stand-alone entity and impart a sense of completeness after reaching each phase's culminating milestone. This is more desirable than having a long series of phases with each ending in a dissatisfying cliff-hanger like some bad soap opera until what will likely be 2025 when the last IPv4 address is finally shut off.

Determining How to Make an Asset IPv6 Capable

As has already been suggested earlier in the chapter, being IPv6 capable is something that applies more to software than hardware. In the majority of cases, even when talking about network assets like routers and firewalls, making something IPv6 capable can be mostly accomplished with a software upgrade. For some network assets the IPv6 capabilities are an inseparable part of the hardware, for example being implemented as Application-Specific Integrated Circuits (ASICs). For others, their IPv6 capabilities are implemented in firmware or the operating system. Such software-centric implementations can typically be upgraded to being IPv6 capable without replacing the old hardware or maybe by also just adding some memory or other less-expensive hardware resource.

Most general-purpose computers, PCs for example, can be considered IPv6 capable (or perhaps IPv6 *compatible*) in respect to their bare-hardware, because the only place IPv6 capabilities are even remotely relevant at that level is on the computers' Network Interface Cards (NICs). These cards are usually only smart enough to push onto the network the bytes the operating system tells them to send. Whatever the NICs receive gets pushed up to the operating system for interpretation. Whether a packet contains IPv4 or IPv6 is irrelevant to the NICs.

As such, nearly the entire decision on whether a general-purpose computer is IPv6 capable rests on the operating system it is running. Like with the routers mentioned earlier, however, upgrading to an IPv6-capable operating system may also require upgrading hardware resources in areas like memory, CPU speed, video display capabilities, and so on. Some of these resources have nothing to do with IPv6 capabilities (for example, the video capabilities), but other parts of the operating system require them. Because you usually can't pick and choose which new features you want, you have to upgrade your hardware to meet all of the operating system's needs. This is where the hardware may not be able to be made IPv6 capable, for example if its maximum memory limit is below the minimum that the new operating system needs, and needs to be replaced as a whole.

Another option you may have to replacing older hardware is to switch to an operating system that demands less from your hardware, can run on the older hardware you have, and is IPv6 capable. Of course, running the operating system is not what your hardware is there for, but only a means by which to run applications. If there are versions of your applications available for other less-taxing IPv6-capable operating systems, the switch mentioned may make sense and you might want to consider it. There is a strong case to be made for running multiple operating systems in your organization; it is good for security and system availability. For instance, security vulnerabilities in one operating system are almost certainly not going to be in any other. Of course, those other operating systems have different security vulnerabilities of their own.

Be aware that, even if your applications are supported by multiple operating systems, most MIS/IT organizations standardize on a particular one for reasons including ease of maintenance and staff training, volume price discounts from vendors, and sometimes even convictions bordering on religious fanaticism regarding the superiority of one operating system over another. In many cases, you are stuck with such enterprise standards and, therefore, have no choice but to replace hardware should older equipment not be able to support the IPv6-capable versions of operating systems. As you will read, those older systems need not be thrown on the junk heap, however.

Determining What You Need to Replace or Upgrade

Transition is, of course, about change. Your asset inventory activities will have gotten you the list of things that need to be changed in some way. You might not, however, have determined what changes were required while performing the inventory exercise. You might have only noted that, for example, an asset was not IPv6 capable and therefore needed to be changed. The next step is to take the list of assets requiring change to the appropriate vendors and finding out what they can do for you.

Your vendors will tell you what patches and upgrades are available to make each asset IPv6 capable. If there are no patches or upgrades for a given asset, the vendor may be able to offer a newer model with all the capabilities you need, including IPv6. If the vendor cannot offer an upgrade or replacement, you may have to seek out another vendor or make do until the current vendor comes out with what you need.

Accounting for Needs Beyond IPv6 Capabilities

When determining the specific changes each asset requires, either during the inventory exercise or afterwards, you should not only assess the need for IPv6 capabilities, but as mentioned in Chapter 5, "Creating Your Transition Plan," each asset also should be assessed to see if any new capacity, performance, security, or other requirements that have come up since it was installed or last upgraded apply to it and, if they do, if the asset meets those requirements. If the upgrade or replacement of the asset to provide IPv6 capabilities is the last one until the next refresh cycle, which may be a ways off, you may have to address those other requirements, as well, when selecting the upgrade or replacement.

For instance, if you need a new feature in your routers (for example, the ability to be managed remotely using SNMPv3) and the current routers don't have IPv6, then you need to find upgrades or replacements from your current vendor(s), or perhaps even new vendor(s), that have both those capabilities.

Dealing with Dependencies between Assets

Beyond the simplistic binary condition of whether or not an asset is IPv6 capable, you may face complexities brought about by interoperability issues between assets. This is typically limited to interactions between software applications, but can pertain to hardware assets, as well.

For example, assume that an upgrade exists for one of your applications, X, that will enable it with IPv6 capabilities, but that new version is only compatible with a non-IPv6-capable version of another application, Y. An IPv6-capable version of Y does exist, but it is significantly different from the non-IPv6-capable version and not compatible with any version of X. Don't laugh. This kind of thing happens more often than you think.

You have a couple of choices here. You can wait for the vendor(s) supporting X and Y to resolve their incompatibility issues and produce new versions of either or both applications that interact properly. You can upgrade X or Y, but not both, to the version with IPv6 capabilities, thereby achieving some level of transition. Which application you choose to upgrade is outside the scope of this example and depends on factors like which application is more pervasive throughout the enterprise. Also, because the new version of Y sounds like a major change in the underlying software, you have to assess how much risk you're willing to take with the vendor's new code. You can replace both X and Y with one or more totally different applications that are IPv6 capable, provide at least all the capabilities that X and Y do, and (in the cases were you'll require multiple applications) are compatible with each other.

Factoring in Remote Asset Management

Earlier in this chapter, you were introduced to the various logical networks that constitute your physical one. Of those, the management network, the one used to monitor and control your assets remotely, is particularly important to consider when deciding how to upgrade or replace assets. Some time between now and when your network is fully IPv6 capable, you have to convert any TCP/IP-based remote management of your assets from IPv4 to IPv6.

Any asset that is managed remotely using TCP/IP stack protocols like FTP, HTTP, SNMP, SSH, Syslog, Telnet, TFTP, and a plethora of proprietary ones, has to be assessed as to whether it can be managed using IPv6 instead of IPv4 at the network layer and whether its other IPv6 capabilities are remotely manageable. The applications doing the managing similarly need to be assessed.

Assessing Whether Your Management Protocols Are IPv6 Capable

Most of the management protocols mentioned previously are unaffected by which version of IP you use to send and receive network management traffic. SNMP is an example of such a protocol. Though SNMP payloads can contain IP addresses (both IPv4 and IPv6), the rigid structure that SNMP requires its payloads to ascribe to clearly describes each payload element and transmits and receives them readily. For an SNMP implementation to be IPv6 capable, there is a requirement for the sending and receiving applications to understand the various IPv6 Management Information Bases (MIBs) in use, but that is a payload issue and does not have anything to do with the protocol itself.

Other protocols, FTP and HTTP, for example, are not as agnostic about the underlying network layer. The typical issue that causes IPv6 compatibility problems for them is their embedding of IP addresses, without regard to the IP address type, within protocol messages themselves and not just as parts of payloads. This was often done for very good reasons, as in the case of both FTP and HTTP, and before IPv6 was even a blip on the Internet's radar. This excuse is especially applicable to FTP, whose roots go back to 1972. In contrast, the original versions of some proprietary management protocols created as recently as 2005 were designed as if IPv4 was all there was, so the type of IP address being exchanged in protocol messages was not specified in the protocol, but rather implicitly defined as IPv4 only. The list of excuses for this kind of design shortcoming is far shorter than the one for FTP.

Overcoming these limitations by adding support for IPv6 addresses to protocol definitions should not be too hard. There are already FTP and HTTP extensions to handle IPv6. In many cases, a good portion of the work is deciding which of several adequate solutions to adopt, but the protocol definition is often the easiest part. The implementations of the protocols then need to be updated, tested, and deployed. Most difficult of all, backward compatibility with non-IPv6-capable assets already in the field has to be taken into account.

Other protocols, including the proprietary ones, have caught up or eventually will provided demand for IPv6 compatibility in the products that use them is there. To help you with your transition, you should be cautious when asking your vendors whether the assets they are providing support IPv6-based remote management. Be sure to verify that they do all the way down to the management protocols in use.

Verifying Your Assets' IPv6 Capabilities Can Be Managed with SNMP

Putting the preceding discussion of IPv6-capable management protocols aside for the moment, it's safe to say that if your assets can communicate using IPv6, then they likely can be managed using IPv6. For example, an IPv6-capable and SNMP-managed asset can almost certainly have its SNMP server configured to listen on the well-known UDP port for SNMP irrespective of whether that port is reached via IPv4 or IPv6 by a management client, but that does not necessarily mean the asset's IPv6 capabilities can be managed by SNMP.

There are several documented cases where parts of or entire IPv6 MIBs have not been implemented, even though the asset is IPv6 capable and SNMP managed. This is likely just the SNMP software group lagging the rest of the product development team and the vendor wanting to get an IPv6-capable product out sooner. There is nothing inherently more difficult about implementing the SNMP MIBs for IPv6 than any other MIB. It just needs to be done. Until the MIBs are implemented on the assets in question, you will likely have to manage those assets from their local consoles or by using some other means of remote management.

In addition to unimplemented MIBs, some implementations are also just plain broken. SNMP has been around a long time and its implementations have been vetted and the bugs rung out over the years. There have been some pretty spectacular ones, including an extremely security-relevant bug back in June of 2002. Barring any new front-page news, SNMP seems pretty stable. That is, until IPv6 came along.

Most of the MIB work nowadays takes place in vendor private MIBs. Those are the ones that pertain to monitoring and controlling specific features a given vendor supports. Though those implementations surely have their bugs, the bugs are often localized to some boutique feature that is either rarely used or whose failure would have minor impact. Plus, vendors don't change their MIBs all that often and it's unlikely that any two vendors will significantly change theirs in the same general time frame.

The IPv6 MIBs, on the other hand, had to be implemented by every vendor, the implementations affected the public portion of the MIB, and all the vendors implemented the changes over a fairly limited time frame, perhaps a couple of years or so. These are all conditions that can lead to much more pervasive failure modes than some new obscure feature implemented by one tertiary vendor. If you find the MIBs on some of your assets broken, your remedies are the same as if the MIBs were absent. That is, use the local console to manage IPv6 or use some other means of remote management, SSH for example.

No matter what you decide to do, knowing how thoroughly and correctly your vendors have implemented SNMP-based management of their assets' IPv6 capabilities is something you should verify when discussing what needs to be done with those assets for IPv6 transition.

Managing IPv6 Capabilities Via Remote Consoles

If you don't use SNMP-based remote management or some of your assets don't have management of IPv6 capabilities implemented in SNMP yet, or the implementations are faulty, you have other remote management choices. Many products have alternate remote management mechanisms other than SNMP, for example HTTP, SSH, Telnet, or TFTP. Some products rely on those methods alone and don't even implement SNMP.

Unlike SNMP, with its well-defined and industry-standard public MIBs, the other remote management choices are typically extensions of a product's local console. Logging in to an asset using SSH or Telnet presents the same user interface as logging in at the hardwired serial port with the look and feel being unique to a given vendor. Therefore, the same tools to view and configure your IPv6 capabilities locally are available with such remote consoles, giving you the maximum, but not necessarily most convenient means of controlling them.

A good security tip to bring up at this point is that if you are using remote consoles to manage your assets, choose SSH over Telnet wherever possible. SSH supports several types of authentication and communications confidentiality. Almost every remote user, administrator, or security officer should find at least one of those types suitable for their environment. SSH's security properties are well understood and there are publicly available versions that include source code for the paranoid. Telnet, on the other hand, also has well-known security properties, in that it is clearly not secure at all. There is no encryption and authentication without encryption is almost pointless. You may have mitigating factors, like overall link-layer encryption of your network traffic, that make Telnet acceptable, but in the general case Telnet (and FTP and TFTP, for that matter) are synonymous with insecurity.

Managing IPv6 Capabilities Via the Web

Many products today support being remotely managed over the web, either with HTTP or HTTP/SSL. Using the same argument that favors SSH over Telnet, choose HTTP/SSL over HTTP without SSL whenever possible when selecting products with web-based remote management.

Usually more intuitive and visually pleasing than command-line based remote consoles, though not always, web-based remote-management is like its command-line cousin in that the user interfaces are different for every vendor and, in many cases, every product. This is not as important with the web-based interfaces because they rarely require you to remember convoluted command or options sequences, instead using English and other human languages to describe what you're seeing and how to control it.

From a software developer's point of view, the implementations of web-based interfaces are usually less complex and easier to update than SNMP implementations. Therefore, if an asset is manageable over the web, it's likely the IPv6 capabilities will be manageable that way, too. Nevertheless, implementing the web-based management still requires work on the part of the vendor and, if a vendor is looking to implement the bare minimum to get a product out on time, the web interface may not be updated for IPv6. With that in mind, like with the SNMP example, if a product you are looking to upgrade as part of your IPv6 transition boasts being able to be managed by the web, make sure all of its capabilities, including IPv6, are included in that boast. Otherwise, you're back to working with remote command-line consoles.

Making Sure Your Management Systems Are IPv6 Capable

There are two sides to the remote network management street, specifically in this case when it comes to managing IPv6 capabilities. You've read in great detail how your assets may need to support remote management of their IPv6 capabilities in order for you to consider them truly IPv6 capable. On the flip side, the applications doing the managing must be IPv6 capable, as well. As with the assets, determining that the management applications are IPv6 capable is a multi-faceted analysis.

Given all the protocols listed previously that could be used for remote management, there are many applications that can fall into the category of network management tools. The list ranges from simple general-purpose SSH, Telnet, and TFTP clients to web browsers, and culminates in complex remote-management applications like HP's OpenView and IBM's Tivoli. The conditions to be satisfied to consider applications in each of these classes to be IPv6 capable for remote network management vary, but they all have common requirements they must meet.

For any application to perform remote management using IPv6, it must of course be able to communicate via IPv6 itself. That is, it must be able to accept an IPv6 address specified by a user, connect to the asset at that address, and carry on an IPv6 conversation with the asset. This is the only requirement on an application used for remote management via web-based interfaces or remote command-line consoles, because the information being communicated between the managing application and the asset being managed is handled as a simple and opaque data stream. It is left to the user to interpret and respond correctly to what they are seeing on the screen. Moreover, though command-line sessions or screen shots of the web pages can be saved for later viewing, what is saved is nothing more than those character streams or images with no inherent meaning to the applications manipulating them as to the nature of their contents. For remote management of this type, versions of applications that communicate using HTTP, SSH, and Telnet and that are IPv6 capable are readily available for all the major operating systems.

In the case of SNMP-based remote management, the applications are much more involved in and highly specialized for that function. Making an application like OpenView or Tivoli IPv6 capable is no small job. As with the simple web browsers, the SNMP-based applications must be able to communicate over IPv6, but that's only the beginning. As discussed earlier, SNMP-based applications must support all the new IPv6 MIBs (or at least the ones you're interested in) in order to be considered IPv6 capable. That doesn't just mean knowing where to find the IPv6 data in the MIB tree (SNMP data is represented as a huge tree-like data structure). It means knowing the format of the data in the MIB elements and being able to store, search on, and aggregate that data, including IPv6 addresses and address block information kept in the application's proprietary databases.

One of the most basic, but cumbersome, functionalities that must be added to a network management application to make it IPv6 capable is the ability to manipulate 128-bit IPv6 addresses efficiently, in other words comparing two addresses, computing the number of addresses represented by a range, determining whether an address belongs to a given address block, and so on. Such applications have been able from their earliest incarnations to produce a list, for example, of all the active IP addresses in a user-specified CIDR block like `192.168.0.0/16`. The application takes all the active IP addresses in its database, and performs a straightforward Boolean AND operation to test each one for membership in the block being searched.

Doing this test on IPv4 addresses is simple arithmetic for 32-bit computers, which have been around about as long as IPv4, and takes as few as three to six machine instructions, including the overhead of moving values from memory into the CPU for computation. For IPv6 addresses, the Boolean math is no different, but the implementation changes from those few instructions to a loop applied against each address that requires at least 4 times more work and more likely closer to 10 times more. Though this doesn't sound like a significant increase for a simple search that took perhaps a second or two with IPv4 and will take 10 with IPv6, for applications that rely heavily on searching, aggregating, and reporting on sets of IP addresses, especially in near real-time, the performance degradation can be detrimental. There are optimizations that can be applied, including indexing the database appropriately, which will bring the time it takes to do the IPv6 search back to the range of IPv4 searches, but you have to be careful about how much housekeeping data you're adding to the database so as not to impact your data storage needs too much.

applications IPv6
ght may take your
ork management
OpenView and
ly applies to sec-
Tivoli class, but
pplications. It is,
ur management
need it to, you
gement applica-
need, you may
se applications,

more-recently
systems, say
t least partly
most as good
IPv6 capable
res from one
ou e-organizing
IPv6 yet to
al government, that

et were already fully
IPv6 capable, you would still have to develop an IPv6 numbering plan and

configure all the network assets with IPv6 addresses, routing information, and so on. Because developing and instituting an enterprise-scale numbering plan is no simple chore, it is covered in more detail in Chapter 7, "Identifying Common Transition Preparation Tasks."

Making Sure Your IPv6 Capabilities Work as Advertised

As is the case with network management systems, where you need to verify that your assets' IPv6 capabilities can be remotely managed, for assets you already own that came advertised with IPv6 capabilities, which you didn't need at the time you got them, you need to verify whether they actually work before declaring the assets truly IPv6 capable. Other hardware asset capabilities, beyond the SNMP ones presented previously, are whether:

- Interfaces can be configured with IPv6 addresses and whether they compute correct dynamically generated addresses, for example, link-local and EUI-64
- Multiple IPv6 addresses are supported on each interface, which becomes important as your IPv6 infrastructure grows
- Routers and other network hardware correctly forward IPv6 traffic and do so efficiently
- Fragmentation and path MTU discovery work correctly
- Extension headers, multicasting, and IPsec are properly supported, if you need them to be

All of your assets must satisfy the conditions in the first four bullets for you to declare them IPv6 capable, and thankfully the conditions are fairly easy to test. The advanced capabilities listed in the last bullet require the development of complex tests and you must determine, based on the specific capabilities you require, which of those complex tests actually need to be created and passed to declare assets IPv6 capable for your environment.

For software assets, you need to check that at least the following IPv6 capabilities function:

- Server applications can be configured to listen on IPv6 addresses, including multiple ones simultaneously
- Client applications can connect to servers at IPv6 addresses
- Intermediate or proxy applications, for example web proxies, that act as front ends to sets of back-end servers support the IPv6 format
- Protocols or data formats, be they open standards or proprietary, containing IP addresses supports both the IPv4 and IPv6 formats
- Storage of IP addresses supports both the IPv4 and IPv6 formats

Doing this test on IPv4 addresses is simple arithmetic for 32-bit computers, which have been around about as long as IPv4, and takes as few as three to six machine instructions, including the overhead of moving values from memory into the CPU for computation. For IPv6 addresses, the Boolean math is no different, but the implementation changes from those few instructions to a loop applied against each address that requires at least 4 times more work and more likely closer to 10 times more. Though this doesn't sound like a significant increase for a simple search that took perhaps a second or two with IPv4 and will take 10 with IPv6, for applications that rely heavily on searching, aggregating, and reporting on sets of IP addresses, especially in near real-time, the performance degradation can be detrimental. There are optimizations that can be applied, including indexing the database appropriately, which will bring the time it takes to do the IPv6 search back to the range of IPv4 searches, but you have to be careful about how much housekeeping data you're adding to the database so as not to impact your data storage needs too much.

As you can see, making dedicated network management applications IPv6 capable involves non-trivial changes to them, so getting it right may take your vendor(s) some time. Whereas HP, IBM, and other big network management application vendors have integrated IPv6 capabilities into OpenView and Tivoli, your vendor may not have done so yet. This especially applies to second and third tier vendors who are not in the OpenView or Tivoli class, but still face the same issues with their network management applications. It is, therefore, important that while you are assessing whether your management network is IPv6 capable or can become so within the time you need it to, you check not only the assets being managed, but also the management applications. If the applications don't support the IPv6 capabilities you need, you may have to substitute other remote management methods for these applications, at least temporarily.

Maximizing What You Can Leave As Is or Swap

Your ideal IPv6 transition is to have no transition at all. Your more-recently acquired network assets, operating systems, and management systems, say those deployed in the last year or two, may make that goal at least partly achievable, because they are likely to be IPv6 capable already. Almost as good as not changing anything is swapping out those assets that are not IPv6 capable with those that are from your existing asset inventory. Reusing spares from one location in others is discussed shortly. This section talks about re-organizing existent IPv6-capable assets from areas you're not upgrading to IPv6 yet to where the IPv6 transition is occurring. For the U.S. federal government, that would be the network backbone.

Unfortunately, even if every network and software asset were already fully IPv6 capable, you would still have to develop an IPv6 numbering plan and configure all the network assets with IPv6 addresses, routing information, and so on. Because developing and instituting an enterprise-scale numbering plan is no simple chore, it is covered in more detail in Chapter 7, "Identifying Common Transition Preparation Tasks."

Making Sure Your IPv6 Capabilities Work as Advertised

As is the case with network management systems, where you need to verify that your assets' IPv6 capabilities can be remotely managed, for assets you already own that came advertised with IPv6 capabilities, which you didn't need at the time you got them, you need to verify whether they actually work before declaring the assets truly IPv6 capable. Other hardware asset capabilities, beyond the SNMP ones presented previously, are whether:

- Interfaces can be configured with IPv6 addresses and whether they compute correct dynamically generated addresses, for example, link-local and EUI-64

- Multiple IPv6 addresses are supported on each interface, which becomes important as your IPv6 infrastructure grows

- Routers and other network hardware correctly forward IPv6 traffic and do so efficiently

- Fragmentation and path MTU discovery work correctly

- Extension headers, multicasting, and IPsec are properly supported, if you need them to be

All of your assets must satisfy the conditions in the first four bullets for you to declare them IPv6 capable, and thankfully the conditions are fairly easy to test. The advanced capabilities listed in the last bullet require the development of complex tests and you must determine, based on the specific capabilities you require, which of those complex tests actually need to be created and passed to declare assets IPv6 capable for your environment.

For software assets, you need to check that at least the following IPv6 capabilities function:

- Server applications can be configured to listen on IPv6 addresses, including multiple ones simultaneously

- Client applications can connect to servers at IPv6 addresses

- Intermediate or proxy applications, for example web proxies, that act as front ends to sets of back-end servers support the IPv6 format

- Protocols or data formats, be they open standards or proprietary, containing IP addresses supports both the IPv4 and IPv6 formats

- Storage of IP addresses supports both the IPv4 and IPv6 formats

IPv6 features have only recently made their way into many products and the changes required to incorporate IPv6 into a product, especially a network-centric one, can be quite pervasive. Therefore, for products you don't have yet and that are billed as fitting your IPv6 and other needs, make sure to get evaluation copies or trial systems. If you can't, be sure to get strong (perhaps legally binding) commitments from your vendors saying that they will address any problems found.

You may be asking yourself why there's so much written in the last few sections about making sure that products advertised to be IPv6 capable actually are. You know that all products have their problems and, if they come from decent vendors, the products will likely function correctly for the most part. The reason for the level of coverage provided is that the scene on the IPv6 product front at this time is often one of a vendor promising IPv6 capabilities to U.S. federal customers knowing that IPv6 is a hot button with those customers, but the vendor has no other customers for IPv6 (because it has nearly zero acceptance in the U.S. private sector), making the vendor only mildly incented to make IPv6 work. It's, therefore, better for you to get trial versions of the actual systems and prove to yourself that they work, and if not go to another vendor. There are plenty of vendors out there that do the job correctly. This sort of thing will peter out as IPv6 becomes more commonplace and especially when the commercial markets heat up. Until then, make sure you're getting what's advertised.

Moving IPv6-Capable Assets to Where They Are Needed

In a large enterprise there are a number of regional offices and other larger locations, not to mention the enterprise headquarters, of which there also may be several world-wide, that utilize similar large-scale network hardware. This hardware includes top-of-the-line routers, switches, and other network infrastructure, as well as large-scale servers. Depending on how refresh cycles are scheduled in different regions, divisions, and so on, some locations or business units may have much more recent versions of hardware than others. During your asset inventory, where you also cataloged your IPv6-capable assets, you may have found IPv6-capable hardware in places that won't be undergoing an IPv6 transition immediately. In theory, you could use those assets elsewhere where IPv6 capabilities are required.

Consider the following example, where your department runs the local network backbone and is using a non-IPv6-capable router for that backbone's connectivity. You are also responsible for the outward-facing portion of your network locally in the form of several websites, an e-mail server, and a split-DNS server. The router providing the outward connectivity is IPv6 capable, but has no reason to be, because it's servicing outward-facing IPv4 connections only and will continue to do so for some time. It just happened to be purchased more recently than the backbone router and had the IPv6 capabilities built into it at the factory.

For the sake of the example, both routers are satisfactory for either role in terms of the bandwidth they support, security, and anything other than the IPv6 capability issue. You could swap those two routers and effectively upgrade your local backbone to be IPv6 capable with no additional hardware cost. You still have to reconfigure each router, possibly physically move one or both, and schedule downtime both of your outward-facing services and your backbone to make the switch, but it could be done if this path is better than spending money on upgrading the backbone router. It is worthwhile for you to take a look at your asset inventory, capabilities requirements, and transition plans to see what's being upgraded and what isn't. You may have similar scenarios in your enterprise and swapping equipment could save you some money over buying upgrades or replacements.

Be warned that, though swapping may look like a good idea in this simple example, it has so many potential pitfalls that it should only be considered in cases where the organizations involved cooperate closely and are on friendly terms. They almost certainly must be geographically close to each other, as well, to save the costs of shipping hardware world-wide. Issues of organizational territorialism, the effort involved in reloading the non-IPv6-capable systems that an organization gets in return for those that are IPv6 capable, plus nightmarish inventory-tracking accounting issues that come from transferring assets between departments in enterprises where organizations have almost as many "colors of money" as they have departments, all make swapping a hard pill to swallow. The concept is presented here to offer an alternative that can work, for example, intra-departmentally or between two closely tied departments where one department, for example, runs the network backbone and the other supports an application that does not need to be IPv6 capable, yet.

Consolidating Systems Into a More Capable One

As you upgrade or replace your systems, you may find that newer systems can do the work of several older systems. For example, two routers can be consolidated into a bigger one, thereby reducing the amount of maintenance work required overall. This may lower your overall IPv6 transition costs, because replacing two routers that are not IPv6 capable with one that is often costs less than two IPv6-capable routers of similar size. This presumes the older routers cannot be upgraded to IPv6 and must be replaced, because the upgrade costs will likely be less than the single bigger router.

When looking to consolidate systems, you have to account for where you're intentionally using redundant hardware to provide greater network availability. If those same two routers are providing two different paths into your network for the purpose of assuring that you'll have connectivity should one router (or the ISP serving it) fail, then you probably don't want to consolidate them. That is, unless you can do so with some sort of high-availability router at a reasonable cost. Unfortunately, high-availability systems tend to be expensive, so it's likely your consolidation won't make economic sense. You'll have to run the numbers yourself for such scenarios to be sure.

Using Virtualization to Consolidate Systems

A new arrow has been added to the application manager's quiver in the last few years, and that is virtualization. Virtualization allows you to consolidate the functions of multiple smaller physical systems into one larger system. Virtualization has been around since the 1970s in the mainframe world, but it has only become popular with smaller computers, recently. This is probably because these smaller computers have only recently become powerful enough to run multiple virtual systems with any kind of reasonable performance.

With virtualization, you run a host operating system on the bare hardware and install and run the virtualization software on that host operating system. You can then create as many Virtual Machines (VMs) as the resources of the host system will allow while still maintaining reasonable performance for each VM and for the host. Some vendors of virtualization tools also sell operating systems and have the two tightly coupled. There are also virtualization products sold by vendors not affiliated with any hardware or operating system manufacturer.

Each VM appears like bare hardware to software running on it. That is why the first thing you typically install on a VM is an operating system, often called a guest operating system. Once the guest operating systems are installed, you can install applications native to each on the different VMs and have a smorgasbord of operating systems and applications running on one computer. It is not uncommon to have one system running a Linux host operating system with multiple Windows XP guests or vice versa. Some virtualization software even allows you to create a virtual LAN to connect all those virtual machines together for a true network in a box.

By using virtualization to consolidate multiple systems, you can, for example, replace several computers that themselves cannot be upgraded to being IPv6 capable with one larger system that is. A financial argument for doing something like this can be made if the one-for-one replacement cost of a dozen smaller old systems is $2000 each and a bigger one that can do the work of all of them is $20,000. You're $4000 ahead right at the start and, if after subtracting the cost of virtualization software, you're still ahead, then this might be the way to go. In addition to the financial savings, consolidation both frees the old hardware for other uses that are within its capabilities and reduces the level of maintenance work required on the now single hardware unit.

Before making the leap to consolidate applications onto one server, you must consider that the same hardware redundancy arguments that were raised earlier regarding routers arise with virtualization. You wouldn't want to consolidate a pool of a dozen web servers redundantly serving as front ends for a back-end database server without considering the availability requirements of the web services the systems represent.

Using Consolidation to Re-purpose IPv6-Capable Systems

When consolidating, you will typically be replacing sets of systems where none of the systems is IPv6 capable. As you'll read more about shortly, those systems can be re-used as spares in parts of your enterprise where IPv6 capabilities are not yet required. In some consolidation situations, you may find one or more of the systems you're consolidating to be IPv6 capable. For example, assume you have a collection of routers throughout one building that can be consolidated down to one or two newer IPv6-capable routers. Some of the routers you'll be replacing are themselves new enough to be IPv6 capable. It would be inefficient to leave them in place just for that reason *and* buy the bigger IPv6-capable system. You can, therefore, free those smaller IPv6-capable routers for use in other areas.

Similarly, if you have several systems deployed running an application that isn't IPv6 capable, when you upgrade that application, you also may choose to replace the hardware with a more powerful system. Replacing the hardware may not even be optional, because the IPv6 version of the application may require more resources than your old hardware provides, as per the discussion about operating systems earlier. If you have to get the bigger hardware anyway (and even if you don't), you may want to consider whether getting hardware capable of running more than one instance of the new version of the application makes sense, either by virtualization as described earlier or by simply putting more resources at the application's disposal on the more capable hardware.

By getting hardware capable of supporting two or more (or all) of the instances of the application you need to be running, you could replace all the old hardware with a single system, freeing that hardware for use elsewhere. Again, keep in mind, while deciding what to do, what hardware redundancy you need to meet your application availability requirements. If the old systems were themselves IPv6 capable, which they probably were, you could use them to replace antiquated hardware that cannot run IPv6-capable software, thereby saving the costs of buying additional new systems to replace the antiquated ones.

Re-purposing Assets to Other Parts of Your Network

During your IPv6 transition, there may be some network assets that are no longer suitable or required for use in the network backbone. They may be unable to be upgraded to IPv6, or they may be IPv6 capable (or upgradeable), but have been made redundant through consolidation. These assets may be able to be re-purposed to other areas of the network. The assets that are IPv6 capable or upgradeable can be re-purposed to areas of your network undergoing the IPv6 transition and having lesser requirements than area from which the assets came. Even if the transition is not occurring in a given area at this time, the assets could replace those that are not IPv6 capable to get a head start on future transition activities.

Finding Other Uses for IPv4-Only Assets

The assets that are not and cannot be made IPv6 capable can still be re-purposed, but are limited to areas of your network where IPv6 transition is scheduled for later on or the transition is coming about via the use of tunneling, dual stacks, or some other mechanism that allows IPv4-only equipment to remain in place. Though the assets cannot be used to expedite or facilitate your IPv6 transition in those areas, they can be used to meet other needs. In this way you can save the financial resources that would have been spent on increasing capacity, implementing hardware redundancy, or deploying additional applications or services in these IPv4-only areas. Depending on how your enterprise manages its finances, that saved money can be re-allocated to IPv6 transition elsewhere or applied to the IPv6 transition later on in those IPv4-only areas, thereby reducing your overall net transition costs.

Where Can I Re-use the IPv4-only Assets?

There are many systems today that are outdated for whatever function you originally purchased them. Their capabilities have not changed, but your enterprise's expectations have as to what is satisfactory in the areas of software features, processor and I/O speeds, and storage capacity. Though no longer acceptable in their originally designated roles, such systems are fine for the plethora of smaller application services required throughout the enterprise or as user workstations. For example, a system with a 1.2 GHz Celeron processor and 256MB of RAM may not be able to handle a new IPv6-capable operating system, but it should be perfectly fine for many other roles.

To make them more useful, systems being re-purposed can be reloaded with lighter weight operating systems, as long as the features that are required in the system's new role are supported and versions of the required applications are available for the new operating system. Web servers, for example, are available on lightweight operating systems that hardly tax the underlying hardware. They can be used to augment the redundancy or performance capabilities of existing web server farms, though depending on the complexity of the web content being served, some development may be required.

There's little to consider beyond performance and storage capabilities when deciding whether to re-purpose an older system as a lightweight server or part of a server cluster elsewhere. When considering re-purposing a system as a user workstation, however, you have to take human factors and esthetics into account. You don't want to put a rack-mount system with fans that sound like turbine engines on somebody's desk (or next to it), but re-purposing a small tower or desktop form-factor server may save the cost of an upgrade for somebody who's running on something that's only 400 MHz now.

The replacement system may not look new and shiny, but with some cleanup of the case (both inside and out) and a new keyboard and mouse (costing under $100), the user will get a fine upgrade and it will cost you nearly nothing. The user will have more capabilities, may be more productive, and might possibly even feel you've done them a favor. From your perspective, that's one more upgrade you won't have to pay for and you've re-used a system you might have otherwise thrown away or junked for parts (which, by the way, is also not a bad thing to do with systems that no longer have any other use).

Before contemplating either type of re-purposing (servers or user workstations), you have to determine if your enterprise has equipment standards for the various categories of assets. Because you're probably in the organization that sets those standards, if they exist, this shouldn't be too hard. All your servers, for example, may be Vendor 'D' rack-mount systems and therefore unsuitable as workstations. Your workstations may all be required to come from Vendor 'H' and, though they could be used as servers from a pure capabilities perspective, the enterprise standards negate that. There may be no reason, however, that an older server or workstation couldn't be re-purposed to a similar role where the asset currently in place is even older. Whatever the case, it is important to understand that such equipment (and software application) standards are there for good reasons because they simplify the lives of the MIS/IT organization and save the company money. They are not to be taken lightly when deciding about re-purposing equipment.

CHECKLIST: Asset Disposition

Apply the following checklist to each asset in your inventory, whether individually or in groups or by asset type, to determine whether the asset can remain in place as is, needs to be upgraded or replaced, or can be eliminated or declared a spare for use elsewhere. The checklist also aids you in determining if any spares can be used as part of your IPv6 transition or in an

IPv4-only capacity. There is a wide spectrum of choices for what to do with an asset based on its capabilities or limitations. These choices depend on the type of asset, the asset's role in the enterprise, and many other things specific to your situation. As such, all the possible answers cannot be provided for the following questions. Part of your planning is to figure out the answers for your specific circumstances.

❑ Are the asset's capabilities or the asset itself required in the post-transition network? If not, the asset can simply be disposed of once its pre-transition role is complete.

❑ Is the asset IPv6 capable for the definition of that term relevant to the given asset? In other words, can it meet its IPv6 requirements? If not, it must be upgraded, replaced, eliminated, or its capabilities need to be provided by another asset. The asset may be able to be deployed elsewhere in the enterprise where IPv4-only assets can be used.

❑ Does the asset possess all the other capabilities it will require, beyond the IPv6 ones, for its intended lifetime in the network? In other words, can it handle the necessary capacity and performance required of it, does it have all the features needed, and so on? If not, it must be upgraded, replaced, eliminated, or its capabilities need to be provided by another asset. The asset may be able to be deployed elsewhere in the enterprise, including areas where IPv6 capabilities are required.

❑ If the asset is not IPv6 capable or lacks other required capabilities, can it be upgraded to obtain those capabilities? If so, is the cost of the upgrade acceptable? If the asset cannot be upgraded or the upgrade cost is not acceptable, the asset may be able to be deployed elsewhere in the network.

❑ If the asset is not IPv6 capable or lacks other required capabilities, can it be replaced by one with the required capabilities from the same vendor or another vendor? Is the cost of the replacement acceptable? If it cannot be replaced or its replacement cost is not acceptable, then its required capabilities need to be provided by another asset.

❑ Are there complex interdependencies between this asset and others related to one being IPv6 capable and others not being? Can the interdependencies be resolved at a reasonable cost? If not, some or all of the interdependent assets may need to be replaced with one or more new assets that can interoperate and provide the required IPv6 and other capabilities.

❑ Can the asset be remotely managed using IPv6? If not, you need to retain IPv4-based remote-management capabilities. Or, you may need to replace the asset.

❑ Can the asset's IPv6 capabilities be remotely managed? If not, you will have to manage them locally or set up remote connectivity directly to the asset's local console. In some enterprises this may be a violation of security policies and not possible. Another alternative is that you may have to replace the asset.

❑ Can the asset's IPv6 capabilities be managed using SNMP? If not, then you will have to manage the asset's IPv6 capabilities via a remote command-line–based console or web interface. Or, you may need to replace the asset.

❑ If the asset must be replaced, is there a spare asset available from else-where in the enterprise that has all the capabilities required for this asset's role? If not, you may have to purchase a new asset.

❑ Can the asset's capabilities be consolidated into those of another asset while still meeting the required performance, reliability, and hardware redundancy values? If not, can the other asset be upgraded to meet those requirements or a replacement asset acquired to replace both this and the other one? Are the costs of the upgrade or replacement accept-able? If not, you may not be able to consolidate the assets.

❑ Can the assets made spare by consolidation be used elsewhere in the network? If so, their return to unallocated inventory should be commu-nicated to the appropriate people assessing the disposition of other assets.

Confirming the New Configuration Satisfies Its Mission

As was the case when you defined your current network configuration's capa-bilities, confirming that the post-transition network configuration meets your needs means determining what your requirements of your network are and creating a way to test that those requirements are met. By having documented your use cases from the capabilities assessment, you will be able to determine whether the current network's capabilities that are also required after the tran-sition are still functional. You also should have created use cases for all the new capabilities you're adding to make sure they work. Such capabilities include IPv6 connectivity, routing, remote management, and so on. If you haven't cre-ated those use cases, you can still do so as the transition progresses, just as long as they are complete for when they are required to be used to test the net-work's capabilities.

In addition to IPv6 capabilities, you may have specified new post-transition capabilities not directly related to IPv6, like improved network performance or capacity, new features like IPsec, or new applications like the latest accounting software. If you wrote the use cases before these capabilities existed on your network, the uses cases may not be completely correct and may require some tuning. Also, in the process of making your transition you may have changed your mind about how existing and new capabilities need to behave in the post-transition network configuration. That too requires updating the use cases.

Documenting the New Configuration

The use cases discussed in the previous section provide the documentation for your network's capabilities after the IPv6 transition. The more detailed such documentation is, the more useful it is for validating your network's capabilities, while at the same time the more difficult it is to create and maintain. There is a minimum amount of documentation you must perform if you decided to pursue use cases to document network capabilities. Otherwise, what little you do write will be all but useless (no pun intended) and not worth the effort spent creating it.

The modern-day MIS/IT organization has far more to do than it has resources, so the mindset that has developed is one of doing as little as possible and still getting the job done satisfactorily. This thinking describes one of the core tenets of engineering itself (that is, the building of economical solutions). Nevertheless, to get the full value out of your capabilities documentation, you should adopt a slightly different mindset, where you focus as much effort as you can on the documentation to the point just before you start depriving *other* projects of satisfactory results. In other words, prioritize the documentation effort. You will appreciate it later.

You also have to update your inventory documentation, in other words your CMDB. If you didn't have one before (or you didn't feel it was satisfactory), your IPv6 transition inventories should provide plenty of information to create or update one properly. CMDBs are all the rage right now with network and asset management vendors and for good reason. Though networks have been more complex for some time than the tools used to manage them can handle, the tools are finally starting to catch up thanks to improvements in software engineering and how networks operate and are used. Chapter 11, "Knowing What Assets You Have," discusses CMDB tools available to you. You're strongly encouraged to jump on that bandwagon because it will make your job much easier once you get past the hurdle of populating the CMDB. Efficient means to do that are also covered in Chapter 11.

Communicating the Plan

In Chapter 5, "Creating Your Transition Plans," you learned how to create your IPv6 transition plans. As you created them, you presumably communicated them to the audience of network and application administrators who will be executing them, the software engineers and other internal resources that will be supporting the execution, and the management of all these internal organizations. You also communicated to your vendors and outside contractors what was required of them during the transition's execution. The other people you need to communicate with are both those in your enterprise and the ones external to it who are affected by the plan, specifically its execution and the potential failure modes more so than the final result.

Chapter 5 addressed when your overall IPv6 transition needed to be completed, but didn't cover when each individual transition step should occur and what decisions needed to be made in ordering those steps. This is because, until you developed the asset inventory and capabilities list discussed in this chapter, from which you then derived the post-transition network configuration, you did not have enough information to go into sufficient detail to order the steps of your transition, nor set intermediate milestones. These topics are covered in Chapter 8, "Defining the Transition Execution Steps." Also covered in Chapter 8 are the necessary communications steps you need to take as the transition is happening so as to keep your management, network and security monitoring staff, and the occasional curious bystanders, informed. This chapter discusses the preparations you need to make to establish and validate the communication channels required and to facilitate communications during the transition.

Why You Should Tell People What You're Going to Do

Now that you have your plans in place and your asset inventory, capabilities list, and post-transition configuration completed, this is a good time to share them outside of the organization(s) actually making the transition. It is not uncommon in many enterprises for the network management staff to have no idea of some critical deadline or upcoming event for which the network is a key participant. By communicating your plans, you are not only alerting your user population to upcoming changes (and significant ones at that), but you are also providing them a communications channel back over which they can yell, "STOP!"

In the private sector, most people are aware of the sensitivity of introducing changes into the network at the end of a fiscal quarter and especially the end of the fiscal year. There are other such well-known times specific to particular industries or companies. For example, financial firms tend to like to keep everything in the network quiescent while the stock markets are open. Given the world-wide economy, this is a tall order, but at least the New York office can be kept stable while the NYSE is open and the Tokyo office can be left alone while the Nikkei is doing business.

Each enterprise also has its own unique internal critical times when the last thing anyone wants is the network to go down, because somebody thought it would be a good time to upgrade a router. The FAA, for example, surely leaves its air traffic control network's scheduled maintenance for when the least number of aircraft are in the sky. By reviewing airline schedules, that looks like it's probably during the wee hours of the morning on weekends, as long as it isn't Thanksgiving weekend. Similarly, the IRS probably leaves the routine stuff for April 16th. Perhaps the IRS even leaves that stuff for the 17th or 18th, to give its staff a day or two off.

While some critical times requiring the utmost network stability are well-known, at least within the enterprise, information about other times may be held closely by those involved for a variety of reasons from simple corporate propriety regarding the launch of a new product to national security regarding the launch of a new spy satellite. If you communicate your IPv6 transition plans and such a critical time exists within the time frame slated for your transition, those affected may not inform you of the details as to why the time is critical, but they will inform you (and if they don't feel you got the message, their management will inform your management) that the time you've selected to upgrade the main router serving their data center isn't convenient.

Keeping Monitoring Organizations in the Loop

You may have already spoken with the people that monitor your network for outages, most likely because they are within your organization. In some enterprises, however, such monitoring is outsourced and you may only know the phone number to call if something is about to be taken offline intentionally. This kind of communication channel to external (and internal) monitoring organizations is provided so as to prevent an alarm triggered by an expected outage from being generated or escalated. It's similar to the phone number you're given for your home alarm system for the case where you accidentally open a window with the burglar alarm set or burn a roast in the oven and set off a smoke detector. You don't want the police or fire department showing up for no good reason. In case you haven't spoken to the network monitoring staff, both those that monitor network availability *and* network security, this is a good time to do so.

In most cases, the monitoring organization doesn't care when you do your IPv6 transition. They just want to be informed of the times you'll be taking equipment offline to avoid false alarms such as those just described. As importantly, if something goes wrong during the transition that you weren't expecting and that you don't detect yourself, those monitoring the network are likely to be the first to know. The monitoring organization also can inform you more readily if they know you are doing something to the network that may cause an unexpected outage. By knowing to contact you, they save a lengthy escalation and discovery process as to the cause of the outage, if in fact you caused it.

Posting Contact Numbers for All Key Transition Staff

It's much easier now than in the past to maintain what are called "living documents," in other words documents that can be easily modified and distributed as conditions change or new information is gathered. The term has been in use for a while, but the living documents before the World Wide Web were not as alive (that is, dynamic) as one would desire. The web makes it possible to include in planning documentation information that you had no hope of keeping up to date in the pre-web days. One such set of information is the contact information for all the key participants in your IPv6 transition. These players include:

- Anyone managing the IPv6 transition planning, especially the owners of the planning documents themselves.

- Team leads for the IPv6 transition execution, so they may be contacted while transition activities are occurring.

- Network and security monitoring contacts, either internal to the enterprise or in external monitoring service providers. If at all possible, try to get the pager or mobile phone number of people in these organizations and not just some toll-free contact number. A good rapport with these people is very helpful in cases where the transition activities accidentally generate alarms in network or security operations centers.

- Vendor technical support, so as to diagnose problems quickly and get answers to questions about product capabilities and limitations. As with the monitoring staff, contact information for actual humans is preferable to having just the vendor's customer support toll-free number.

- Representatives of the enterprise's internal and external user population who are dependent on the network's capabilities being available. This will allow IPv6 transition planners and those doing the transition execution both to inform the user organizations of the state of the transition and get their input on how the transition is going and whether any changes are needed.

When creating your IPv6 transition plan, make sure to include in it a separate section, appendix, or link to an appropriately secure website with the contact information for all these people or to their organizations' support numbers when you can't get a specific person's information. Include each contact's e-mail, office and mobile telephone numbers, and their mailing addresses. Though you probably won't be sending written correspondence through the postal system, the technology to transfer matter over the Internet still doesn't exist. So, if you need to ship hardware or a DVD to somebody, having their mailing address handy will make it that much easier.

Just as it is important to post contact information for all the key players, it is equally important to dictate the rules of engagement for using that information. For example, if your CIO's phone number appears on the list and the list is accessible by vendors for IPv6 transition purposes, vendors should not interpret that as authorization to pass the CIO's number to their sales teams so as to start soliciting the CIO. Restrictions on the use of the contact information for non-sanctioned purposes should be communicated along with the information itself, and with the penalties for misuse. It is also a good idea to mark the list as proprietary to the organizations represented on it or as For Official Use Only (FOUO) so as to limit its distribution and provide additional legal protections.

Scheduling Transition Events

In the preceding section, you read about some of the constraints that might be placed on you regarding when you can execute your IPv6 transition, most of them revolving around when your network must be stable and quiescent. This section covers the periods where network change is expected and acceptable, so as to help you pick the optimal times for your transition activities. When reading this section, don't forget the constraints mentioned earlier as you devise your overall transition schedule. To keep the discussion that follows more focused, it's assumed you've accounted for all those constraints, especially when they might contradict the following material.

Using Off-peak and Maintenance Times for Transition

As you've read, every enterprise has its peak times of network use where the network must be reliable and any activities that could destabilize it are discouraged or forbidden. On the flip side, there are times when the network, either by the nature of its mission or the cycles of human activities (for example, sleeping, working 9 to 5, taking summer vacations), tends to be under minimal loads. Such times are the best ones for your IPv6 transition activities.

Most enterprises understand the highs and lows of their network's utilization well enough to establish pre-defined maintenance windows during the least critical off-peak periods. There are many possibilities for when such windows can be placed, for example, between 2 a.m. and 6 a.m. nightly, or the network may be in such demand that there are shorter maintenance windows nightly (for example, only from 2 a.m. to 3 a.m.) and a longer window on Saturday (and perhaps Friday) night. Just because these periods are set aside for maintenance, thereby telling the rest of the enterprise to exercise caveat emptor if they happen to be working on the network (if they are even allowed to be) at those times, that doesn't mean any maintenance activities will occur.

It's certainly possible that when a particular maintenance window comes up, there is no maintenance to be performed. In that case, the window passes with nothing happening and the MIS/IT staff can stay home snug in their beds. The point is, something could have happened, and the rest of the enterprise was already prepared as if something might.

Maintenance windows are used for many different kinds of activities, including hardware and software upgrades of network assets or major application servers, re-cabling of critical segments or large numbers of segments, deployment or retirement of significant sets of assets, and updates to network configuration parameters like static IP addresses and DHCP-managed IP address pools, routing, DNS services, and firewall rules. There are two things all of these activities have in common:

1. They are all things you will be doing during your IPv6 transition.

2. They all present the possibility, if performed incorrectly, of causing some level of non-trivial damage or outage to the network.

In addition to predefined maintenance windows, there are also ad hoc or event-based ones. An event-based maintenance window is sometimes first communicated by an e-mail from your system administrator that goes something like this:

```
Dear users,

The mail server is hung, so we are rebooting it right now. There will be
no mail services for the next 30 minutes.

Sincerely,

Your friendly system administrator
```

There are less-extreme cases where a new piece of critical equipment is expected from a vendor and its installation can't wait until the next predefined maintenance window, so it will be installed as soon as it arrives.

All of these impromptu maintenance events have one thing in common, which is that they are in response to a need that suddenly arose. If the mail server hadn't hung, it may have been rebooted as part of normal maintenance next Saturday night. Because action had to be taken immediately, a maintenance window of sorts was created. This is not how your IPv6 transition should go. With all the planning you're doing ahead of time to define exactly what you want the outcome to be and how you're going to get there, you should be able to work within predefined maintenance windows.

Working within a Predefined Maintenance Window

Your IPv6 transition is (or should be) about as well-defined a series of maintenance events as there ever was. As such, the scheduling of your transition's
activities should, with rare exception, fit into your enterprise's predefined
maintenance windows. Because the transition's execution will be spread out
over weeks, or quite possibly months, that gives you a lot of choices on how to
do your scheduling. That's good, because scheduling is not only about fitting
activities into time slots. It is also about determining dependencies between
activities or, in other words, which activities must precede others. You learn
more about ordering your IPv6 transition activities in Chapter 8, "Defining the
Transition Execution Steps." For now, assume you've got the order figured out.

An additional factor to consider when working within predefined maintenance windows is that the activities will all fit in the windows. That may
require breaking up some activities. For example, if re-cabling a building in
preparation to install new IPv6-capable routers is expected to take 24 hours in
total, but you only have 6-hour maintenance windows to work within, you'll
have to break up the re-cabling activity into smaller pieces, each of which fits
in a 6-hour window. That doesn't necessarily mean four equally sized pieces
either, because the smaller sets of tasks need to have clean beginnings and
ends; in other words, you can't leave a bunch of cables hanging from the ceiling just because a maintenance window ended.

You may wind up having to break up the overall 24-hour activity into three
4-hour chunks, a 6-hour chunk, and finally two 5-hour chunks. The mathematically inclined may have noticed that the total amount of time allotted is
now 28 hours. This is because, in order to have clean breaks in the smaller
tasks, additional work has been added to close up wiring closets, along with
ceiling and floor spaces, and then re-open them when starting the next maintenance window's activities. To make matters worse, the total amount of possible maintenance time is 36 hours, because all but one of your smaller sets of
tasks takes the full 6 hours of the maintenance window. Hopefully, you can use
the remaining time in the other windows to accomplish work required for
other activities, like renumbering systems or upgrading software. That way, at
least the overall schedule won't be extended too much.

Staying within Your Allotted Maintenance Time

It's a fact of life that, no matter how much you plan and how hard you work,
something will go wrong sooner or later, or something will simply take longer
than the time you expected and allotted. Somebody could arrive late for the
maintenance activity, burning valuable time in the window. It may take longer
to get started, because you forgot the right cable or tools. There are all kinds of

things that can go wrong. When it comes to your enterprise, the needs of the many outweigh the needs of the few (that came out better than I hoped). That means, if while you're performing your transition activities you determine that you can't complete the work before the maintenance window closes, even if it's only an hour into a 6-hour window, for example, then you should call it a day and go home. Take your lumps with your boss and try again next time. This is a much better choice than trying to fit things in and realizing all too late that you're going to have a partly broken network when 1,000 other workers show up in 5 hours.

So as not to waste the night completely, and it always seems to be at night for some reason (usually around 2 a.m.) when you find a problem, you may be able to perform alternate IPv6 transition or other maintenance activities, since everyone's already there. To prepare for such contingencies, you can do additional planning ahead of time and prepare alternate activities for each maintenance window, should the primary ones not be possible for some reason. To maximize your flexibility, sets of smaller work units for the alternate activities will allow you to fill in a larger variety of gaps. This is also true for planning the primary activities as well, but you should realize that some activities will simply take a long time and making them more granular than is realistic is wasteful and misleading.

Should you realize after starting your transition activities during a given window that you will not be able to finish within the window, take a lesson from the flight-safety people; that is, in an emergency: aviate, navigate, and communicate, in that order. In the flying profession that means to first fly the plane, because if you hit a mountain that will just compound the emergency. Second, figure out where you're going next, and third, tell others (namely air traffic control) what you did so you can a) warn them to clear others out of your way, and b) get any help possible.

Applied to the maintenance problem you're now facing, that means you first figure out what you absolutely must do to get the network in the best shape before the maintenance window closes and then start doing it immediately. As you're doing those critical steps, figure out what else you need to do to get the network back into an acceptable state. The difference between the preceding two steps is that the first one may still leave you with problems or some level of outages, but the network will be in the best shape that you could get it into with the time provided. The second step gets the network running as it should have been at the end of the maintenance window, had you not gone over your time limit.

Once you're working on patching up the network and have figured out how to get it back to acceptable levels of operation for the coming day, communicate to whomever you need to what has happened. This may include calling the network and security monitoring organizations, your management, other groups dependent on the capabilities you won't have back in time for the morning rush, and so on. Tell them the state of things, what you plan to do to fix them, when you will be done, and then ask if there's anything they would like you to do differently or if they can help. Maybe you'll catch a break. Maybe the full capabilities of the network are not required for a while and, once you've returned any critical capabilities disabled by your transition activities, you can do the rest of the work at a more leisurely (that is, less error-prone) pace.

Even if you get no relief and have to work your tail off, at least the powers that be are aware of the situation. That's why it's important to have contact numbers handy and everyone who needs to know aware of what you were planning for this maintenance window beforehand. The last thing you want to do with you precious time is explain to a bunch of groggy people why you're calling them in the middle of the night and that there's a problem. Whether they're happy about the state of things is a different issue, but you can get some comfort from knowing that they're likely to be far less happy if they walk into the office the following morning to find no Internet connectivity or some critical application down for the count.

Engineering easily reversible transition activities so as to minimize the chances of overrunning your maintenance windows (or simplifying backing things out should you realize you're going to run over) is covered in more detail in Chapter 8.

Staging Resources for a Speedier Transition

The purpose of your maintenance windows is to perform sometimes risky changes to your network infrastructure or applications during times of low utilization and when people are aware such changes may be occurring. There is no reason you cannot do non-risky transition work during times other than just maintenance windows.

Preparing Replacements and Upgrades for Installation

When installing new network assets, it's a rare practice (and a discouraged one) to connect the new asset to the network infrastructure with no pre-installation configuration and then start to configure it. For example, unless you're using DHCP to set the device's IP address, which is unlikely for many core network assets, you can configure the address before ever connecting any cables. Similarly, such trivial configuration items like the system's time and time zone can be set offline. Even if your network is using the Network Time Protocol (NTP) or something like it to set system times accurately, you can still set the approximate time (something that's plus or minus a minute or two off is pretty easy); if NTP doesn't function correctly at the start, at least your error logs will have reasonable time stamps. NTP, by the way, is another thing you can configure ahead of time. Then, simply ignore the errors until network connectivity is established.

Swapping Hard Drives as a Means to Upgrade Software

Performing a software upgrade, especially of a complex application, can be a time-consuming, tedious, and error-prone process for all but the most-robust (or simple) of applications. Though you have the luxury of powering down the application's server and doing whatever you want to it during a maintenance window, introducing so much risk and having a clock running to provide additional pressure should be avoided. A way to reduce the amount of work you have to perform during the maintenance window, that also reduces the risk level of the remaining work in the window, is to create a duplicate of the hard drive for the application servers you are upgrading.

There are many ways to create a duplicate hard drive, but that aspect of the process is not germane here. Assuming you have created the drive, you can use another system similar to the target application server to upgrade the software on that drive. Depending on the application, the upgrade may require information that is specific to the target server, its IP address for example. You may be able to substitute the IP address of the substitute system for the time being and change it later, or you may be able to enter the IP address of the target system right away, provided the server does not have to be connected to the network during the upgrade.

Another good argument for the drive-swapping strategy is that it provides you the ability to revert to the original configuration, should something not work correctly after the swap. Backing out changes that didn't work correctly, and other measures for reacting to things that don't go as planned, are covered more in Chapter 8, "Defining the Transition Execution Steps."

There are conditions where it could be easier to perform the software upgrade on the application server's existing hard drive than to swap drives. For example, the application might have components installed on multiple hard drives, perhaps many of them, on the application server. In that case, a complete set of duplicate drives may need to be created. Parameters to account for in that situation include the overall cost of the duplicate drives and if you can re-use the drives being replaced. If you subscribe to an enterprise hardware standard as mentioned earlier, you should have little trouble finding uses for spare hard drives that fit into perhaps every other application server you own.

If you're thinking about using the drive-swapping strategy to upgrade software and your application server has multiple drives, even if the application resides on fewer than all of those drives, there's a strong argument for swapping all of them. Unless you're sure the application is contained on the drive(s) it purports to be using, the inconsistencies and instabilities (sometimes myste-rious and never-before seen by the vendor) that could come about from acci-dentally mixing and matching versions of the software on different drives are not worth the risk. The additional effort of duplicating the server's remaining drive(s), the ones the application is allegedly not using, and swapping all the drives is well justified and will almost certainly avoid headaches later.

Licensing may also make upgrading software using substitute hardware too difficult to be practical. Software license keys are often tied to some hard-wired attribute of the application server, the MAC address for example. If that's the case for your application, the upgrade may refuse to install on any hardware other than that to which the license applies. Oddly enough, some of the most expensive applications have little or no software-based license enforcement. The reasons for this are varied and all boil down to the vendor's cost-benefit analysis of implementing such license controls indicating that the controls are impractical from a business point of view. For you this means that, if you're upgrading some of your bigger applications, dealing with licensing may be a non-issue technically; however, you are still bound by your license agreements. Once the duplicate drive(s) is installed and running, provided its creation is allowed by your license agreement in the first place, you must destroy the copies of the software on the original drive(s) if your license requires it.

Should you run into license-related problems, an alternative to abandoning the drive-swapping strategy for this particular application, you have the option of contacting the vendor and asking for a temporary license key for the substitute hardware, just to perform the upgrade and swap. Depending on your clout with the vendor (or how eager they are to keep you a happy cus-tomer), they may be willing to oblige. One thing to consider with this option is that you may be unable to change the license on the software afterwards, pos-sibly making the application inoperable on the server that is to be the soft-ware's final home. Your vendor should be able to tell you if this is the case when you ask for the temporary license key. Just remember to tell the vendor what the key's intended purpose is.

Pre-configuring Hardware to Reduce Maintenance Window Work

Setting things up prior to installation is not limited to software configuration. In many cases, there's no good reason you can't install a network asset in its intended data rack, hook up power and cooling, and run cables to within inches of where they need to be connected. If the system is a simple replacement for another one, the maintenance window activities may thereby be reduced to nothing more than switching cables and validating the new configuration. If the replacement is meant to go in the same physical space as its predecessor, you may have to cable and configure it in an alternate rack space (if there's one free) or on the floor nearby, but that still reduces the maintenance window workload to just one short physical move followed by the aforementioned cable switching and validation of functionality.

Getting What's Needed Where It's Needed Ahead of Time

In order to install or upgrade network or software assets, you need to get the relevant hardware and applications to where they are needed. Like pre-configuration, transporting assets into place is something you can do, with rare exception, during normal business hours (or any time that's convenient). If the asset's delivery will disrupt business for other workers, for example if it's a huge piece of network hardware or many crates of smaller assets, you may have to time the delivery and coordinate a time where those workers can factor it into their own activities, but that should still be possible at more convenient times than when typical maintenance windows are placed.

As the previous paragraph suggests, getting assets into place ahead of time is as true for software media and configuration information as it is for hardware. Even with the hardware in racks and ready to go, if the software CDs, license key disks, or other required software components are sitting on someone's desk across town or weren't in today's expected deliveries from vendors, there's not much you can do to complete your activities for the maintenance window in question.

Checking That Everything's Ready Before You Start

By staging the items you need for your IPv6 transition activities into place ahead of time and pre-configuring as many of the systems and applications as you can beforehand, you greatly reduce the amount of work to be done during the maintenance window. You also reduce the risks of something going wrong, because there is less work to be done. As a final preparation step for your IPv6 transition activities, you should verify that all the various items you require are present and ready to go *before* the transition activities scheduled for your about-to-open maintenance window begin. That includes:

- All the required hardware, including checking that model numbers, firmware version numbers, and in some cases serial numbers match the ones you expect and need.
- Tools required for installing the hardware, including diagnostic tools and the correct associated connecters and cables.

- Pre-assigned rack space, including power, cooling, and other support services.

- Network and other communications connectivity in the form of the appropriate number and types of jacks in patch-panels, including making sure those jacks are functioning and configured properly.

- Configuration information for the new hardware and for other hardware or software services it requires or that require it, for example DHCP, DNS, SNMP community strings, and so on.

- All the required software media, license keys, and other items required to install or upgrade your applications.

- Passwords and other authentication or access control tokens you need to perform privileged operations on the servers for which you're installing or upgrading software.

If you find everything as it should be, then you are ready to start you transition activities. If not, then you have to take appropriate actions depending on what is missing or incorrect. Such actions may include delaying or cancelling the transition activities for this maintenance window. Other actions may be as simple as driving across town and getting the application CD you forgot. If you can do so and get back with enough time to perform the activities within the maintenance window, then the minor mistake will have no further consequences. If, on the other hand, you find that a vendor has configured the wrong firmware in one of your new routers, you may be stuck or you may only be able to complete part of the transition activities. You'll have to assess whether the part you can complete will leave you with an adequately functioning network when you are done and before the maintenance window closes.

As you can imagine, the list of what could go awry is endless as is the list of remedial actions. In making your decisions how to proceed, remember that the primary goal is to have all the required capabilities of the network functional when others in the enterprise expect them to be there.

Getting the Right Approvals

In any organization composed of two or more people, someone almost certainly has to approve the activities of someone else. Scale that up to the typical enterprise preparing for upgrading to IPv6 and there's surely a whole lot of stuff you have to get signatures on or at least verbal nods. The sooner you start working on those, the better. Don't formulate all your plans, fill out all your purchase orders, and schedule your downtimes and then expect things to get rubber stamped.

Even if you run the whole MIS/IT organization, no matter what the OMB believes (that is, that the IPv6 transition can be accomplished with existing MIS/IT budgets), you'll surely have to get funds from the CFO for your transition activities. You'll likely also have to get approval for the maintenance windows you'll need to execute the transition (and there will probably many of them required). This is because, as any MIS/IT manager knows, even though you run the network those for whom you provide services may have more control as to when it can be brought down than you do. This is especially true for enterprises with significant missions like the DoD, FAA, and IRS in the government sector and banking and other financial firms in the private sector.

You may be very familiar with the approval processes in your enterprise, in which case this section serves only as a reminder. If you are not, consult those in your organization that should be. There is surely some kind of central body that manages, audits, and validates your enterprise's functions. Ask them what you're required to do. Be careful how you approach this. Word your queries about what is the right thing to do in ways that don't cause alarm. If you don't and instead present your plans with an (unintentional) underlying message that you're going to tear down the network, re-build it, and hopefully get a much better network as a result *and* everyone's just going to have to deal with that, because OMB said you had to do it, you may find you'll need more signatures than the U.S. Constitution just to order the pens and paper to get the approvals.

Complying with Existing Procedures and Practices

A sure way to improve the chances that you'll get the approvals you need, and in a timely manner, is by staying within the lines drawn by those in your enterprise whose job it is to draw lines. Those lines are, of course, the collection of your enterprise's best practices, standard procedures, and whatever other name you've chosen to give them. Like the enterprise standards on hardware and software mentioned throughout this chapter so far, the practices you've taken the time to socialize, document, and standardize on (or reach for, if they're still only goals right now) are meant to facilitate getting work done, keep everyone in sync regarding the enterprise's direction, and save money by optimizing good practices and eliminating bad or haphazard ones.

Your enterprise's best practices, as the collection of all the preceding rules and guidelines are called here, should be consulted from the beginning of your IPv6 transition process. If there's a process for socializing a new plan and getting consensus, you should follow it when putting out the initial drafts of your transition plan. If there's an approval cycle for various levels of the draft and the final releases, you should follow that, too. Whatever process you use to authorize the procurement of new hardware and software, or get the budget for those things, the closer you follow that and keep those that control the purse strings happy and informed, the more likely you'll get things done efficiently.

As a casual read of a sufficiently large sample of Dilbert comics (and the sample doesn't have to be that big) will clearly show, there's a lot of best practices out there that are not, shall we say, the best. Like the law and taxes, they are what you have to work with and you should strive to work with them. There may be places in your enterprise where bucking the system gets better results, but it can also leave bad taste's in people's mouths and may eventually start to work against you. So just like laws and taxes, if you don't like them work to get them changed. Until they are changed, however, uphold them the best you can. Your job is executing an IPv6 transition, not tilting at bureaucratic windmills.

Making Sure You Have Approvals in Writing

There's a great scene in the movie *Clear and Present Danger* where a CIA Deputy Director named Ritter is operating outside the law, allegedly for the good of the United States. To protect himself, he gets a signed letter from the president authorizing his activities, thereby transferring or at least spreading the blame should something go wrong. The hero, Jack Ryan (played by Harrison Ford), cooperates with Ritter, but has no such protection. At the risk of ruining this 1994 movie for someone, the dialog (courtesy of `www.imdb.com`) that is pertinent to this section goes as follows:

```
Jack Ryan: If I go down you're coming with me.

Ritter: Wrong again. I have an *autographed get-out-of-jail-free card*!
"The President of the United States authorizes […]" You don't *have* one
of these, do you Jack?
```

Like Ritter, but for far-less nefarious purposes, it behooves you to get your IPv6 transition approvals in writing. Your reasons should not be to transfer blame to others, but to prove that you followed the correct procedures and that everyone that needs to be is on board with your plans. All kinds of things can happen during the time that it will take for you to complete the IPv6 transition. For example, people with whom you worked closely to develop your transition plans may move on in their careers and their positions could be filled by others who are unaware of what you're doing. Written approvals provide something more than just your word that what you're doing to the network is authorized.

Testing Your Knowledge

This was a long chapter, but preparation is half the battle. Answers are in Appendix A.

1. What are the four goals of your IPv6 transition for it to be considered a success?

2. In the context of this book, what's the difference between an asset inventory and a capabilities assessment?

3. What are the three goals of your asset inventory and capabilities assessment efforts?

4. What are two required attributes for each asset in an inventory?

5. What do you want to associate with every software asset?

6. How many logical networks are typically in a physical one?

7. How can you make an asset IPv6 capable?

8. What capabilities must an asset have to be fully remotely manageable in IPv6 terms, in other words if all IPv4 access was turned off?

9. Silly Trivia: Who is Jack Ryan, and why is he important to IPv6?

Identifying Common Transition Preparation Tasks

Perfect numbers like perfect men are very rare.
— René Descartes

This chapter focuses on common tasks everyone will have to perform while preparing for their IPv6 transitions, no matter the nature of their enterprise or the market segment it occupies. If not performed during the preparation phase, these tasks must be performed very early in the execution phase. If you're to have a successful transition, you'll need to acquire IPv6 addresses and external connectivity, and you'll need to document properly what you get and how you use it. The preceding sentence summarizes what 80 percent of the chapter covers and, in doing so, trivializes it to the point where many organizations don't put enough forethought into the work involved and wind up numbering themselves into a corner. With such organizations, the moment they open a new facility or launch a new program or product line, they find their numbering "plan" coming up short and have to renumber a whole site or more. Your aim (as well as that of any other MIS/IT professional) is to do the legwork up front so you won't have to renumber for the next five years after your upgrade is done.

What You'll Learn

No matter which IPv6 transition project you're currently undertaking, be this the first one that establishes an IPv6 backbone and perhaps a few outposts in the network's outer rim, or a subsequent one that adds new capabilities or brings new facilities or subnets into the IPv6 fold, there are some common tasks to all transitions. This chapter is written in a style useful for first-time "transitioners," but those extending the reach of their IPv6 network should review it, too.

The most important thing you'll learn in this chapter is that there are many aspects of IPv6 that are quite different from those in IPv4. You will learn that IPv6 addresses come with rules regarding who provides them, how they can be used, and how multiple providers of external connectivity need to go through more effort to implement network redundancy for your enterprise than they do with IPv4.

On the positive side, you will learn that your internal provisioning of IPv6 address spaces is far easier than with IPv4. All LANs are the same size (that is, huge) and your biggest provisioning chore is not doling out limited numbers of addresses, but rather the much simpler task of creating subnets without having to worry about how many devices are on each one.

You will learn to organize your IPv6 address assignments into a numbering plan and to develop hierarchies within your enterprise and its sites. This is not something new for IPv6, because you should have a numbering plan for your IPv4 address spaces; however, the architectural freedom that IPv6 provides you with its effectively unlimited LAN sizes eliminates some of the more burdensome chores in network numbering (for example, tuning your plan down to the device level).

The other thing you'll learn in developing your numbering plan is to consider a product to manage it versus home-grown spreadsheets. IPv6 addresses are more difficult to manipulate, due to their size, and typical office spreadsheet programs are not able to handle them without a great deal of complexity that overshadows the ultimate purposes of the numbering plan. In addition, the hierarchies IPv6 addresses contain as an artifact of their allocation and assignment strategies may be accounted for and simplified by dedicated asset-management products, which is more work you won't have to do.

The chapter concludes with an analysis of how IPv6 will affect your network bandwidth needs (here's a hint: not much) and then takes you through some of the details of advanced IPv6 features you were introduced to earlier in the book. These features include IPsec, secure auto-configuration, and mobile IPv6. You are given the necessary information to investigate whether these features are right for your enterprise network as part of your first transition project, a later one, or none for the foreseeable future.

Provisioning Your IPv6 Address Space

Even if your network is completely ready for IPv6 without any upgrades or replacement of equipment or software (an unlikely, but not farfetched, possibility), you still have some tasks to accomplish for your IPv6 upgrade. One of those tasks is to acquire and configure IPv6 addresses for all your routers, workstations, laptops, printers, and other assets with network interfaces. If you're in the U.S. federal government, your first transition (remember, you're going to have several to get the whole network upgraded) may cover the backbone assets only, but you still have to get addresses for them.

Developing an IPv6 Address-space Mindset

Unless you've been in computer networking for many years, you may have never needed to get new IP addresses from an external registry. Most enterprises got the bulk of their IPv4 assignments in the mid to late 1990s during the Internet revolution. With talk of the supply becoming scarce even then, they've managed to live off those addresses for the most part. New assignments do get handed out, but since the dawn of the twenty-first century, assignments have become increasingly smaller and you need a pretty strong case to get even a few dozen new IPv4 addresses from the registries today. As such, when you talk to network managers about acquiring new address space, they may act as if you're talking about mining rare gems. It wasn't always that way, even with IPv4.

Recalling When IPv4 Addresses Roamed the Internet in Huge Herds

Before the mid-1990s and the huge increase in demand, the IPv4 address space, with its 4.3 billion addresses, seemed like the prairies of the Old West full of roaming buffalo, and those controlling the IP addresses were liberal with their assignments. Who could blame them? When Mozilla was released in April 1993 (per `http://en.wikipedia.org/wiki/Mosaic_(web_browser)`), there were only 1.5 million hosts on the Internet. That was over 2800 addresses free for every one in use (all those unused addresses are not assignable to hosts, but that's splitting hairs). Who knew that in April 1995 there would be over 5 million hosts and in April 1998, five years after Mozilla's debut, there would be over 100 million users of the Internet? That's only 43 free addresses for every one in use. By June 2007, the ratio of users to free addresses was less than 1 to 4. Considering that most enterprises manage their address spaces with 1-percent efficiency or less (meaning 1 address in use for every 99 unused), it's impressive (and can mostly be attributed to NAT) that the addresses haven't run out yet. The preceding statistics are quoted or interpolated from:

■ `http://www.mit.edu/people/mkgray/net/internet-growth-raw-data.html` and

■ `http://www.internetworldstats.com/emarketing.htm`

Add to the impressive growth figures that there was a set of organizations with large historical assignments from the early days of the Internet. These organizations had been assigned whole Class-A networks of addresses. A Class-A address block is a '/8' in CIDR-based terminology and contains 16.8 million addresses. The reasons for the assignments ranged from the receiving organizations being part of early Internet technologies and deployments or having worked closely with other organizations (for example, defense contractors) that were. In some cases, it seems in hindsight like they simply asked for the addresses and got them.

Several of these organizations have been the topic of discussions regarding wasteful address assignments for years, because there is no clear reason why they need all that space. Imagine if you had all the land in the United States to hand out and someone came to you with a request for a parcel the size of Delaware, Maryland, and Washington, DC combined. That's what a '/8' amounts to in IPv4 space. Because the land is free (as IP addresses were then), the price for a big chunk is the same as the price for a single address. Given that money doesn't buy IP addresses (or more correctly, the right to use them, because they are explicitly stated not to be treated as property), what criteria would you use to give such a big parcel to someone and, therefore, deprive everyone else of it? How about asking what they planned to do with the parcel?

You can find the present-day owners of those prime Class-A IP address blocks at `http://www.iana.org/assignments/ipv4-address-space`. Many have not changed hands since the mid-1990s or earlier. Some of the owners have obvious reasons for the space they own. For example, `12.0.0.0/8` is owned by AT&T and its WorldNet Internet access service was built on it. That was not the block's original intent, but AT&T found it mostly unused and realized it was valuable real estate. One might argue that the multiple Class-A address blocks owned by the various agencies of the U.S. DoD are rightfully theirs as eminent domain for funding all the early and ongoing Internet work. You may not agree, but the argument is not without merit. Even after accounting for these and other such seemingly reasonable assignments, there are still half a dozen or more Class-A address-block owners whose uses for 16.8 million addresses are not as clear.

How Can There Be Progress with No Space to Grow?

Of course, the scarcity of IPv4 addresses doesn't mean there hasn't been a lot going on in enterprise networks these past few years. Ignoring for the moment the argument about them not being property, IPv4 addresses are like real estate, where the old saying goes "nobody's making any more." Like land in Manhattan, you have to tear something down to put up something new. Enterprises are using what IP-address space they have more carefully, augmenting the public addresses with RFC 1918 private ones. Also, as companies acquire each other, sometimes the acquisition brings a new source of IP addresses. This could be because one company has extra assigned space that's not in use. Or, through duplication of functions, one company can eliminate a couple of departments that are redundant after the merger. With that, the IP addresses the defunct departments were using are now free. Even such conservation of address space cannot last forever (that's why you're starting to see skyscrapers in Queens and Jersey City).

Getting Back to Those Days of "Unlimited" Space with IPv6

With your IPv6 transition, you're entering an exciting new realm. Instead of being limited to the Great Plains of the not-so-Old West, now cluttered with strip malls, fast-food joints (serving SPAM), and never-ending tracts of housing developments, imagine that you've discovered new land, and it's not a new island or continent; it's a new galaxy. A galaxy where every planet is as reachable as any in the IPv4 universe you're in now. For the networking old timers, it's both a change of mindset and invigorating not to have to worry about conserving every last IP address.

Starting at the Top with RIRs

When provisioning your enterprise's IPv6 address space, a good place to start is with your RIR (that's Regional Internet Registry, in case you forgot from Chapter 2). The RIRs are not quite the top of the IPv6 numbering pyramid, because they get their address-space assignments from the Internet Assigned Numbers Authority (IANA). Much like the Wizard of Oz, nobody talks to IANA, not about getting IPv6 addresses, at least. That's the RIRs' and their subordinate registries' job.

There are presently five RIRs that together provide IPv6 address allocation and assignment coverage to the entire world. Their names and coverage areas are:

- AfriNIC for Africa,
- APNIC for Asia-Pacific,
- ARIN for North America, excluding Mexico,
- LACNIC for Latin America and the Caribbean, and,
- RIPE for Europe.

You can find a map showing the coverage areas of each of the RIRs at `http://www.arin.net/community/countries.html`.

You'll want to see what your RIR's policies are regarding to whom they'll allo-cate address space directly and how they recommend their subordinate reg-istries do so. All the RIR policies are similar and you can find a comparison at `http://www.nro.net/documents/nro45.html#3-1`. For the rest of this chapter, unless stated otherwise, examples will use ARIN's policies, guidelines, and so on, available at `http://www.arin.net/policy/nrpm.html#ipv6`.

Whom do the RIRs Serve?

You'll quickly realize on reading their policies that ARIN (or any other RIR) probably won't be your direct source of IPv6 addresses. Part of the reasoning for this is organizational efficiency. Because of the total number of possible assignments (literally millions) in the decades to come, ARIN does not want to deal with you directly, except in the three cases cited in the next sections, unless you can show proof of the need for 200 '/48's or more. Even if you have a reasonable plan for using at least 200 '/48' subnets (which for a single enterprise is impressive), unless you're assigning those subnets to other orga-nizations, you probably can't get them directly from ARIN. In other words, you have to be Local Internet Registry (LIR) or Internet Service Provider (ISP). Furthermore, you need to provide connectivity for all those addresses you're assigning to allow them to route to the other IPv6 networks world-wide through your one aggregate allocated space.

That final requirement is very important. Recall from earlier in the book how the IPv6 addressing structure is far more hierarchical than IPv4. This is because the people who manage world-wide routing of the Internet and other extremely large infrastructures saw the efficiencies in a strict routing hierarchy. Sadly, the IPv4 networks primarily grew organically, especially the Internet, so the chance to instill more than a partial hierarchy was lost. IPv6 is starting from scratch and the RIRs (among others) want to do IPv6 routing right. You'll see an example of the routing hierarchy in action in the next section.

If you meet the preceding criteria and have a level of demand suitable to work with ARIN directly, for example if you're with the Defense Information Systems Agency (DISA), the DoD's ISP, then you'll initially be allocated a min-imum of a '/32' of IPv6 addresses. With that, you'll have the ability to assign as many IPv6 *subnets* as there are total addresses in the IPv4 space, in other words more than 4 billion of them with each subnet able to handle 2^{64} interface IDs.

Seeing the Hierarchy in Action

The best way to understand how the routing hierarchy works is by example. Figure 7-1 shows the partial results of a traceroute from TowardEX's site in Waltham, Massachusetts to the `www.kame.net` site in Japan. TowardEX is a managed IP solutions provider in New England that was chosen for this example because it provides free network tools including an IPv6 traceroute capability at its website. The example results were gathered using the IPv6 traceroute form at `http://www.twdx.net/`. Some of the intermediate hops were eliminated to make the example clearer.

KAME is one of the first IPv6 implementations and includes a famous website with a turtle (which is what *kame* means in Japanese) on it. If you visit the website using IPv4, there is a static image of the turtle. If you visit using IPv6, you get a short animation of the turtle dancing. The difference is there to show people when they've got IPv6 running correctly on their systems. It also is a mild incentive for IPv6 adoption in the software development and computer networking communities, because everyone wants to say they saw the turtle dance.

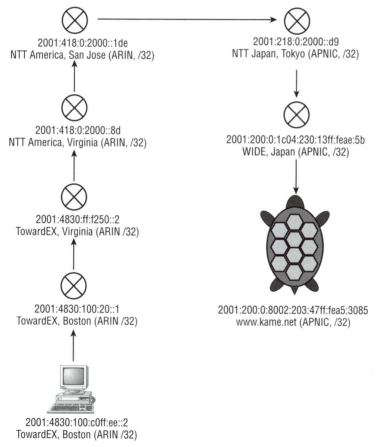

Figure 7-1: The path of typical IPv6 packet showing hierarchical routing

If you're familiar with how traceroute works, then with the exception of the IPv6 addresses versus IPv4 addresses, Figure 7-1 should be easy to understand. Each hop shows the IPv6 address and to whom it is assigned. Parenthetically, the RIR that allocated it and the size of the allocation are also shown.

There are several pieces of information in the figure that result from the routing hierarchy used by IPv6. Note at the top of the figure how, on hopping from San Jose to Tokyo the ISP does not change, but the network prefix (and RIR) does. This is because even the RIRs are not immune from the rules of hierarchical addressing. NTT (though technically two different companies in the USA and Japan) presents the view that it is one ISP. This can be seen from the DNS names of all of NTT's routers in the figure. The DNS names (not included in the figure) all end in ".ntt.net" to create the perception that the routers all belonged to the same network. Because NTT is getting its addresses from APNIC and from ARIN, it must use two different allocations to cover all of its territory. In IPv6 routing, nobody cares if you're a multi-national corporation. They care that you get your addresses from the same area that you're going to use them.

You can also see that there are only four RIR allocations in use throughout the entire traceroute. This is because the allocated address spaces are so huge that all but the largest ISPs can readily provision their networks with just one allocation from an RIR. This will become less true as IPv6 adoption proceeds and ISPs get bigger. For now, there are few with more than one allocation for reasons of needing more space.

In the example, you see that TowardEX splits its allocation from ARIN, using 2001:4830:100::/48 for its site in Boston and 2001:4830:ff::/48 for its site in Virginia. Multiple subnets are in use throughout TowardEX's network, as can be seen by the fourth value in each network prefix (that is, c0ff, 20, and f250), but there are only two sites. Also note the cute use of numbering to create the word "coffee" in the address of the device starting the traceroute. This kind of device numbering is covered later in the chapter when you learn how to create a network numbering plan. As you might imagine, if you don't want your devices to be easily found by hackers, the kind of numbering used here is not such a good idea. On the other hand, if you want people to remember the IPv6 addresses of key routers and other devices, using words as mnemonics is a great idea.

Among the NTT-owned routers in Figure 7-1, you can see that the ones in the U.S. are on the same subnet (2001:418:0:2000::/64). This is probably a backbone network connecting ingress and egress routers throughout NTT's presence in the U.S. The site portion being '0' reinforces that theory. When you hop to Japan, the RIR-allocated portion of the network prefix changes for the reasons mentioned earlier, however NTT has chosen to leave the site and subnet numbers the same in both Japan and the U.S, making the Japan-side network prefix 2001:218:0:2000::/64. Though this may be a coincidence, it is more likely a planned way to identify its backbone network across RIR-allocated boundaries.

Understanding the Hierarchy's Downside

A hierarchical network structure from the "top" of the Internet all the way down to the lowliest device sounds like a great idea. For one thing, it makes for fewer IPv6 entries in the Internet's routing tables (far fewer than the nearly 200,000 entries the Internet uses for IPv4). Unfortunately, it's not all good news. As you saw in Figure 7-1, hierarchical IPv6 address allocations and assignments go all the way down to local ISPs before your enterprise sees them. That means if you pick ISP 'A' to provide your IPv6 Internet access service, you'll be assigned addresses from an allocation the ISP received from its LIR or RIR.

Realizing Your ISP Choice Decides Your Internal Addresses

Because IPv6 did away with NAT (and the following is a case for why NAT may come back), all the devices inside your enterprise will bare the brand of ISP 'A' in the network portion of their addresses. That has some implications in security, for example if ISP 'A' is known to have poor security practices, then your devices' addresses may entice somebody to hack your ISP and then you. This is not too different from the IPv4 world, however, because a few quick searches of the RIR databases will find the same weak ISP and what IPv4 address spaces it provides to its customers.

The more troubling problem you'll face arises if you want to leave ISP 'A' for ISP 'B'. Because ISP 'B' has different allocations of IPv6 addresses, that means you'll have to renumber all your internal assets. That could be like going through a mini-IPv6 transition every time you want to get better reliability, features, or rates for Internet access. Even with IPv6's advanced automated configuration mechanisms, you may still have to reconfigure multiple DHCP and DNS servers, along with any statically configured interfaces on devices. Moreover, you will have to orchestrate the switch from one ISP to the other very carefully so that connectivity is maintained both between internal systems and to the outside world during the transition.

IPv6 does offer a solution that is part of the auto-configuration mechanisms. A Router Renumbering (RR) protocol is defined in RFC 2894 and it lets you renumber your assets remotely, provided you've set it up during your upgrade. As the RFC states and as should be evident to a security-conscious network manager, RR is a very powerful protocol that could be used to disable your whole network if compromised. Therefore, you have to be very careful in its implementation to make sure strong authentication is in use to prevent spoofing. The details of such an implementation are beyond the scope of this book and as of August 2007 no vendor or open-source project is advertising that they support RR. You'll have to do your own digging to see if your router and management system vendors support it.

You'll see shortly that with ARIN there are ways around the dilemma of ISP-centric addressing, but with RIPE in Europe, a recent pair of articles shows the ISP 'A' versus ISP 'B' problem has become a thorn in the sides of IPv6 adopters. According to the articles, unlike ARIN, RIPE currently has no exception for direct allocation or assignment of IPv6 addresses to anyone other than ISPs. A proposal has been raised to add such exceptions so that end users can get "provider-independent" addresses directly from the RIR. This may pass, but given RIPE's long cycle for policy changes, it may take on the order of five months. That's a long time to wait for those looking to switch to IPv6 as IPv4 addresses become increasingly scarce and enterprises want to grow. For the original articles, see:

- `http://news.zdnet.co.uk/communications/` `0,1000000085,39287566,00.htm` and

- `http://www.circleid.com/posts/what` `_prevents_ipv6_deployment_europe/`.

Balancing Hierarchy and Aggregation with Reality

The balance between wanting a hierarchical and ISP-centric world-wide topology of networks versus the realities of how those networks are used make for interesting times as IPv6 is adopted more broadly. To get around the issues of ISP-dependent address blocks, look for solutions to arise in the future including geography-centric addressing schemes that divide countries, states, provinces, cities, and so on, into *areas* where each area has its own dedicated address blocks, and all ISPs in a particular area are required to support all those blocks.

The U.S. DoD is already doing something similar with its address space by overlaying a hexagonal grid on the entire world and assigning a distinct IPv6 address block to each hexagon. Such an addressing scheme plays very well with one popular interpretation of how IPv6 addresses should be viewed. That is, the interface ID (the lower 64 bits) should indicate who you are and the network prefix (the upper 64 bits) should indicate what (or where) you are.

Geography-based network addressing may sound familiar to you, possibly because that's how telephone systems have worked successfully for more than 100 years. You may also see other concepts from telephony applied to IPv6 addresses. For instance, number portability may evolve, probably along with the geocentric addressing schemes. In the telephony world, if you leave carrier 'X' for carrier 'Y', you can take your number with you, provided you stay in the same general geographic region. This might make a popular solution with IPv6 addresses, as well.

Who Else Can Get Addresses Directly from ARIN?

One way you may be assigned IPv6 addresses directly from ARIN, thereby avoiding being locked into a given ISP, is if you qualify for a direct assignment of *IPv4* addresses. As you may have guessed, the IPv4 policy is more restrictive than the IPv6 one, due to the scarcity of IPv4 addresses. There are criteria to be met regarding the minimum portion of the space you have to put to use immediately on getting the assignment, as well as criteria for efficient utilization of the total assigned space in a timely manner.

So as to retain the routing hierarchy as much as possible (not to mention keeping its bookkeeping from turning into a nightmare), ARIN limits the minimum size of IPv4 spaces assigned directly to end users, making satisfying the utilization criteria all the harder. Unless you're also adding infrastructure (not just renumbering existing assets) while you're performing your IPv6 upgrade, you may not be able to get IPv6 addresses directly from ARIN using the IPv4-assignability exception. The restrictions are less severe if you're running BGP and have multiple Internet connections (that is, you're multi-homed). In any case, you should consult the current policy when it's time for you to request addresses, because it's likely to remain fairly fluid for years to come.

If you should qualify for a direct assignment of IPv6 address space under the IPv4-assignability exception, ARIN will give you no fewer than a '/48' of IPv6 addresses, for the same reasons as mentioned previously for why there are minimum size limits on the IPv4 direct assignments. The block will be taken from the pool of free address space such that there is room to grow it to at least a '/44' should you need more space at a later time.

Though getting addresses directly from ARIN avoids locking you into a given ISP, this option also has its drawbacks. According to ARIN, its directly assigned provider-independent addresses are the least likely to be globally routable (see `http://www.arin.net/registration/guidelines/ipv6_assignment.html`). What this means is not entirely clear, partly because no RIR guarantees IPv6 global routability at this time (as also stated in the RIRs' policies). It does not mean, however, that you can't upgrade to an IPv6 backbone infrastructure for internal use (and meet your June 2008 mandate, if you have one) and put off or limit external IPv6 connectivity until things settle down.

Making Exceptions for Critical and Internal Infrastructure

There are two other exceptions to ARIN's policy regarding to whom it will assign IPv6 addresses directly. Most enterprises will not be able to use these exceptions, but because a primary focus of this book is to help those performing IPv6 upgrades on U.S. government networks, the odds that you can use one of them is better than with the average enterprise.

Provided you meet all the criteria in the policy exception, ARIN will assign you an address block of as few as a '/48' if you are one of the critical infrastructure providers of the Internet. Examples of what constitutes such a provider are given in the policy at `http://www.arin.net/policy/nrpm.html#six10`.

The other exception where ARIN may assign you addresses directly is if you need it for non-routed internal infrastructure. You will have to justify why a subset of your existing IPv6 address space is inadequate. For this exception, examples are not provided in the policy at present.

Comparing ARIN to the other RIRs

All the RIRs' policies basically stick to the '/32' minimum for ISP assignments and '/48' minimums for all direct assignments. Moreover, all the RIRs leave how their ISPs assign addresses up to those ISPs. The guidelines from ARIN have much in common with the policies of the other four RIRs. ARIN is the only one that recommends assigning a '/56' for smaller sites. It is also the only RIR (with the exception of APNIC) that does not explicitly recommend a '/128' be assigned when it is certain that only one device is connecting to the ISP. APNIC is the most flexible, stating that how each ISP assigns its allocated addresses is purely up to the ISP.

What Address Spaces Are Currently Assigned to the RIRs?

To help you recognize the different RIRs' addresses when you see them, the list of network prefixes assigned to the RIRs by IANA as of December 2006, as documented at `http://www.iana.org/assignments/ipv6-unicast-address-assignments`, is:

AfriNIC: `2001:4200::/23, 2C00::/12`

APNIC: `2001:200::/23, 2001:C00::/22, 2001:4400::/23, 2001:8000::/18, 2400::/12`

ARIN: `2001:400::/23, 2001:1800::/23, 2001:4800::/23, 2600::/12, 2610::/23, 2620::/23`

LACNIC: `2001:1200::/23, 2800::/12`

RIPE: `2001:600::/23, 2001:800::/22, 2001:1400::/22, 2001:1A00::/23, 2001:1C00::/22, 2001:2000::/20, 2001:3000::/21, 2001:3800::/22, 2001:4000::/23, 2001:4600::/23, 2001:4A00::/23, 2001:4C00::/23, 2001:5000::/20, 2003::/18, 2A00::/12`

Getting IPv6 Addresses from ISPs

If you won't be getting your IPv6 addresses from an RIR, which is likely for at least some of your addresses, you'll have to find one or more ISP. You'll learn about two of the ISPs' functions in this chapter. One function is assigning IPv6 addresses. The other is providing external connectivity, which you'll read more about later in the chapter.

Checking with Your Existing ISPs

As part of an enterprise MIS/IT department, you probably deal with one or more ISP already. You can start by asking them about their IPv6 offerings. Even some of the biggest ISPs, however, are not setting foot into IPv6 territory in earnest yet, so your ISPs' offerings may be non-existent, merely lip-service to their roadmaps for IPv6 deployment, or functional but unreliable for production work.

As you vetted your hardware and software vendors' claims of having IPv6 features, you should similarly vet your ISPs. If they claim they have deployed IPv6, ask for reference customers. It's highly likely any of the early-stage deployments came with discounts to the customers to adopt IPv6 in trade for a reference or testimonial. Find those customers and get their opinions of the ISP. If the ISP has not deployed, but has a plan in place as to when they'll do it, ask for estimated dates of service availability and what the ISP's comfort level is with those dates. If they want your business, they may even sign contracts with clauses saying you'll sign up provided they hit the target dates. This way, you can back out if they fail and they have the comfort of knowing there's at least some financial reason for deploying IPv6 technology.

Searching for New or Additional ISPs

If you are not satisfied with the offerings, or lack thereof, of your current ISPs, then you will need to find new ones from whom to get IPv6 addresses. In addition to the ones you are using, you are probably aware of others in your area that you did not choose to use for any number of reasons. This would be a good time to find out about their IPv6 offerings and timelines and see if they can meet your needs. Of course, you should vet them at least as much as you did your existing ISPs and other vendors.

To augment the list of ISPs you already know about, here are some other places you can look for new ones. In most parts of the world, ISPs serving your enterprise's local areas should not be hard to find. Many of the big telecommunications and cable companies are ISPs, plus some well-known names on the

Internet, like AOL. You can also check the membership lists of the RIRs, though not all members are ISPs. For four of the RIRs, those lists can be found at:

AfriNIC: `http://www.afrinic.net/foundingMembers.htm`

APNIC: `http://www.apnic.net/apnic-bin/memlist.pl`

ARIN: `http://www.arin.net/cgi-bin/member_list.pl`

RIPE: `http://www.ripe.net/membership/indices/`

At present, there is no published list of LACNIC members. There may be by the time you read this, so check their website at `www.lacnic.net`. Also, the only list available at AfriNIC's website is for founding members. A more complete list may be available from AfriNIC at a later date, too.

In addition to the RIRs, you can do a search for ISPs at `http://www.ipv6-to-standard.org/index.php`. Select "ISP" in the "Product or Application or Service" drop-down list or type "ISP" into the "Free Search" text box. Another resource for ISPs world-wide is "The List" (`http://www.thelist.com/`). In existence since before 1995, The List was one of the first websites on the burgeoning commercial Internet and is still a definitive source for locating ISPs. Neither of these websites allows you to search for or calls out IPv6 capabilities specifically, so you'll have to do some digging once you've narrowed your search by country or type.

Unfortunately, in the United States it's very hard to find an ISP that offers IPv6 addresses, because they have no connectivity service with which you can use those addresses. To extend the analogy presented at the start of the chapter equating the scarce IPv4 addresses to rare gems, if IPv4 addresses are such, at least the mines (ISPs) where you can look for them are easy to find. For IPv6 addresses, the mines are bountiful with gems, but the mines themselves are hard to find.

If you're in the U.S. government, you stand a much better chance than private-sector businesses or residential customers. If you're in the U.S. DoD, then DISA is your ISP. DISA already has its addresses from ARIN and its mission is to get you connected, so you can be comfortable that at least this portion of your transition should be manageable.

To address (no pun intended) the rest of the U.S. government, under the Networx Universal and Networx Enterprise telecommunication programs, awarded by GSA in March and May 2007, respectively, several vendors including AT&T, Level 3, MCI, Qwest, and Sprint offer IP protocol services. You can find out more about Networx, how to contact the vendors, and getting IPv6 addresses at `http://www.gsa.gov/Portal/gsa/ep/channelView.do?pageTypeId=8199&channelPage=%2Fep%2Fchannel%2FgsaOverview.jsp&channelId=-16201`.

Understanding ISP Address Assignments

ISPs have some latitude within which to assign their allocated IP address spaces to customers downstream. The RIRs publish guidelines for ISPs that vary in how much the ISP must comply. All the guidelines stem from recommendations in RFC 3177, but each RIR's guidelines are slightly different. Continuing with examples based on ARIN, recall from Chapter 2, "Demystifying IPv6," that ARIN recommends its ISPs assign IPv6 address blocks in the following sizes for the situations indicated:

- A '/64' if only one subnet is needed,
- A '/56' (256 subnets) for those sites requiring only a few subnets over the next 5 years, and,
- A '/48' (65,536 subnets) for larger sites.

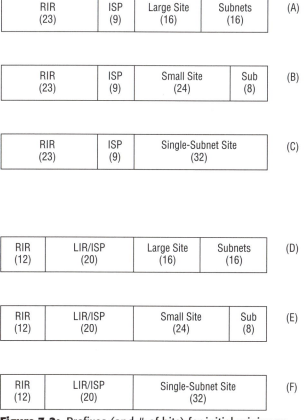

Figure 7-2: Prefixes (and # of bits) for initial minimum ISP assignments per ARIN

The odds are that you can get as much as a '/48' for your enterprise with a minimum of fuss, and certainly a lot less fuss than if you asked for even a handful of new IPv4 addresses.

To help understand the different types of address-space assignments you may receive, Figure 7-2 shows all the common combinations of network prefixes (the high-order 64 bits of an IP address) for first-time minimal allocations. How you grow your address space after that (or if you get more than the minimum initially) depends on your individual circumstances and network size and layout, but most enterprises will start with assignments from the set in Figure 7-2.

Interpreting Network Prefixes

When IANA and the other bodies at the top of Internet "management" first started distributing the huge IPv6 address space to the RIRs, they were commendably conservative and gave out sets of '/23's to each RIR. Even such conservatively sized blocks allow the RIRs to allocate up to 512 address blocks to their ISP members. Though this may not sound like much, to put it in perspective "The List" mentioned earlier shows there are 321 ISPs in the United States as of August 3, 2007. ARIN could allocate at least one '/32' (the minimum size) to each of those ISPs allowing the ISPs to assign addresses to tens of thousands of their customers.

Combining the RIR and ISP components of the network prefix with ARIN's guidelines for how ISPs should assign address blocks produces the set of address formats shown in (A) through (C) of Figure 7-2. In other words, the RIR's assignment from IANA is represented by the first 23 bits. Being that an ISP allocation is no fewer than 32 bits in length, this leaves 9 bits within each RIR allocation to identify the downstream ISP. Depending on the needs of the ISP customer, the next 16 to 32 bits is used to represent the customer's site. For single-subnet sites (for example, residential customers), the ISP defines the entire network prefix. If you're part of a large enterprise, the ISP allows you to distribute the assignment across up to 65,536 subnets. The middle category represents small sites, allowing the ISP to conserve space by giving fewer addresses to those who don't have much infrastructure.

Interpreting the Newer Prefixes

As IANA gained knowledge on how to manage IPv6 address spaces, it saw cause for being less conservative with assignments to the RIRs. Starting in May 2004, larger assignments were doled out, especially to APNIC and RIPE because their regions were deploying IPv6 the fastest. The largest and most recent jump in address-space assignment size occurred in October 2006 when each of the five RIRs was given a huge '/12' block (see the list of RIR assignments earlier in the chapter). Examples of allocations formats the RIRs could provide to LIRs and ISPs from their '/12' spaces are show in (D) through (F) of Figure 7-2. Because an RIR is represented with fewer bits in the newer network prefixes, instead of 9 bits for the LIR/ISP portion, the new allocations allow up to 20 bits. This means an RIR can allocate more than a million '/32' address blocks before the space provided it by IANA runs out.

There will be cases where RIRs make larger allocations than '/32' to some ISPs. Also, ISPs will assign more than a '/48' to larger enterprises. Such situations make for many other combinations of bit-field sizes for the ISP, site, and subnet portions of network prefixes. By using the formats shown in Figure 7-2 as examples, you should be able to figure out how to interpret those other formats, as well.

Interpreting Prefixes Directly Assigned by RIRs

As mentioned earlier in the chapter, some RIRs have provisions for assigning address space directly to organizations that are not ISPs or LIRs, in other words, end-user enterprises. Figure 7-3 shows the bit fields contained in network prefixes directly assigned from ARIN. Both the old and new RIR field sizes are shown in (A) and (B), respectively. You'll see two main differences in the directly assigned network prefixes from the ISP-assigned ones.

One difference between ISP-assigned addresses and directly assigned ones from ARIN is the size of the field ARIN uses to distinguish your direct assignment. The field ranges in length from 21 bits to 32 bits. In other words, the ISP portion has been eliminated or seems to have been. What is actually going on is that the directly assigned address spaces lie in the same overall ARIN space as the ISP ones. ARIN has set aside some portion of its assignment from IANA for direct assignments to non-ISPs. The portion set aside is probably identifiable from the high-order bits of the directly assigned field. That way it still looks like there's an ISP component; the "ISP" just happens to be ARIN. Of course, ARIN does not provide connectivity, so you will have to find somebody to route your addresses for you, if they need to be reached from outside your enterprise.

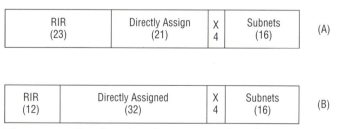

Figure 7-3: Directly assigned ARIN network prefixes (and number of bits)

The directly assigned addresses are also given out with growing room built in, as indicated by the 'X' (for eXpansion) field in Figure 7-3. Though ARIN assigns you a '/48' initially, they reserve a '/44' block should you require more space (and can present a case why you should get it). ISPs probably get their addresses with room for expansion built in, but it is not directly called out in ARIN policy. One reason that may be is because the minimum '/32' blocks that are assigned to ISPs are much easier to manage and track. ARIN is probably easing its management workload by simply cordoning off a whole '/44' for you to use, even if you never do need it.

What About Assignments of Smaller Address Spaces?

As you saw earlier, ISPs have a lot of control over how they assign addresses to their customers. With the exception of '/128's for single devices, however, the ISPs are discouraged from crossing over to the right side of the network prefix boundary at '/64'. This is to allow the final recipients of the assigned addresses to control completely how they construct their interface IDs. There are parts of the IPv6 addressing architecture that allow smaller interface IDs than 64 bits, but they are not in use by the RIRs.

Earlier in the history of IPv6, there was discussion about allowing ISPs to assign network prefixes of '/80', '/96', and other sizes that encroached on the interface ID field. This was due to the shear size of the interface ID and trying to account for large groups of IPv6 users (for example, residential customers) for whom providing 64 bits just to connect one or two computers in their homes or small offices was viewed as a colossal waste. As the total amount of IPv6 space became clearer in the grand scheme of things, arguments for such assignments fell out of favor in the name of better routing, network management, and standardization in how interface IDs are computed.

That said, should you ever find yourself being a residential IPv6 user with 64 bits of address space to play with, how you organize it behind your gateway router is solely up to you. Even enterprises may eventually encroach on the interface ID space so as to create more subnets with smaller ISP assignments (though this is probably a long way off). Like squatting on IPv4 addresses that don't belong to you (see Chapter 6, "Defining the Transition Preparation Steps"), what you do with your IPv6 address assignment behind your gateway routers is your business. Just make sure you block the egress of squatted-on IPv4 addresses and aggregate the IPv6 addresses correctly before routing out of your enterprise to the Internet.

Getting Addresses from Multiple ISPs

Internet connectivity has become such an important business tool that there probably isn't a single organization that's gone as far as renting office space that it hasn't also hooked up to the Internet. Moreover, if Internet connectivity is in any way related to the organization's business (for example, website development, e-commerce, and so on), then it's likely the organization has engaged at least two ISPs to assure that connectivity will be maintained in the event of outages. Certainly for any organization that can call itself an enterprise, all of the above holds true, and that is why you need to understand the special issues in using multiple ISPs with IPv6. You'll read more about using multiple Internet connections to improve the redundancy of your network later in the chapter. In this section, you'll read about what you have to consider when getting addresses from multiple ISPs.

Getting Addresses for Multi-Regional Enterprises

As you read earlier in the chapter, IPv6 addresses are tied to the region where they will be used, not just where an enterprise's headquarters may be located. Therefore, a multi-national (technically, multi-regional) enterprise will have to engage several ISPs to provide IPv6 addresses for all its network assets. Excluding provider-independent addresses, that means the enterprise will have at least one assignment of IPv6 addresses for every RIR region within which it has assets requiring them.

If you have managed a multi-national enterprise network before, having multiple address assignments world-wide is nothing new. Even in IPv4, where addresses are not as closely associated with RIR geography, local ISPs get theirs from local RIRs and you in turn get yours from the ISPs. In addition, business reasons (including the advantages of incorporating separately in each country where your enterprise has a presence) make the details of having and managing region-specific assignments much the same with IPv6 as they are with IPv4.

Getting Addresses for Network Redundancy

In addition to your enterprise requiring multiple ISPs to provide IPv6 addresses to its sites world-wide, many of those sites (certainly any of reasonable size) will require multiple ISPs for redundancy purposes. By procuring Internet connectivity (and therefore IPv6 addresses) from both ISP 'A' and ISP 'B', each of your sites protects itself from the situation where an outage at either ISP also takes the site offline. You'll read more about redundancy in external connectivity later in the chapter. Here you will read about assigning addresses from both ISP assignments to each of your network assets within the site.

Using Multiple IPv6 Addresses on an Interface

With IPv4 you are probably accustomed to any given interface on one of your network assets having one IP address. The interface is part of one network, though the asset may be part of several, for example, in the case of a router. This limitation is no longer true with IPv6. It is not uncommon for each interface to have multiple IPv6 addresses. For example, each interface will have an automatically generated link-local address for communications with local infrastructure prior to (and in parallel with) the assignment of any routable IPv6 address (for example, by DHCP). An interface may also have multiple routable addresses, and therefore belong to multiple overlaid networks at the same time.

Recall from earlier in this chapter that an IPv6 address is composed of two parts, a network prefix and an interface ID. The interface ID, in theory, does not have to change no matter what network that interface is on and it represents "who" that interface is. As such, it is often tied to the link-layer MAC address of the interface hardware. The network prefix, in other words the vehicle by which an interface receives routing and other services, is the part of the address that tells other devices "what" or "where" the interface is.

Think of network prefixes like the various cards in your wallet. In a typical case, you'll have a driver's license, a credit card or two, an ID card for your place of employment, a library card, supermarket discount card, and so on. Each one of these items has your name (or interface ID) on it. Each one also ties you to a different network via a different network prefix (your driver's license number, credit card numbers, employee ID number, and so on). As with the cards in your wallet and the many different associations they bind you to, the same is true for interfaces in IPv6 networks.

A given interface on one of your devices may be part of several networks simultaneously. For example, it may be part of the enterprise's world-wide MIS/IT infrastructure for e-mail, accessing HR and other company-internal websites, and so on. At the same time, the interface may be part of a departmental or project-specific network that is cordoned off for privacy or merely manageability reasons. The interface may also be part of the enterprise's management network so that patches can be pushed to the device. You can probably come up with as many different networks that the interface could be a part of (and the business associations those networks imply) as there are ID cards in your wallet. The collections of addresses on your interfaces that are the most applicable to this section, however, are those used to implement redundant external connectivity.

Tying an Interface to Multiple ISPs

As with other associations derived from the network prefixes used on an interface, connectivity to two or more ISPs can be accomplished by using multiple IPv6 addresses on that interface. By assigning an IPv6 address from ISP 'A' and one from ISP 'B' to an interface, the device can communicate with devices external to the enterprise using either ISP.

As long as both ISP connections remain functional, the interface (or more accurately, an application on the device) can freely choose from which of its IPv6 addresses to originate communications and the rest of the given conversation (be it a simple response to a one-time UDP query or a full TCP session) will occur between the IPv6 address chosen and the external device. It is when one of the ISP connections becomes unavailable that more processing must be performed for new connections and connections that are in progress.

When one of the enterprise's ISP connections goes out of service, as long as a multi-homed (meaning having multiple IP addresses) interface continues to choose the other ISP by virtue of the originating IPv6 address it picks, nothing different occurs from when both ISPs are available. If the interface chooses the IPv6 address belonging to the incapacitated ISP connection, then any packets sent will not go through. Depending on the distance (measured in the number of hops) between the originating interface and the point of the outage and how well the outage is communicated to upstream routers, the interface may get no response from the network regarding its lost packets or the network may issue a redirection message saying that the other ISP's connection is the better way to go.

For either situation, a lot of burden is placed on the device to which the interface belongs to create a new packet with a new originating IPv6 address (the one from the functional ISP's assignment). Not all devices are clever enough to do that, unless the network also has some way of communicating that the out of service ISP's addresses should not be used to originate connections until further notice. That could mean the device needs to be tied into the local routing protocols like OSPF, RIP, or even BGP. This is not common for many end devices. Some devices offer "dead gateway detection" which, if the network communicates the loss of the ISP as the loss of the local default gateway, can be used to switch to the gateway servicing the other ISP. This, in turn, might force the interface to pick only the IPv6 address provided by the active ISP's assignment.

The preceding paragraphs describe the origination of new connections, but what if an ISP goes down in the middle of a session? This is quite possible for longer-duration sessions like FTP downloads or Telnet or SSH interactive terminal sessions, which are all TCP-based. Because a TCP connection is tightly coupled with the originating IP address, the chances that the session can simply hop to the interface's other address are very poor. Newer session-oriented protocols like SCTP (see RFC 2960) strive to handle multi-homed devices better, but the replacement of TCP is a long way away and you need to have redundancy now.

Because this section focused purely on getting IPv6 addresses, the solutions it offers to implement redundancy are limited to multi-homing of your interfaces to addresses from all of the ISPs you're using. The section on external connectivity that you'll find later in the chapter covers other solutions for using multiple ISPs to implement redundancy beyond simple address assignments.

Using Addresses in 6to4 Space

An alternative to getting IPv6 addresses from ISPs or even RIRs is to leverage your existing IPv4 address space. Via an addressing mechanism called 6to4 (see RFC 3056), anyone who has been assigned IPv4 address space automatically also has IPv6 space available from which to number their assets. In fact, the amount of IPv6 space you have available is quite vast. For every single IPv4 address assigned to you, you have a '/48' worth of space available in IPv6. The assignment is automatic once you have the IPv4 addresses, meaning there are no forms to fill out, nobody to call for permission to use the addresses, and so on. You will need somebody to terminate the other end of the tunnel that must be created to get 6to4 traffic to other IPv6 networks, but you'll see that's not difficult when you read more about it in the external connectivity section later in this chapter.

Figure 7-4 shows the format of a 6to4 network prefix. The first two octets are hard-wired with the hexadecimal value 2002. The next four octets contain the IPv4 address on which the IPv6 addresses are piggy-backing. The IPv4 address must be assigned to you, routable, and not from private (RFC 1918) address space. The last two octets are yours to use for setting up subnets, just like any '/48' assignment from an ISP or RIR. You will find that, beyond acting as a bridge to the IPv4 universe, there is nothing else special about 6to4 addresses or network prefixes. The addresses are assigned to network interfaces the same way, and the prefixes can be used in routing tables just like native IPv6 prefixes.

2002 (hex) (16)	IPv4 Address (32)	Subnets (16)

Figure 7-4: Network-prefix format for 6to4 IPv6 addresses

Because the 6to4 addresses are almost exactly like native IPv6 addresses, an enterprise can select one of its externally routable IPv4 addresses (for example, 19.12.4.15) and use the associated 6to4 network prefix (2002:130c:40f::/48) to number all the assets at a site. As you'll have the ability to assign up to 65,536 different subnets, even the largest of sites should be readily addressable with only one network prefix. All the assets at the site that you do number will have to be IPv6 capable, of course, because the addresses you assign from this network prefix will be IPv6 ones.

A typical network architecture choice is to use 6to4 addresses only at border gateways between the enterprise and the Internet. Though you have the ability to provision thousands of subnets, you may choose to provision only one or two using 6to4, in other words just enough to set up routing from a site to the outside world. The remainder of your enterprise can draw from site-local ULA addressing (see RFC 4193) or provider-independent addresses with the routing infrastructure using those addresses internally on intermediate routers and only using the 6to4 gateways as the last hop out of the network. This way, when you get native IPv6 connectivity you will only need to renumber the 6to4 gateway interfaces and change the routing infrastructure (be it managed by OSPF and so on, or statically assigned) of adjacent systems to point to the gateways' new addresses.

You can even use 6to4 to augment your ISP-assigned spaces by provisioning addresses from both to your device interfaces. This is possible via the ability to assign multiple IPv6 addresses to a given network interface. Here, too, you may limit your 6to4 use to gateway routers to augment your natively addressed ones.

If you go with 6to4 addresses, be aware that if you decide in the future to switch to native IPv6 ones, be they ISP-assigned, ULAs, or provider-independent ones, you will have a renumbering job on your hands. This is no different from the example cited earlier in the chapter regarding changing IPv6 ISPs. Think of 6to4 as another ISP. You will also have to renumber if you change the underlying IPv4 address because this will change the 6to4 network prefix. It is for these reasons that it is recommended several times in this book that you automate your address configuration, provisioning, and management systems as much as possible.

What Should You Do Until the Policy Dust Settles?

What you should take away from the chapter so far is that many of the policies and practices on provider-independent address spaces, site-local ULA addressing, and addressing in general are still very much up in the air. For those interested in a more technical discussion of the state of things, an excellent one is provided by the transcript of a March 2007 ICANN conference session in Lisbon (see `http://www.icann.org/meetings/lisbon/transcript-tutorial-ipv6-25mar07.htm`).

Remember that your responsibility is the transition of your enterprise's network to IPv6, not following Internet politics (at least no more than their decisions affect your plans). You can still perform all your hardware and software upgrades and replacements, no matter what the IPv6 address policies from the RIRs turn out to be. Depending which policies win favor regarding ISP-centric versus provider-independent addressing, for example, your choices in network topology and external connectivity might be affected. Other than that, however, IPv6 addresses are just numbers and when the Internet powers that be figure out which ones they want to give you and how, you should be ready for them.

The other lesson you should take away is that, if there's any reason to be cautious and possibly even hold off your transition, the addressing policy one would be it. If you're subject to the OMB mandates for June 2008 and have to press on in the face of uncertainty, you should consider the following recommendations:

1. Simplify what it takes to number (and renumber) the devices on your network as much as possible. Use IPv6's automated configuration wherever you can within the constraints of your security and other policies. For devices that must be manually configured, document well the procedures to change their addresses because you may be doing so several times as policies settle down to a steady state in the years to come.

2. Document any dependencies your addresses have. For example, if they are tied to a particular ISP, make sure everyone managing them knows it. This way, you can factor that in when deciding whether you want to replace that ISP. Also document which RIR you got the addresses from so you know where to go to extend the allocation or assignment.

3. Investigate asset management tools that can also push out addressing changes to your devices. See Chapter 11, "Knowing What Assets You Have," for a snapshot of the tool landscape. If you find ones that meet your needs, use them. You'll be glad you did. For you network management software vendors out there, this is an excellent emerging market.

4. Design your topology to be flexible to address-policy changes. If provider-independent addressing doesn't catch on as more than an exception case (and the driving goal of all the RIRs is aggregation, which is in direct conflict), be ready to handle ISP-centric addressing. You'll read about that more in the next section.

5. Choose your ISPs carefully. Until the provider-independent addressing issues are settled, you'll probably want to stick with whomever you picked.

6. Assign someone to follow the discussion groups of the RIRs that affect you, as well as the central authorities to whom they answer, including the IETF, ICANN, and IANA. If your enterprise is a big enough player, get involved and join the discussion to make things the way you want them to be.

7. Consider using 6to4 addresses and tunneling, at least in the parts of your IPv6 network that require access from outside the enterprise. The addresses are provider independent, though you will have to renumber your infrastructure when you get "real" IPv6 addresses that aren't based on IPv4 addresses.

Creating and Maintaining an IPv6 Numbering Plan

The address-space provisioning section earlier in the chapter encouraged you to think of the overall IPv6 address space as an essentially limitless resource. Even the address spaces you are assigned from the global pool (which itself has barely been tapped), though huge, represent only an infinitesimal portion of what is available. Although it would be hard to imagine you exhausting your assigned resources no matter how wastefully you deploy them, there are other reasons you need to plan and then track how you number your network These reasons include the need to:

1. Document which ISP, RIR, and 6to4 network prefixes are in use in your enterprise and where they are deployed so as to be able to track down assets and problems with them.

2. Organize your address-space assignments further into enterprise-local subnets for efficient routing and aggregation at the borders of your network leading to your ISPs.

3. Define your interface-ID generation methods so as to assign values to your devices' network interfaces with a minimum number of conflicts between devices on your LANs.

4. Track what percentage of your IPv6 addresses is in use and when you may need to go for additional address assignments.

Bidding Farewell to IPv4 Network-Numbering Headaches

Think about that new web server farm you have to set up for your customers to access downloads of the important documents, software, and so on that your enterprise produces. In IPv4 provisioning you have to compute how many servers you'll need based on customer demand and other parameters. Whether it's 2, 10, or 100 servers affects how big an IPv4 space you have to assign to the server LAN. If the estimate is on the edge of an address-space size boundary (for example, 16, 32, 64, and so on addresses), you'll probably have to play it safe and go with the larger assignment. That means, if you think you'll initially need 200 servers, you might assign 512 addresses and waste more than half of an already precious resource. In contrast with IPv4, each IPv6 subnet has enough address space in its interface ID field to hold every network device made to date or that will likely ever be made. You can safely wager that when the device that overflows the 64-bit interface ID field is finally created, the Y10K (year 10,000) problem will be ancient history.

Enjoying Network-Architectural Freedom with IPv6

Unlike the IPv4 example, IPv6 has made your network provisioning job one of counting subnets, not devices. If you need to deploy that same web server farm under IPv6, and for some reason it can't go on an existing subnet (because there will certainly be room), all you have to do is take a subnet from your assigned pool and provision the servers' IPv6 addresses from there.

In reading the IPv6 address-space provisioning section earlier in the chapter, you were probably able to create a ballpark estimate of how much IPv6 space you'll need without even thinking about counting your network assets. You probably just counted the number of sites in your enterprise and guessed at the number of LANs you would need at each site. If you're getting your addresses from an ARIN-allocated ISP, you might have toyed with whether you could get away with '/56' assignments at some sites while at others you simply need '/48's because you would need more than (or come close to needing) 250 subnets. It's so doubtful a site will need more than the 65,536 subnets in a '/48' assignment that ARIN and the other RIRs have special sections in their policies devoted to that contingency.

It is with this freedom from having to determine almost the exact number of addresses required on each subnet that you might dare say network design is fun again. If you're not willing to go that far, you must concede that there's a lot less stress in getting away with simply drawing the footprints of the rooms in your network's house than having to figure out where every door, window, and electrical, telephone, and cable TV receptacle has to go before you even get started deploying equipment.

Numbering Your Networks

As suggested earlier, a first swag at numbering your IPv6 network can be accomplished by assuming each of your sites is assigned addresses from a local ISP. Most ISPs likely will follow their RIR's guideline of assigning a single initial '/48' per site. A site may be composed of one building or an office park full of them, and you'll see that for most cases a '/48' will cover all that you need. In the case where a site can show a need for more than a '/48' from an ISP, you can consider this as multiple '/48' assignments and what follows can still be applied with little change.

ARIN, unlike other RIRs, suggests its ISPs assign '/56' address blocks to smaller sites, but you can ignore such smaller sites for the time being so as to first focus on getting the '/48's done right. You'll next be reading about decomposing the ISP-assigned '/48' into smaller blocks to be distributed internally to buildings, departments, and so on. Once you've mastered the '/48' numbering, you can think of any ISP-assigned '/56's the same way as those smaller distributions you manage within your '/48's, except the aggregation is at the ISP, not your gateway routers.

Understanding That It's Not All One Flat Space

Reviewing Figure 7-2 through Figure 7-4, you might assume that the subnet portion of the network prefix defines a flat plain of subnets all one hop away from a gateway router to an ISP. This will rarely be the case, because most enterprise topologies don't look like that and the physical limitations of building construction, cabling, and so on would not let you deploy your networks that way. If you currently manage an IPv4 '/16' (65,536 addresses) or larger, consider the sub-netting that occurs, even though all the addresses may ultimately be aggregated at your gateway routers.

Creating Subnet Hierarchies within Your Sites

Though the name of the game in IPv6 routing is aggregation, it doesn't have to be done all at once at your network gateways. Just as IANA, the RIRs, and the ISPs impose multi-tier hierarchies external to your network, you too should do so using sub-netting within your sites. There are three main drivers for the kind of hierarchy you should impose on your subnets:

1. Physical topology of your network, which drives network topology or, in other words, where you place your routers. You can think of your routers as an army thinks of its supply depots or as the telephone company thinks of its repeaters in undersea cables. A given router can only cover so much, given physical limitations in cable lengths, for example. To cover a large site fully, you will need to have a hierarchy of routers serving different buildings, floors, and so on, all aggregating to common gateways.

2. Differing security levels between sites and within them, which drive where you place access controls, some of which will be implemented on your routers. Security may drive you to set up ten subnets where one would do, and in IPv6 you've already seen that one subnet would do for your whole enterprise (given the 64-bit interface ID), if it weren't for the external factors cited here. Each subnet may require Internet access, for example, but none of the subnets may be allowed to communicate directly with each other.

3. Separation of mission-critical or production networks from administrative, development, experimental, and other general-purpose networks. This is encompassed in the preceding item, but you may not see such separations as being security related, instead being more comfortable considering them reliability or disaster-avoidance related, so it is called out specifically.

Balancing Your Hierarchies with Efficiency

Hierarchies are meant to organize things, be they books in a library, organized by the Dewey Decimal System, or IP addresses in a network. Using them comes with a price, however, so you should balance the complexity of your hierarchies against your actual needs. For example, if one of your sites is a huge production facility full of thousands of IPv6-enabled robots building cars, there may be little reason to have more than one subnet serving what could be acres of devices. You might even choose link-level switching over network-level routing to extend the reach of your subnet to such a large physical space. The reason you would consider this is because, though hierarchies help you organize things, they consume resources to produce overhead and they can be inflexible to new things.

Understanding the Overhead of Hierarchies

In the case of IPv6, the overhead produced via hierarchies consumes parts of your address space, making them unavailable for numbering devices. You may not think you have to worry about losing part of an address space that lets you create 65,536 subnets, but once you impose a hierarchy on that 16-bit subnet field, the space may no longer look that big and you may find yourself coming up short. The overhead produced by imposing hierarchies is made worse when you are dealing in the binary values associated with IP addresses. Whenever you have a level in the hierarchy that doesn't fully utilize a power of two's worth of values (for example, 2, 4, 8, 16, 32, and so on), you introduce waste.

For example, if you have a bag containing marbles that are red, green, or blue, to organize the marbles by color requires the use of a field that is two-bits wide. Because two bits can contain four values, you have wasted a quarter of your space (unless you get some yellow marbles). With IP addresses, in the worst case the overhead imposed by a hierarchy can consume almost half of the values at a given level. Take the case where you have 513 research laboratories at a site and you want part of your hierarchy to subnet down to the lab level. Because nine bits can only represent 512 values, you will have to use ten bits (which can represent 1024). In doing so, you have created a nearly 50-percent overhead because 511 of the values of that field are not being used.

You may be asking, "What about space for growth?" That's covered in the next section. What you should take away from this section is that, when defining your subnet hierarchies, look for each layer to come as close to a power of two as you can without going over.

Limiting a Hierarchy's Intolerance to Change

Hierarchies work best when describing things that don't change. This allows the most optimization so as to incur as little overhead as possible. The hierarchies you work with describe subnets that constantly change, and therefore you will have to account for growing room.

Take a slight twist on the earlier example and assume you only have 500 research laboratories at a site. You can represent that with nine bits, however do you really feel comfortable that you won't reorganize the site or create as few as 13 more labs over the course of the hierarchy's lifetime (which could last many years)? That's less than a 3-percent increase or margin of error in your design. If you aren't comfortable with that idea, you may make that level of the hierarchy ten-bits wide despite the initial waste. That "waste" may prove valuable when you add Lab #513, because you won't have to reorganize the entire site's networks to accommodate the addition.

Hierarchies can also change such that a particular level shrinks making it available for reorganization to use fewer values to represent its remaining members. This would be the case if your subnet hierarchy accounted for buildings on a site and you sold off half of the buildings, thus removing them from your network. Other than the loss of efficiency, there is no immediate cause for concern if part of your hierarchy becomes underutilized. The exception to that would be if you can transfer the bits that are now spare to a field that is using nearly all of its possible values. This is easier said than done, however, because it requires re-engineering the whole hierarchy and possibly renumbering all the assets at your site. This is why a reduction in utilization and the inherent inefficiency induced is almost always tolerated by network engineers and managers.

Analyzing Some Basic Hierarchy Choices

Some typical choices you may make in designing your subnet hierarchies are shown in Figure 7-5. None of the hierarchies shown is meant to be adopted by you unchanged, and you are encouraged to mix and match or even roll your own.

Hierarchy (A) in Figure 7-5 shows a generic format with three tiers or levels of subnets leading to LANs containing servers and workstations. This format can be interpreted as having up to eight routers at Tier-1 (which presumably connect directly to your enterprise's border gateways). Each Tier-1 router can support up to 16 Tier-2 routers, each of which in turn can support 16 Tier-3 routers. The Tier-3 routers can each support 32 LANs. This hierarchy is driven entirely by the network topology and allows you to have more than 2000 routers at a site. Tier-1 could represent the core routers in each building at the site or there could be two core routers in one of the larger buildings. The beauty of this format is that the number of buildings and so on doesn't matter. The limitation, as you read earlier, is that if you should want to add a ninth router at Tier-1 or similarly go over one of the maximum values at a lower layer, your hierarchy has no tolerance for it. On the other hand, you may be nowhere near those maximums in your current network and you may have devised this format for growth. Of course, you then incur the overhead of wasted address space that comes with planning for growth.

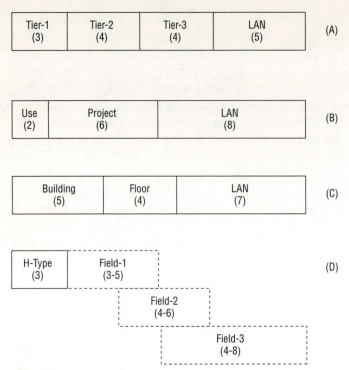

Figure 7-5: Example hierarchies to use on your network prefix's subnet bits

Hierarchy (B) in Figure 7-5 shows how subnets may be distinguished by their use. The first two bits can represent the development, quality control, and production subnets at a site. This kind of hierarchy is useful for creating firewall rules, because you can with one rule protect all the production networks based on their "Use" field. As you read earlier, the lesson to be learned from such small fields as "Use" is that you should try to assign values to all the combinations of bits. With the current example, one of the values is unassigned and, therefore, 25 percent of your subnets are unusable. If you don't have a fourth category readily available, you can mark it reserved and assign a value later. This is also good practice to allow room for growth. Though, with fields of three bits or fewer you should try to define as many of the bit combinations as possible.

Because Hierarchy (B) leaves 14 bits undefined after the "Use" field and it's somewhat unlikely that any of the uses of the subnets will require over 16,000 LANs, you might choose to do as the example shows and create a "Project" field. This way, you can simplify your inter-project access controls, for example, based on this field and still have more than 250 LANs per project.

Hierarchy (C) in Figure 7-5 numbers subnets based on the building they're in, the floor in that building that they're on, and then a flat LAN number. If all the buildings have between nine and sixteen floors, then the "Floor" field is used fairly efficiently, but if there's only one ten-story building at the site and all of the other buildings (of which there are apparently more than sixteen) have three to four floors, then one of the bits in the "Floor" field is mostly wasted. Also, by virtue of encoding the buildings and floors into the hierarchy, the space for the "LAN" field is so small as to make you think whether there's enough space for growth. Are 128 LANs on a floor enough? Some buildings and their floors could be a city block in size. You could easily put more than 100 LANs on a floor, especially if it's some kind of network hosting or other production facility. That's something you'll have to decide, because you're the one who knows the size of your buildings.

Hierarchy (D) in Figure 7-5 shows a hybrid approach. Because a site may have several heterogeneous functions, trying to force all the subnets into one hierarchy may be extremely wasteful. Instead, by using the first few bits of the hierarchy format to define an "H-Type" or type of hierarchy, you have extensive latitude for future growth, and each "H-Type" value does not have to be a different hierarchy. You can use ranges of values to carve out larger spaces for hierarchies requiring them. For example, you could encode a good portion of Hierarchy (C) from Figure 7-5 into Hierarchy (D) by declaring "Field-1" to be the five-bit building value and "Field-2" to be the four-bit floor value. By further declaring that values in the "H-Type" field ranging from 0 through 3 represent a format similar to Hierarchy (C), you effectively still have six bits left for "Field-3" to represent 64 LANs.

Using Consistent Numbering at All of Your Sites

As you define your sub-netting strategy and hierarchies, think about taking commonalities across all your sites into account. Recall the routing example from Figure 7-1, where NTT used the same value in the subnet field in both the United States and Japan. Hierarchies (A), (B), and of course (D) in Figure 7-5 are readily adaptable to this methodology. For example, using Hierarchy (B), your enterprise's international "Project Alpha" could use the following network prefixes for its LANs world-wide:

2400:5552:6153:0100::/56 for production in Japan

2600:6E65:616B:0100::/56 for production in the United States

2A00:794F:6E65:0100::/56 for production in Europe

2400:5552:6153:4100::/56 for quality control in Japan

2600:6E65:616B:4100::/56 for quality control in the United States

2A00:794F:6E65:4100::/56 for quality control in Europe

2400:5552:6153:8100::/56 for development in Japan

2600:6E65:616B:8100::/56 for development in the United States

2A00:794F:6E65:8100::/56 for development in Europe

In this case, the "Use" field is defined as '0' for production, '1' for quality control, and '2' for development.

Creating Interface Identifiers

Compared to numbering your network prefixes, the interface IDs should require almost no thought at all, that is once you've made a few simple decisions. As you've read earlier in the chapter, the 64-bit interface ID space in use by the RIRs and their subordinate ISPs is effectively infinite, unlike the tight spaces you typically have for devices in an IPv4 network.

There are a few classes of devices that will go into each of your LANs: those that everyone (at least everyone on the LAN) needs to know about, those whose addresses can remain anonymous or difficult to remember, and those that you want to hide from network threats. The interface ID numbering options presented in this section are designed to help you deploy your LANs' assets in the manner that meets all your needs and may even add some fun to the task. Note that not all the following options are compatible, and if you choose one, you may not be able to choose any other on a particular LAN. Such limitations are pointed out as the options are presented.

Letting Devices Choose Their Own Interface IDs

IPv6 is far less reliant on devices getting their addresses (or at least parts of them) from other systems than IPv4. Optimally, network prefixes should still come from other devices, notably routers using Router Advertisements (RAs), which you can read about in RFC 2461. By automatically getting your devices' network prefixes you also enable the renumbering of the entire network using the RR protocol mentioned earlier in this chapter. This will make your job managing the numbering of your network much easier.

As for your devices' interface IDs, you can choose whether to get them from an external source like a DHCP server or have the devices determine the values themselves. The preferred choice in IPv6 is for devices to set their own interface IDs. The downside of this choice is that, without a central authority, devices risk creating interface IDs that are in conflict with other devices on the LAN. IPv6 has foreseen this possibility however and provided a Duplicate Address Detection (DAD) protocol for devices to determine if they're colliding with something else on the LAN. If a device is in conflict, it can pick a different value for its interface ID, or if the device uses a hard-wired value, it can get off the network so as not to cause conflicts. See RFC 2462 for details on DAD and RFC 4429 for optimizations of mobile networks. With DAD, the risk of collision is eliminated, thereby allowing devices to set their own interface IDs and offload network-based resources.

The next few sections acquaint you with several interface-ID generation methods so as to help you pick what is right for you. Most of the methods that follow can be implemented by a device choosing to set its own interface ID or by the device getting the interface ID from a DHCP server. The exception to this is the EUI-64 method, which requires knowledge of the device's MAC address and is better off implemented locally rather than via a DHCP server.

When numbering your interfaces, there is one rule that applies to all of them and is new for IPv6. The traditionally forbidden IPv4 values at the start and end of the address range for a subnet (for example, '0' and '255' in an IPv4 '/24' block) are fair game in IPv6. The concept of broadcast addresses does not exist in IPv6 and, therefore, all interface IDs are available. Keep that in mind and you may even want to get gutsy and number a router or two as '0' just because you can.

Using 1, 2, 3, and So On

An old favorite LAN numbering scheme, and the first one you might think of for numbering your IPv6 interfaces, is to start at the bottom of the address space and assign IP addresses to devices in an increasing sequence. In IPv4 addressing, assuming you're numbering a '/24', the LAN's gateway router often is assigned the lowest address (for example, 192.168.0.1). Some networks provision the routers at '254'. Some number the workstations starting at '1' with an increasing sequence while numbering the servers from '253' with a descending sequence. Others create finer standards and put all DNS servers at '3', all Intrusion Detection Systems (IDSs) at '17', and so on. As you can imagine, there are many possibilities.

This manual numbering method is compatible with any other method that does not require the full interface ID space. That includes the EUI-64 method described later, provided you adhere to the use of the universal/local bit. You may find manual numbering impractical, however, especially if you ever have to renumber your interfaces when changing ISPs or switching from 6to4 to ISP-assigned address space.

When considering this or any other manual method, you should include as a deciding factor whether the equipment you're numbering allows you to set the interface IDs separately from the network prefixes. If you can do so, then you can hard-wire the interface IDs manually once and allow the devices to pick up their network prefixes from a local router using RAs, for example, to construct the full IPv6 address. If your equipment requires you to choose either fully automatic configuration (that is, the interface ID *and* the network prefix) or having to configure the entire IPv6 address manually, then you will have to revisit each device every time you change network prefixes, even if the interface IDs don't need to be changed. Over the course of your network's lifetime, this can become frustrating, not to mention error prone.

In addition to being possibly labor-intensive, this method doesn't take advantage of one of the greatest capabilities offered by IPv6, that is, the ability to hide your devices from casual hackers and network worms. Unlike even the largest of IPv4 LANs, the IPv6 interface ID space is large enough that you can make the job of someone or something looking for your devices in order to harm them totally impractical. You'll read more about that shortly. If hiding your assets is not something you feel you need to do, and the other limitations mentioned previously are also acceptable, then this method should be fine for you.

What Is Modified EUI-64 and What Are Its Faults?

EUI-64 is a mechanism defined by the IEEE for devices to create autonomously their own unique 64-bit identifiers from 48-bit link-layer MAC addresses, like those found on Ethernet and other link-layer interfaces (see `http://grouper` `.ieee.org/groups/msc/MSC200407/OnlineTutorialsB/EUI64.htm`). The IPv6 standards (see RFC 2464 and RFC 4291) modify EUI-64 encoding slightly. The modification allows network administrators to create locally unique interface IDs that are as short as possible (presumably because the administrators will have to enter them manually) while at the same time not colliding with the EUI-64 space. This is the reason for the designation "Modified EUI-64." In this book, you'll be reading only about the modified form, so it will be shortened to EUI-64.

Learning to Create an EUI-64 Address

As shown in Figure 7-6, EUI-64 maps 48-bit MAC addresses to 64-bit IPv6 interface IDs by concatenating the high-order 24 bits of the MAC address, the literal hexadecimal value 'FFFE' and the low-order 24 bits of the MAC address. Deviating from standard EUI-64, the high-order MAC-address bits are modified. The seventh-most significant bit (known as the "universal/local" bit) in the interface ID is zero in standard EUI-64 for all universally unique MAC addresses. This bit is complemented for modified EUI-64; in other words, if it's set in EUI-64, it is cleared in the modified form and vice versa. As such, the effect of complementing this bit adds two to the first octet of any globally unique MAC address. The following example shows the mapping of a typical Ethernet MAC address to an EUI-64 interface ID:

```
00-0e-a6-22-e1-0a      (MAC Address)
::020e:a6ff:fe22:e10a  (EUI-64 Interface ID)
```

Note the insertion of the 'FFFE' value into the middle of the address and the change from '00' to '02' of the most significant octet. By complementing the universal/local bit, the modified EUI-64 method allows network administrators to create short interface IDs (for example, '::2') for local use without fear of colliding with the EUI-64 space. If the bit had been left as originally defined in EUI-64, it would have to be set in all locally unique interface IDs (for example, ‘::200:0:0:2’), leading to a lot of extra typing and mistyping by administrators.

Mod MAC High (24)	FFFE (hex) (16)	MAC Low (24)

Figure 7-6: Modified EUI-64 format for interface IDs

Arguing EUI-64's Pros and Cons

EUI-64 is recommended by many for creating interface IDs, because it can be fully automated and is therefore suitable for IPv6 auto-configuration. In that respect, EUI-64 is a great thing. If you are trying to keep your devices hidden from worms and other attackers, however, this makes the search for devices on your LANs much easier than the random-numbering scheme you'll read about shortly.

Networking purists also argue that EUI-64 violates one of the primary rules of stack-based networks, that is, using information from one level of the stack in another. By encoding the MAC address in the IPv6 address, you are creating an artificial and unnecessary association between the link and network layers. Also, EUI-64 has only limited usefulness if the link layer doesn't use MAC addresses, for example, with PPP and other serial-line based protocols.

Putting the religious aspects of intermingling the layers aside for the moment, a more practical matter is that by encoding MAC addresses in your IPv6 addresses, you are advertising who manufactures your devices to the rest of the world. This is information that is better off not being made public, because hackers look for exactly this sort of thing to find potentially vulnerable systems.

Hacking EUI-64

EUI-64 addresses, while useful for auto-configuration, greatly reduce the potential size of your LAN's address space. This is not a problem from a provisioning point of view, because every device is supposed to have a unique MAC address and therefore will have unique EUI-64 interface IDs. The problem comes up when a hacker or a worm is trying to find a system to exploit. Remember, IPv6 has not eliminated the vulnerabilities associated with TCP, UDP, or the applications that use them. A bug in an e-mail or web server is as exploitable in IPv6 as it is in IPv4. The only defense IPv6 adds is that the server can be harder to find on the LAN in order to be exploited.

A comparison of how hard it is to find devices that use randomly generated interface IDs versus those that use EUI-64 IDs should serve to clarify the magnitude of the vulnerability in EUI-64. Assume you have a LAN with 1000 devices on it, each with one interface. If the interface IDs are randomly generated, then a brute-force search for the devices is pointless. Even if the time to test for the presence of each possible interface ID is only a millionth of a second (which is far too short to be realistic in terms of the required network traffic), to try enough values even to have a 50/50 shot of finding a device would take almost 300 years. In fact, the chances of an attacker finding a single one of your devices, if the devices are using random interface IDs, are about the same as winning the U.S. Mega-Millions lottery *twice*.

EUI-64 reduces the amount of address space that needs to be searched, making a brute-force search practical. This is because most of the MAC-address space on which EUI-64 is based is empty. Most MAC addresses consist of two equally sized parts:

- An Organizationally Unique Identifier (OUI) encoded in the upper 24 bits of the MAC address to represent the address's owner uniquely, for example the company that built the network interface hardware.

- An additional unique identifier encoded in the lower 24 bits of the MAC address and assigned by the OUI's owner to distinguish each of the network interfaces of the devices that it builds.

There is room for almost 17 million values in each of the preceding fields, but neither is fully utilized. The far-less utilized of the two fields is the OUI. As of August 2007, there are only approximately 10,000 OUIs registered with IEEE at http://standards.ieee.org/regauth/oui/index.shtml. That reduces the possible number of interface IDs by almost 1600-fold.

There are several assumptions you can make about the other unique identifier field, but even if you commit yourself to searching all 2^{24} values, the combination of the underutilized OUI field and the hard-wired 'FFFE' reduce the search space to a manageable 38 bits. That means if you're looking for an active interface in the previous 1,000-device LAN (at a more reasonable rate of 10,000 tries per second), you can expect to find one in fewer than four hours.

To close out the preceding glimpse into the hacker's mind, imagine you are looking for devices from a particular vendor, because you just discovered a vulnerability with their equipment. Focusing on one vendor allows you to reduce your search further by selecting only a handful of OUI values (most big vendors have more than one OUI assigned). The search space is now as few as 24 bits. With 10,000 tries per second, you'll find one of those vulnerable devices (or determine that there is none on the 1000-device LAN in question) in less than a second.

The preceding discussion clearly shows that EUI-64 is excellent for automatically numbering interface IDs, as long as it's OK that those IDs are readily discoverable by an intruder on the network. That implies you believe the devices using those interface IDs are patched and resilient to attack. If you believe in a layered defense (and that it's only the LAN owner's business what his or her interface IDs are), then you may prefer randomly generated interface IDs, which you'll read about next.

Using Random Interface IDs

If you have a background in cryptography, on first seeing IPv6 addresses you may have made an association with the large keys used in modern encryption systems. In fact, cryptography is the only other discipline where numbers the size used in IPv6 have any real meaning (as you may have gleaned if you answered the last test question in Chapter 2). A close relative to cryptography is random number generation. Without truly random numbers, most modern cryptographic systems become breakable, sometimes trivially so. By applying modern random-number generation technology and fully utilizing the 64 bits of the IPv6 interface ID, you can hide your devices from any form of brute-force search imaginable and render worms and casual hackers wandering through your network powerless.

Operating system products that support random interface ID generation include Microsoft Vista and Windows Server 2008. There may be others, but only Microsoft advertises this feature online. A search of DHCP products available in August 2007 yielded nothing that advertised the capability to generate random interface IDs, but this is not a complicated feature and if the market demands it, the products should follow shortly. Market demand may not be forthcoming, however, because the same reasons that make you want to use random interface IDs also encourage you to generate them on your devices, not get them from DHCP.

Understanding the Security Limitations in Random Interface IDs

Though randomly generated interface IDs prevent brute-force searches, you must not take this as a panacea to prevent all forms of attacks on your devices. Most attackers today, including automated ones, rely on e-mail directories, DNS searches, weak SNMP servers, and sniffing network traffic to discover new IP addresses. Brute-force searches are becoming the last choice and are only used if none of the preceding methods turns up any targets. It is for this reason that the decision to use random interface IDs is not a simple one. The benefits of more mainstream automatic configuration (for example, EUI-64) or ease of remembering important IP addresses (by manually configuring your default router and DNS server interfaces) should weigh in your decision regarding which method to use.

Dealing with Collisions in Random Generation

Random generation, like most of the other numbering methods, has the potential to cause conflicts between devices on your LAN. Practically speaking, the chances that two truly randomly generated interface IDs conflict with each other or that a single randomly generated ID conflicts with a manually configured or EUI-64-based ID are infinitesimally small (though not impossible). What is much more possible, however, is that the random number generators that create the interface IDs are flawed and limited to far less randomness than 64-bits' worth. In that case, collisions may be a practical concern.

As you read earlier, IPv6 deals with collisions using DAD, but DAD has a downside in that you have to advertise the address you want to use to everyone on the LAN in order to see if there are any conflicts. Because one of your reasons for using random interface IDs may be to hide your IP address from others, broadcasting it with DAD would defeat that purpose. If you don't want to use DAD for this reason, your only alternative is to trust that there will be no collisions and just have your devices generate their interface IDs and hope for the best. You can feel quite comfortable that this is a safe bet.

Using Cute Hexadecimal Names

Another manual method at your disposal employs the letters "A" through "F" from the hexadecimal system to create *hexwords* useful for assigning interface IDs that are easy to remember. In addition to the actual hexadecimal letters, many people map some of the digits to similar-looking letters not represented in hexadecimal, for example the numeral "5" is often used as the letter "S" in creating hexwords.

Interface IDs created using this method can be assigned to systems whose addresses should be memorable, like gateway routers, DNS, e-mail, web servers, and so on. You can see an example of the use of hexwords in Figure 7-1 with the "c0ff:ee" router. Someone has actually gone to the trouble of producing a comprehensive list of hexwords for the English language, which you can find at http://nedbatchelder.com/text/hexwords.html.

As you might imagine, if you don't want your devices to be easily found by hackers, using hexwords is not advisable. On the other hand, if you want people to remember the IPv6 addresses of key routers and other devices, using words as mnemonics is a great idea. As for conflict resolution, besides DAD, that's totally up to you.

What Other Numbering Methods Are There?

In terms of automatically generated interface IDs, the EUI-64 and random methods are the two most popular and the only ones available in product form. If you have access to software development resources, you can create your own, if you really feel the need (which you probably shouldn't). Be aware that if you do go making up your own automated numbering method, the one requirement you must meet for a workable solution is conflict avoidance so as not to overload your network with DAD traffic. In particular, you should avoid setting the universal/local bit so as to prevent future conflicts with EUI-64-based interface IDs. Otherwise, the parameters for automatic assignment are wide open.

For manual interface ID numbering, the same rules apply as for automatic generation, except you don't need software development resources. If you're not happy with the existing automated methods or any of the manual methods presented in this chapter, your choices of alternates are all but limitless. You can go with dates in history, the birthdays of your family members (though this is a bad idea from a personal privacy point of view), the numbers of the players on your favorite sports team, or your favorite lottery numbers. Do whatever you want that works for you.

Whatever numbering method you come up with, automatic or manual, remember to keep extensibility in mind. Don't use a method that runs out of numbers before you run out of interfaces to number. Think big and choose a method with far more numbers than you will ever have interfaces. To clarify the importance of extensibility, here's a real-world example from naming computer systems. The first time a newbie administrator set up a lab, he named the systems after planets in the solar system. He learned his lesson when the tenth system showed up (Pluto was still a planet then). The administrator named the next lab's systems using elements in the periodic table.

Managing Your Numbering Plan

While developing your numbering plan and for maintaining it afterwards, you will need a place to store all the network prefixes and manually configured interface IDs. The asset inventory you read about in Chapter 6, "Defining the Transition Preparation Steps," is an excellent place to put your numbering data, especially for associating the various numbers with the assets to which they apply. Moreover, there are many products for asset management that support IPv6, have friendly user interfaces, and simplify the daily work associated with managing a network's assets and IP addresses. If you weren't convinced while creating your asset inventory that a third-party asset-management product is the most productive and cost-effective way to take care of your network management data, perhaps in creating your numbering plan you will change your mind. You are encouraged to think about it while considering the following comparison of managing IPv4 addresses versus IPv6.

Because IPv4 addresses are small, they can be treated as integers and general-purpose spreadsheet applications can handle them with only a modest amount of work on your part. If you're not proficient in spreadsheet macros, then representing an IPv4 address in a form that the spreadsheet program can sort and search and that you can read in its familiar dotted-quad notation takes as few as 6 columns to implement, though 10 columns is more realistic.

Though viewing and searching for data is tolerable, entering and modifying it can be challenging and prone to errors, but many who manage IPv4 have learned to deal with the pain.

For IPv6, a similar solution would take at least 10 columns and lead to spreadsheet formulas the likes of which you've never seen (unless you deal in plasma physics or computational fluid dynamics). A more manageable solution would take at least 18 columns. In either case, all your addresses would be in their canonical form with all eight colon-separated groups of 16 bits intact (whether their values were zero or not), unless you add even more complexity to reduce them to the double-colon short form.

As suggested earlier in the book, to make a business-wise decision, you need to weigh the costs of building a tool to manage your numbering plan versus buying one. Though every enterprise's circumstances are different, it sure looks like managing IPv6 numbering is something you would want to pay somebody else to do for you.

Getting External IPv6 Connectivity

You saw earlier in the chapter that, with IPv6, in most cases getting your addresses and getting external connectivity are tightly coupled. ISPs are the preferred source for IPv6 addresses, and the addresses they provide are routed by them (and in many cases by them alone) into the global aggregated and hierarchical IPv6 routing infrastructure. You can feel comfortable that, if you find an ISP to provide you IPv6 addresses, they can also provide you the external connectivity you need.

For the U.S. government, there's no explicit requirement for external IPv6 connectivity, not in the June 2008 mandate, at least. It is assumed an agency's backbone will support IPv6, either natively or in a dual-stack mode. You would further assume that a given Agency X's and Agency Y's backbones should be able to communicate with each other using IPv6. That can be accomplished with dedicated circuits between agencies, and true "external" connectivity (for example, to the IPv6 pieces of the Internet) is not mandatory. By the time the June 2008 mandate comes due, all of the interesting and useful content on the Internet will still be available using IPv4 and much of it will likely not be reachable using IPv6. This gives very little reason for an agency to engage an IPv6 ISP. That's good, because there don't seem to be very many of them.

Finding Native Connectivity

As of the August 2007, very few ISPs offer native IPv6 services, at least in the United States. Europe is doing a little better and Japan has quite a few. Because this book focuses on the U.S. government's IPv6 transition, the search for connectivity will be limited to the United States.

In the U.S., NTT offers connectivity and IPv6 gateway services to its dual-stack backbone with Points of Presence (POPs) around the country, particularly in Washington, DC (`http://www.us.ntt.net/products/ipv6/`). NTT is also on the GSA schedule for its IPv6 services. U.S. government employees should go to `https://www.gsaadvantage.gov/` and enter GS-35F-0322T in the text box under "What are you looking for?" The contract is good until March 2012.

Other ISPs offering native IPv6 connectivity at present are Hurricane Electric in California (`http://www.ipv6.he.net/`) and Global Crossing in Reston, Virginia (`http://www.globalcrossing.com/ipkc/ipkc_ipv6.aspx`). Sprint is talking about native IPv6 connectivity with a planned debut in early 2008 (`http://www.sprintv6.net/Sprintv6.html`). You can presume that the various telecommunications companies listed for the Networx program earlier in the chapter also offer native IPv6 connectivity, at least for its government customers and probably for the private sector, too.

Going with Tunneled Connectivity

The majority of IPv6 connectivity in the U.S. is still via tunneling as of August 2007. NTT offers tunneled IPv6 connectivity through its GSA contract mentioned in the previous section, which means it should be available outside the contract, as well, for those enterprises that cannot go through the GSA. It should be safe to assume that the other native-connectivity providers listed earlier also offer tunneled connectivity, but you should contact them to be sure.

Make sure the ISP or tunnel broker you're thinking about using offers business grade services, because some tunnel brokers are collaborations of researchers and ISPs working on advanced IPv6 features or trying to promote IPv6 adoption. These are fine goals, but you need rock-solid connectivity and the research-based sites clearly state the tunnels' reliability and availability are not guaranteed.

Many such research tunnel brokers, however, offer free access to anyone, giving you the opportunity to experiment with external IPv6 connectivity and other features before committing to a connection or address space of your own. An excellent place to look for tunnel-broker POPs located near you is at `http://www.sixxs.net/pops/`.

Using 6to4 Relays

A special case of tunneling is 6to4, described earlier in the address-space provisioning section of the chapter. As you read then, connecting via tunneled addresses in 6to4 space is available to anybody who has been assigned at least one public IPv4 address. You might consider using 6to4 for redundancy with your IPv6 ISP connections. This way your enterprise's sites connected to IPv6 ISPs can also be on the IPv4 Internet, which is currently far more robust than the IPv6 version.

Though the IPv4 Internet is quite robust, not all the 6to4 relay sites (see next) are. They fall more into the category of experimental sites, like those mentioned in the previous section. In case you can't find a site that meets your reliability or availability needs, you can still use 6to4 for experimentation (because you don't have to engage an IPv6 ISP or get IPv6 address space), just like the other tunneling mentioned previously.

RFC 3068 created an IPv4 anycast address to get you to the 6to4 relay router closest to your site. Each site using 6to4 may wind up at a different relay router using this anycast address, and that's exactly what the anycast address is there for (optimal access to 6to4 relay services). A list of relay routers, should you not want to use the RFC 3068 anycast mechanism for some reason, is available at http://www.kfu.com/

Connecting Externally at Many Points

Any organization that can call itself an enterprise is using multiple ISPs for external IPv4 connectivity and will want to do so with IPv6, as well. You got a glimpse into the problems with multi-homing (as using multiple ISPs is called) earlier in the chapter when you were reading about provisioning your IPv6 addresses. In this section, you'll learn some of what is being proposed to overcome these problems so that redundant and load-balanced connections from enterprises to multiple ISPs can exist as they must in an IPv6 world. You'll also learn that the IPv6 multi-homing problem is nowhere close to being solved yet.

IPv4's address space is rather orthogonal to the routing infrastructure, which means that every ISP has to provide a path for almost every IP address to travel through it. This has led to nearly 200,000 global routing table entries on the Internet over the life of IPv4 and the people who designed IPv6 do not want to repeat that mistake.

The preferred hierarchical network architecture for IPv6 (not including a limited set of provider-independent addresses) requires each ISP to have its own allocations of addresses, which are further assigned to the ISP's customers (your enterprise, for example). To get to the rest of the IPv6 Internet, those addresses are aggregated by the ISP and presented to its upstream routers as a single block. There is no other way for those addresses to be routed to the rest of the Internet, except through the ISP. Should the ISP go offline, your enterprise and its addresses from the ISP go with it. You can attempt to mitigate the risk of your ISP going down by engaging another ISP for redundant connectivity. That ISP will provide you with a different set of IP addresses, which you can dutifully assign to your devices. This is actually not too bad, because each IPv6 interface can handle multiple addresses unlike

IPv4 interfaces. What is missing is a mechanism to switch from the failed set of addresses to the live ones when an ISP goes offline.

Many solutions have been suggested to alleviate the multi-homing problems in IPv6, some apparently coming from the late Rube Goldberg. Among the ones currently in favor is Shim6, a mechanism for assigning temporary values that look like IPv6 addresses for protocol layers above IP to use. Your web browsers, e-mail clients, and so on would see these addresses, as would you when you typed them in or got them back from a DNS lookup. These values would remain constant even through ISP outages and a thin layer or "shim" within the network layer would translate them to a currently active IPv6 address on an available ISP. Shim6 is still an Internet Draft (that is, non-standard) as of August 2007 and you can find its details at `http://www.shim6.org/draft-ietf-shim6-proto-08.txt`.

Other solutions that have been proposed to solve IPv6 multi-homing problems include using the RR protocol for automated network renumbering should an ISP fail (but that will not be instantaneous like current IPv4 failover is) or possibly mobile IPv6 features. Solving the multi-homing problem is extremely important and, at this point, it is too soon to tell which solution will prevail, including the possibility of falling back to a solution similar to what IPv4 uses. With ever-increasing CPU speeds and memory sizes in routers, as long as the routing tables don't grow any faster than the underlying hardware's capabilities, the extra overhead in the Internet is worth the elimination of extensive amounts of complexity at every multi-homed site world-wide. The best thing you can do is to see, when you contact your ISPs for multi-homed IPv6 connectivity, what their current strategy is and what commitments the ISPs can make regarding redundancy and transparent failover. If it all makes sense, use those ISPs. If not, find others or factor the potential for loss of connectivity into your overall network risk analyses.

Assessing Whether to Deploy IPsec with IPv6

Preceding chapters suggested you consider deploying IPsec during your IPv6 transition, because you're going to be visiting most (if not all) of your assets for inventory purposes and almost certainly will be upgrading or replacing some of them. While you're undertaking that exercise, laying the foundations for IPsec may be worth your while. With a foundation of IPsec in place, you can customize specific servers or whole sections of your network to operate with different (sometimes otherwise mutually exclusive) security profiles while sharing the same physical infrastructure, thus saving you money, as well.

Imagine a network where you could encrypt sensitive employee data while it's in transit from one HR system to another across the country. Many companies employ WAN-based VPNs, but leave the local network segments wide open. This is ironic, because report after report in the security community points the finger at insiders being the biggest threat to an enterprise's security.

In addition to protecting employee information, if you are in a field that, for example, manages medical records, being able to protect that data in transit with something like IPsec may soon become mandatory under regulations like HIPAA (see `http://www.hhs.gov/ocr/hipaa/`). Other fields are being subjected to similar regulatory scrutiny to keep sensitive and private information protected. IPsec may even have application in your classified environments, if you have any.

Possibly the largest IPsec deployment (and enterprise-wide IPv6 deployment, for that matter) is going on at Microsoft. Microsoft's Server and Domain Isolation (SDI) technology (`http://www.microsoft.com/sdisolation`) is a well thought out solution for network security based on IPsec to provide real protection in a practical manner. If you're even considering deploying IPsec (now or later), then you should investigate SDI.

Determining What Deploying IPsec Entails

You'll find that much of the work in implementing IPsec is made easier with proper planning, just like much of the IPv6 transition work is. During that planning, you'll need to come up with:

- A security architecture for how you want to distribute and manage your identification and authentication information for users and devices, which is the basis for how devices decide whether to trust each other and establish secure communications.

- Estimates of the resources required to deploy IPsec, what exactly must be done (for example, equipment upgrades and replacements, procurements of new software), and the costs of the deployment.

- Use cases (see Chapter 6, "Defining the Transition Preparation Steps") or some other means to determine that your deployment was successful, has all the capabilities you need from it, and functions correctly.

Note that there are many vendors, both of network infrastructure as well as server and desktop software that can help you with each of these items. Despite that, during your planning process, you may come to the conclusion that you do not have the resources to deploy IPsec or that you do not want to take the risk of making two big changes at the same time. This is perfectly sound thinking. Should you, however, want to deploy IPsec in part of your network or take the opportunity presented by your IPv6 transition work to assess what such a deployment would entail (for example, while you're inventorying your assets), this section provides some basic information on how IPsec works and what you will need to deploy it.

Getting to Know the Basics of IPsec

This book is about IPv6, not IPsec, so the following is not meant to be a comprehensive tutorial. Instead, it is meant to give you the vocabulary to have meaningful discussions with your vendors and to understand better the literature available from them as well as what is publicly available in the RFCs and so forth.

An important thing to know about IPsec is that it is not an all or nothing deal for your network. Down to the device and user level you can configure security policies defining to whom a device is willing to speak and how. This allows you to deploy IPsec piecewise, much like IPv6, so that you can get a feel for what it means to your enterprise before implementing it everywhere.

Wherever you do decide to deploy IPsec, you have the option to make its use mandatory or merely optional down to the device and user level. In other words, you can configure device 'A' to initiate a conversation with 'B' asking to use IPsec, but if 'B' cannot do so (or has an incompatible security policy), 'A' can choose to proceed anyway without it. Of course, 'B' may have its own requirements on anyone communicating with using IPsec that 'A' cannot meet. In that case, 'A' and 'B' may not be able to find a common ground for communications. Sometimes, however, that may be exactly the way you want it to be.

Introducing the AH and ESP Headers

IPsec is implemented using two extension headers to the IP protocol. They are the:

- Authentication Header (AH) defined in RFC 4302
- Encapsulated Security Payload (ESP) defined RFC 4303

As the name suggests, the AH extension provides authentication services tying some form of identity (for example, a user's) to each IP packet. It does not provide any kind of confidentiality for the payload and it does not protect the entire IP packet header. The ESP extension provides authentication *and* these other features. In practice, the AH extension is not used often because the ESP extension can emulate it simply by using null encryption, discussed shortly.

Recalling how IPv6 packets are constructed from Figure 2-3, the AH and ESP extensions insert headers between the IP header and the ultimate payload, TCP for example. The ESP extension also uses a trailer after the encrypted payload to account for any padding added by the encryption.

Understanding Common Algorithms and Key Lengths

IPsec offers a variety of algorithms for authentication and encryption. This is to facilitate interoperability world-wide, as well as handle the situation where one of the algorithms is cracked and rendered insecure. It's unlikely you'll be rolling your own IPsec software, so the details of the implementations of these algorithms are unimportant, but you should know the names and a little about each so as to recognize them and help select those that are appropriate for your particular applications. To that end, each algorithm's name, order of preference or relative strength, and its key lengths are provided here.

Both the AH and ESP extensions support a large variety of algorithms. In order to assure some minimum level of interoperability between implementations, however, RFC 4305 defines the official preferences as follows. For the AH extension, the algorithms in order of preference are:

SHA-1. This is the best choice for compatibility and algorithm strength. See RFC-2404 for the implementation details.

AES. This is an encryption algorithm adapted for authentication. AES is an up and coming algorithm that may replace SHA-1 in the years to come. See RFC 3566.

MD5. This is an older algorithm with some weaknesses in other applications (but purportedly not for authentication). It remains in use for compatibility with legacy implementations. See RFC 2403.

Note that SHA-1 and AES are U.S. FIPS standards, which may be important for government implementations.

The preferred authentication choices in RFC 4305 for the ESP extension are the same as for the AH extension, except a null algorithm has been added. See the next section for details. For encryption, the ESP choices are (in order of preference):

Triple DES. This is the old DES algorithm applied three times in series over the data to encrypt it. The key length is therefore up to three times that of DES or 168 bits. For details of Triple DES's use in IPsec, see RFC 2451, which is a little dated and mentions other algorithms you can safely ignore.

AES. The same algorithm used in authentication, this time for its intended purpose of encryption. There are two modes of AES supported in IPsec, one with a 128-bit key (see RFC3602), and the other with 128, 192, or 256-bit key (see RFC 3686). AES is gaining popularity and is expected someday to take the #1 spot away from Triple DES.

DES. This is an oldie (and not so goodie) algorithm around since the 1970s that has had known weaknesses for years. NIST issued a statement declaring DES inadequate in July 2004 (see the US Government

Federal Register, Docket No. 040602169-4169-01). It remains supported purely for compatibility with legacy equipment and for use where export controls forbid anything else. See RFC 2405 for details of the DES implementation for IPsec.

NULL. See the next section and RFC 2410.

In a further effort to promote compatibility, RFC 4308 defines suites of algorithms based on implementations in common use. Suite "VPN-A" matches commonly used corporate VPN security at the time of RFC 4308's publication (December 2005). It employs the ESP extension using Triple DES encryption with SHA-1 authentication. Suite "VPN-B" is expected to be the commonly used corporate VPN security within a few years of RFC 4308's publication. It also employs the ESP extension, but uses one of the AES encryption modes (and 128-bit keys) along with AES for authentication, as well.

All of the preceding algorithms, excluding the null one, are known as block ciphers. That means they operate on multi-byte blocks of data and, if the input is not a multiple of the block size, padding is introduced to make it so. The output (which is the same size as the input) will therefore be larger. Most of the ciphers use blocks in the 8-byte to 16-byte range, meaning that smaller IP packets (for example, 40 bytes or so) could suffer up to 50-percent growth due to padding and IPsec headers. Larger packets will suffer less growth as a percentage (as little as 4 percent for typical "large" packets), but an additional 4 to 8 bytes will be added on average due to padding alone. You should account for this when planning your bandwidth of IPsec will be deployed.

What Is Null Encryption?

Null encryption is exactly what it sounds like. It is a pass-through algorithm that copies its input to its output with no changes. RFC 2410 defines null encryption in a tongue-in-cheek manner that is certainly worth a read if you're into cryptography. If you didn't know it was serious, it could be taken for an April Fool's RFC.

The purpose of null encryption is far from a joke, though. The algorithm (more like an option) is useful for implementing your IPsec infrastructure without obfuscating the packets while debugging. It also gives you a way to turn things off later at a segment or device level for troubleshooting. Null encryption also allows standard Intrusion Detection Systems (IDSs) and other traffic monitoring equipment to continue to work in the less-sensitive areas of your network without having to become part of encrypted conversations.

Perhaps most importantly, null encryption allows you to outfit your entire enterprise with IPsec homogeneously with only the already-tunable authentication and encryption algorithms changing from LAN to LAN or device to device. This is far easier than implementing parts of the network with AH extensions only, because you don't think you'll need encryption in those segments, only to find out later that you do. Should such a situation occur and you are using ESP extensions and null encryption, you can simply substitute a real algorithm and within the blink of an eye have an encrypted and secure network.

Getting Keys for All Those Algorithms

IPsec consumes a lot of keys in its daily life, due to the frequent instantiations and dissolutions of Security Associations (SAs) between communicating entities. New keys also need to be generated to replace those that have been in use too long or that have been used on too much data and that might be in risk of compromise. This is especially true on high-throughput sessions. The more information that is encrypted by a given key or the more time that passes with that key in use, the better the chances that an attacker can guess the key, and eavesdrop on the session or falsify authentication information. For that reason, keys are changed out or "rekeyed" regularly.

The keys just described can be thought of as secondary keys in that they are derived automatically from other primary keys. That's not the correct terminology, but for purposes of keeping explanations simple, it's accurate and concise. With the frequent turnover of secondary keys during all the IPsec sessions that can take place on a typical enterprise network, manual key generation at the session level could never keep up. The other function the primary keys serve is to enable authentication of the two sides of an IPsec SA to each other. This allows each side to apply its security policy to the other in a trusted manner to see if they're allowed to communicate.

The IPsec folks defined the Internet Key Exchange (IKE) protocol to use the primary keys to establish SAs and to generate secondary keys securely. IKE is the end result of several other efforts in distributed key exchange and management with names like ISAKMP, Oakley, Photuris, and SKEME. IKE is composed of parts of some of those protocols plus some new stuff. IKE version 1 (IKEv1) is defined by RFC 2409. Like the algorithms for which it supplies keys, IKE supports secure authentication and key exchange using combinations of Triple DES, AES, SHA-1, and MD5. IKEv1 has been made obsolete by IKEv2 (see RFC 4306 and RFC 4307), but IKEv1 implementations are still in use.

IKE supports authentication of communicating parties using digital signatures, public-key encryption, and shared secrets. So, if you have a Public-Key Infrastructure (PKI), you can use IKE with ease. If not, that's OK, too. You can just use shared secrets. The shared secrets need to be distributed to the parties that wish to communicate in order to set up an SA from which to create secondary keys. There are numerous ways to distribute shared secrets securely. Microsoft, in its SDI technology mentioned earlier, uses the Kerberos protocol, which you can read more about in RFC 4120.

Factoring in any Bandwidth Requirements

As mentioned in a prior chapter, your IPv6 transition is not occurring in a vacuum. You are not upgrading your assets to produce a network that is exactly the same, except that after the transition it will use IPv6 headers whereas before it used IPv4 ones. Simultaneous to your IPv6 transition needs, you have to deploy more applications, bring new users online, connect new sites and improve connectivity and speed of access to existing sites, and so on.

For all those reasons, you need to assess not only whether your network assets are IPv6 capable, but also whether they can handle the bandwidth you'll need. Other than the IPv6 transition, it's assumed you've faced all these upgrade and new functionality issues before. However you addressed them then will work here, too. The purpose of this section is to show you what additional bandwidth IPv6 will draw, so that you can factor it into your overall build-out plans.

Determining the Effect of Increased Header Sizes

In a realistic comparison, IPv4 headers are 20 octets in size because nobody really uses IPv4 options. IPv6 headers, without any extensions in use, are 40 octets in size, making them twice as large. This argument has caused several IPv6 naysayers to warn that IPv6 will clog the pipes of the Internet and your enterprise network by doubling the amount of traffic. For the purposes of the following, assume that when your transition to IPv6 is completed, your network will handle the exact same number of packets as it did with IPv4. If your network was filled with empty (header-only) IPv4 packets before the transition, then it is true the number of octets of traffic would have doubled from IPv4 to IPv6. You know very well, however, that this is not even close to realistic.

The majority of the traffic on your network is probably e-mail and web transactions. Those are TCP-based and the TCP header is at least 20 octets long. Assuming no data in the TCP payload (another absurdity), then IPv6 has only increased the number of octets flying around your network by 50 percent. If you add data, say 40 octets for an HTTP query of a typical web URL, the total packet size is now only 25-percent bigger with IPv6 than with IPv4. Finally, if you increase the payload size to 1,000 octets, which is representative of a medium size HTTP response or a roughly 25-line e-mail message (with no graphics, images, and so on), the overhead increase with IPv6 is less than 2 percent.

The preceding analysis did not cover ICMP and UDP, which are lighter-weight protocols and fairly prevalent on your network. ICMP is used for returning error codes or testing connectivity. The biggest UDP contribution is probably DNS or one of the Microsoft SMB protocols. If you believe the analysis though, that TCP is by far the most prevalent IP-based traffic on your network, then you can see that worrying about header size is unjustified.

Estimating Other Packet Size Changes

Other than the marginal increase in packet size from the bigger IPv6 headers, you can expect to have larger packets after your IPv6 transition for the following reasons:

- Tunneling, because you'll be adding a 20-octet IPv4 header to every tunneled packet. This will likely be your most frequent cause for packet inflation. You can see it isn't a big increase.

- IPsec, should you choose to deploy it. The cost is the same in IPv6 as it would be for IPv4, so the IPsec bandwidth decision is orthogonal to the IPv6 one.

- Fragmentation, if your end hosts decide to send packets larger than the MTU. This should occur only in isolated cases. In other words, if you're not seeing fragmentation with IPv4, you probably won't see it with IPv6. If you are seeing it with IPv4, then you already know from earlier in the book that you have to deal with IPv6's increased minimum MTU size and upgrade your equipment or implement link-layer fragmentation handling. You are also encouraged to implement path-MTU discovery so as to avoid fragmentation even more.

There are other IPv6 extension headers that will increase the size of a packet (you can read about them in RFC 2460), but they are likely to be as popular as their IPv4 cousins, so no appreciable increase in network bandwidth utilization is expected.

What Additional Traffic Can You Expect?

When factoring for additional bandwidth requirements, the biggest increase you're going to get is from all the auto-configuration traffic, should you choose to implement any or all of those IPv6 features. Between routers announcing the network prefixes they offer to workstations looking for network-layer connectivity and configuration information, while at the same time avoiding conflicts with other devices on the LAN, IPv6 networks can become awash with auto-configuration messages. RFC 2461 and RFC 2462 define these different messages, under what circumstances, and how frequently you will see them on your network.

Before you panic too much, there is already a lot of this kind of traffic flying around networks in the form of periodic log messages, Windows SMB messages, and so on, so the net increase is minor. For example, the default interval between unsolicited Router Advertisements is five minutes. That's hardly enough traffic to worry about. Other messages, like DADs, are sent on demand, meaning when a new device comes online and wants to find a non-conflicting address for itself. Again, this is a rare event.

Investigating More-Advanced IPv6 Capabilities

As you've read several times so far in this book, IPv6 offers advanced features that promise to enable many new, useful, and exciting capabilities in your network. Most of these new features, except maybe IPsec, are probably best left to later upgrade projects. Your primary goal for your first transition should be to assure you establish a solid beach-head in IPv6. Two IPv6 advanced features worth considering for your first transition, however, are secure auto-configuration and mobile IPv6. This section introduces them both and gives you enough information to jump-start your own investigation or decide that you can wait until a later time (perhaps when more resources are available) to implement them.

Adopting the New Secure Auto-Configuration Features

Understanding the security features in later forms of IPv6 auto-configuration (or put another way, the lack of realizable security in the earlier forms), and assessing your need for them, obligates you at least to investigate whether the overhead they require is worth the security benefits they offer.

IPv6 defined Neighbor Discovery (ND) in RFC 2461 to enable auto-configuration of networks, routers, and other devices. Without some form of authentication of the ND protocol, several attacks can be launched to cause denial of service, misdirection of traffic, and so on. RFC 3756 provides an excellent analysis of the weaknesses in ND when too much trust is placed (or misplaced) by one device on another one without knowing a little about the other device first.

The original ND implementation relied on the use of IPsec in areas where the trust among devices was suspect. Due to complexities in defining IPsec security policies for the ICMPv6 messages associated with ND, as documented in `http://tools.ietf.org/html/draft-arkko-icmpv6-ike-effects-02`, the original plan to secure ND with IPsec became problematic. To meet the security goals required for ND that were originally charged to IPsec, Secure Network Discovery (SEND) was created.

SEND is defined in RFC 3971 and deliberately does not use IPsec to meet its security requirements. It still uses cryptographic mechanisms like those in IPsec, but they are incorporated into the SEND protocol, rather than separate IPsec extensions. One of SEND's mechanisms introduces chains of trust between devices desiring to use a router as their Internet gateway, for example, and a router purportedly offering such gateway services. If the chains meet at a common point that both parties trust, then the devices can feel comfortable using the router. If not, the router is suspect and perhaps shouldn't be used.

No matter how trusted your network is, SEND is a good idea. As mentioned earlier, insiders are the greatest source of attacks and requiring routers (and other devices for that matter) to identify themselves in a trusted manner eliminates a host of vulnerabilities. Because SEND is quite new (as of August 2007), there are few implementations. None of the vendors you would expect to offer it in their network infrastructure product lines is promoting it, so it's probably not implemented in them yet.

There is an open source implementation of SEND from DoCoMo USA Labs (not surprisingly an NTT company, given its interest in IPv6) that runs on Linux and FreeBSD and that you can use for experimentation or if you have software development resources with which to incorporate it into your production infrastructure. The implementation is available at `http://www.docomolabs-usa.com/lab_opensource.html`. By the time you're ready to make your transition, SEND should be available from sources other than research labs, too.

Introducing Mobile IPv6

Mobile IPv6 is an exciting feature that allows your mobile devices to be found and communicated with even if they are connected on the other side of the world from their usual home. The best part is that they can be found using those well-known home addresses. Think of mobile IPv6 as call forwarding on steroids.

Part of the need for mobile IPv6 stems from the ISP-centric addressing hierarchy discussed earlier in the chapter, which ties IPv6 addresses to both geographic regions managed by the RIRs and furthermore to the territories of the ISPs from which the addresses are assigned. Even if this were not the case, it is impossible for most mobile devices to retain the same IP address regardless of where they are in the world. In IPv6 terms, the best you could hope for is to retain your interface IDs as your devices move around.

Not all networks presently have a need for mobile IPv6 (you got away without it this long, right?), but networks with large numbers of mobile assets (for example, the modern military, cell phone networks, and so on) benefit from an easier way to stay connected while their devices are on the move. And as mobility becomes more commonplace, there will come a time in the not too distant future where mobility services will be required by most enterprises, if not all of them.

RFC 3775 defines IPv6's mobility features. In addition to the basic call-forwarding functionality, mobile IPv6 also allows you to communicate the visiting addresses your devices are using while away from your home network to calling parties, so they can contact the devices directly. Those wishing to connect to one of your mobile devices (which they may not know is mobile) can use your home address to start a session. Like with call forwarding in telephony, an agent you have running in your home network can assist your mobile device in providing the address you are visiting to the calling party, who can then use it for all future conversations until you move again. This makes for more efficient routing, especially if the caller is sitting next to you on a business trip and your home network is a continent away.

If you are deploying IPsec, your mobile devices can benefit from that deployment, as well. RFC 3776 defines how IPsec is applied to mobility to protect the signaling between a mobile device and its agent back home. With the various updates to IPsec in recent years, the application of it to mobility has also been updated and is reflected in RFC 4877.

To round out your tour of mobile IPv6, you should know that RFC 3963 extends mobile IPv6 with the Network Mobility (NEMO) protocol to allow for more seamless and uninterrupted connectivity as devices move around to different networks. Finally, from the network management side of things, RFC 4295 defines the SNMP management aspects of mobility including a mobile IPv6 MIB.

In keeping in line with the goals of this book, the preceding discussion was not meant to make you a mobile-IPv6 expert. Instead, it was meant to give you enough of an idea of what mobile IPv6 is about to decide if it's something you need to think about for your present transition or whether you can put it off until later, or perhaps not implement mobile IPv6 at all. For far more thorough coverage of the technical details behind mobile IPv6, refer to Blanchet's book cited in "Further Reading" in Chapter 1. You can also read the RFCs mentioned here, but Blanchet conveys the information more clearly. Refer to the RFCs, though, for the final word on the bits and bytes of the implementations and standards, should you have the need.

Testing Your Knowledge

You were introduced to many important concepts in this chapter, so there are a few more questions than in prior ones. The questions aim to get you thinking about IPv6's unique attributes that aren't part of the IPv4 universe to which you are accustomed. As before, a little bit of trivia is thrown in to impress your friends at cocktail parties (though, you should probably consider alternate cocktail parties, if this impresses your friends). Answers are in Appendix A.

1. What are AfriNIC, APNIC, ARIN, LACNIC, and RIPE? What do the abbreviations mean?

2. What properties do IPv6 addresses have, particularly in how the addresses are acquired, that IPv4 addresses do not? What do you need to be aware of, as an enterprise customer, based on those properties?

3. In what sizes should ISPs assign IPv6 address spaces to their customers, given the recommendations of the RIRs?

4. Can you get IPv6 addresses directly from an RIR?

5. Can you use 6to4 with dynamically allocated (for example, via DHCP) IPv4 addresses?

6. If IPv6 addresses are so plentiful, why do you need a numbering plan?

7. If you are setting up three IPv6 LANs, the first requiring 30 single-interface devices, the second requiring 900, and the third requiring 8200, what size network prefixes would you provision (including the subnet portion) and how many addresses would be set aside for each LAN for growth based on those provisioned sizes?

8. What are the three drivers for how you should implement sub-netting in your enterprise's sites?

9. In defining your hierarchical sub-netting, what should you take into account when determining the levels of the hierarchy and their sizes? What may have Hierarchy (C) in Figure 7-5 failed to take into account?

10. What are EUI-64-based interface IDs and what do you need to consider before using them?

11. What is arguably the most important question you should ask your potential IPv6 ISPs that you would take for granted with IPv4?

12. Extra Credit (or, Irrelevant Trivia): It would take 64 coin tosses to produce a random IPv6 interface ID. If you had a six-sided die, how many tosses of that would it take?

13. Truly Irrelevant Trivia: Which RIR covers Antarctica?

CHAPTER 8

Defining the Transition Execution Steps

I'm okay to go! I'm okay to go! I'm okay to go...
— **Eleanor Arroway,**
played by Jodie Foster
in the film, *Contact.*

I enjoy painting the rooms in our house. My wife is the interior decorator (and she does an inspired job) and I see to the execution. Over the 12 years we've lived in the house, I've done nine rooms, some of them twice. Because we bought the house brand new, it was great to watch the "builder white" walls take on color. Like I said, I enjoy the painting. What I don't enjoy is the other 90 percent of the work, which is the removal of most of the furniture, the taking down of pictures (which, if you know me, are a real pain to get back up and level just right), the covering of the floors, windows, and remaining big furniture, and the sanding. I hate the sanding most of all, because the builder's painters must have mixed pebbles into the original paint when they applied it. When the last of the sanding is done, I actually consider the job done. The painting is almost incidental. I bring this up, because you've probably come to the point by this chapter to ask, "When will I actually upgrade something in my network to IPv6?" Well, this is the last chapter of covering floors and sanding walls. When this chapter ends, you'll have started executing your IPv6 transition activities. Hopefully, as the tasks reach completion as smoothly as my sanded walls, you'll appreciate all the preparation you did.

What You'll Learn

This chapter covers what you need to know to execute the steps of your IPv6 transition. The chapter is not about the steps involved in installing software, running cables, or putting equipment in racks. You should already know how to do that. Instead, the chapter covers organizing all the tasks you planned in the previous chapters into groups of activities containing work items and executing in maintenance windows. You'll learn how to identify and resolve dependencies between tasks and how to use the knowledge of those dependencies to put your tasks into an optimal order for execution. You'll also learn the best locations in your network for your first transition activities, so that you might learn the ropes someplace where you can do the least damage.

You'll learn other ways to make your transition activities less risky, as well, like trading off speed of execution for resilience to failures, both predictable ones and unforeseen ones. Where you can't avoid risk completely, you'll learn to define reversion paths that will allow you to restore your network to a normal state, should your transition activities not go as planned.

The chapter concludes with some final tasks you must perform before you can start your transition activities, the last task being the informing of everyone who needs to know that you're finally ready to get started.

Organizing the Transition Execution Activities

Your IPv6 transition is (or should be) as well-defined a series of maintenance events as you have ever planned and executed. This is because you will be upgrading or replacing core assets across your network's entire infrastructure, thereby impacting every network user. Despite this large amount of change, by pacing yourself over a well-managed time frame, the scheduling of your transition activities should, with rare exception, fit into your enterprise's predefined maintenance windows.

Seeing as there are many activities to execute across your whole enterprise and that the transition execution will be spread out over months, you have many choices on how to do your scheduling. Having many choices is good, because your scheduling is not only about fitting activities into time slots, but also about determining the dependencies between activities and which activities must precede others. This section helps you to organize your activities, first by helping you decide at a strategic level how you want to proceed and then by providing guidance for organizing the daily details.

Picking What to Switch Out and in What Order

The asset and capabilities inventories you created with the help of Chapter 6 Defining the Transition Preparation Steps gave you the information you needed to decide which assets to upgrade or replace, as well as what network capabilities to preserve during the process and after its completion. At this point, you're ready to start execution and only have to figure out what to do first. You should have a list of equipment and software applications that are not IPv6 capable. You are most likely not going to include every single one of those assets in your first transition exercise, but the complete list is still helpful for you to decide a strategic direction.

If you're part of the U.S. federal government and, therefore, subject to the June 2008 OMB transition mandate, then you need only concern yourself with your network backbone assets for now. Even if you're not affected by the OMB mandate, the backbone is a good place to start your transition, because it will make connecting newly upgraded IPv6-capable sites to the overall IPv6 network infrastructure easier in later transition exercises. There are several different backbone architectures and which one your network falls more into will affect your transition choices. The next section delves further into backbone architecture issues.

Another strategy you can employ, based on the results of your asset inventory, is to complete the transitions of network segments or sites that are already most of the way there. For example, if you find from your inventory that 90 percent of the assets at a given site are already IPv6 capable, you may want to complete the upgrades and replacements of the other 10 percent of the assets and then provision IPv6 addresses to all the assets and external connectivity to that site. By making that site fully IPv6 capable with a minimum of transition effort (and capital), you will get the experience of a full transition cycle on a smaller scale and possibly with less impact or risk to your overall network capabilities.

Taking a page from modern software development methodologies, smaller-scale projects, like the example just described, that undergo the entire transition cycle in a much shorter time than it would take to execute a full IPv6 transition of your entire enterprise network, are useful for learning all the possible pitfalls of IPv6 transition quickly. The alternative breadth-first approach exposes you repeatedly to the earliest phases of your IPv6 transition and you will surely become an expert in handling those phases optimally. The breadth-first approach's downside, however, is to leave any execution of the later phases of the transition cycle for future activities that may be months away, which means you are leaving the risks of there being planning errors or that your knowledge of how IPv6 transition should occur untested until much closer to your transition deadline.

From the preceding discussion, you should see that, even if you choose your first IPv6 transition project to be changing something as significant as your whole network backbone, one or two mini-projects that first change out parts of that backbone from soup to nuts in the early days of the transition will help you clarify the risks in all phases.

The depth-first methodology described earlier applies particularly well to your IPv6 transition, because replacing assets that aren't IPv6 capable with new IPv6-capable assets whose overall capabilities are the supersets of their predecessors is often the easy part. For example, a router that is IPv6 capable replacing one that isn't, where both have exactly the same IPv4 capabilities and where those capabilities are managed in exactly the same way, is hardly a transition and should be a non-event when dealing with any reputable vendor. It's in the later network numbering and connectivity exercises that your true IPv6 experience is gained, because those activities are where you'll actually be using the new router's IPv6 capabilities.

Chapter 12, "Selecting an Enterprise Transition Strategy," covers what is involved in deciding whether to plan and execute your IPv6 transition from the network backbone outward or the network edges inward. Because this book is tailored to the federal mandates for IPv6 transition, the focus until that chapter is on backbone-centric transition activities. No matter how you decide to proceed with your enterprise's IPv6 transition, keep the depth-first methodology in mind when organizing your transition activities and use it where possible, because it is an excellent way to eliminate risks in your overall IPv6 transition.

Comparing Network Backbone Architectures

Your enterprise network surely doesn't look like any other one in the world, but all network architectures share common traits. In this section, you'll read about two general network backbone architectures that are used by all enterprises. Some enterprises favor one of these architectures over the other, whereas others mix and match the two throughout their network. The choices each enterprise's network management makes are based on the network's mission, the past experiences of the network management staff, and several other factors. All network backbones, however, have traits of either the symmetric or asymmetric architectures described in the following sections. After describing these two architectures, you'll read how to tune your IPv6 transition activities to each one.

Understanding Symmetric Network Backbones

Symmetric network backbones (a term that, as far as I can tell, I made up because it returns zero hits on both AltaVista and Google as of August 24, 2007) are composed of network elements that are fundamentally the same in size, capacity, and so on, across the whole backbone. Figure 8-1 shows an example of such a backbone, loosely based on the logical network diagram in Figure 4-1. In Figure 8-1, you'll note that each backbone router is physically located in one of the facilities symbolized by the clouds. This differs from the Figure 4-1 backbone that is represented by a logical cloud tied at no particular physical location.

The symmetric backbone shown in Figure 8-1 is composed of eleven, "Series '7'" routers, which are presumably heavy-duty equipment, but not the top of the line from the given vendor. Such upper-middle class routers are less expensive, have very good performance characteristics, and reasonable scalability. They differ from their top-of-the-line counterparts perhaps by supporting fewer total connections, topping out at lower aggregate bandwidths, or not being as resilient to faults. They may support hot-standby configurations or they may not. In summary, they're good routers for their lower price point and one of them can handle a smaller enterprise location just fine. Larger locations may need to utilize two or more such routers to meet their connectivity, bandwidth, or fault resilience needs.

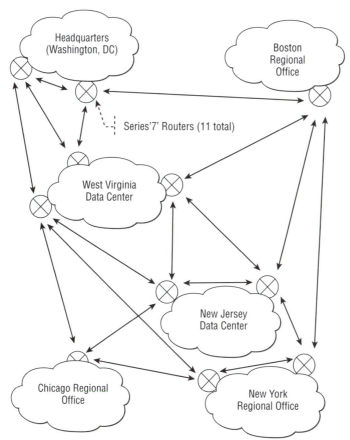

Figure 8-1: Example of a symmetric network backbone

The backbone in Figure 8-1 doesn't have a center, per se, but is instead composed of six locations that are essentially peers. Each location has connectivity to at least two others, partly for fault resilience and perhaps partly for better aggregate bandwidth. Similarly, almost every router has at least two paths out for traffic, plus the path going back the way the traffic originally arrived. The latter path is wasteful, however, because any traffic directed back the way it came should never have been directed to the given router in the first place.

You'll note that the Boston and Chicago regional offices are not as large (or perhaps as important) as the other locations, because they do not have redundant routers connecting them to the other locations. You'll also note that the ~~ing of lines connecting the outlying locations so that, should connectivity~~ to the West Virginia or New Jersey data centers be lost, there are still ways for the regional offices and headquarters to communicate.

One of the negative tradeoffs in choosing a symmetric backbone architecture, like the one in Figure 8-1, is the increased distance between locations in terms of network-layer (for example, IP protocol) hops. Certain locations are one hop apart, but many are three hops. In addition, keeping the hop counts minimal throughout the network requires running dedicated lines from the Washington headquarters to Boston, for example, and from Chicago to New York. Such lines are not cheap, but not using them increases your hop counts further. Obviously, in such a small example the hop counts are all going to be small, but you can imagine the network expanding to include offices in more distant places like Dallas, San Francisco, and Seattle with the hop counts increasing accordingly, along with the number of expensive dedicated lines required to keep hop counts down.

The specific choices in hop counts versus number of dedicated lines are based on parameters outside the scope of this example, but you can see there are tradeoff decisions to be made. Other benefits of symmetric architectures that offset the cost of increased hop counts can include less training for network management staff (they only need to learn how to manage a few types of devices), more readily managed "canned" router configurations, and perhaps better vendor discounts when buying in bulk. Other downsides include putting all your eggs in one security basket, should a vulnerability unique to the Series '7' routers be discovered.

Understanding Asymmetric Network Backbones

Asymmetric network backbones have network elements that tend to be bigger and more capable as you approach the network's center and you may have only a handful of really big nodes at the network's core. An example of such an asymmetric backbone is shown in Figure 8-2. Instead of all the network elements being mid-size Series '7' routers, as in the architecture in Figure 8-1, the network elements in Figure 8-2 that are located in West Virginia and New Jersey are larger Series '10' routers.

The Series '10' routers provide more capabilities in bandwidth and fault resilience, along with better scalability to handle more connections. In centering the core network in the data centers, the enterprise may also have decided to consolidate the lion's share of its network management activities to those data centers, where land and salaries are less costly than in the big cities. Whatever the reasoning, the network is no longer one composed of six peer locations.

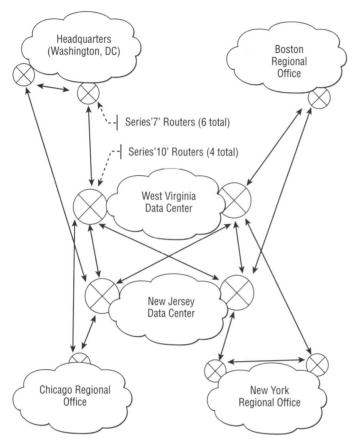

Figure 8-2: Example of a symmetric network backbone.

The network in Figure 8-2 clearly has a center, which is composed of the two data centers. They are heavily cross-connected and all the outlying locations connect to the enterprise network through the data centers. The risks of losing connectivity, should one of the data centers go down, are presumably mitigated by the more powerful routers, as well as by other factors including higher-reliability electrical power, the use of better ISPs, and other mechanisms not covered by the figure.

The negative tradeoff in using the asymmetric architecture is the cost of the more expensive equipment, but the upside is being able to eliminate several of the (also expensive) dedicated circuits. The lines that form the perimeter network in Figure 8-1 are not present in Figure 8-2, specifically the long-haul lines from New York to Chicago and Washington to Boston. For redundancy purposes, some long-haul lines are necessary, like the ones from Boston or New York to West Virginia, but the cost tradeoff there was apparently worth it.

Applying coarse distance weights to all the dedicated connections in both Figure 8-1 and Figure 8-2, the savings are a little over 10 percent and the dedicated-circuit line count is reduced from 15 to 12 in the asymmetric architecture. These are crude calculations at best, but you can see that there are merits to having a network core rather than a collection of peer-like locations.

The other improvement in the Figure 8-2 architecture over the symmetric one in Figure 8-1 is a reduction in hop counts between locations. Several paths between locations are only one or two hops long and no path goes over more than three hops of expensive low-bandwidth dedicated circuits. This assumes the intra-location connections in Washington and New York are over high-speed LANs that introduce little routing delay. Moreover, the routers in the data centers also may be connected via various methods proprietary to each vendor that eliminate or significantly reduce the penalties of intra-location hops, effectively making each pair behave like one router. That would make all the enterprise's locations no more than two hops apart.

Tuning Transition Activities to Your Network Architecture

The preceding discussions of network backbone architectures left much unsaid about the decision process behind selecting one of the architectures over the other. Most enterprises use combinations of both, peering local sites symmetrically while relying on core data centers and the like for long-haul connectivity. The purpose of the preceding two sections was to introduce the symmetric and asymmetric network architectures and provide a frame of reference for the transition tuning discussion that follows. Your enterprise presumably decided a long time ago which architecture(s) to use, where to use them, and how. It's now your job to upgrade that backbone to be IPv6 capable.

If you're fairly new to IPv6, which is a distinct possibility, then you probably want your first transition activities to occur off the beaten path. This way, you can mitigate the risks of learning on the job a little better and not crash the whole backbone if something goes wrong.

Preserving Network Redundancy During Transition Activities

Because your IPv6 transition activities will temporarily shut down (or risk the unintentional shutdown of) part of your network connectivity, it's a good idea to select your first transition locations in such a way that as much redundancy as possible is preserved in the remainder of the network.

With a symmetric backbone, you have a greater number of choices of where to start your transition, because no one location is significantly more critical to the whole backbone than any other. Referring to Figure 8-1, with the exception of Boston and West Virginia, if you lose all connectivity to any location, you still have redundant connectivity between all other locations. If you lose either Boston or West Virginia, you still have complete network connectivity for the rest of your locations, but the connectivity between some of your locations is no longer redundant.

The redundancy aspect is important, because you would like to perform your IPv6 transition activities in such a way that, should you break something and take down a particular location's connectivity *and* coincidentally another network outage occurs elsewhere, the rest of the network is still operational. It's superstitious, but by forcing part of the network out of service intentionally, some people (including myself) are wary that another part of the network will crash sympathetically. Whether basing your decision on risk management or superstition, it's a good idea to retain as much of your redundant connectivity as possible and perhaps not make Boston or West Virginia your first transition location in Figure 8-1.

For the asymmetric network in Figure 8-2, picking your first IPv6 transition location based on preserving redundancy is more black and white than in the symmetric backbone case. The loss of any of the outlying locations has no effect on the connectivity of any other location, so you can select Washington, Boston, Chicago, or New York for your first transition activities with no fear of a sympathetic crash elsewhere disabling more than that local connectivity, as well. For the data centers, taking either one down immediately removes all redundancy from your network. Should the other data center crash, your outlying locations will all be disconnected from each other. As a side note, it is that criticality of those data centers that caused you to spend the extra money on better equipment, power, and so on when you went with the asymmetric architecture.

Selecting Locations for Depth-First Transitions

Recall the earlier discussion on using one or more depth-first transition activities to shake the bugs out of your whole IPv6 transition process, rather than just repeating your earlier transition phases and then moving on to the unproven later phases only when you're uncomfortably close to your overall transition deadline. Should you decide to undertake any depth-first transition activities, your network backbone architecture can help you determine where to conduct those activities.

Using logic similar to that behind preserving redundancy during your transition activities, you want to perform any depth-first activities off the beaten path. Ignoring the desire to preserve redundancy in the network for the moment, two good choices you have in the symmetric architecture of Figure 8-1 are the Boston and Chicago locations.

Assuming you have everything you need ready to go when the maintenance activities start (the importance of which is covered near the end of the chapter), the complete IPv6 transition of either the Boston or Chicago locations should be less work than any of the others. This argument is based solely on there being only one backbone router at each location, but given the scope of the example, that's all you really have on which to base your decision. In the real world, there will surely be other factors.

When you factor in the desire to preserve redundancy in the event of an outage from the previous section, then your best choice is probably Chicago. That location is not critical to any connectivity, whereas Boston is the only way out of Washington, should West Virginia go offline.

For the asymmetric architecture in Figure 8-2, as with the redundancy discussion, any of the outlying locations are acceptable candidates for initial depth-first transition activities to get your team skilled in all aspects of IPv6 network management, not just replacing router hardware. Boston and Chicago are again the best first candidates and in this case, unlike with the symmetric backbone example, Boston is not a critical location for redundant connectivity.

Mitigating Risk in More-Aggressive Transition Activities

When the time comes to upgrade a more critical part of your network backbone to IPv6 capabilities, your architecture will help you decide where to shore up your defenses in other parts of the network. Looking at the asymmetric network backbone in Figure 8-2 first, when the time comes to upgrade one of your two data centers, a prior activity might be the validation of the functionality of the other data center. This includes coming up with acceptable resolutions for all trouble tickets of a certain priority or higher, as well as verifying that all equipment and applications are functioning correctly, perhaps using the automated test suites discussed in Chapter 9, "Defining the Transition Verification Steps."

For the symmetric backbone in Figure 8-1, a similar criticality analysis of the your network is required, from which you should determine that Boston and West Virginia are your critical locations and, before upgrading one to IPv6, you should execute the same kind of validation on the other location as described for the asymmetric backbone case.

For either architecture, your goals for critical locations like those just described should be to get the site undergoing IPv6 transition back online as quickly as possible. Because all IPv6-capable equipment is also IPv4 capable (and there's nothing in the OMB mandate that says you have to turn the IPv4 functionality off), you should strive to get the new IPv6-capable equipment up and running with the same IPv4 functionality as their predecessors and only then start configuring IPv6 features. The remainder of the chapter expands on that methodology significantly, but it's mentioned here in the network architecture section because this is where you figure out which of your locations, subnets, and so on are more critical than others and can afford the least downtime.

Identifying and Resolving Execution Dependencies

There are few activities in your IPv6 transition that don't depend on the prior success of other activities, certain resources being available, or completion by a certain time. The challenges in resolving the dependencies in your transition are first in identifying them and then in ordering your activities so all the dependencies on a given activity are resolved before that activity starts. If the activity must start or complete by a certain time, you can consider that another dependency.

Some dependencies are simple to identify and resolve and you'll need no assistance to do so. For example, it's obvious that, before you can install new routers in an equipment rack, you have to remove any old equipment from that rack. You also have to switch the old and new equipment within the bounds of the relevant maintenance window. More subtle dependencies in a seemingly simple activity like replacing equipment include having adequate power, cooling, and network connectivity available at the time of the switch (should what was available for the old equipment be insufficient for the new equipment).

There are so many potential dependencies in the IPv6 transition of an enterprise network, many of which are specific to your situation, that they can't all be covered with any degree of useful detail here or anywhere else. Instead, this section is written to provide guidance to facilitate your identification and resolution of all the dependencies in your specific transition activities.

Identifying Dependencies in Your Transition Activities

Resolving dependencies in a set of activities is typically straightforward, once the dependencies have been identified. Identifying dependencies, like cooling, electrical, and networking mentioned in the preceding section, requires a disciplined analysis process that unfortunately comes mostly from years of experience executing large IT projects. This section tries to impart the principals of that disciplined process by suggesting approaches on how to implement it as related to your IPv6 transition.

One approach to implementing a disciplined process for identifying dependencies on a given set of transition activities hinges on asking yourself a series of questions regarding dependencies after the work items of those transition activities have been defined. The questions you need to ask yourself are:

1. What do I need to start the given set of transition activities?
2. Who (or what) is providing what I need?
3. When must what I need be provided?
4. Where do I need the things to be provided?
5. Why does this dependency exist (and can it be eliminated)?

These questions should remind you of the journalistic approach recommended in Chapter 5, "Creating Your Transition Plans." The underlying logic is the same. You can argue that the first question is simply a reformulation of "What are my dependencies?" and you wouldn't be entirely wrong. The subtle wording change is important, however, because the questions in the list lend themselves more readily to being asked about each work item in your transition activities. The more abstract question, that simply asks what your dependencies are, needs to have derived from it the more concrete questions in the preceding list.

As an example of the process, consider the work item of deploying IPv6 addresses to a set of your network devices. Asking yourself the preceding list of questions, you can identify dependencies such as having to get the IPv6 addresses from your ISP before being able to deploy the addresses further. That answers the first two questions. Perhaps you need to deploy the addresses by a certain time, because another team that is porting applications to IPv6 needs to use the addresses as part of its transition activities. In that case, asking the third question identifies the dependency that you need the IPv6 addresses from your ISP a sufficient amount of time before your deadline, so you can deploy them to your devices. For IPv6 address deployment, the fourth question reminds you that you have to get addresses from multiple ISPs, if you're deploying them to devices in different parts of the country or different regions overseen by different RIRs.

For this example, the fifth question is straightforward. You need the addresses because you're supposed to be deploying IPv6 and there's no way around not getting them. For other activities, asking yourself why a dependency exists may actually initiate a train of thought that allows you to eliminate the dependency and thereby reduce your workload.

The more methodical and detail-oriented you are in asking yourself the questions regarding dependencies on your IPv6 transition activities, the more likely you are to identify more of those dependencies and be able to resolve them.

Using Dry Runs and Simulations to Identify Dependencies

Sometimes, the subtle dependencies of your transition activities get lost simply because it's difficult to envision every work item at a sufficiently granular level to determine every last thing you need. To counter this risk, a dry run or simulation of the work items can help.

Continuing with the earlier example of deploying IPv6 addresses, you can perform an effective dry run by getting out the manuals for your various network devices and going through the motions of programming IPv6 addresses into those devices. When you read about the fields that you have to populate in a configuration web page or the parameters required by a router's command line, you should quickly conclude that you will need to put IPv6 addresses into those places. That should further force the conclusion that you need to go get those addresses from someplace first. Following that train of thought, you then need to enumerate all the locations where you'll be doing these address deployments and determine which local ISPs you'll need to contact to get addresses assigned to you.

The trick to getting the most out of a dry run or simulation is to take nothing for granted. For example, on encountering a configuration web page requiring you to enter a valid IPv6 address that's assigned to you, don't just wave your hands and assume you'll have the address when you need it. Record the need for the address as a dependency, along with everything else for which you don't have an immediate and concrete resolution as you're executing the dry run, no matter how trivial those dependencies seem.

Your first encounter in the dry run with an apparently trivial dependency may seem unimportant, but if that dependency continues to show up repeatedly as the dry run plays out, you may decide that it has become important enough to determine exactly what needs to be done to resolve it, by whom and when. Conversely, if you never see a particular trivial dependency again, and your experience tells you that you will surely have it resolved by the time you need it, you can choose to strike it from your overall dependency list.

Depending on the transition activities in question, you may only be able to simulate so much. For example, until you actually perform the related transition activities, no dry run will tell you how your network will perform while routing live IPv6 traffic. In those cases, your simulations may be limited to mathematical models of traffic flows and bandwidth utilization. If those models say that the current bandwidth available is not sufficient, then you need to address the dependency of upgrading your physical infrastructure. If the bandwidth you have is sufficient, then no dependency exists.

Decomposing the Activities to Better Identify Dependencies

Prior chapters have touted the merits of decomposing large tasks into sets of smaller ones, and dependency identification and resolution are no different. Your need to use maintenance windows to perform your transition activities already requires that you decompose your IPv6 transition into sets of work items. Each set of work items needs to fit into one of your maintenance windows and, at the same time, the set of work items must be self-contained and accomplish a transition goal in such a manner as to have a functional network when the maintenance window ends.

By making small sets of self-contained work to fit your maintenance windows, you have also simplified your dependency identification process. Smaller sets of work ideally should have fewer dependencies and the dependencies should be more readily identifiable, because the identification process is less complex and less susceptible to human error. It is, therefore, less likely you'll miss a dependency. To further reduce the risk of missing an important dependency in a set of work items, you can decompose your IPv6 transition activities over a dimension other than the windows of time in which you must perform the activities.

Identifying dependencies between your IPv6 transition activities is a lot like assembling a jigsaw puzzle. In a jigsaw puzzle, some people assemble the border first, seeking out edge pieces readily identifiable by their having one or two perfectly straight sides. Other people look for particular colors or patterns, like the sky, the ocean, or a grassy field, and organize the pieces that appear to belong together into groups. That creates a set of smaller sub-puzzles each with fewer possible combinations that have to be checked for correct fits.

By organizing your IPv6 transition activities along other dimensions than just time, you may be able to spot sets of work items that all have a given dependency and that also have other traits in common. If you then analyze a new work item and discover it has the same trait as others already in the group, you can immediately assess whether the common dependency also applies. This kind of grouping also serves as an audit process. In other words, if a work item you encountered earlier has the same trait as the group with the common dependency, but you didn't assign the dependency to the work item when you first assessed it, that should cause you to check whether the dependency truly doesn't apply or you just missed it the first time around.

Identifying Dependencies Before Starting Your Activities

As with many other aspects of your IPv6 transition, the dependencies on your activities are things you should figure out *before* you start any work that threatens to disrupt the network and its capabilities. You probably won't find every dependency, because no amount of planning, dry runs, or simulation will uncover them all. The best you can strive for is that, by being thorough, methodical, and disciplined in analyzing your work items for dependencies, you'll probably get all the big dependencies and most of the little ones.

What's left undiscovered should be little more than minor inconveniences that may require you to reorganize your remaining activities to address a missed dependency or two that hasn't been resolved yet. At worst, you may have to abandon a transition activity and waste the remainder of that maintenance window if you discover an overlooked and unresolved dependency at the last minute. With good planning ahead of time, including reviewing exactly what you're going to do just before a maintenance window starts, there shouldn't be too many of those last minute discoveries.

Balancing Efficiency with Resilience

If you were certain that nothing would go wrong in your IPv6 transition, then you would likely strive for the most efficient transition possible, which often means the transition that is the shortest in duration. For every piece of equipment and every software application you upgraded or replaced, you would immediately configure all the required IPv6 capabilities and restore only the old IPv4 capabilities you still needed, if any, after the transition. There would be a "before" state and an "after" state on each part of the network as it underwent transition with not much in between except the transition activities themselves. In other words, there would be no intermediate states of transition.

The reality of the situation, of course, is that something will go wrong or, even if it doesn't, you should plan as if it will. Aside from errors in your transition plans and assumptions, there are countless mishaps that could occur at any time during your transition activities, many of which can't be predicted on a timeline. These unpredictable events include natural disasters, outages in places outside your control (like at your power company, ISPs, or in the national and local telecom infrastructure), disk crashes and other hardware failures, and cables or fibers that are accidentally cut as you slide a new router into its rack.

Though you can't predict these events, you can organize your work such that they have a minimum impact and that you have safe configurations to fall back to should an external event (or simply an error in your own planning or execution) halt your transition progress. In organizing the work items for any particular set of transition activities, you should divide them into the following classes and perform the activities associated with the first class first, the second class second, and so on:

1. Replacement of old IPv4-only equipment that can't be upgraded with new IPv6-capable equipment.

2. Upgrading of old IPv4-only equipment to give it IPv6 capabilities.

3. Configuration of the new or upgraded equipment to restore the IPv4 capabilities previously provided.

4. Configuration of the new or upgraded equipment's IPv6 capabilities in phases, for example interfaces, addresses, and routing, then auto-configuration, and then more advanced features.

You may be wondering why replacement activities precede upgrade ones. This ordering pertains more to hardware assets than software. In software, it's hard to distinguish an upgrade versus a replacement from a configuration point of view. If you're replacing a hardware asset, you can usually perform a great deal of the new asset's configuration offline and reduce the amount of work in the third class of activities significantly. Moreover, while the new asset is being configured, the old asset is still in place and keeping the network running.

For the second class of activities, if you're performing an upgrade of a hardware asset, then the asset almost certainly must be taken offline for the upgrade, which means network down time unless there is a redundant asset backing up the one being upgraded. There's a chance the asset's upgrade procedure will fail, in which case you now have to reload the old version of the asset's firmware, for example, and reconfigure that old firmware. In the case of an asset replacement, should there be something wrong with the new asset, you can often just put the old asset back.

As you perform each class of work items during a set of transition activities, you incrementally add capabilities to the network while simultaneously creating plateaus of stability so you don't have to abandon all your changes should something go wrong late in the maintenance window. The cost of creating such plateaus may be a longer duration for your transition activities, because you will likely need to save intermediate configurations as each plateau is reached so that you can restore those configurations in the event of a mishap or outage.

As an example of how you can trade off efficiency to gain resilience against unpredictable outages, assume IPv4 and IPv6 configuration of a newly installed asset each takes an hour by itself, but if you did both configuration work items together in parallel, you could be done in 90 minutes. By performing both configuration work items together, you would be done half an hour sooner, but you would have a 90-minute window of vulnerability where you could lose power, for example, along with all the configuration work completed so far. If you perform the two configuration work items in series, there would only be an hour-long period where an outage would require the asset to be totally reconfigured, followed by another hour where only the IPv6 features would need to be reconfigured. Should an outage occur in that second hour, you would have the latitude to decide whether to try the IPv6 configuration again or restore the (presumably previously saved) IPv4 configuration and get the asset online with IPv4 capabilities only. This is especially useful if you're nearing the end of your maintenance window or if the IPv6 configuration is not a critical part of the current transition activities and you don't know when power will be restored.

Later in the chapter, you'll read more about staging transition activities, including how to be ready to recover to a normal state should something go wrong, and how to know when you must begin such a recovery in order not to violate your maintenance window constraints.

Grouping Your Transition Activities

At this point, you've organized your IPv6 transition activities into the order in which you want to upgrade the various locations, subnets, hardware, and software in your enterprise. In creating the ordering, you've factored in the interdependencies between activities, so that when a given activity is set to start, everything it needs is already in place. Ideally, you have a master transition activities list or something equivalent that is sorted into those time-ordered steps, but without actual times assigned to the activities, because you still need to fit them all into the appropriate maintenance windows.

To determine which activities should go into which maintenance windows is not as easy as taking 500 hours of work and distributing it on a first come, first served basis into the next 500 hours of maintenance windows. Before you can assign activities to maintenance windows, you need to organize the activities further into groups that must be executed together.

Those of you familiar with databases may be aware of the concept of transactions. A transaction, in database terminology, is a set of steps that must all complete successfully. If any one step doesn't succeed, then that step and all the ones that precede it in the transaction must be reversed, leaving the database in the same state it was in before the first step of the transaction started.

The groups you must organize your IPv6 transition activities into are similar to database transactions. The consequences of one activity in the group not succeeding are not necessarily as dire as having to reverse the effects of all the preceding activities, however. Depending on the types of activities in the group, should the latest activity you're performing fail, you may be able to recover to an intermediate plateau of stability, as described in the previous section. In grouping your activities, you should also be looking to define such plateaus and what recovery steps are required to reach them.

An example of a group of activities that must succeed together is the one from earlier in the chapter regarding replacing some old IPv4-only routers with IPv6-capable ones. The three distinct activities that would make up a group that must be executed together are removing the old equipment, installing the new equipment, and configuring the IPv4 capabilities you require into the new equipment. Depending on the requirements of the transition activities, the IPv6 configuration may also be required, which would make it part of that group. If the IPv6 configuration is optional and can be postponed to another maintenance window, then you don't have to include it in the group. If the length of the maintenance window permits, however, you may include the IPv6 configuration as an optional activity whose execution is contingent on all the preceding activities in the group succeeding. You'll shortly read about how utilizing such optional activities can reduce the amount of unallocated time in your maintenance windows.

Once you've organized the activities into groups, you need to find a sufficiently long maintenance window for each group. A group must fit completely into the maintenance window, because you cannot exit the maintenance window with any of the group's activities incomplete. A maintenance window does not necessarily need to be devoted to a single group of activities, however. If you can fit two or more complete groups of activities into a maintenance window, there's no reason why you shouldn't.

Because the recovery process from a failed activity will also likely take some time, you have to make sure that you have enough time in the maintenance window not only to complete all the activities in the group successfully, but also to recover from the failure of any of those activities. An example of scheduling a group's activities, including failure recovery, into a maintenance window is provided later in this chapter.

Identifying Any Irreversible Steps

Many projects have steps that are irreversible. In skydiving, the most obvious irreversible step is the step out of the airplane. Before you take that step, you can still coax the jumpmaster or pilot to turn around and land, because you've changed your mind. After you step out of the plane, you're going skydiving whether you like it or not. Hopefully, you've resolved the "put on parachute" dependency before starting that last step.

As should be obvious, an irreversible step is one where there is no going back. If you're replacing an IPv4-only application with an IPv6-capable version, you might consider the deletion of the old application an irreversible step. If you don't have backups of the old application, then the deletion would be truly irreversible and you would be in a rough spot if the new application doesn't do everything you need it to do or if it is faulty. Of course, you should have backups and a plan for the case where the new application fails or turns out to be insufficient to meet your needs.

Between the backups of applications and their data, hardware configurations, and so on, and the inherent nature of IPv6 transition, there should be very few irreversible steps. Remember, you're adding capabilities to your network, not removing any. Every IPv6-capable device and application will also be IPv4 capable. If you were forced to throw out all the IPv4 equipment and functionality as part of the IPv6 transition, that would be another story.

Despite the fact that there shouldn't be any irreversible steps in your IPv6 transition activities, you should still be on the lookout for steps that look like they are. When formulating your transition activities, groups, and schedules, you should frequently ask yourself and your teammates, "What will we do if this step fails?" Any time there isn't a clear answer, the next thing to do is to start the process of creating a plan to deal with the failure of the given activity.

Sometimes, the only choice may be to retain the old hardware, software images, and so on for a complete reversion to the normal state you had before you started the group of activities in which the given failure occurred. Though it can be disappointing to lose an entire maintenance window's worth of work, especially if you're within minutes of completing that work, the alternative of having a non-functional or unstable network when the maintenance window ends is much worse, as your users will communicate to you, should it occur.

Verifying Capabilities to Create Checkpoints

Verification is a critical part of your IPv6 transition and there should be at least one work item devoted to it in every maintenance window. Before you can call a group of transition activities complete and go home or continue to the next group, you have to make sure what you just did works correctly and that all the capabilities your users need from your network are there. Because verification is a complex step, the details (including how to recover, should verification fail), are left to Chapter 9, "Defining the Transition Verification Steps."

Using Optional Work Items to Fill Spare Time

Once you group your IPv6 transition activities and assign them to maintenance windows, you're likely to find that there is rarely a perfect fit. There may be some groups of activities that fit fairly well, leaving only an hour or two spare in a maintenance window. That time is a welcome buffer, should something go wrong that your plans overlooked. It's also a nice treat occasionally to get to go home early, especially when considering that over-planning to fill those last little bits of time often leads to unrealistic schedules and you suddenly find yourself scrambling to get all the work done before the maintenance window ends. That can lead to more mistakes, plus it can be demoralizing to be in a rush constantly.

Because your IPv6 transition, and the groups of activities that you've organized it into, has an overall order, you can't always pick and choose which groups to put into which maintenance windows. You may, therefore, find that some maintenance windows have only one four-hour group of activities assigned to them and there's no group nearby in the transition order that you can use to fill out the rest of the spare time in the window. Leaving most of a maintenance window empty seems like a waste, especially since you already have to stay late or drive to work in the middle of the night, anyway. Sometimes you may be able to find additional work that is scheduled for later in the transition order, and that you can start (but perhaps not complete) sooner. Such "optional" work (though it is not optional in the overall transition) can be scheduled into the maintenance window to reduce the amount of wasted time.

There are constraints on which optional work items you can use to pad out your maintenance windows. The most important constraint is that you need to finish all the mandatory work items (or be very certain you'll be able to finish them), before starting optional work items. The transition ordering has dictated which work items you must get done during the maintenance window in question. If you don't get those work items done, you'll likely delay the overall transition, and you may be leaving a dependency unresolved that could affect other teams performing transition activities.

The other constraint on any optional work items you consider to fill out your maintenance windows is that whatever work you perform from them, be it everything required to complete the work item or only part of that work, when you cease work (possibly leaving the work item incomplete), the network must be in a normal state for your users. For example, after installing the new IPv6-capable routers mentioned earlier, configuring their IPv4 capabilities, and verifying everything is working properly, you could configure all the IPv6 interfaces as well, but leave the IPv6 routing configuration for later. The routers will not be able to move IPv6 traffic outside the LAN without that routing configuration, but because nobody needs them to do that at present, that's an acceptable state for the network.

Adopting the Expect-To-Revert Mindset

One of the basics of learning to fly is to be constantly ready for something to go wrong and to react appropriately to whatever the event is. In instrument flying, that is, flying in the clouds with no external references to which way is up or North, emergency preparedness is particularly emphasized when flying an approach for landing. When you start the approach, based on weather information you received before your flight and en route, you assume you will "break out" (exit the clouds) at some specific altitude, often called the decision height. Decision height altitudes are usually 200 feet above the ground and you're descending at 300 to 500 feet per minute or faster, so you don't have a lot of time to think things over if you get that low and the clouds don't magically part. That means you need to have a plan ready to go beforehand. For instrument approaches, that plan is called the missed approach.

Missed approaches consist of a set of well-documented instructions published by the FAA and specific to the airport and approach that you're using. The instructions are known by you, the other instrument pilots in the vicinity, and the controllers on the ground. Everyone knows when you will use a missed approach, from where, to where, and how. There is no mystery as to what will happen next if you declare to Air-Traffic Control (ATC) that you're "going missed."

An important part of missed approaches is that they return you to some place in the "normal" ATC infrastructure, once the pseudo-emergency (in reality, missed approaches aren't even close to emergencies) is over. At that point, you can advise ATC what you plan to do next in a more orderly and less rushed manner. You can choose to try the approach again, but if the airport is "socked in" (not a technical flying term), you may choose to go to an alternate airport.

In cases where you're suspicious before even taking off that you may not be able to land at your originally intended destination, based on the weather forecast for your arrival time, you are required to tell ATC what your alternate airport would be. You also need to bring enough fuel to get to the alternate from your original destination (plus some spare fuel) and be certain that the weather at the alternate will be acceptable for you to land.

The types of disasters possible with poorly planned instrument flying are far nastier than the MIS/IT problems you might encounter during your IPv6 transition, but every aspect of the preceding discussion has an analog in your transition's execution. That the stakes aren't as high (which your managers and network users may disagree with, especially if you're with the FAA and run the ATC network) is no excuse. You should adopt a mindset that expects undesirable (but not always unforeseen) circumstances to come up during your IPv6 transition activities. With that mindset, you can determine the critical points in your transition steps, identify potential failure modes, and have backup plans prepared *beforehand* to mitigate the failures.

Defining a Normal State for Your Network

In this chapter, you've already seen and will continue to see terms like "stable configuration," "normal state," or something similar. For the chapter, the term has a precise meaning. It means that, from the perspective of your users, the network is in one of a handful of states that allows the users to do their work. Those states are usually limited to no more than two. In other words, the network is either in the state that you told your users it would be in at the end of a set of successful transition activities, or the network looks like it is in the state it was in when the users last saw it before those activities. Remember, normalcy is from the users' perspective. Many transition activities are likely to produce a normal state that looks to the users exactly like the state before the activities, which is often the most desirable outcome of all.

Reaching a New Normal State via Successful Transition Activities

On the successful completion of a particular set of IPv6 transition activities, your network will be in the upgraded state that was advertised as the outcome of those activities. For example, certain application servers may have been upgraded to IPv6-capable versions. The users may not care about the IPv6 capabilities, yet. All they may have been told is that Application 'X' is being upgraded from version 4.0 to version 6.0.

The users may have been advised of a set of new capabilities (not necessarily related to IPv6) to expect from the new version of the application. They definitely should have been told how to work with any differences in the new version, as they pertain to capabilities in the old version. For example, if the old version's interface was a custom client application and the new version uses a browser-based web interface, then the users should have been told to cease using the custom client and start using their web browsers. Depending on the differences between the old and new clients, the users may also have received training on the new client.

In summary, the first definition of "normal state" is that the network looks to the users like it was advertised to look on completion of the most recent transition activities. Moreover, as mentioned, if the users don't care about the IPv6 capabilities and there are no other changes from the transition activities, then the post-maintenance normal state may look no different to them from the pre-maintenance one.

Returning to the Old Normal State when Transition Activities Fail

The other definition of "normal state" is that, again from the perspective of its users, the network looks as it did before the most recent transition activities. It is irrelevant to the users whether those activities took place (with no visible changes), were cancelled, or failed. All the users know (and often all they need or care to know) is that you were going to upgrade Application 'X' from version 4.0 to version 6.0, yet version 4.0 is still running as of when the users walked in the door this morning.

To prepare the users for all cases of normality, you should have done a few things. The previous section covered preparing the users for a new version of software with appropriate training and a message saying when the upgrade would occur. You also have to tell them that, should undesirable circumstances arise, the upgrade may not occur at the time planned. Assuming no users are dependent on the capabilities promised by the upgrade being delivered on time in the upcoming maintenance window, the warning that the upgrade may not happen is sufficient.

If the users, or another transition team, are reliant on the success of the transition activities in the upcoming maintenance window, then they should be prepared for the potential failure of those activities, as well. Preparing other transition teams for all of the potential outcomes of your transition activities, especially those activities on which the other teams are dependent, is covered elsewhere in this book. For the user population, the negotiation and planning surrounding new capabilities is something you go through all the time and is not specific to IPv6 transition. You should already have processes in place for communicating to your user population the expectations for deployment of new capabilities, the risk that those capabilities may not be provided when expected, and what steps you will take should the deployment fail.

Communicating to your users what to expect of upcoming transition activities and when those activities will occur are covered later in this chapter.

Knowing When to Revert

When a project begins to show warning signs that it may not succeed, it's human nature to press on as long as some hope for success remains. Unfortunately, as you're pressing on, your concept of reality changes. Think to yourself how many failed projects you've been on, and if you've been in MIS/IT any appreciable time, it's likely there's been at least one or two. In retrospect, you often can identify where the point of no return was in the project, and it's usually long before when you gave up.

Changes in your objectivity as a project starts to fail are why it's critical that you determine the conditions for reversion *before* getting started. Nobody can say that the project wouldn't have succeeded with a little more effort five minutes after you gave up, but the conditions aren't meant to define the point of irreversible failure. They are meant to draw a line in the sand where you can pull back and live to fight (and possibly succeed) another day.

Before continuing with this section, a dose of reality is in order. As has been said many times in this book, the best laid plans can still fail. That includes reversion plans. There is nothing special about them and you should not expect them to be some panacea that can save you from every untoward circumstance.

You can safely assume that there will be unforeseen failures in your IPv6 transition, hopefully minor ones. Among those failures may be cases were reversions themselves don't work as expected. For example, on restoring an old router because you couldn't get the new one to work, you may find that the old one won't power up. Hopefully, you've planned at least a little bit for such contingencies and have alternate connectivity options for the network segments this old router used to serve.

The types of fallbacks on fallbacks you have will depend, of course, on how much damage the failure of the reversion path (or of its reversion path, if your backup plans need backup plans) can cause. The bottom line is to restore network capabilities as soon as possible, perhaps even in phases. For example, a smaller router that you have spare may be able to handle some of your network segments until you can get the new router configured or the old router restarted. The types of scenarios and their fallback plans are infinite. What you should take out of the reversion discussions in this chapter is the need to plan for failure and have prudent actions that you can take should failure occur.

Establishing Measurable Conditions for Reverting

When determining the conditions that dictate the need to revert to a prior normal state, you must remain objective. That means the reversion conditions *must* be readily measurable and anybody doing the measuring should get essentially the same results as anyone else. The reason instrument flying uses decision heights is that they are easy to determine while you're flying an approach, and it's crystal clear when the reversion-triggering event occurs. For your IPv6 transition activities, a readily measurable and unambiguous indicator for signaling the need for reversion is time.

When you think about all the possible things you can measure during your IPv6 transition activities, they all boil down to some measurement associated with time. Whether you have to get ten subnets configured on a new router or fifty servers upgraded with the IPv6-capable version of some application, the underlying criteria is always, "by when?" If you haven't completed the given work item(s) by some time, then you have to revert to a prior normal state. The sections that follow help you determine and work with reversion times.

Determining the Revert Time for Your Transition Activities

Think of the simple concept of day and night. As a child I had trouble grappling with the fact that it was still light out after sunset. I recall my father saying that, once the sun has set, night comes quickly. What I didn't grasp was that, just because night didn't come instantaneously after sunset, that didn't mean it wasn't coming soon. As an adult I am still caught by surprise by how quickly day turns into night, and that's why I've done some of my most efficient painting and wall-papering to the glow of half a dozen table lamps.

Returning to the aviation theme for a moment, the FAA has several definitions for night, depending on what topic is being discussed. The common thread is that they are all defined as amounts of time before or after sunset. Sunset is a hard and fast measurable parameter with no ambiguity. When the Sun's disk goes below the horizon, in one hour (for example), that's nighttime. In some parts of the country, you may still have plenty of light for what you need to do an hour after sunset. That doesn't matter. If the rule is "no painting at night," then you're done at 8:17 p.m., if the Sun sets at 7:17 p.m. Much more importantly, as you're working through the day, you need to remain certain that you *will* be done by that time, or you may need to stop work and put things back into a usable state for however you've defined normal *before* the deadline arrives.

Stopping work early sometimes causes the perception of wasted time, especially if returning things to normal is a long process. For example, if you have to perform a one-hour upgrade activity, the reversion from which requires two hours of reassembling a bunch of equipment (probably because there was an activity of disassembling that equipment to prepare for the upgrade), then you have to make a go/no-go decision at a time that gives you the two hours you need to reassemble things. You should not think of those two hours as wasted, but rather as insurance. Moreover, as mentioned earlier and demonstrated in the example later in this chapter, you may be able to fill that spare time with optional activities, in case everything goes according to plan.

Reverting When You Planned to and No Later

Too many projects have failed from people soldiering on "just a little while longer," because some minor task in the overall scheme of things had a successful outcome, but at a time well beyond when it was supposed to have succeeded. Such successes create false hope that everything else will proceed on time (or even more quickly than originally planned, to make up for the slip of the prior item).

Remember that the purpose of setting revert times is not to determine when you should be done. Those completion milestones will usually precede the revert times. What revert times dictate are the times when you have to stop trying "just one more thing" and start putting the network back together again. If you had all the time in the world, there would be no reason to set revert times. For all reasonable projects (excluding the bleeding edges of research and development), you will eventually succeed. That's not the point. The point is your users need a functional network when the maintenance window ends. If the revert time for your activities is 4 a.m., because your maintenance window closes at 6 a.m. and you need two hours to revert to a normal state if things don't go to plan, then when the clock strikes 4 a.m., you have to assess whether your activities are finished. If they're not, then you have to stop those activities and start reverting, period.

Applying Your Real-World Experience to Revert Times

The previous section's draconian guidance may seem naïve to you, if you've been managing networks for a while. To temper the rules with reality, recall Chapter 5, "Creating Your Transition Plans," suggesting that you might choose to defer to your professional experience and perhaps bend some project management rules without adding undue risk. When applied to revert times, a little fudging now and then may not hurt, especially if you're certain you'll be done with your activities only five or fifteen minutes after you should have started reverting.

The basis for your rationale for working past a revert time should include the realization that you may be adding some risk, despite any feelings that you are not. Moreover, the blame for working past your revert time, should the upgrade (or a reversion started later than it was supposed to have been) not go smoothly or violate the end of a maintenance window, will be placed squarely on your shoulders, even if your choice to press on when you should have retreated was not a contributing factor.

Because you are probably not executing your IPv6 transition activities alone, don't forget to account for your team's level of experience in any decisions related to working past your revert time. If your team is new or you haven't worked with them before, just because you can move mountains and leap tall buildings in a single bound isn't relevant. You need to know what your team can do. Moreover, if your team is new, its members may not yet know what they can realistically accomplish. If you have a team that's fairly inexperienced, they may have a totally different concept of what's reasonable from yours. Conversely, if you're the new kid on the block (at least for this particular type of work) and your team has executed dozens of projects of the scope of an enterprise IPv6 transition, heed their words despite what you think is reasonable.

To round out what you need to consider in your assessment of whether to work past a revert time is that the revert time may be set (due to the duration of the reversion work required) long before an obvious failure is in sight. Returning again to the aviation theme, for missed approaches, 200 feet is a lot from the pilot's point of view and there's always that nagging feeling of unnecessary surrender when you have to abandon an approach. Having been in a plane with my wife as we broke out at what looked to her like tree-top level, I can unequivocally say that not all people think 200 feet is very high in the air, at all. In this case, where the important factor was not that the ground was 200 feet below, but rather that it was fewer than 30 seconds away, they were correct.

Getting Back to a Normal State

Once you've decided to revert, you need to get the network back to a normal state. That can mean a host of things including reassembling equipment, restarting servers, and re-enabling connectivity. The normal state you're striving for, depending on how many of your transition activities were completed successfully, is either the configuration in place before the current transition activities started or an intermediate configuration that offers all the capabilities the users need from the network.

If the goal of your current transition activities was, for example, to upgrade an application to an IPv6-capable version and, for whatever reason, you couldn't get the new version installed, configured and running correctly in time, then you'll probably have to revert to the old version. In that case, from your users' perspective at the end of the maintenance window, nothing has changed, which is exactly the perspective you're seeking.

The application-upgrade example may have some intermediate normal states that you can revert to (upon completing any prerequisite transition activities), thereby allowing you to come away from your maintenance window with at least some progress. For example, once you've installed the new version of the application, you may not have to uninstall it just to restart the old version. Every application is different, but you can assume in this case that two installed versions can co-exist. If that's so, then you may be able to revert to running the old version of the application with the added benefit of only having to schedule enough time to configure the new version and get it running. Depending on the complexity of the application, that could reduce your later workload significantly.

The other property required by an intermediate normal state is that any loose ends from your transition activities, for example any partially installed new versions of applications, are not accessible by users. Communicating to users how the transition activities turned out will prevent most users from stumbling across a partially installed upgraded version of an application. For those who don't read their e-mail frequently or are just overly curious, you must take the extra step of turning off any of the new version's network listeners and such, especially if the application is mostly functional.

In reality, the closer the partially installed application is to being functional, the worse off you are. As ignorant or curious users poke around the partially installed application, they can break it and cause more work for you in repairing the problem. If the application is only partly functional, you may get tech support calls saying the application isn't working, which you already know.

Moreover, if the application is far enough along to look like it's 100% functional, those same curious users may start entering data into it causing two more potential problems for you. If users start accessing the new version of the application before it's fully and correctly configured, you may have to scrub the data from the new version's database, and you may have to get the users to re-enter that data into the correct version of the application, which will certainly not make them happy (and somehow it will be your fault). If the application versions share the same database, you may even have to deal with database corruption or inconsistency issues. To avoid all these problems, don't expose the new version of the application to users until you've completely verified it, as you'll read more about in the next chapter.

Regrouping and Trying Again

Once you've reverted and reached a configuration where your users have the capabilities from your network that they need and you have stabilized the MIS/IT side, you need to review your situation and decide what your next steps are. This requires knowing what caused you to revert, beyond just time running out in your maintenance window. You need to determine if your plans were formulated with false assumptions or excessive expectations, whether you missed work items in the planning that turned up during the execution, or whether something undesirable and beyond your control happened (like you had a flat tire and didn't get to the data center until well into the maintenance window).

Trying Again After an Unpredictable Event

Sometimes it's just dumb luck that causes a good plan to fail. The flat tire just mentioned, hard disk crashes, and power outages are all examples of unpredictable events that are sufficiently rare that you probably didn't plan their effects into the transition activities' work items or schedule and, therefore, the events threw a monkey wrench into the works. After reading the earlier part of the chapter, however, you hopefully did organize your work so the unexpected event that caused you to abandon all that transition work had a limited impact from which you can recover quickly.

If you determine that your transition activities had to be reverted due to an unlucky fluke, then your overall plans and schedule for those activities are probably sound. In that case, you simply need to schedule the activities into a new maintenance window and try again. Be sure, however, that you are being honest with yourself and that the cause of the reversion was not from flawed planning.

Reformulating Over-Ambitious Scheduling

If the reason you had to revert from your recent transition activities is because you bit off more than you could chew in the chosen maintenance window, then you'll have to try again either during a larger maintenance window or by distributing the activities into a set of windows that provide more overall execution (and potential reversion) time.

If you decide to split the activities across multiple maintenance windows, you need to make sure you continue to satisfy the condition that the network will be in a normal state when each of those maintenance windows ends. That may mean adding additional work items to the end of some of those maintenance windows to return the network to an intermediate normal state. Those work items would not have been necessary if you could have completed all the transition activities in one maintenance window, and therefore the sum of all the work in the multiple maintenance windows may exceed that amount of work that was in the original one. This may, in turn, push out your overall schedule further than just the amount of time due to the reversion that led to the re-scheduling.

Adding Missed Steps to Transition Activity Schedules

Sometimes during the execution of a project, you discover work items that you missed in the planning and preparation phases. Depending on the scale of the missed work items, you may be able to absorb them into the original maintenance window and not have to revert. If you can't absorb the additional work, you will have to revert to some intermediate normal state or even the original configuration from before the maintenance window started.

Factoring in the missed work items should be a straightforward exercise, because it's simply the same planning, dependency resolution, grouping, and scheduling tasks that you had to perform with your original work items. The results of the exercise, however, may cause you to have to change other parts of your plans and schedules and shuffle transition activities into different maintenance windows from where they are scheduled now. If you were diligent in your original planning, however, the missed work items will hopefully be minor ones and the disruption equally minor.

After having factored the missing work items into the current IPv6 transition activities, it's also worth performing an assessment of the other remaining transition activities to see if those new work items apply to them, as well. For example, assume you discover that you need two new license keys each time you upgrade a given application to be IPv6 capable, instead of your original assumption that you only needed one key for each instance. This just happened to me in real life. In that case, you may have to add a work item for procuring another license key from the application vendor to any other transition activities that install instances of that application.

What Else Could Have Gone Wrong?

Other than freak mishaps, over-optimistic planning, and missed transition work items, there are many reasons why you might have to revert during a maintenance window. For example, you may have received the wrong parts or software from your vendors. In that case, you'll have to get the right items and, if there's no reason to doubt your initial plans, schedule a repeat of the transition activities.

Similarly, there may have been preparation work required at your facility that was not complete. I once worked at a facility that ordered several big Uninterruptible Power Supplies (UPSs) to allow for more servers to be installed. On arrival the UPSs were found to have a different type of power plug from the old UPSs. Nobody thought of this (so you could call it a planning failure) and an electrician had to be called in to set up the correct outlets.

Whatever the cause of your reversion, what you must do before performing the given set of transition activities again, is assess whether your plans and schedules are sound (in which case trying again the same way as before should be OK), or whether you need to reassess and modify those plans and schedules to achieve a better probability of success on your next attempt.

Creating a Sample Transition Activity Schedule

Now that you've read how to organize your IPv6 transition activities and you've adopted an "expect to revert" mindset for transition execution, an example showing all these skills in action should finish connecting the dots.

Table 8-1 shows an example of how to prepare a transition activities schedule for a typical evening's maintenance window, in this case a window that runs from 9 p.m. to 6 a.m. the following morning. The format is simple and conveys a lot of information with only a few words. Obviously, your transition activities need more detail than just "basic configuration" and the like, but the schedule shown in the table acts as a checklist and allows the people executing the transition work items in the middle of the night to know quickly and conveniently how much time they have to perform a work item, when the work item is planned to start, by when it must be completed in order to move forward with the next work item, and what to do if it isn't completed on time.

Table 8-1: An example of Transition Activity Work Items with Revert Conditions

WORK ITEM (#)	DURATION (START)	REVERT @ (OPT)	REVERT WORK
Window for all activities	9 hrs (21:00)	N/A	N/A
(1) Remove old equipment	1 hr (21:00)	23:00 (22:30)	Restore old equipment (2 hrs)
(2) Install new equipment	1 hr (22:00)	00:00 (23:30)	Remove new / Restore old (3 hrs)
(3) Basic configuration	2 hrs (23:00)	02:00 (01:30)	Remove new / Restore old (3 hrs)
(4) Verify/Save basic capabilities	1 hr (01:00)	03:00 (02:30)	Remove new / Restore old (3 hrs)
(5) Advanced configuration and verification (not mandatory)	2 hrs (02:00)	04:30 (04:30)	Restore basic capabilities (1.5 hrs)

The example uses 24-hour local time because I find that the most convenient for those directly involved in the execution of this kind of work. This way, there's no need to do complex subtractions in the wee hours of the morning (and after midnight, most subtractions are complex). If you're communicating the transition activities across time zones, then inclusion of the local time zone or the use of Greenwich Mean Time (GMT) should be used for those communications. Some organizations' MIS/IT departments operate regularly on GMT, in which case your transition schedules are probably most easily managed in that format, as well.

Plugging Known Values into the Activities Schedule

On starting the task of creating the transition activities schedule for your maintenance window, you should know several things from your transition planning exercises. You should know the order in which the work items need to be executed, because you worked out their dependencies during your planning. Putting your work items in order is where those dependencies show their value. You also should know the expected duration of all of your transition work items.

Because the concept of reverting has only been mentioned in passing before this chapter, you may not yet have estimated the amount of time it would take to revert from each of the network's transitional configurations to a normal state. Before completing your transition activities schedule, you need to estimate the durations of your reversion activities so as to plug them into something like Table 8-1, where they are shown parenthetically in the fourth column.

Plugging your work-item estimates into an activities schedule is where you must have the discipline to stick to the results of your prior planning exercises. Unless you're talking about the tiniest of fractions of the overall maintenance window, one of the worst things you can do is try to force a 3-hour work item into an hour simply to have the maintenance window mathematics work out.

If you thought a work item was going to take 3 hours when you created the IPv6 transition plan details, then second-guessing yourself (or simply ignoring the planned number for scheduling convenience) both introduces risk and reduces the value of the original planning exercise. If you're going to pick random durations for work items now, you might as well not have planned too hard in the first place. The forced transition activities schedule may look good on paper, but you'll almost certainly have to revert in some maintenance window sooner or later and the time wasted will likely not be made up for by the earlier schedule "optimizations."

Computing Your Activities' Revert Times

From what you knew going into the transition activities scheduling exercise, you should have been able to fill out all the columns in Table 8-1, except perhaps the "Revert @" column. The values in that column are the missed approach decision heights described earlier for your transition activities, in other words, the times by when each work item must be completed, or a reversion started. They are arguably the most important values in the table and they can be complex to compute if you want to come up with optimal results and not over-budget and schedule too much slack time to potential reversion activities.

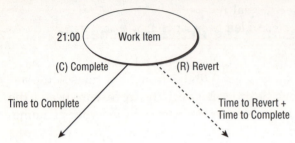

Figure 8-3: Graphical depiction of a work item and its two possible outcomes.

Figure 8-3 shows a graphical depiction of one of the work items in your schedule along with its two possible outcomes, completion or reversion. The name or ID number of the work item appears in the oval and the lines leaving the oval represent execution paths to take when the work item is done based on whether you completed the work successfully or had to revert to a prior normal state. For clarity, the figures that follow have the completion and reversion lines marked with a (C) or (R), respectively. Each line also has its distinct thickness and solid or dashed appearance to help identify it.

A numerical value (labeled "Time to Complete" in Figure 8-3) next to the completion line shows the time required to complete the work item successfully. The completion time value comes directly from your planning exercise results and is the same value as listed in the "Duration" column in Table 8-1. You can assume for the moment that these values represent reality accurately (and, if you're a good planner, they do). Shortly you'll see just how much your estimates can be off before you risk extending your work outside your maintenance window.

Similarly to the completion line, the reversion line shows the sum of the time to revert and the time to complete the work item successfully. The reason for the successful completion time estimate being added to the reversion time estimate in the reversion path is to account for the case where the work item has nearly been completed when the need to revert arises. Those familiar with network management surely understand this concept because there seem to be an inordinate number of times during maintenance activities that you are 99 percent done, but the last configuration parameters just aren't being accepted or the new server simply won't boot when all the configuration work is complete. The unfortunate truth of the matter is that, even when you're that close to completion, if the new network configuration isn't working or is unstable, the only thing to do is revert.

The value to the left of the oval in Figure 8-3 is the expected start time of the work item. This value and the durations symbolized by the values associated with the execution-path arrows will be used shortly to determine the total amount of time required for the work items in a given maintenance window to be completed (accounting for potential reversion) and the amount of spare time you have based on what work is left to be done.

Representing Your Work Items Graphically

Using the data from all but the "Revert @" columns in Table 8-1, and the graphical depiction of a work item from Figure 8-3, you can construct a timeline in graphical form, as shown in Figure 8-4. In stringing your work items together, note that all the reversion paths terminate the transition activities and point to the expected worst-case time for relevant reversion to take. All the completion paths point to the next work item, except for the completion path from work item #5, because that is the last work item scheduled for this maintenance window. The start times of the work items the completion paths lead to are based on the sunny-day execution of all the preceding work items. Work item #5 doesn't lead to another work item, so only its sunny-day completion time is shown.

You can think of Figure 8-4 as the flight plan for your transition activities. The relevant characteristic to know here regarding any flight plan is that the plan becomes obsolete the moment you take off. In both flying and network maintenance, there are many sources of delay, and there are also ways to speed things up safely to make up for lost time and get your activities back on track. In any realistic example, it is absurd to think that work item #4, for example, will start at exactly 1 a.m. (01:00). Assuming your maintenance activities are standalone (meaning you don't need to coordinate with anyone else's work efforts), if you finish work item #3 at 12:45 a.m. and then start work item #4, that's no big deal and you may even be able to get home early.

What you can't do is finish too late, because that jeopardizes the successful completion of the remaining work items. That means you need to decide for each work item what it means to be too late, and as emphasized earlier, you need to decide that *before* you start work.

Computing Revert Times Based on Work Remaining

As hinted at earlier, when you schedule your transition activities, the "Revert @" column is typically filled in last, because the revert time for each work item is a function of the duration of the completion or reversion efforts for all the work items that follow that work item. In this section, you'll learn how to compute the revert time, based on all those values. With the graphical timeline you created in the previous section, the revert-time computations amount to little more than reading the right numbers off Figure 8-4 and doing some simple arithmetic.

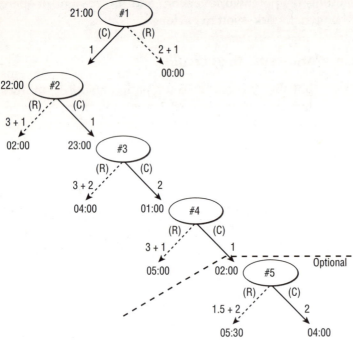

Figure 8-4: Timeline for example transition activities in Table 8-1.

Computing Revert Times for Your Mandatory Work Items

The "Revert @" column in Table 8-1 is defined as the latest time a particular work item can complete while still allowing for completion or reversion of the remaining work items. Ignore the parenthetical values for a moment, because they pertain to optional work items and are covered in the next section. The non-parenthetical values in the column represent the revert times associated with your mandatory work items only.

You can see that the revert times in Table 8-1 are not shown in Figure 8-4, per se. They can be computed readily from the figure, however, using the times shown at the end of all the reversion path arrows and the completion path arrow for the last work item. Ignore work item #5 for the moment, because it is optional. Instead, use work item #5's sunny-day start value of 2 a.m. as the sunny-day completion value for work item #4. The set of worst-case times that reversion is expected to complete for work items #1 through #4 consists of 12 a.m., 2 a.m., 4 a.m., and 5 a.m., respectively. The successful completion time for the set of all four work items is 2 a.m. (that is, the completion time of the last mandatory work item, #4).

Given the set of times just listed, the latest time that you'll complete your mandatory work items successfully or by reverting is 5 a.m., which is the time to revert from a worst-case failure in work item #4. Because your maintenance window runs until 6 a.m., that means you have one hour of spare time to apply across all of your work items. It's therefore simple to compute the times that your work items must complete while still getting work item #4 done successfully or reverted. Apply that one hour of spare time to all of the work items and you'll be able to compute the (non-parenthetical) revert time values shown in the "Revert @" column in Table 8-1.

For example, take the revert time for work item #1, which is 11 p.m. Assuming your other work estimates are correct and you don't have a safe way to accelerate your remaining work items, if you don't complete work item #1 by 11 p.m., you will not be able to complete all the remaining work items *and* have enough of a buffer should you have to revert work item #4. Because all the work items are mandatory, once you start work item #1, your only choices are to proceed with successful completions of all your work items until you finish work item #4 or revert somewhere in the middle. There is no intermediate success case where you can stop and put off the rest of the work for another day. In the literal interpretation of the process described in this section, if you're not done with work item #1 at 11 p.m., then you must revert to the normal state the network was in prior to the start of your transition activities and call it a night, even with six hours left in your maintenance window after the reversion is done.

Taking a Moment for Reality

The hard part of all this, of course, is having the discipline to start a reversion at 11 p.m. with seven hours of maintenance window remaining. The real-world aspects of mitigating factors like "knowing" you'll be done in five more minutes, or that you can (safely) accelerate the remaining work items, are hard to capture mathematically. As you gain experience, you'll develop a gut feel as to what's doable and what isn't and nobody should expect a seasoned network engineer to follow a schedule like the one in Table 8-1 to the letter. For the experienced network engineer, the schedule acts as a guideline, pointing out things that might not be obvious, an example of which is provided shortly for a case where one work item's reversion takes significantly more time than others.

The situation you don't want to get yourself into is when it's 3 a.m. and you've finally finished the new equipment's basic configuration (work item #3 that was to have reverted no later than 2 a.m.). By not reverting at the pre-decided time an hour ago, maybe you were being overly optimistic as to the outcome of your pending verification in work item #4. If the verification fails, you may have only two hours to get things back to normal, despite having budgeted three hours for that same work when perhaps you were being more objective.

As you take risks by casting doubt on your original work estimates, consider the people who expect your network and its capabilities to be available the moment the maintenance window ends. The losses in productivity that they may suffer range from simple frustrations to financial loss and even to loss of life when you account for some of the defense and intelligence networks facing IPv6 transition. Fortunately, the administrators of the utmost critical networks (at least all the ones that I have met) understand their responsibilities and always err on the side of safety. A reminder every now and then doesn't hurt, though.

Applying Spare Time Across the Whole Schedule

The one hour of spare time you computed using Figure 8-4 does not need to be applied against one work item only. If, for example, you are running 15 minutes behind on work item #1 and complete at 10:15 p.m., you still have 45 minutes of spare time left that you can apply against the remaining work items. As long as the total time lost, for whatever reason, does not exceed the amount of spare time available, the distribution across work items of that time is irrelevant.

Factoring in Your Optional Work Items

The revert times you computed previously only took the mandatory work items into account. By only looking at the mandatory work, you computed the maximum spare time for completing all the work you must get done in the maintenance window. If all goes well, however, you'll finish the mandatory work by 2 a.m., leaving four hours of maintenance window, which feels like a waste. As suggested earlier in the chapter, to better utilize that extra time, you included some optional work. It would now be helpful to know how your revert times change if you factor in wanting to complete all of your work items, both the mandatory and optional ones.

Factoring in the completion and reversion times for work item #5 at the bottom of Figure 8-4, you can see that all of the maintenance window's revert times need to be half an hour earlier to account for the reversion path of work item #5. In other words, instead of having an hour of spare time in your maintenance window, by including item #5 you only have 30 minutes. The revert times that factor in the optional work items are shown parenthetically in the "Revert @" column in Table 8-1.

Working with More-Complex Reversions

The example based on Figure 8-4 assumes some fairly uniform amounts of effort to revert from various work items. The two main components of the reversion work are removing new equipment (if you got as far as installing it) and restoring old equipment. Once you've started installing the new equipment, from any time past that point it's no more than 3 hours to get back to the pre-transition configuration. What if, however, one of the work items comes with a significantly longer reversion effort?

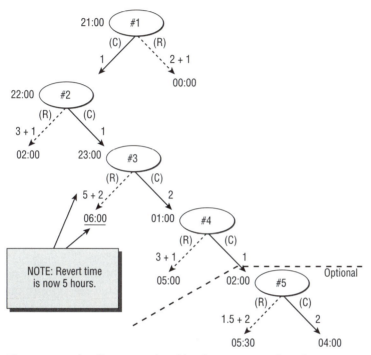

Figure 8-5: Timeline example with a longer revert time than example in Table 8-1.

Figure 8-5 shows a modified version of the transition activities graph with a 5-hour reversion effort required to recover from a failure in work item #3. Because this work item pertains to configuring the new equipment, perhaps the extra effort comes from configuration changes in other parts of the network necessary to bring the new equipment online, which needs to be restored to its pre-transition values when the old equipment is returned to service on reversion. Attributing a real-world reason to the longer reversion effort is not important, because the example is not for that purpose. What you do have to do is determine what the new revert times are for your other work items.

Because the change in the example occurred in a reversion path, work items #4 and #5 are not affected. That is, as long as you successfully complete work item #3 by 2 a.m., you still have time to complete the remaining mandatory work items. Finishing work item #3 by 1:30 a.m. leaves you time to safely fit in the optional work, also.

Given the change in the reversion path of work item #3, work items #1 through #3 now have no spare time and must execute as scheduled or quicker. If everything goes well, you'll finish work item #3 at 1 a.m. and earn an hour of spare time within which to finish work item #4 (or 30 spare minutes if you want also to try to get work item #5 done). Until work item #3 is done, however, you have no room for slippage. At 1 a.m., five hours before the maintenance window ends, you must start your reversion efforts if work item #3 is not completed.

The preceding example shows how the spare time in a maintenance window isn't always spread evenly across all the work items. There can be critical parts of the transition activities schedule that must execute on time, while other parts have room for slippage.

Verifying That Your Schedule Makes Sense

The graphical depiction of the transition activities schedule in Figure 8-4 is not only useful for computing revert times. You can also use it to verify that a schedule, like the one in Table 8-1, is mathematically correct and fits into the given maintenance window.

In formulating your transition activities schedule, you'll possibly make changes and tweak things, like the starting times of work items, in ways that you can accidentally and unknowingly create a schedule that doesn't work or make sense overall. To reduce the risk of creating such a schedule, when you think your schedule is ready, you should execute it on paper, using a graphical depiction like the one in Figure 8-4, checking the completion and reversion paths for each work item to make sure you have enough time in your maintenance window to complete the mandatory work and enough time to revert in case of mishap during any of the work items. You can also check that nothing starts before something it depends on completes.

Once you're satisfied with the mandatory portion of the schedule, check the schedule again and factor in the optional work items. If there are multiple optional work items, you can choose to limit yourself to checking only the no-option and all-option cases, meaning you check that the schedule makes sense for performing all the optional work items or none of them. You can also choose to check combinations of optional work items, but be warned that this kind of checking can get complex fast if there are more than two or three options. Based partly on the complexity of checking schedules with numerous options, as a rule you're probably better off putting no more than one or two optional work items in a transition activities schedule.

Keeping Your Transition Schedules Manageable

As you can see, the durations of work items, the amount of time it takes to revert in case of mishap, and whether a work item is mandatory or optional all weigh into the creation of your transition activities schedule. Creating such schedules gets more complex the more work items you put in them. The simple example in Table 8-1 took over two hours to compose, but it was designed to exemplify as many special cases as possible.

There may be software out there that facilitates the scheduling process. Basic project-management software or spreadsheets (at least the ones I've seen) won't fit the bill completely, due to the reversion paths in the schedules. I haven't looked for custom applications, because I prefer the approach of keeping the schedules simple enough to manage by hand. For a typical 2-hour to 8-hour maintenance window, you shouldn't force too much work and anything that looks more complex than Table 8-1 is probably overly aggressive.

For longer maintenance windows, like weekends or even weeks when a particular facility shuts down to retool or such, you're better off creating a master schedule of what's to be accomplished each day. That master schedule is built from daily schedules on the order of complexity of Table 8-1. The daily schedules must factor in intra-day dependencies so that all the work items in Day #2 have their dependencies completed in Day #1.

Don't be overwhelmed by the complexity of Table 8-1, Figure 8-3 through Figure 8-5, and the logic that underlies them all. Creating your own transition activities schedules of this sort should be much easier than the comprehensive example shown, because you really only have to ask yourself three questions:

1. How long will it take me to complete this work item? You already know that answer from your planning exercises.

2. If I can't complete the work item before I need to revert, how long will it take me to revert to the normal state that I've chosen?

3. Is this work item mandatory or optional?

After those questions are answered for all the work items you wish to perform in a maintenance window, you can create a schedule like the one in Table 8-1 and the associated graphical depiction, like the one in Figure 8-4. You can then follow the process outlined in the preceding sections and compute your revert times and check your schedule. Try it on a few simpler cases. In some of those cases, you'll maybe even start being able to do the math in your head.

Making Sure Everything and Everyone Is Ready

All the work required for starting a set of IPv6 transition activities is almost complete. Your work items have been organized and scheduled into maintenance windows. You've resolved all the dependencies required to start the next maintenance window. Your revert times have been computed and you know what to do in case of unforeseen surprises. This section covers the last few tasks that you must perform to be sure you are ready to start your IPv6 transition activities. Each time you prepare to start a maintenance window and perform the transition activities assigned to it, the following tasks must be performed. Once these tasks are complete, you're ready to start (or continue) upgrading your network to IPv6.

Backing Up Data and Configurations Before Starting

As a seasoned network manager, little needs to be explained to you about how important it is to create backups of your network configuration information, the firmware on your routers and other equipment, your software application programs, data and configurations, and so forth. You're changing a lot via your IPv6 transition, however, so a quick reminder about the importance of backups is warranted, in case you have to abandon a set of transition activities and revert to an earlier network configuration.

As important as creating backups is, verifying them is equally important. You can verify your backups immediately after creating them, and many backup applications allow you to do so easily and automatically. In the case of automated verification, make sure to check the backup application's logs to be certain that the verification phase didn't find any discrepancies. As an alternative, you could compare your backups to the live data they duplicate some time after the backups are created, but that is a much more difficult task given the frequent changes a network undergoes. Whatever you choose to do, you need to be sure that, before the live copy of the data is put at risk of being lost forever (by the execution or failure of IPv6 transition activities), you are not under the false belief that you're doing proper backups only to be storing blank tapes in your data center or offsite.

Regarding what you need to back up, how often you need to create backups, how many copies of the backups you need, where you store them (for example, offsite or locally), and other factors associated with protecting your data, these are all decisions you have to make with your specific backup policies and goals in mind. IPv6 transition should be achievable without changing your backup practices and procedures too much, because your transition activities will be less disruptive than a natural disaster or other significant outage for which you should already have recovery plans in place (and of which performing regular backups is an integral part).

If you do not have satisfactory backup and recovery procedures in place, in other words if they don't cover the effects of IPv6 transition and its potential failures, then you should not start any IPv6 transition activities without them. If you need help creating such procedures, there are several good system and network administration books available, along with online references. You can also hire one or more well-qualified system or network administrators or contract with a vendor that specializes in network management and disaster prevention.

Because establishing satisfactory backup and recovery policies, practices, and procedures is outside the scope of this book, it is assumed from here on that you have addressed your specific needs. This is an important assumption, because you have already read about reverting from failed transition activities, which often requires restoring data or configuration information from back-ups. You will read in the next chapter about restoring from backups in case the verification of your IPv6 transition activities fails. In both cases, that means you should know how to perform those backup and restoration functions, should the need to do so arise.

Communicating the Details of Your Transition Activities

The communication of what you're going to do, what you're doing, and how what you did turned out is important throughout your IPv6 transition. Chapter 6, "Defining the Transition Preparation Steps," described in detail the reasons and means for communicating your plans during the transition preparation phases. The next chapter describes how to communicate the results of your transition activities, like their success or failure. The focus of this chapter's communications section is on getting the word out regarding what you're going to do in the near term, in other words, your upcoming maintenance window. The recommendations in Chapter 6 for communicating plans apply equally well for communicating the details of impending transition activities. For example, it's a very good idea to provide a list of contact telephone and pager numbers to all the other network management and user support organizations in your enterprise (and affected customer and vendor organizations) before the transition activities start. Via the contact numbers on such a list, your team members can be reached if a transition activity causes an unexpected bad effect somewhere out on your network (or somebody else's) beyond where your team can see.

Communicating When Your Transition Activities Will Occur

In communicating transition activity execution information, there are a few more things that can be (and need to be) said, than there were when you communicated planning information in Chapter 6. Your planning information was at a sufficiently high level so as not to include anything more than perhaps crude timelines. The execution information you now must communicate needs to have the exact time that your transition activities will start in the maintenance window, along with the expected latest completion time. Within the period bracketed by the activities' start and completion times, anyone outside your team will want to be sure to have appropriate safeguards in place, in the event that something goes wrong on your end. Those external organizations may also want to put off any critical work of their own so as to avoid the risk of disruption by your activities.

Network and security monitoring organizations need your start and end time information to help pinpoint the causes of any anomalous events they detect. Knowing you have transition activities in progress helps such monitoring organizations determine whether those events are harmless ones related to your transition activities or more serious events that must be handled using your enterprise's event resolution and escalation procedures.

Communicating the times when you will be performing transition activities also gives external organizations the ability to attempt to veto your plans, should you be infringing on the time windows of more important activities. Determination of whose activities are more important is a negotiation process external to your IPv6 transition and outside the scope of this book. The part of that process that is relevant here, however, is that to make sure your team acts like a good network citizen, you need to make the times for the execution of your activities known.

Communicating Possible Side Effects of Your Activities

Closely related to activity execution times in importance to other organizations external to yours are the expected effects of those activities. On being told about your upcoming activities, some organizations may expect and prepare for the worst. By communicating enough of what you're doing, what will be changed in the network, and what the potential undesirable side effects are, you provide other organizations the information they need to prepare more accordingly and rationally.

For example, if an entire site or region like the north-eastern United States will be offline for an hour or two, organizations in other parts of the country (and the world) need to know that. This is especially true if there is greater than a nominal risk that the region may not be returning to service at the expected time. Obviously, a planned outage of such magnitude requires extraordinary proof that your transition plans are sound and that you have highly reliable procedures ready for getting things back to normal before the maintenance window ends. As your activities are assumed to have been approved, it is further assumed here that you have all the things you need to everybody's satisfaction.

An important aspect of communicating the times and expected effects of your transition activities is to do so with a sufficient amount of prior warning to the other organizations involved. Some enterprises have formal approval processes that include reviewing proposed maintenance window activities and requiring those activities to be approved by a network management oversight board or similar body. Other enterprises' processes require review by and approval from the heads of the major divisions. If you don't have such processes for your enterprise, at least consider the golden rule when deciding how much warning time to give for your transition activities. Put yourself in the position of an applications management group that suddenly finds half the country inaccessible by its monitoring systems and (false) alarms going off right and left. You wouldn't want that to happen to you. Don't inflict it on others.

Communicating the Expected Results of Your Transition Activities

As mentioned, part of your communications regarding your upcoming transition activities must include what the expected state(s) of the network will be. Given the earlier example, there will either be an upgraded version of Application 'X' running (for which the users might have gotten all the required training, and so on, before the transition activities started) or the previous version will still be in place.

In some cases, you need to give instructions for what users need to do to work with the new application. They may need to go to a different website to use the application, for example, or they may need to reset their passwords. The instructions don't have to be too detailed, because any complex training can be provided outside the transition activity communications before or sometimes after the activities complete. Ideally, the instructions you send with the transition communications should be limited to references to the training material or other documentation provided with the new application.

Communicating the results of your transition activities is covered further in Chapter 9, "Defining the Transition Verification Steps," where you will learn to tell your users and other interested parties what the actual results were. This way, you can reduce the communications described in this section to just indicating that the transition activities are about to occur and a summary of the potential outcome(s). You also reduce the communications described in the next chapter by only needing to provide instructions on working with what actually happened, as opposed to all the possible contingencies.

Choosing a Means of Communications

Your communications need not be elaborate, as long as you are comfortable that they have been received and understood by everyone who needs them. The delivery mechanism can be something as simple as an e-mail to all affected users (or their managers if the size of your organization prohibits a bulk e-mail to everyone), other transition teams, management, network monitoring organizations, your network security group, and any other organizations that might see the effects of your transition activities, both the good effects and the bad ones.

With the unfortunate reality of modern SPAM filtering, there is some chance your message may not reach everyone you want it to, so phone calls to the heads of departments or other business-unit managers can help distribute the workload and assure that the message gets out. If it makes you more comfortable, you can request responses from a limited part of your audience (that is, those same business-unit leaders) acknowledging that they understand the potential effects of your activities and that they are ready for your activities to commence at the appointed time. Such acknowledgments are no guarantee that those same people won't raise a fuss later, should something go wrong, but at least you can feel comfortable that you provided fair warning.

Getting the Green Light for Your Transition Activities

The last step before starting your IPv6 transition activities is telling network operations and various other organizations that you are ready to begin. This typically happens at the start of your maintenance window or very shortly into it, so you can get the maximum time possible to perform your activities.

Because you are probably in one of the groups that need to be informed, approval from that group is certain. As for the other groups, including network monitoring, security monitoring, customer support, and so on, you should have already done all the preparation work and communication so that approval to start comes quickly, if it hasn't already been provided ahead of time.

There may be cases where an external group needs you to wait before starting, or requires you to give up the maintenance window because there is some fire being fought somewhere else in the network that is more important than your transition activities. Should that occur, you can chalk it up to the freak accident category covered in the reversion section earlier and simply try again when the next maintenance window rolls around. You may have to adjust your plans a little more, should some of your dependencies come undone while you're waiting for the next maintenance window, for example. In most cases, however, you shouldn't suffer more than an irritating time delay.

Once you have the last of the approvals you need in hand and you've indicated to everyone who needs to know that you are starting, you can begin your transition activities and continue your journey into the brave new world of IPv6. Good luck and I'll see you in the next chapter, where you'll read about verifying that all the activities you just performed worked out correctly.

Testing Your Knowledge

The following questions address some of the key points of getting ready to start your IPv6 transition activities and recovering from failures during their execution. As always, the answers are in Appendix A.

1. When deciding the factors for when you have to revert to a prior normal state, whose views should you listen to, what do you need to establish, and when do you need put the factors in place?

2. In the context of this chapter, what does the "normal state" of your network mean?

3. What qualities should you look for when determining the locations where you'll be executing your first IPv6 transition activities?

4. What are the advantages to executing a "depth-first" transition at some of your sites?

5. What methodology advocated previously in this book is also good for identifying dependencies between IPv6 transition activities?

6. What must any group of transition activities assigned to a maintenance window achieve when, regardless of whether they complete successfully, the maintenance window ends?

Defining the Transition Verification Steps

The strongest arguments prove nothing so long as the conclusions are not verified by experience...

— Roger Bacon

I had a great manager years ago who knew the value of testing, and observed that I was particularly good at getting other people's programs to fail. He gave me a copy of *Peopleware* so that I might read the chapter on the Black Team, IBM's infamous testers of the 1960s who would revel in making developers' software fail. To the uninitiated (or software development managers), the chapter reads like a story about a bunch of jerks who nowadays would be accused of subjecting software to unrealistic tests and wasting the company's resources. My contrarian opinion is formed by an excerpt from near the end of the chapter that reads, "Needless to say, the company was delighted. Every defect the team found was one that the customers wouldn't find." You do not have software customers. Your customers are the users of your network and its applications. As you complete your IPv6 transition activities, remember the importance of verifying the results. If you're one of those people concerned about the happiness of others, think of all the users who will enjoy high-quality network services and capabilities. If you're the selfish type, think of all the trouble tickets and 3 a.m. phone calls you won't get, if you verify that your transition activities got done right the first time. It's a win-win either way.

What You'll Learn

Hand in hand with the execution of your IPv6 transition activities goes the verification that those activities resulted in the correct changes and upgrades to your network. Moreover, the purpose of verification is to make sure that you didn't break anything else along the way while upgrading your network to IPv6. In this chapter you learn how and where to fit verification into your IPv6 transition activities. You learn what to verify and in what order, from the most required capabilities to semi-optional capabilities that you can verify at a more leisurely pace.

Emphasis is placed on the importance to verification of having good requirements pertaining to what your IPv6 (and IPv4) capabilities should do, how well they should perform, and how secure they should be. You will also be introduced to a few different testing paradigms, some of which you may be familiar with and some of which may be new to you. The importance of regression tests and automation in testing is also presented. In the event your tests should fail, you'll learn to identify the cause of the failure and what steps you need to take to recover.

The chapter wraps up by reminding you of some final steps you need to take once a given set of transition activities is complete. It also reminds you to tell all the affected parties that your activities are complete and how they went.

Testing the New Configuration

In the preceding chapter, you (finally) started executing your IPv6 transition activities. As you finish those activities, you need to verify that they achieved the desired results. In other words, you have to verify that the transition activities were successful. The amount of verification you'll want to do to satisfy yourself that the transition activities were successful is dependent on what the specific activities tried to accomplish. For simple configuration of devices and applications that are already IPv6 capable, sufficient verification can be provided by some simple tests. If you're replacing assets with entirely new models, possibly from completely different vendors from those who sold you the old assets, you may want very elaborate verification suites.

Verification of your IPv6 upgrade, like so many endeavors in computer-related disciplines, is still in the realm of "gut feel," meaning that sufficient coverage is defined by what makes the people performing the transition activities comfortable that everything is working correctly. As a consequence, sometimes you'll test too much, which is satisfactory from the point of view of pure verification, but can be a waste of a few or many resources. On the other hand, you may test too little, perhaps because you're overconfident based on the belief that the changes you are making to the network are straightforward or minimal. Overkill in verification can be difficult to spot (partly because it is so rare), whereas determining that you're verifying too little is usually spotted quickly, typically by your users. Though it is desirable to keep the trouble tickets and support calls to a minimum, you can at least feel some comfort in having that feedback process to improve your network's quality.

As has been recommended in this book before, the best way to proceed with verification is to rely on your prior experience when deciding the depth and breadth of your coverage. You are not performing completely alien work to what you normally do in network management. Whatever verification you perform to roll out an enterprise-wide release of a new operating system, application, or hardware upgrade (that isn't IPv6 related) should also apply to your IPv6 upgrade. Don't get consumed by all the hype about IPv6 and just focus on the network management job of deploying the capabilities.

Benefiting from Good Requirements

The level of effort involved in verifying your network's new IPv6 capabilities, and that all of the old IPv4 capabilities your users continue to need are still there, is directly related to how well you prepared for your transition way back when you were defining your requirements for IPv6. The better you described what IPv6 capabilities your network and its applications must have, the easier it will be to verify that those capabilities work as desired. Moreover, if you didn't already have good requirements for your IPv4 capabilities, preparing for your IPv6 transition will have been the right time to create or update those IPv4 requirements, as well.

In addition to needing the IPv4 requirements to verify that all your required IPv4 capabilities are still present, you should also have reviewed those requirements to see if any of them were modified by way of the IPv6 transition. In your first upgrades, like your network backbone for example, your IPv4 requirements will likely remain the same as they were before you started working with IPv6. Later transitions, however, like those that move applications, departments, or sites from the IPv4 realm to IPv6, may allow you to eliminate IPv4 support (or at least reduce it) in parts of your network.

Covering the Multiple Types of Requirements

Your requirements should cover what capabilities are necessary in terms of functionality, performance, security, and other areas, some of which may be unique to your enterprise. For example, some enterprises may have compatibility requirements to allow them to interoperate with other organizations. Other enterprises may have standard hardware or software configurations that must be used on their equipment for maintainability or any number of other reasons. Because there are so many possible areas where requirements are needed, this book cannot cover all of them fully and will be limited to functionality, performance, and security. For your particular requirements issues, good requirements are the basis for overall success in a project. Refer to the numerous requirements-management books (for example, *System Requirements Analysis* by Jeffrey O. Grady), software products, and courses available.

Assuring You Create Testable Requirements

If you've been in project management for a while, you'll have heard the term "testable requirements." This is a requirement, if you will, on the requirements themselves. A requirement is of little use if determining whether it has been met is not possible, in other words, if it isn't testable.

The need to have testable requirements is also the primary reason why the appropriate testing organizations in your enterprise should be intimately involved in defining your IPv6 requirements. If you're doing your own testing of the IPv6 capabilities being deployed (and a later section argues why it's better that you don't), then you'll be the one in charge of determining that all your requirements are testable. Otherwise, you should include the people testing your work in the definition of the work's requirements. Those people can tell you not only whether a requirement is testable, but also the level of effort required to test it.

For example, one likely requirement that applies to all your applications and network management tools is that all web pages and other displays that show IPv4 addresses must also be able to show IPv6 addresses. Though that's a trivial requirement to state, the verification (not to mention the implementation) of the requirement could require dozens (or hundreds) of hours of work. Such a requirement should be decomposed to address specific applications and tools directly, if only to provide some hint to the readers of the requirements as to the level of effort involved. Moreover, either the requirements or the IPv6 transition plans and tasks derived from them should go further to enumerate all the web pages, displays, and so on, involved. This allows for better resource management and scheduling.

Reviewing IPv6 Transition Terminology

Chapter 8 introduced terminology that defined your enterprise's IPv6 transition as being achieved via transition activities composed of work items, which take place during maintenance windows. Earlier chapters discussed planning your IPv6 transition and creating tasks for executing it. The relationship between your IPv6 transition plans and your transition activities is shown in

Figure 9-1. For roughly each one of the tasks in your plan, there is a transition activity to execute that task. This is not a strict formula that must be followed, but more of a guideline and a way to think of your overall IPv6 transition in terms you can manage and communicate to others.

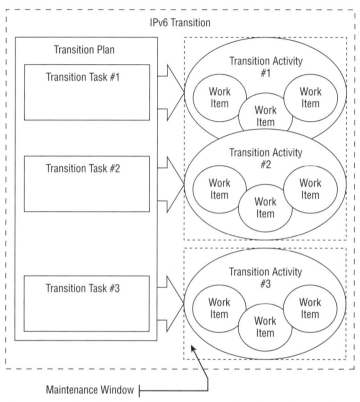

Figure 9-1: Organization of your IPv6 transition into plans, tasks, activities, and so on

Another IPv6 transition planning and execution guideline is that more than one transition activity can occur in a maintenance window, but all transition activities should fit into their windows completely. In other words, you shouldn't split a transition activity across two maintenance windows. If you do, you definitely need a step at the end of the first portion of the transition activity to "button up" the network and get it back to normal operations before the maintenance window ends. This may require additional steps at the beginning of the second portion of the transition activity, performed in a subsequent maintenance window, to "unbutton" the network back to the state required to upgrade it. These two steps are unnecessary, if you keep a transition activity contained in one maintenance window.

Don't Some Activities Happen Outside of Maintenance Windows?

There are some IPv6 transition activities that need not occur during mainte-nance windows, for example certain types of verification, which you'll read about shortly. In addition, the software development work to upgrade your in-house applications to have IPv6 capabilities occurs outside maintenance win-dows. That work is performed by your software development teams as part of their daily jobs during normal business hours (whatever that means for soft-ware development). It is only when a release of that in-house application is being deployed that maintenance windows get involved. Because the software development work of upgrading any in-house applications is an important part of your IPv6 transition (and subject to its own verification efforts), but not one constrained to maintenance windows or affecting users or network stabil-ity until deployment, it is not covered in this chapter. Refer to Chapter 13, "Using Pilot Programs to Facilitate Your IPv6 Transition," because the pilot programs covered therein include software development examples for upgrading applications to IPv6.

Understanding the Role of Work Items in Your Activities

A typical IPv6 transition task and activity is the upgrading of all of your routers at a particular site (or a subset of buildings, departments, or floors at that site), as in the example from the previous chapter. This is a good descrip-tion of a self-contained and fairly significant bundle of work that can be staffed, scheduled, and otherwise manipulated during the planning process. It is not, however, a sufficient description for executing the work.

The details of what work must be done during transition activities are described by the work items contained in those activities. You saw work items being defined and used for transition activity scheduling in Chapter 8, "Defin-ing the Transition Execution Steps," specifically in the sections associated with Figure 8-3 through Figure 8-5. A work item must be sufficiently detailed to describe what must be done by the staff executing the work. Examples of work item descriptions include "remove all the old routers" or "install and config-ure the new routers." The preceding are, of course, overly simplistic examples of work items, but you should get the idea. Depending on the level of experi-ence of your IPv6 transition staff, the work items can be more or less detailed. Seasoned network managers may know exactly what it means to replace all the routers in Building 14, for example, whereas less-experienced staff may require a list of the routers in that building (or at least a reference to where the list can be found).

Including Verification in Your Transition Activities

Verification, as shown by the router-upgrade example in the previous chapter, is implemented as another work item (or set of work items) in your transition activities. Verification is a critical part of your IPv6 transition and there should be at least one work item devoted to it in every transition activity. In some cases, you might choose to include a single verification work item at the end of a particular transition activity, or you can include verification steps throughout the transition activity. In the latter case, you may choose to verify that subsets of capabilities being implemented by the transition activity are functional, before proceeding to the next implementation work items. For example, in upgrading routers you might first verify that IPv4 capabilities are functional, and then move on to implementing and verifying basic IPv6, and finally advanced IPv6 capabilities, rather than verifying all of those capabilities at the end.

By having multiple verification work items in a transition activity, you can create checkpoints in case the need to revert to a prior configuration arises during work items later in the maintenance window. This way, you don't necessarily have to revert to the configuration as it was prior to the maintenance window starting, which would lose all the work you accomplished during that window. You can instead revert to one of the checkpoints and reorganize the remaining work items into a shorter transition activity that can fit in a smaller maintenance window at a later time.

Separating Execution and Verification

Taking a page from software engineering, it's always a good idea to maintain a separation between the development team and the team that tests the software. The closer the two teams are to each other in the enterprise's organizational chart, the more likely you are to get inferior software. The worst case is when the two teams are one and the same. The same logic can be applied to the execution and verification of your IPv6 upgrade.

Software development and testing are fairly serial activities, in other words, you have to develop something before you can test it. Translating the execution and verification separation concept directly to your IPv6 transition activities might leave you with the verification team sitting idle while the "development" team is implementing the changes in your network. That's no fun for the testers at 2 a.m. (though they could be called in later when the development portion of the transition activities is close to complete). Instead, you may want to separate your transition activities team into two groups or schedule two or more transition activities in a given maintenance window. That way, both teams can do their actual changes to the network and then verify the handiwork of the other team.

The other option you have for separating execution and verification during your IPv6 transition activities is to include the network and security monitoring organizations in the verification phase. A useful attribute of the changes you're making as part of your transition is that most of the changes can be detected and verified from afar. That means, as they complete their work items, your execution team can inform the network monitoring team that the capabilities those work items implemented are available for verification. This is a natural way to test the network in any case, because once your assets are restored to normal operation, the monitoring organizations will be verifying them constantly in a sense anyway.

Nowadays, it's understandable that you may not be able to deploy separate execution and verification teams. Whatever your resource and scheduling limitations, the point of this section is to teach you that separating execution and verification of work items leads to better quality overall and that you should strive to achieve such separation whenever possible. You'll be surprised what an independent verification team can find wrong compared to the network engineers who implemented the capabilities, not because those engineers aren't any good, but rather because they are too close to the implementation to see all the potential problems. The savings in not having to go back to rework items that weren't done correctly in the first place may justify better verification up front, though you shouldn't be disappointed to find that hardly anybody believes that until they see all the trouble tickets generated by insufficient verification.

Verifying the Different Types of Capabilities

As mentioned earlier in this chapter, the types of capabilities and the verification of them discussed in this book are limited to the domains of functionality, performance, and security. Each one of those capability domains has its own unique way of being verified. This section covers all three capability domains and offers examples and suggestions you can apply to your verification efforts.

Verifying Functionality Capabilities

Verification of feature functionality is in some ways the easiest, because the testers are given a set of features, via the requirements, and testing reveals which features work and which don't. A functional requirement might read:

[R1]   All IPv6 traffic must be routable by the enterprise backbone so that accessing any IPv6-based service external to the enterprise is possible.

This is one of those requirements that can only be verified in theory by showing that every external service with an IPv6 address is reachable from within the enterprise. Such a broad requirement is usually covered by a handful of test cases, created with knowledge of the network's routing behavior and covering a wide enough range to exercise all the ISP connections. It should be sufficient to have the test cases attempt to access some publicly available IPv6-based web servers to verify connectivity. If all the selected external sites are accessible during verification, then the requirement can be deemed to have been met.

Verifying Performance Capabilities

Verifying performance requirements takes more work from the verification team, because the previously discussed functionality test cases have to be instrumented to measure the performance of connections in addition to having to detect that the targeted external sites are accessible. The preceding section's requirement, written with performance in mind, might read:

> [R1]   All IPv6 traffic must be routable by the enterprise backbone so that accessing any IPv6-based service external to the enterprise is possible at *no less than* 1.5Mbps.

Using proper requirements management, the functionality and performance requirements would be separate, but for illustration purposes the two are combined here. The performance portion of the preceding requirement necessitates that the verification team has a way to measure the throughput of the connections they are making to external services. The team also must have the means both to generate network traffic at the required throughput rate or faster *and* to sink the traffic at the destination side.

For the 1.5Mbps requirement (a T1 line), any common PC should be able to produce that throughput rate. For requirements specifying aggregate throughput rates suitable for a large enterprise, special equipment may need to be procured. Don't forget the other half of the test case, which is the need to sink all that network traffic. Sending HTTP requests to the IPv6 versions of popular websites may verify accessibility, but may not give you enough measurable traffic to verify performance requirements. Bombarding those same sites and measuring the output rate at your end verifies the output half of your performance requirement, but may not verify the incoming rate, because the sites may not respond at sufficient speeds. You also may upset the sites' owners with all the unwanted traffic.

To sink large quantities of traffic externally, you may need to place your own test devices "outside" your network, which could amount to simply attaching them to the external-side LAN segments of the firewalls leading to your ISPs. An additional advantage to such a verification configuration is that you will be measuring only the performance of the part of the connection that you can control. Your performance requirements should only address the performance from your network perimeter inward, not the whole Internet. By attaching your data sinks just outside your network, even before traffic goes to an ISP, you eliminate the cases where a given external site is responding too slowly or the networks along the path to that site are congested.

Verifying Security Capabilities

The most difficult requirements to verify are invariably security requirements. This is because they almost always are written as a negative statement. Adding a security component to the requirement from the preceding section produces:

[R1]   All IPv6 traffic must be routable by the enterprise backbone so that accessing any IPv6-based service external to the enterprise, *except Telnet*, is possible at *no less than* 1.5Mbps.

You can see why it is recommended that you separate requirements into their distinct functionality, performance, and security capability domains, because the preceding combined requirement is now somewhat ambiguous. Does it mean that Telnet is forbidden, or that Telnet simply doesn't have to meet the performance requirement?

Assuming IPv6-based Telnet traffic is forbidden from exiting your network, you have to verify that no Telnet services external to your enterprise are accessible from within the enterprise. You can use modified versions of the test cases you created earlier for functionality verification, and simply reverse the success and failure conditions. If you can't get to a given Telnet service, the test case passes.

To be truly sure your network is secure, you need to know why you couldn't reach an external Telnet service. For example, the external service simply may have been down when you were testing against it, so the connection failure had nothing to do with your network's security. This is another case where a closed-loop verification environment, like the one discussed for performance verification, is valuable. By having an "outside" Telnet server running, the state of which is well-known and controlled by you, you can be sure that, if a connection cannot be made to that server, it's because of network security being correctly configured, not the server being down.

Using Black-Box, White-Box, and Grey-Box Testing

To create a manageable set of test cases, especially security test cases, you need to combine elements of testing paradigms called black-box and white-box testing. Black-box testing requires testers to operate as users, working solely from the documentation and other information provided to users for the capabilities under test. If the testers are verifying that network connectivity is present at a satisfactory level of throughput and only for the types of services authorized by the enterprise security policy, all the testers might be given are a connection to the enterprise network, the list of proxy servers (if applicable) to access external services, and the DNS names or IPv6 addresses of the external services to be tested against. The testers have no idea which of the enterprise's ISPs is being used for each connection (though they might be able to infer it from the IPv6 address they are assigned). They also have no idea what the network's internal routing looks like. Black-box testing promotes the separation of execution and verification mentioned earlier, but it can lead to a lot of test cases, because the testers don't know enough about the environment to optimize testing.

White-box testing is, as you might guess, the opposite of black-box testing. The testers are given every possible scrap of information regarding the network topology, proxy locations, ISP connection points, and so on. White-box testing is best for verifying security requirements because it negates the "security by obscurity" crutch that many development and network management teams use to create solutions quickly. If the testers know the same things as the network engineers, for example, that there is a special secret proxy server that allows all connectivity to external sites, then the Telnet security test cases will likely fail.

An intermediate testing paradigm that combines the best of black-box and white-box testing is called grey-box testing. Each organization chooses a different point in the spectrum and some grey-box testing is blacker and some is whiter. The goal is to know as little as possible about the thing you're testing, while at the same time reducing the number of test cases to something you can manage. For example, if the testers know there are only three external connections to the outside from a given site, then they can test the Telnet security requirements against the firewalls of those three points. Security experts reading this will likely consider this insufficient testing; who's to say that just because network management thinks there are only three external connections, there aren't more? Quite true, but this is only an example.

Verifying the Minimum Required Capabilities

Many of your IPv6 transition activities will implement capabilities that nobody may need for some time. Recall that the Federal OMB transition mandate only requires your network backbone *to be able* to route IPv6 traffic. There are no mandates due June 2008 for any application or other IPv6 functionality that would actually generate IPv6 traffic.

Because the IPv6 capabilities you're deploying will have a limited audience for some time, there are two distinct classes of capabilities that come out of your transition activities. There are the required capabilities that were there prior to the transition activities occurring and there are the optional capabilities, like IPv6 functionality. Technically, by virtue of the OMB mandate, the IPv6 capabilities are not optional, but there won't be too many people on the proverbial Monday morning that will miss those capabilities if you didn't get them working in last weekend's maintenance window.

Of the required capabilities, there is a subset that contains the minimum required to declare the network usable. Depending on the specific transition activities, that minimum set may include all the required capabilities affected by the transition activities. In other cases, the minimum set may be missing some esoteric capabilities that your users can go a short time without. You'll have to restore them as soon as possible, if you didn't by the end of the maintenance window, but you have a few hours or even days of breathing room. One way you can decide whether a certain required capability falls into the minimum required set is to ask yourself whether you'll be allowed to go home at the end of the maintenance window if the given capability hasn't been restored yet. You might also ask yourself what the user reaction and feedback associated with that capability's absence will be.

Verifying the Less-Required and Optional Capabilities

Once you've verified the minimum required capabilities (and remember, in many cases that may include *all* the required capabilities), you have some latitude how to proceed with verification. If you've verified all the execution work items completed so far in the given maintenance window, then the next thing to do, depending on how much time is left in that window, is either to go on to the next work item or go home.

If your transition activities didn't go as smoothly as planned, then you may have chosen to verify your minimum required capabilities first and then move on to verifying any other capabilities you implemented via the execution work items. For example, you may have changed out all your old routers with new IPv6-capable ones and found yourself tight for time due to some unexpected delay or problem. Instead of running all your verification test cases in parallel, you chose to verify minimum required functionality (IPv4 routing) first. Once those capabilities were verified, you moved on to the SNMP-management test cases, in other words, whether the new routers' IPv4 capabilities could be managed using your SNMP tools. The requirements said the routers had to be manageable by SNMP, the vendor said they were, and now you need to verify the claims. If you run out of time in the maintenance window, you can continue the SNMP verification later on, because the users don't care about SNMP management. They just need the routers to route.

A word on running verification test cases while the network is in use: Once you've achieved the minimal necessary configuration or capabilities for the network to provide what the users need, you can continue verification after the network is back online, however such verification should be limited to activities that exclude:

1. Disabling or hindering basic or required network capabilities, unless users have been told ahead of time of such a possibility and everybody who needs to sign off has done so. Beyond informing the users, it's also up to your network policies whether you can introduce instability during business hours. The users may be OK with it, but your accountants and lawyers may not be.

2. Changing network or application configuration parameters, because any time you change a configuration, you risk changing something that you didn't want to change (and it usually changes in a bad way) or you wind up changing something that you did want to change, but incorrectly.

3. Adding any test or troubleshooting equipment, because that usually involves breaking connectivity, which could cause a loss of capabilities. Even a temporary loss may be significant, if a critical session were in progress between a user and an application server, for example.

As has been mentioned before, your upgrade to IPv6 is no different from any other large MIS/IT upgrade, and you should know by now what's allowed to happen on your network during business hours, what's strictly forbidden, and what's a grey area open to discussion and interpretation. Just keep Hippocrates in mind when working outside of maintenance windows; in other words, do no harm.

Using Regression Tests to Expedite Verification

Some transition activities are so simple that you may question the need for elaborate functionality, performance, and security verification after performing the work items in the given activity. For example, if you already have an IPv6-capable router in place serving a building at one of your sites, configuring it for IPv6 routing should take fewer than 30 to 60 minutes and you won't even have to disable the IPv4 capabilities while you're doing the configuration.

Once the IPv6 configuration is done, "pinging" another internal or external IPv6-capable device may suffice to verify the new capabilities. What about the IPv4 capabilities? You can probably issue an IPv4 ping to an appropriate device to be more comfortable that the newly configured router is still functioning for IPv4. That doesn't cover performance, however, and some IPv6-capable devices are alleged to be slower with IPv6 enabled. Given that information, you might want to repeat part of your performance verification. As for security, if you made changes to the router's filtering rules, it's probably a good idea to verify those changes, as well.

As you can see, prudence requires you to verify anything that *might have* been changed by your transition activities, not just those things that you believe have changed. To make such verification easier, most organizations implement regression testing. Regression tests are composed of a set of test cases to be run no matter what the intended changes to the network. Test cases typically included in regression tests cover basic connectivity, throughput, and security (for example, making sure the nastiest TCP ports are still blocked against inbound traffic to your network). It's impractical to run your whole verification test suite for every trivial change, but regression tests allow you some level of comfort at a minimal cost of time and effort.

To choose which test cases you should include in your regression test suite, start by looking at those test cases that verify your minimum required network capabilities. If that's all you can verify regularly and be sure is working properly, you're ahead of many other organizations. Also, look for test cases that give you the biggest bang for the buck. For example, a simple ping of a device external to your network verifies your network addressing and routing to and from the LAN sourcing the ping traffic. It also verifies your DNS services, and provides some performance information via the round-trip time of the ping. In contrast, a complex test case to verify some esoteric application feature, even if that feature is on the minimum required capabilities list, probably shouldn't be included in your regression tests.

Automating Your Verification Tests

To improve the coverage of your verification efforts, and especially your regression test suites, you should consider automating as much of your verification as possible. There are many different kinds of software tools available to enable test automation. Some, like those from Spirent, comprehensively cover much of your IPv6 verification needs. Even if you can't afford or don't care for such store-bought tools, a simple UNIX-based system (Linux or FreeBSD), for example, and some shell scripting goes a long way in automatically verifying network functionality. For verifying IPv6-capable applications, especially your Microsoft Windows-based ones, you'll probably need to buy tools, because creating those test cases requires issuing mouse movements, clicks, and so on, which can range from being difficult to being impossible to do any other way.

Another advantage of automated test cases is that you can create many more tests. This way, if you find a particular problem with the network once, for example, a firewall apparently "forgetting" to filter a certain form of traffic, you can add the automated test case for that failure to your regression tests. That allows you to check that the given firewall is still working correctly every time you run your regression tests. Moreover, automation enables you to run your test cases whenever you want. You can schedule a nightly job to verify functionality, performance, or security. Such tests can even be run during the day using automation, provided you obey the principles cited earlier regarding not disturbing the network while users are on it and expecting full functionality.

Recovering from Failure

Once you introduce verification of capabilities, you also introduce the possibility for that verification to fail. If a verification work item fails during your transition activities, you need to figure out why it failed and what to do about the failure. Typically, you need to do so quickly because either there are other work items to execute or the end of the maintenance window is approaching.

Determining the Cause of a Verification Failure

When a verification test case fails, the first thing you have to do is figure out why it failed. Test cases focus on verifying capabilities, or more accurately, the requirements that describe those capabilities. When a test case fails, you know the functionality of the capability being tested is suspect. If your test cases are well written, you also should be able to identify the device or application that is suspect. The reason I say "suspect," and not "broken," is that part of your triage process to find what failed includes eliminating all the causes that are not related to the capability the test case declared a failure.

Finding the Root Cause of Verification Failures

Just because a given test case fails doesn't immediately mean the capability being tested is what's broken. For example, if you're testing the functionality of an application and you can't connect to the application server, the server may be fine. The actual problem may be located between your client workstation and the server in the form of a network-connectivity outage. Other alternate possibilities as to why the test case failed are that the operating system on the application server crashed or that the data center housing the server lost power.

Relying on the results of one test case to isolate a failure can lead to a lot of wasted time and effort trying to fix something that isn't broken. Unless the cause of the failure is obvious, for example you connected to the application server via a maintenance console and found the application had crashed, you should look at the results of all your test cases to determine whether there is a pattern that points to a root cause. This is another excellent argument for automated regression tests, because you can test a larger portion of your network and its applications readily if you're having trouble isolating the problem using only the test cases pertinent to the current IPv6 transition activities.

Accounting for Incorrectness in Verification Tests

Just like you can make mistakes in your execution work items, your verification test cases can be wrong, too. Don't rule out checking your test suites, because they might be testing the requirements incorrectly. Requirements tend to be underspecified, especially for a project as large and complex as an IPv6 transition of an enterprise network. Interpretations by different organizations, including project management, those executing the transition activities, and those verifying the work, may differ. That means some upfront planning work is required to achieve consensus on what the requirements really mean. Moreover, as execution plans and verification test cases are created, you should be putting them out for review to all those involved in requirements, execution, and verification to make sure that the test cases match what the requirements intend and also that the engineers executing the work items implement those intentions.

Fixing Non-Critical Failures without Reverting

Once you have identified the root cause of your verification failure, you need to figure out what to do about it. Provided you have the time during your maintenance window, there's nothing forbidding you from fixing any problems found during verification and then running the verification tests again. This cycle can be repeated until the verification tests pass or until the maintenance window's end is so close that you have to revert to an earlier stable configuration. If there are verification work items that you can perform outside your maintenance window, the same cyclical process can be applied in that case as well, provided you adhere to the guidance offered earlier as to what types of activities to avoid when the network is online for your users.

The ability to do quick fixes to parts of the network during verification is augmented by having automated test suites. In addition to the savings in time and ease of use associated with automated test suites, automation eliminates the possibility of human error that arises when a manual task (like a test case) is repeated multiple times in quick succession.

When you repeat the cycle of trying to fix a problem and then testing your latest attempted fix, it's just human nature that you will eventually skip a key step or make some other mistake that will lead to either falsely passed test cases or configuration errors in the network or its applications. That's why it's a good idea, if you don't have the benefit of automation, to be particularly attentive (as the expression goes, "measure twice, cut once") when performing more than a few iterations of alternating between manual test cases and fixing any problems discovered on the live network.

Reverting from Backups

If you determine that the cause of your verification failure cannot be repaired *and* re-verified in the time remaining in your maintenance window and you can't work past the end of the window, then you have no choice but to revert to a prior stable configuration before your maintenance window ends. This is where your backups come into play.

As discussed in the preceding chapter, backups range from the kinds most system administrators think of, which are near-mirror images of servers and workstations, to much smaller backups representing configuration parameters pulled from routers and other network devices via TFTP or similar protocols. You should have made backups prior to starting the transition activities you are reverting from now. In some cases, like network device configurations in particular, you may also have made backups following intermediate steps of your transition activities. For example, you may have backed up an upgraded router's configuration after you verified its post-upgrade IPv4 functionality, but before you started configuring the IPv6 capabilities.

Reconciling Compatibility Issues of Upgrades and Backups

You should be aware that backups taken of a given version of network-device firmware and configuration data or software application configurations and user data may not be restorable to later versions. Vendors typically support backward compatibility across most releases, perhaps excluding major releases. If there's any doubt as to whether your old backups are restorable to an upgraded device or application, contact the vendor for their assistance.

In some cases, especially across major releases, a vendor may support restoration from older backups as a manual procedure (or via a special restoration application) where the raw backup from the prior version might be loaded to another system. The necessary data is then extracted from that system, reformatted to be compatible with the new version, and then restored to the upgraded device or application. Such services are not always free, so discuss what your options are with the given vendor, including the financial aspects, *before* you execute the upgrade of the relevant systems or applications. Many vendors are happy to upgrade you to the latest version of their products (if you're under a maintenance agreement or elect to partake in one as part of the restoration services) and give you free services to do the restoration. Other vendors may not provide the services for free, even if you are already paying support fees, because an upgrade isn't always considered maintenance.

Verifying the State of New Features Not Stored in Backups

If you managed to upgrade a network device's firmware or an application's software and the use of a prior version's backup is supported to restore configuration and user data, then your reversion to a prior stable configuration may allow you to keep the upgraded firmware or software, shortening the total time you need to re-try the transition activities that you are reverting from this time. Next time, you will still need to configure the device or application, but you won't need to upgrade its firmware or software.

When restoring from the old backup, you still have to verify that any new features unique to the upgraded version, like the IPv6 features, for example, are set to acceptable values for your environment. The configuration parameters for the new features won't be stored in the backup, because the new features did not exist in the backed-up version. The restoration functionality of the device or application will set those new parameters to default values, leave them untouched, or set them to random values. How the restoration functionality behaves is entirely vendor dependent, because there are no standard behaviors. Vendors of good quality products will have thought of some reasonable behavior, but there are many reasonable choices, so you still have to ask the vendor how the restoration functionality behaves.

As an example of the preceding discussion, assume you are upgrading a router's firmware. The newer firmware version is IPv6 capable, but the older version is not. Assume further that a backup of the older version's configuration parameters can be loaded into the newer version, thus restoring all your IPv4 configuration information. What you need to verify, in addition to whether the IPv4 capabilities are working correctly, is whether the IPv6 capabilities are set to what you want them to be. It's possible that the router's default behavior is to have all IPv6 auto-configuration features on, or none of them may be enabled, or something in between might be the case. Whatever the behavior of the upgraded device is, you need to make sure it's what's right for your network. If you're only upgrading firmware and restoring the old IPv4 configuration, but not configuring IPv6 during the current transition activities, then you need to make sure that the IPv6 capabilities are turned off.

Knowing When You Are Done

Simply put, your transition activities are done when your verification test cases all pass. In reality, you're not really done until the users have tested the configuration by working with it, but that kind of testing takes place over the days and weeks after the transition activities are done. As such, it is best to keep backups around for possible reversion use for quite a while until you feel comfortable.

Making Sure to Clean Up Any Loose Ends

There are a few final things you need to be sure to do after the verification of functionality, performance, and so on is complete, but before telling everyone you're done with your IPv6 transition activities. Referred to earlier as "buttoning up" your network, these final activities include removing any test equipment from the network and from maintenance ports on routers, switches, and so on. You need to reset any devices or applications that you placed into "debug mode" or on which you enabled more than the usual amount of event logging. Both debugging modes and increased logging rob your systems and applications of performance required for user activities. Debug mode may also open security vulnerabilities that must be closed before users return to the network or start using an upgraded application.

Communicating When Activities Are Complete

In the execution phase of your IPv6 transition, you told a number of parties when you were starting your transition activities, what you were doing, and what the various potential outcomes would be. For example, you told the users that they could expect either an upgraded version of an application or no apparent change, depending how things worked out and what the goal of the particular transition activities was. You also possibly provided intermediate status on your activities to network monitoring, external organizations, and other interested parties.

As the last step of your IPv6 transition activities' verification phase, you will tell those same parties that your work is done, how it turned out, what it is they can expect from the network, and if there are any caveats to be aware of in using the network's capabilities. Depending on how much you briefed the user population on the successful transition scenario of your activities, once the transition activities succeed, you may need simply to tell them to start using those new versions of applications, procedures, and so on.

Congratulations on completing your first (or fiftieth) IPv6 transition activity. Because you are likely now to start preparing for the next set of activities, you can refer to earlier chapters to remind you of what's required for a successful transition, but first, if you haven't already, you may want to read the chapters that follow this one for additional information about the security aspects of deploying IPv6, the best ways to perform your asset and application inventories, selecting the transition strategy that's right for you, and using pilot projects to learn about IPv6 in a controlled manner before deploying it throughout your network.

Testing Your Knowledge

To verify that you gleaned the pertinent information from this chapter, here are a few questions regarding testing the results of your IPv6 transition activities. Answers are in Appendix A.

1. What are the downsides of too much testing or too little testing?

2. What is the primary component of a successful verification phase?

3. Are there any transition activities that can occur outside of maintenance windows? If so, what are they?

4. Name some of the testing concepts and paradigms that can provide you with a more successful transition verification phase.

CHAPTER 10

Factoring IPv6-Specific Risks and Limitations into Your Plans

Call before you dig.
— **Underground Utility
Industry slogan**

I recall there was a time that lasted quite a while after we moved into our newly built home that when I attempted almost any minor fix-it or improvement job, I found a problem in the original construction. The job I recall most is installing an over-the-stove microwave oven to replace the vent fan that came with the house. On removing the old unit I found that the hole in the wall leading to the outside world was four inches from where the fan's "ideal" output was. The builder had "jimmied" (a technical term) the unit in so it was actually able to vent, but the microwave was far more rigid and less forgiving. The simple installation job became a full day task. The whole affair reminded me of an episode of one my favorite shows, *Malcolm in the Middle*, where the average middle-class dad aims to change a light bulb and winds up lying under the car working on some unrelated problem, the latest of a succession of chores he found on the way to locating a bulb. His wife comes in and asks him, "What are you doing?" He answers, "What does it look like I'm doing? I'm changing a light bulb." The point of this little story is that your IPv6 transition will have its misaligned kitchen vents and broken light bulbs, because like my home all those years ago, it's brand new. Despite what the RFCs and vendors say, the implementations will behave differently. Moreover, what the RFCs don't say is as important, in other words how all this complex technology will interact, which is still unknown.

What You'll Learn

Throughout your IPv6 transition planning, execution, and verification phases, you've surely been considering the risks that may cause your transition to fail. You've probably also considered what limitations IPv6 has, other than its lack of significant adoption, at least in the United States. This chapter takes all those risks and limitations and organizes them into one central location for you to review, before you deploy a particular set of capabilities.

This chapter covers the risks associated with you being one of the first IPv6 adopters, a pioneer if you will. The chapter encourages you to seek out answers to your IPv6 transition questions, and it directs you to the right venues in which to get your questions answered. The chapter also points out that, with all the changes in the implementations of TCP/IP stacks and applications to support IPv6, surely a fair share of bugs has also been introduced. The lesson taught is that, until all these technologies are more mature, you should be careful in deploying all but the basic IPv6 functionalities in your first few transitions.

The chapter goes into more detail than prior chapters did regarding all the new extension headers and options available with IPv6. This is to give you the context to understand the vulnerabilities that are described and the mitigation advice that is provided. The chapter ends by analyzing some of the risks associated with Mobile IPv6 as a prelude for your own more detailed research to determine if the features associated with Mobile IPv6 are ones you need and can afford from the network performance and security perspectives.

What Risks Are There with Your IPv6 Transition?

Like all major MIS/IT projects, your IPv6 transition comes with some inherent risks. You may have underspecified the transition requirements or created requirements that are far too "aggressive" to achieve, especially within the allotted time. You may have underestimated how long the transition will take, which will either lead the project to failure, costs overruns, or lots of overtime for your staff. You may not have budgeted enough money to obtain all the equipment, vendor services, external consultants, and so on that you need, or you may lose a key member of your staff at an inopportune time.

If you are a seasoned CIO or network manager, you have encountered the preceding risks time and time again and, if you have been successful in your career, you have learned to mitigate them as much as possible. With your IPv6 transition, however, there are some risks that may be new to you or that are more significant than you might normally be used to, due to their magnitude.

The risks specific to your IPv6 transition, or amplified by the nature of the transition, fall into three broad categories:

1. A lack of publicly available information regarding practical IPv6 experiences in production environments.

2. A lot of changes in hardware, firmware, and software. With changes come bugs.

3. Many new networking concepts, core designs, and especially advanced features that are largely untested in production or mission-critical environments.

In the sections that follow, all three of these distinct types of risks are addressed, along with their realistic effects and what you can do to mitigate them. In some cases, especially for the advanced features, mitigation may just mean falling back on less glitzy solutions and waiting for someone else to deploy the new stuff and publish their experiences.

In addition to the risks just mentioned, IPv6 does have its limitations, which might make your transition more difficult. At the very least, the limitations might slow down the rate of your transition. Some of the limitations are temporary ones that will disappear as more support infrastructure goes into place. Both the temporary and more permanent limitations are covered here, as well.

Acknowledging That You Are a Pioneer

By far the biggest risk of an IPv6 transition is that you are one of the pioneers. Recall the old joke asking how you can tell who the pioneers are. The answer is that they're the ones with the arrows in their backs. There have been some fairly large successful experiments with IPv6, for example the 6BONE and MOONv6. None of the experiments in the U.S. to date, however, could be called a production network, at least not one that Wall Street CIOs would consider a satisfactory technology proof or one that you would want to have as a critical part of landing an airliner on which your kids are passengers.

Dealing with the Lack of IPv6 Lessons Learned Online

The most challenging aspect of your IPv6 transition probably won't be the need to learn all the new IPv6 capabilities and what's required to deploy and configure them. You can acquire that information by reading some good IPv6 technology books and taking classes offered by your vendors or independent training organizations. You'll likely be more challenged by the eerie silence online about anything related to real-world IPv6 deployment experiences and lessons learned.

Classes can teach you about all the knobs and gauges on new tools, even complex tools like IPv6 and its associated technologies. To find out, however, that a given feature is impractical in certain environments (like large enterprises), or that a certain vendor's implementation is broken, typically requires looking online through all the archived blogs, mailing lists, and newsgroups that are replete with information that you can't learn in a sterile classroom. If you want opinions, for example, on "Windows versus UNIX", you get almost 17,000 of them by typing that string (logically OR-ed with "UNIX versus Windows") into a search engine. Your IPv6 results won't be nearly as robust.

Instead of learning, for example, neat network management tricks to get particular vendor's arcane implementation of an IPv6 feature working, the search-engine results you'll get back for most IPv6-related queries will primarily point to hardware and software vendors and consulting organizations talking about how they can help you manage a successful upgrade. You'll also see discussions and arguments about the good and bad of an IPv6 feature, but mostly within the context of hypothetical scenarios. There are very few case studies of successful transitions or lessons learned after a full-scale enterprise-wide deployment.

One that came up for me was a U.S. Department of Energy case study of the successful transition of the Energy Sciences Network (ESnet) to IPv6. That was a research network, however, and the study was from 2002. In other words, very few organizations or vendors have managed to get to the other side of the transition tunnel (pun somewhat intended) to tell the world how they succeeded (or failed) on an enterprise scale for a production or mission-critical network.

Before you get too disappointed, there are some who have had successful deployments or who have a comprehensive enough knowledge of both network management and IPv6 to put you on the right track. The next section covers who they are and what they have done or can do for you.

Seeking Out Those Who Went Before You

Not having many sources of information online, the next thing to do is find people who know enough about IPv6 to deploy it in a production environment. You've adopted new networking standards before on a large scale where you didn't know all the details as much as you knew the stuff you worked with every day. You often had people in your organization who knew those things. If the technology was new to everyone nearby (organizationally), you could go to conferences, symposiums, and trade shows. The reality with IPv6 is that many of those venues mostly talk about what a wonderful world it will be when IPv6 is deployed, or they focus on small-scale technology demonstrations or aspects of the technology that they "still have to figure out." This is useful information, for sure, but it doesn't help you with your immediate needs.

With all that gloomy stuff said, there are many IPv6 experts out there and quite a few have deployed real networks of appreciable size. How large those networks are and the details of those people's experiences are not easily found because the operations community (as opposed to the academic and research communities) has not gelled around IPv6 enough yet to form a global consciousness. If you're in the U.S. federal government, however, you can take great comfort in the knowledge that you probably have access to the best minds for operations-grade knowledge, because that's where IPv6 is actually being deployed in the U.S. Alternately, those overseas (especially in Eastern Asia) are doing great things with IPv6 and perhaps you should look there for help. A fact-finding trip (and a visit to the Emperor's palace while you're there) can be quite informative. If your boss won't sign off on a junket to Tokyo or Beijing, however, where else can you look?

Starting with the Usual Suspects

On September 2, 2007, Lockheed Martin announced that it would be deploying IPv6 on its Global Vision Network from California to the U.K. (`http://www.pcworld.com/article/id,136689-pg,1/article.html`). Though this may take many months or even years to bear fruit that Lockheed Martin is willing to share publicly, you can be sure that they will apply what they learn privately to their customers undertaking IPv6 upgrades. This makes Lockheed Martin a valuable resource to search out and work with as they deploy their own IPv6 networks.

The other large systems integrators, defense contractors, and MIS/IT outsourcers are surely working on similar programs, because they are in the same boat regarding having to help their government customers with transitions. If you don't work with Lockheed Martin at present, see what Northrop Grumman, General Dynamics, EDS, and so on are doing in the realm of IPv6. If you outsource any significant part of your MIS/IT infrastructure, contact your outsourcers. You're paying these people to serve you and solve your networking problems. Get answers.

Asking Those Who's Job It Is to Know

For expert information in specific areas of your transition, look to your router vendors. The people who make the routers, switches, and other network hardware, specifically Juniper and Cisco for enterprise-grade IPv6 equipment, are at the center of the IPv6 universe and, if they don't know how to make IPv6 work at the enterprise scale, nobody does. You surely have contacts and service agreements with at least one of those companies. If you haven't done it already, have them come in and help you along. To sell hardware, their services may actually be among the least expensive.

On another specific IPv6 topic, this time at your enterprise's periphery, look to the vendors servicing the Networx contract mentioned in Chapter 7, "Identifying Common Transition Preparation Tasks." In addition to getting you ISP connectivity and IPv6 addresses, they have knowledge regarding enterprise-scale deployment, because they had to build the IPv6 infrastructure to act as your ISPs. Considering the Service Level Agreements (SLAs) these organizations are used to adhering to, their IPv6 networks are probably about the most robust in the world.

Learning from Those Who Walked the Walk

When looking for vendors that both sell solutions in a given space and claim customer-relevant expertise in it, you should always favor those who have eaten their own cooking, as the saying goes. Two companies that stand out in the IPv6 domain are Microsoft and Command Information.

For several years now, Microsoft has been deploying IPv6 in its own campus networks with a great deal of fervor and those networks now represent some of the largest corporate IPv6 deployments in the world. You can be sure Microsoft learned a lot about what works and what doesn't in IPv6 deployment and you should take advantage of that knowledge. A comprehensive place to start getting Microsoft's take on IPv6 is at `http://technet.microsoft.com/ en-us/network/bb530961.aspx`. Moreover, if you are running Microsoft infrastructure in your network (and few aren't), contact your customer representatives and have them help you with the aspects of your transition associated with Microsoft's servers, workstations, and applications. Contrary to some common misconceptions, they have quite a bit of knowledge in the networking realm, too.

The other company that stands out as a center of IPv6 knowledge is Command Information in Herndon, VA. Its federal branch is in Vienna, VA. This company is composed of some of the top minds and leading-edge implementers in the IPv6 domain. Several of them have come from the U.S. DoD's IPv6 projects, plus they have close ties to other IPv6 experts within the government, academic, and research sectors. This is probably the single biggest nucleus of IPv6 talent in the U.S. government sector. Along with all the other resources mentioned, you should see what they have to say. You can reach Command Information at `http://www.commandinformation.com/`. In case you're wondering, I have no ties to the company, except a couple of former business associates who knew what they were doing, so I think it's worth plugging talented people.

Publishing Your Experiences and Questions

Now that you've been on one side of the IPv6 information abyss, wouldn't it be nice if people published the good, bad, and ugly experiences of their IPv6 transitions? Every now and then, in many fields of endeavor, you'll see "lessons learned" papers. In modern times, you'll see online blogs of people's experiences with new projects. Because you've probably just spent a good deal of time digging up the few scraps of practical IPv6 knowledge that are out there, perhaps you should consider it your duty to make the next person's transition that much easier. That person may be sitting in an office much like yours in a different branch of your enterprise. If he or she knew what you knew about IPv6 transitions, there would be a far better chance that what they do would interoperate with what you implemented for your part of the overall enterprise migration.

As a member of your organization's MIS/IT department, you should publish your transition experiences internally, however raw or incomplete they are, so other parts of your organization can learn from your experiences and know what transition path the organization is taking. You may already have best practices websites. You may even have official programs to disseminate information to other teams. You should use these forums to the fullest, primarily to help others, but also in the karmic hope that your publications will encourage others to publish their results.

If you're in the U.S. federal sector, your publication choices are more limited. First, there's the issue of classified information. You can't very well publish your transition experiences if your network's mission or capabilities are not for public knowledge. There is also the issue of For Official Use Only (FOUO) information, which is not strictly classified, but it's not for public consumption, either. Though you can't necessarily publish in a public forum, you can still socialize your experiences with other government bodies.

There are plenty of MIS/IT venues that are open to government employees and contractors only, but that span all the organizations undergoing IPv6 upgrades as part of the OMB mandate. Even in the classified realm, there are ways to distribute information that has global relevance (and need to know) within your agency or community. You are probably already aware of what avenues of communication are open to you, because IPv6 transition is not the first large-scale MIS/IT project you've undertaken. You should employ those communications paths for IPv6 knowledge exchange.

If you're in the early stages of an IPv6 transition, you probably don't have many answers to publish, but you can publish your questions. The same venues mentioned previously can be used to get information about what you don't know about IPv6 transition from those with very similar problems to yours who do know. In the public domain, you can also post your questions to IPv6-specific forums like the ones hosted by the Go6 IPv6 Portal, whose mission it is to be an online meeting point for the sharing of experiences with IPv6. You can try those forums at `http://forum.go6.net/`.

Creating an Enterprise Transition Knowledge Base

As hinted in the previous sections, you may want to consider creating an enterprise-wide repository of your IPv6 experiences, as well as a centralized location for unanswered questions your people may have. The model of forums and blogs used by sites like Go6 is an excellent basis from which to build your knowledge base. A good technological choice for your knowledge base is a wiki, which has the attractive property of letting anyone with access to the knowledge base site also post to it. With some wikis, you're on the honor system not to trample or intentionally damage another person's content, but that's usually not a problem. All the people given access to a particular wiki are meant to collaborate and it doesn't help any of them not to play nicely with each other. Also, at least the wikis I'm familiar with, stamp any changes with the name of the person who did them. That's a strong incentive not to goof around.

A wiki with which I have lots of personal experience and which I can recommend for quick and easy publication of knowledge like what you'll need to distribute during IPv6 transition is TWiki. It's billed as an open-source wiki for the enterprise and you can find it at `http://twiki.org/`. You may have your own preferred publication means or wiki-like tools, but if you don't, TWiki is a good choice.

Realizing That with Changes Come Bugs

Throughout this book, I've been espousing that IPv6 and IPv4 are not all that different from each other and that your IPv6 transition shouldn't be much more effort than any other technology upgrade. Looking at the IPv4 and IPv6 packet headers in Figure 2-1 and Figure 2-2, you can see that there aren't any weird new fields in IPv6. The traffic class and flow label are the most complex fields in the header and only one of them is truly new. The traffic class in IPv6 is defined the same way as the one in IPv4. As for the flow label, most traffic isn't going to care about it, and it will be set to zero and ignored in most cases. Even the new ICMPv6 messages and IPv6 extension headers and options discussed later in this chapter are fairly tame, once understood. So, you might ask yourself, what's the big deal with an IPv6 transition? The answer to that is that there's theory and there's implementation.

On paper, deploying and configuring the basics of IPv6 looks pretty straightforward. Ignoring for the moment all the details about getting address space assignments and external connectivity, and the sheer scale of the transition (again, calm down and remember that you've done other big technology roll-outs before), the actual mechanics of assigning addresses and deploying networks for IPv6 isn't much different from IPv4. That doesn't factor in the side-effects of all the changed products and new products, however.

The implementation of IPv6 in vendor products affected software associated with lots of old code that had been running just fine (mostly) and that nobody had really touched for years. In Vista, Microsoft tore out and rewrote the entire TCP/IP stack. Aside from being a very large piece of software, by looking at any fraction of the more than 5,000 RFCs associated with TCP/IP networking (granted not all in the stack), you can see that the TCP/IP stack is probably one of the most complex subsystems of any networking product, and in Microsoft Vista, it's all brand new. Other operating systems made less sweeping changes, but complex ones nonetheless. Similarly, the router and other network equipment vendors not only had to write IPv6 and ICMPv6 modules into their products, they had to integrate them with the existing IPv4, TCP, UDP, and so on, modules. That doesn't account for all the advanced features, like IPsec and mobile IP, which further tweak the stack code.

With all the code that had to be changed or added, surely the vendors put in new bugs, too. About one bug was added per 1,000 lines of new code, if old rules of thumb for good software development still hold. For bad software development, well, the number of bugs is greater. Add to that that developing network software is particularly hard. Buffer overflows, off-by-one errors, and all kinds of other demons live in that kind of software, with all of its complex data structures and interdependencies between modules.

Recall the conversation about whether to re-write an old IPv4-only application from scratch to have both IPv4 and IPv6 functionality. Remember the recommendation to leave the working IPv4 version alone and write a new IPv6 one. Then, after you've beaten the bugs out, merge the two versions. You could even create a wrapper program that calls the appropriate version based on what types of IP addresses are being used. Without knowing the internals of the various products, I can't say how each vendor implemented their stacks. I can say, however, that they must have reached the final stages of the sequence just described, because nobody is selling you two routers (or operating systems, or web browsers), one for IPv4 and one for IPv6. That means the functionalities have been integrated. With all the IPv6 on IPv4 tunneling and a little bit of vice versa, they're integrated pretty tightly.

The lesson to take away from the preceding discussion is that, even if you become an expert with every facet of how IPv6 is *supposed* to work, the bugs in all that new code will likely make for some interesting surprises. That's why you have to work closely with the very same vendors who inflicted the bugs on you and force them to come clean regarding what works as advertised and what doesn't. Again, that's nothing new in the Byzantine relationship between customers and vendors. It just bears repeating here.

Summarizing Risks from Prior Chapters

I've talked a lot about risks and limitations throughout the book, and rather than repeat here all that has already been said, I'll summarize and refer to the appropriate preceding chapters.

Re-Visiting Auto-Configuration

Auto-configuration is covered in Chapter 2, "Demystifying IPv6," and Chapter 7, "Identifying Common Transition Preparation Tasks." The features we're interested in here are composed of Neighbor Discovery (ND), documented in RFC 2461, and Secure ND (SEND), documented in RFC 3971. Router Advertisements and Solicitations are the key to auto-configuration, but they are also its weakness, because they have limited security in the original ND. There are numerous security issues with ND, and rather than repeat them here, I'll refer you to RFC 3756, which takes a long hard look at ND's security problems. In a nutshell, if you can't trust that your ND messages are genuine, in other words nobody would ever spoof them, then you need to consider seriously whether you should be leaving the numbering of your network's devices in ND's care. With insider threats being a major component of the security landscape, it's hard to see how anyone can assume spoofing won't occur, especially if the devices or networks in question hold valuable information.

Understanding SEND's Advantages and Weaknesses

SEND improves things, partly by using Cryptographically Generated Addresses (CGAs), which are documented in RFC 3972. CGAs are nice in that they don't give away private information like a device's MAC addresses, as EUI-64 addresses do. CGAs tie an asymmetric public key to an IPv6 address and require those using those addresses with SEND to prove knowledge of the associated private key. A PKI-like certification hierarchy or similar trust-distribution model completes SEND and makes for something far more secure than the Address Resolution Protocol (ARP) from IPv4 that ND and SEND replaced.

CGAs and SEND also have their weaknesses and limitations. CGAs provide no security as far as spoofing is concerned from anybody who can sniff SEND packets in transit. Such sniffing used to be easy on a LAN, but the mass adoption of switched networks makes sniffing less of a problem than it used to be. In any case, believing a CGA on face value is a bad idea and you should always check that the private key associated with the CGA is known by the sender of the packet. Fortunately, SEND does this. Other protocols using CGAs should do likewise.

Ironically, SEND is also limited in that there is currently no specification for supporting anything other than CGAs. Though you can see how one might go about it by reading between the lines in RFC 3971, venturing off on your own is sure to bring incompatibilities with whatever the standards people finally create. As such, you should assume that SEND requires CGAs and, if you need to use EUI-64 addresses or static addresses (with interface IDs like '::1', '::2', and so on), then SEND isn't for you.

Finally, though SEND doesn't use IPsec, many of the functionalities required by IPsec are also required to implement SEND, for example public-key cryptography and cryptographic hash functions. Like IPsec, that makes SEND computationally expensive, not necessarily for end hosts, but it can be for routers. The generation of CGAs, depending on what level of brute-force protection you want (see RFC 3972), can also become a burden on the end hosts. Apply the same performance considerations when deploying SEND as you do with IPsec.

Choosing DHCPv6 Instead of ND

DHCPv6 is the IPv6 version of a trusted old network configuration favorite and it can be used to meet your auto-configuration needs if ND and SEND don't measure up. DHCPv6 is documented in RFC 3315, with options documented in several other RFCs. Unlike ND and SEND, DHCP hands out entire IP addresses, instead of just network prefixes. There is no client-side computation component to DHCPv6-provided addresses. The clients simply start using the addresses provided by the server. DHCPv6 also provides information about DNS servers, timeservers, print servers, and so on, which ND and SEND do not. A particularly nice improvement over the old version of DHCP is the inclusion of a Reconfigure message, which tells a host depending on DHCPv6 addresses that it's time to renumber. Prior versions of DHCP were passive and required address leases to expire before renumbering could occur.

The downside of DHCP surfaces if you use a lot of "hard-wired" addresses, in other words you number your devices statically and use DHCP to distribute the addresses to your devices, along with DNS server addresses and other information. This departs from DHCP's original intent to draw randomly from a pool of addresses with devices possibly being renumbered as leases expire. If you do use a lot of fixed addresses, then you have to configure every individual IP address on the DHCP server. When the time comes to renumber the network, you will have to change all those addresses. Some DHCP product may make that easier than others, but in any case you still have to change a lot of values in a configuration file or database. If you use ND or SEND, you only have to renumber the router's network prefix and the devices will renumber themselves as soon as the router issues a Router Advertisement with the new prefixes.

Where Are the Products?

Many of the more recent IPv6 features, like SEND and DHCPv6, share the common trait of a lack of mature products. If you're an open source fan, you're in luck because several people have tried their hand at implementing IPv6 features. Microsoft is a big supporter of IPv6, so it, too, is getting code out as fast as it can, but these things take time to get right.

As of September 2007, Microsoft has a DHCPv6 server in Beta 2 of Windows "Longhorn," but that's hardly something you want to deploy in a production environment. A portable open-source version, called "dibbler," which seems to be a living, breathing project with executables for Windows and Linux, along with source code (dated February 2007), is available at `http://sourceforge.net/project/showfiles.php?group_id=147607`. For other platforms, ask your vendors what they offer.

Regarding SEND, although the RFC is over two years old, the usual purveyors of networking hardware and software have not made any noise about products supporting it. As noted in Chapter 7, an open-source version is available at `http://www.docomolabs-usa.com/lab_opensource.html`.

Knowing Where Not to Use Auto-Configuration

Security problems and a lack of products aside for the moment, there are some places you shouldn't be using auto-configuration at all. Auto-configuration is not recommended for routers and other network infrastructure, due to the hard-coding of such devices' IP addresses in, for example, BGP and other configuration files. If you chose to use an auto-configuration mechanism like EUI-64 addressing, the address may change without you noticing it if a faulty network card is replaced, causing applications and configuration files not informed of the change to break, and possibly leading to lots of debugging until you determine the root cause.

If there are any other well-known IP addresses in your network, they too should be statically configured. There probably aren't any such addresses known by people, because DNS eliminates that need. There are places that don't trust DNS, however, in which case static addressing becomes important again. More likely than people, however, there may be applications, especially home-grown ones, that rely on well-known central server IP addresses to operate. Unless such applications have a way to find the servers they depend on other than by IP address, those IP addresses should not be dynamic.

Tunneling with Care

Chapter 3, "The Current IPv6 Landscape," and Chapter 4, "Choosing When to Make the Transition and How," discuss tunneling and its risks in depth, so I won't repeat much here. As a reminder, if you're not interested in reading the details in the other chapters, you should be very careful about where you let tunnels go, especially in network segments where your IPv6 transition is only partially complete. Tunneling IPv6 over IPv4 (using Protocol #41) is especially dangerous, because it can be used to attack improperly configured or secured IPv6 implementations within IPv4 devices. See Chapter 3 for the attack details, if this has piqued your interest.

Avoiding EUI-64 or Knowing Its Limits

Chapter 7 covers EUI-64 in great detail, including attacks based on it, and you should go read the details there. As an additional note, from earlier in this chapter, don't forget that by tying your IPv6 interface IDs to your network cards, when those cards are replaced the interface IDs are likely to change, as well. The effects of such changes on those depending on well-known IP addresses are covered a few sections back. Another dependency may exist in your firewall rules. If a device with a given EUI-64-based address is allowed to communicate through a firewall (or, if it is expressly forbidden), a renumbering caused by a change of that device's network hardware may affect the security or functionality of the device or the network to which the device is connected. If you're using EUI-64, be sure to check your firewall rules whenever hardware changes are made.

Looking for IPv6 ISPs

Finding and working with IPv6 ISPs is covered in Chapter 7, especially the scarcity of such ISPs. This is one of the greatest limitations many will face for some time when deploying IPv6, especially when looking for external native connectivity. If your enterprise is part of the U.S. federal government, you have more choices because of initiatives like the Networx contract (see Chapter 7). Outside of the federal government, however, at least as of September 2007, IPv6 ISPs are hard to find, and you'll have to do some digging of your own, because the playing field will likely have changed by the time you read this. See Chapter 7 for further information on what is available and where you might start your search.

Coping with ISP-Centric Addressing

Another problem tied to ISPs is the way IPv6 address spaces are primarily being assigned at this time. This is covered in great depth by Chapter 7. To summarize, ISP-centric addressing makes multiple connections to sites (a.k.a., multi-homing) difficult, because each multi-homed device needs at least two IPv6 addresses, one for each ISP through which it wishes to communicate.

Solutions to the multi-homing problem include bump-in-the-stack mechanisms. Applications above the network layer (where the bump is) see a single IPv6 address for the device they are on, but there are multiple addresses visible for the device at the network layer and below. One address is assigned by each ISP in a multi-homed scenario and the device decides how to distribute its traffic between ISPs.

You can bet there will be new bugs in code that implements such convoluted address-mapping schemes. Even if the stack (and bump-in-the-stack) software developers get the code 100 percent correct, debugging network connectivity problems will be a nightmare. Unless there are (possibly administrator-only) ways to view the actual IP addresses in the packets going out, a simple ping to check out firewall rules could take on levels of complexity equivalent to NAT, which is what IPv6 was supposed to eliminate to make network managers' lives easier.

Recalling All the Things That IPv6 Didn't Change

Before you read the next section about all the neat whistles and bells under IPv6's hood, don't forget about TCP, UDP, SNMP, DNS, SSL, and the other protocols above the network layer. They are all still there, largely unchanged in *intended* functionality, but with the added risk that some vendors may have introduced new bugs while integrating their old modules with their IPv6, ICMPv6, and other new modules. Moreover, all the security issues associated not only with the implementations, but with the actual specifications of those components, are still there. IPv6 does not protect you from a buffer overflow bug in a mail server, for example, or a security vulnerability in how PKI certificates were designed.

To reduce your risk of encountering such bugs at an inopportune time, when you analyze your network security as you're performing your IPv6 transition, don't forget to also use your vulnerability analysis tools (those that are IPv6-capable) to validate that your web servers, mail servers, and other applications are still secure. Don't get caught up entirely in the network layer.

Analyzing Other Risks of IPv6 Features

By virtue of being at the network layer, there is a set of common services that IPv6 must provide, the same as IPv4. There are also some features that seem to make sense or be desirable at this layer, but that have security ramifications that reduce their value to the point where they may never be used. Some such features of IPv4 that were a good idea in 1981 became part of IPv6, despite evidence that the features were less than desirable from a security viewpoint. Those features and their vulnerabilities are among those covered in the sections that follow.

One thing to keep in mind as you read the following sections is that the body of experience in a production setting for all the IPv6 features, from the most common to the most esoteric, is quite small. The basics look OK, especially for the more pedestrian features. How the features will interact is a different matter and one that only experience will teach.

As an example of an unforeseen "difficulty," consider why SEND doesn't use IPsec. The answer is because you need to provide keys to IPsec. Those keys are usually handled automatically, but that requires a key server. SEND was created not because the creators of ND didn't care about security. They assumed you would use IPsec and everything would be great, however it's tough to talk to a key server when you don't have an IP address, which is one of the things ND enables you to have. The alternative without a key server, if you still wanted to use IPsec, is to key all your devices manually. That's highly impractical in any realistically sized production environment, so the only practical form of ND is the insecure one. Hence, the need to create SEND arose.

There will be other such realizations of design shortcomings as IPv6 becomes deployed in real-world environments. The best defense you have is to be well educated about how the protocol and its innards work. That way, maybe you can see a problem coming before it gets too big.

Understanding IPv6's Version of ICMP

ICMP was revamped for IPv6 and the new version is named ICMPv6. RFC 4443 defines the basics of ICMPv6 and a few message types. There's the typical error processing already associated with the IPv4 version of ICMP, like destination unreachable, time exceeded, parameter problems (new to IPv6), echo requests and replies (a.k.a., pings), and so on. Much of IPv6's auto-configuration and some of its mobility functionality are implemented using ICMPv6. The associated message types are defined by other RFCs. Table 10-1 organizes the ICMPv6 messages by the IPv6 features that they enable or support. The sections that follow discuss what you should be thinking about regarding these features and your IPv6 transition risks.

Learning the Importance of Path MTUs

In IPv4 every device can fragment packets. That means if a 1500-octet packet came in one interface of a router, three 500-octet packets might exit another interface where the link couldn't handle the bigger original packet. As long as a sender didn't make the packets bigger than its first-hop local link's MTU (defined in Chapter 4), there is little fear that they can't be squeezed down into smaller ones downstream.

IPv6 allows only one device to fragment a packet, and that is the original sender. Fragmentation was (rightfully) deemed as too much work for routers, especially because hosts blind to downstream constrictions could drive a router into overload by sending the largest packets possible all the time. Because routers no longer fragment packets en route, a sender must know the largest packet size acceptable to a given destination. The sender could play it safe and always use the guaranteed IPv6 minimum MTU of 1280 octets, but on paths composed of high-bandwidth links that would be a waste of resources. This is especially true when you consider that most MTUs are 1500 octets by default on Ethernet LANs.

The Packet Too Big ICMPv6 message (see Table 10-1) was created to support path MTU discovery, and it is used much like the Time Exceeded message is used in traceroute. Simplistically speaking, through an iterative process of sending smaller and smaller packets and getting feedback via ICMPv6 as to when those packets don't fit into downstream pipes, a sender can tune each connection to its best possible performance. For details of the actual path MTU discovery algorithm, see RFC 1981.

Low bandwidth is not really a security risk, which is the primary focus of this chapter, but it does introduce an unnecessary limitation, which is partly why it is included in this chapter. The other reason this crucial ICMPv6 message is included is to remind you to let it through your firewalls. If you don't, your devices will either suffer from packets being mysteriously lost (because the generation of the ICMPv6 message causes the originating packet to be discarded, probably by a router in the middle of nowhere), or your network will run sub-optimally.

The Packet Too Big ICMPv6 message is one of the few ICMPv6 messages that does not use multicast. Most of the others do. That means, along with learning IPv6, you're going to have to learn about multicast. The next section gets you on that path.

Table 10-1: ICMPv6 Types for Auto-Configuration and Other New Features

IPV6 FEATURE	ICMP MESSAGE(S)	RFC	MULTICAST?
Path MTU Discovery	Packet Too Big	RFC 4443, RFC 1981	No
Multicast Listener Discovery (MLD)	Query, Report, & Done	RFC 2710	Yes
MLD (version 2)	Query & Report (version 2)	RFC 3810	Yes
Multicast Router Discovery (MRD)	Advertisement, Solicitation, & Termination	RFC 4286	Yes

Table 10-1 (continued)

IPV6 FEATURE	ICMP MESSAGE(S)	RFC	MULTICAST?
Neighbor Discovery (ND)	Router Solicitation & Advertisement; Neighbor Solicitation & Advertisement; Redirect	RFC 2461	Yes, except Redirect
Inverse ND	Solicitation & Advertisement	RFC 3122	Yes
Secure ND (SEND)	Certification Path Solicitation & Advertisement	RFC 3971	Yes
Router Renumbering (RR)	Command, Result, & Reset	RFC 2894	Yes
Mobile IPv6	Home Agent Address Discovery Request & Reply; Mobile Prefix Solicitation & Advertisement	RFC 3775	No

Recognizing Multicast's Role in IPv6

IPv4 has multicast features, but they were never used for much. With the elimination of broadcast in IPv6, multicast takes on an extremely important role. This means that your IPv6-capable devices have to send and receive packets containing multicast addresses. It means you have to do extra work for multicast configuration. That means you have the potential to make a mistake doing so, and that means you should learn about multicast (if you don't already know it), because it's going to become a much bigger part of your network management job.

Many of the multicast addresses associated with ICMPv6 messages are preconfigured on IPv6-capable routers and other devices, and those devices will know how to communicate via Router Solicitations, Router Advertisements, and so on. As far as those features are concerned, you don't need to learn much more than how to manage the features themselves from your router consoles.

As IPv6 becomes more pervasive, however, especially in Internet telephony, and the distribution of video, audio, and so on, multicast that you actually need to understand becomes more important. Your organization may not be interested now, but if you start doing internal videoconferencing or distribution of multimedia training materials, for example, multicast plays a big part in that and perhaps you should bone up on it.

You'll note in Table 10-1 that most of the currently defined ICMPv6 messages use multicast to get their job done. Don't panic, it's mostly the preconfigured kind described earlier. There are several ICMPv6 messages devoted to managing multicast routers and listeners, and you can read RFC 2710, RFC 3810, and RFC 4286 to familiarize yourself with them and how multicast resources are managed by your network's devices.

Before breaking out those RFCs, however, if you're new to multicast you should find a good IPv6 technology book to teach you what multicast is, what it's used for, and how it works. Chapter 15 in [Blanchet], listed in "Further Reading" at the end of the chapter, is particularly clear on multicast and its IPv6 cousin, anycast. You'll also want to look through your router vendors' manuals for configuring multicast, because you won't be putting those raw ICMPv6 and other multicast packets on the wire yourself. You'll be telling your routers what to do.

Noting How ICMP Implements ND and SEND

ND and SEND have already had a good amount of coverage in the auto-configuration section of this chapter and in prior chapters, so I won't beat the dead horse. Suffice it to say, the ND and SEND features are implemented as ICMPv6 messages. Most of them are sent to multicast addresses, like the ones for all routers or all nodes. Inverse ND is for environments where link addresses are known and IP addresses need to be learned, as in Frame Relay, for example. The RFCs pertaining to all these ICMPv6 messages are listed in Table 10-1.

Renumbering Routers the IPv6 Way

Router Renumbering (RR) is the granddaddy of all the new IPv6 auto-configuration features, because a successful secure deployment of it and proper use can make your IPv6 upgrade and subsequent network re-numberings almost painless. Conversely, it is one of the most frightening IPv6 features and one that you will (and should) likely approach with a great deal of trepidation.

RR is no less than the ability to manage your routers' network prefixes remotely, giving you the power theoretically to change the IP addresses of all the interfaces on all your enterprise's routers with one command. The bells going off in your head right now are due to the potential for catastrophic network failure should a security vulnerability be found in the protocol or in one of its implementations.

On the bright side, RR could address the multi-homing problem by allowing an enterprise that is served by two ISPs to use one ISP as the active one and the other as a standby. Should the first ISP fail, the second could be "activated" by issuing an RR command to all the affected sites and changing the routers' network prefixes to those serviced by the second ISP. The routers would then use Router Advertisements to propagate the new prefixes to the devices on their LANs. This is a crude solution with several problems (like dealing with devices with manually configured addresses) and could lead to many minutes of downtime network-wide in the best of scenarios, but it's a way RR could be put to good use, once proven secure.

Because of the impact it can have on your network, RR requires and is protected by IPsec, along with additional safeguards to avoid replay. You can find the details of the protocol in RFC 2894. Though the RFC has been around since August 2000, few implementations exist and probably fewer have been submitted to rigorous testing.

I'm usually not one for blanket statements, but RR is a feature I would leave out of my IPv6 upgrades for the foreseeable future. If your IPv6-capable routers actually support it, you can always deploy RR fairly easily later on after somebody else has worked the kinks out. If you have a lab environment you can play in, though, RR would be something worth experimenting with to see if limited deployments could make life easier for you on a building or LAN scale.

Highlighting ICMPv6's Support of Mobile IPv6

Mobile IPv6 is an advanced topic and probably not part of your first IPv6 transition. For completeness, the ICMPv6 messages defined for Mobile IPv6 are included in Table 10-1. Mobile IPv6 also introduces its own extension header and a new destination option. All of these components are discussed together in a dedicated Mobile IPv6 section at the end of this chapter.

Reviewing the Limited Success of IPv4 Options

IPv4 has numerous options defined for use in its header, none of which have seen widespread adoption over the past two and a half decades. Several of the options have security vulnerabilities that outweigh their usefulness and, therefore, use of these options has been discouraged for a long time. The Source Routing options, which are covered more thoroughly when you read about IPv6 extension headers shortly, are examples of options with security issues. Packets containing such options are often dropped for security reasons by enterprise routers. In security-conscious organizations, the packets are dropped silently, so as not to give a potential attacker any information on what kind of traffic a router will pass or drop.

Other IPv4 options have limited functionality, making them less valuable and less likely to be used. An example of this is the Record Route option. This option allows a source device to provide space in the IPv4 headers of packets that it sends for routers along the path to a given destination to deposit (that is, record) their addresses. The result is that the destination device gets, in addition to the payload of the IPv4 packet, a list of routers that the packet traveled through on its way from the source. If the source device sends a packet that causes the destination to send an ICMP response containing that original packet within it, then the source can also see the router addresses that were along the path. Alternatively, if the source and destination are cooperating, the destination can simply send the recorded route to the source as part of regular communications traffic.

You may recognize the preceding functionality as being similar to the commonly used traceroute mechanism. There are two important properties of the IPv4 Record Route option, however, that can augment traceroute results. First, the addresses that the routers deposit in the space provided in the IPv4 header by the Record Route option are supposed to be the ones facing the destination device, not the source device. Traceroute tends to return the IP addresses of the routers facing the source device. By getting the addresses of both sides of all the routers along a path, this allows for a more thorough discovery of your network's topology and assets.

The second property of the Record Route option that can augment traceroute is that not all routers necessarily respond to traceroute. Traceroute packets may also be blocked by firewalls, except if sourced from specific network management addresses. The advantage of Record Route is that it comes along for the ride in regular IP packet payloads. If two devices are allowed by security policy to communicate, for example a workstation with a web browser communicating with a web server, then Record Route can be used by either device in the process of exchanging regular web traffic to ascertain network topology. The counter to the preceding argument, however, is that routers don't necessarily honor the Record Route option (despite RFC 791 requiring them to), especially if they're already ignoring traceroute for security reasons. Moreover, firewalls can be configured to drop packets containing IP options altogether. Even with these limitations, however, Record Route can be used to augment your knowledge of your network's topology.

Although Record Route sounds like it's a great way to map out network topologies, it is limited by the very IPv4 header in which it is contained (as are all the other IPv4 options). Because the IPv4 header can be no larger than 60 octets, including options, you can't record more than nine hops with Record Route. Though this provides a decent amount of coverage for your local network, for Record Route to be useful on the enterprise or Internet scale, nine hops is not enough. There have been successful implementations of Record Route based network discovery, however, that allow a sort of "short range sensor" functionality with the long range discovery still handled by traceroute.

Coupling all the shortcomings of IPv4 options with the disadvantages of the variable-length IPv4 header field and additional processing required at all routers through which an option-bearing packet travels, you can conclude that IPv4 options have been less than successful. Some new options have been defined recently, the last one as of September 2007 was in January of the same year. As of this writing, the popularity of the latest IPv4 option, a quick-start mechanism for TCP and IP (see RFC 4782) remains to be seen.

Finding Risks in IPv6 Extension Headers

In contrast to the IPv4 options discussed in the previous section, many of the IPv6 extension headers (see Table 10-2) are expected to see a great deal of use as the protocol is deployed. The Internet Assigned Numbers Authority (IANA) is the official registry for protocol parameters and the data in Table 10-2 came from IANA's website at `http://www.iana.org/assignments/protocol-numbers`, with a last-update date of February 12, 2007. The complete protocol list covers more than IPv6 extension headers. In fact, it covers all the registered protocols, even ones that have fallen out of use or that were never implemented. Only the registered IPv6 extension headers are included in Table 10-2, however.

Table 10-2: All the Defined IPv6 Extension Headers

EXTENSION HEADER TYPE	RFC	MUST SUPPORT?
Routing Header	RFC 2460	Type 0 only
Fragment Header	RFC 2460	Yes
Authentication Header (AH)	RFC 4302	Yes
Encapsulating Security Payload (ESP)	RFC 4303	Yes
Hop-by-Hop Options Header	RFC 2460	Yes
Destination Options Header	RFC 2460	Yes
Mobility Header	RFC 3775	No

For an IPv6 implementation to be considered fully functional, all the extension headers indicated in Table 10-2 as "Must Support" need to be implemented. That doesn't mean anyone has to use any of those extension headers, but the implementation must make them available for use.

With the exception of the Mobility Header, the next few sections cover the risks associated with each header type. As mentioned earlier, I'll cover the Mobility Header, along with other components required to implement Mobile IPv6, all in one place near the end of the chapter.

Recognizing IPv4's Source-Routing Problems in IPv6

If you've been in the TCP/IP networking field for a while, then you probably weren't surprised by the news in May 2007 that there are denial-of-service attacks based on the IPv6 Routing Header (Type '0' of that header, to be exact), which is almost a clone of the flawed IPv4 Source Routing options. Those options in IPv4's header allow a packet's sender to specify which IP addresses a packet must go through on its route to destination. Though there are some uses to these features, there are far more vulnerabilities.

Understanding the Vulnerabilities of IPv4 Source Routing

There are at least two classes of well-known security vulnerabilities associated with the IPv4 Source Routing options. The first class of vulnerabilities centers around the fact that, if you can specify what devices a packet must go through on its way to a given destination (a destination that need not be directly accessible from where you are located), then it becomes possible to bypass firewalls and get illegal traffic to enter or exit a network, perhaps through surreptitious secondary connections. This may even allow for attacks to be launched from the Internet against devices in a network's RFC 1918 private address space, which normally cannot be routed to from the Internet. You may also be able to route attack-filled packets around Intrusion Detection Systems (IDSs), so that those systems don't detect the packets and sound alarms.

The other class of vulnerability brought on by IPv4 Source Routing is a denial of service one. In the legitimate uses of Source Routing, you might use the IP4 option to send a packet to destination 'C' via a path including router 'A' and then router 'B'. The attack comes about from configuring a Source Routing option so that the packet is directed to follow a path like A-B-A-B-A-B-A-…C. 'C' is irrelevant to the attack, but only a placeholder that should differ from 'A' and 'B' so that a smart device doesn't realize the packet is actually destined for itself and stop the attack short. The resulting consumption of both network bandwidth and the packet-processing resources on 'A' and 'B' is the crux of the attack.

Augmenting IPv4's Vulnerabilities with IPv6

The preceding classes of vulnerabilities have been identified in IPv4's Source Routing for some time and many experts were also aware that there are similar vulnerabilities in the IPv6 Type-0 Routing Header, but the seriousness of those vulnerabilities in IPv6 were underestimated. The potential damage of denial of service attacks has been found to be much worse in IPv6, because the "improved" IPv6 Type-0 Routing Header can hold far more intermediate-hop addresses than the IPv4 header can. It has been demonstrated that a ping-pong denial of service attack, like the one described in the preceding section for IPv4, and consisting of only one attack packet, can sustain itself for over half a minute. By sending hundreds or thousands of packets, an attacker could effectively shut down targeted hosts or LANs. Moreover, because IPv6 includes end hosts in its definition of legitimate processors of *Routing* Headers (meaning even a device that doesn't route can participate in this attack), two end hosts can be forced by a completely unknown and untrusted outside party to beat each other to a pulp without a router or firewall even getting involved.

The details of the this vulnerability are outlined in a CanSecWest 2007 presentation at `http://www.secdev.org/conf/IPv6_RH_security-csw07.pdf`, and clarifying prose can be found in articles like the one at `http://www2.csoonline.com/blog_view.html?CID=32916`. As of early May 2007, the Internet Engineering Task Force (IETF), which is responsible for the definition of IPv6 and many other Internet standards, has had no instances of this "ingenious" exploit (IETF's words) reported to it (see `http://www.eweek.com/article2/0%2C1895%2C2126099%2C00.asp`). Press coverage of the vulnerability died out by the end of May 2007, given that there were no newsworthy exploits.

Mitigating the IPv6 Routing Header Vulnerability

Per RFC 2460, the Type-0 Routing Header must be implemented for an IPv6 stack to be considered completely functional, so most IPv6 implementations are likely to contain the feature. Based on the discovery of the vulnerabilities discussed in the preceding section, the IETF has moved to require the Type-0 Routing Header be disabled as the default state of IPv6-capable systems. Even with that requirement, you should still make sure the Type-0 Routing Header is turned off in your systems, and you should block the passage of packets containing such headers in your firewalls and router filtering lists.

As you configure your systems and firewalls, note the Mobile IPv6 section later in this chapter, where it states that only Type-0 Routing Headers are vulnerable to exploit, at present. The other non-experimental type of Routing Header still in use is Type-2, which is required for Mobile IPv6 and is considered harmless at this time. If you're using Mobile IPv6, Type-2 Routing Headers must be allowed to pass through firewalls, and so on. All other Routing Header types can be turned off. If you're not using Mobile IPv6, it's probably best to block *all* IPv6 Routing Headers.

The IPv6 Type-0 Routing Header vulnerability is not a cataclysmic one, because there are few legitimate uses for that form of the header (network discovery being a rare example), so few people are left out in the cold if the feature is never used again. This stems from the fact that whatever legitimate uses there were for IPv4 Source Routing, those uses were abandoned years ago, because they were simply impractical given that most routers drop Source Routing traffic. Now in IPv6, the same will likely apply.

One remaining observation from the Type-0 Routing Header experience that bears remembering as you're assessing advanced features for your IPv6 transition is how the IPv6 designers managed to incorporate a flawed feature from IPv4 into IPv6, even with all the years of experience with IPv4's vulnerabilities. This should underscore that IPv6 technology is new, that the advanced features are unproven, and that you should weigh the business risks of deploying anything more than the most basic IPv6 features (addresses, routing, DHCPv6, and maybe IPsec are a good start) in your first upgrade.

Understanding the Exploits Associated with Fragmentation

Like IPv4, IPv6 has the capability to fragment packets so as to fit them onto links with lesser MTUs. A distinction between the two IP protocol versions regarding fragmentation is that IPv6 removes the data fields for fragmentation from the main header and wisely puts them in a separate extension header, because they are unused in most cases. The details of fragmentation have been discussed in Chapter 2 and elsewhere in this book and won't be repeated here.

Starting as early as the mid-1990s, several exploits arose based on IPv4 fragmentation. These exploits were designed to get around access controls or to cause denial of service. You can find examples of the types of IPv4 fragmentation exploits at `http://www.ouah.org/fragma.html`, which also cites vendor-specific vulnerabilities. RFC 1858 also describes one class of these exploits. The exploits can be summarized into the following broad classes:

- Exploits meant to trick a destination host into reassembling fragments to produce an IP packet greater in size than the maximum limit of 65,535 octets. A similar exploit uses fragments that lead to a final re-assembled packet with gaps, in other words, missing fragments. Such exploits are meant to crash sloppily implemented IP stacks.

- Exploits that use tiny fragments to force parts of upper-layer protocol headers, like TCP, into locations other than the first fragment. Poorly implemented firewalls could be tricked into passing forbidden traffic, because they don't detect the split TCP header and therefore don't analyze it. There are similar exploits that use overlapping fragments so that later fragments overwrite otherwise legitimate TCP headers in earlier ones, for example, setting header fields to forbidden values. This occurs during packet reassembly at the destination device, after a firewall has passed all the fragments, which are inoffensive by themselves, into the network the firewall is supposed to protect.

Assessing the Impact of IPv4 Fragmentation Exploits on IPv6

The IPv4 fragmentation exploits described in the preceding section are also theoretically possible in IPv6, because the basic design of fragmentation has not changed much. Many of the exploits described have been around for some time, however, and IPv4 stack implementations and firewalls have been hardened against them. This might make you optimistic that stack implementers aware of the IPv4 exploits also hardened their IPv6 stacks appropriately. That sounds like a reasonable assumption, but you need only to look a few pages back to see how well Type-0 Routing Headers worked out with similar forewarning. As recommended in Chapter 6, "Defining the Transition Preparation Steps," regarding verifying the advertised capabilities of your IPv6 systems, it's probably a good idea to see that they are resilient to the IPv4 fragmentation exploits, modified as necessary for IPv6. I'm not aware of any implementations of these exploits for IPv6, so you might have to roll your own.

What about New IPv6 Fragmentation Exploits?

Because IPv6 fragmentation is not a radical departure from the IPv4 version, it's not surprising that IPv6-specific fragmentation exploits have not arisen yet. There may someday be exotic exploits as yet unforeseen by the designers of IPv6, like using overlapping fragments to replace valid cryptographic data in IPsec or SEND with fakes, to which only some poorly written stacks should be vulnerable. Another class of exploits might involve denial of service via fragmentation against Mobile IPv6 users out in the boondocks where MTUs are small. As long as devices reassembling fragments also process the *entire* packet *after* reassembly and protect themselves from exploits that try to overflow buffers, and so on, fragmentation should be a minor source for new exploits. This is, of course, difficult to predict with any measure close to 100-percent certainty.

Summarizing IPsec

IPsec has been discussed a lot in this book and this section is only to remind you of the AH and ESP extension headers (see Table 10-2) that implement IPsec. If you need more information, Chapter 7 covers IPsec technology at a level less complex than the RFCs, but detailed enough for you to learn how IPsec works. Chapter 4 discusses the performance costs of cryptographic protocols, which translate to higher equipment costs, should you decide to deploy IPsec. That chapter also discusses what you should consider regarding implementing IPsec as part of your IPv6 transition, including the additional transition resources you'll need and the complexity of the work. Look to those chapters and the index for what you need.

Introducing Hop-by-Hop and Destination Options

The Hop-by-Hop Options Header and Destination Options Header (see Table 10-2) serve as containers for variable numbers of options that are processed either by each hop in the path taken by a packet, or by destinations only. The reason for two header types is to reduce router workload by only requiring routers to look at the Hop-by-Hop Options. In fact, the Hop-by-Hop extension header is the only one that routers care about for packets not destined explicitly for them, which is why it is required, if present, to be the first header after the main IPv6 header.

Destination Options are, as the name implies, only of interest to the destinations of packets. The list of packet destinations doesn't include only the final destination of a packet, but also any destinations in the Routing Header, if present. That's why the Destination Options Header can appear twice in a packet, once before the Routing Header for options of interest to all destinations, and possibly again as the last extension header before the upper layer payload (for example, TCP), for options only of interest to the packet's final destination.

The non-experimental Hop-By-Hop Options and Destination Options, defined as of July 18, 2007 (see `http://www.iana.org/assignments/ipv6-parameters`) are shown in Table 10-3 and Table 10-4, respectively. There are also experimental options that should be turned off in your implementations. You can find them at the website mentioned, but they are not listed in the tables.

As you can see from Table 10-3 and Table 10-4, there aren't a lot of options defined at this time. The Padding Options defined by RFC 2460 are simple mechanisms for data alignment in options lists and present little in the way of risk. One type of Padding Option adds a single octet to an options list, and the other is used if more than one octet of padding is required.

The sections that follow summarize the features associated with each of the remaining non-padding options in Table 10-3 and Table 10-4, including any risks or limitations that might apply.

Table 10-3: Non-experimental IPv6 Hop-by-Hop Options

OPTION TYPE	IF UNRECOGNIZED	RFC	MUST SUPPORT?
Padding (1 octet)	Skip option	RFC 2460	Yes
Padding (N octets)	Skip option	RFC 2460	Yes
Jumbo Payload	Discard packet; send ICMP if unicast	RFC 2675	High MTU links only and optional there, too.
Router Alert	Skip option	RFC 2711	No

Telling Devices How to Handle Unrecognized Options

Encoded in the value that represents each option's type is a 2-bit flag indicating what a router or destination device should do if it doesn't know how to process the given type of option. The choices of what to do with an unrecognized option consist of:

1. Skipping over the option and continuing to process the packet

2. Discarding the packet silently

3. Discarding the packet and sending an ICMPv6 error message to the sender, regardless of the destination address of the original packet

4. Discarding the packet and sending an ICMPv6 error message to the sender, but only if the original packet was to a unicast address

What each of the defined IPv6 options causes the processing device to do, if that device doesn't understand the given option, is shown in the "If Unrecognized" columns of Table 10-3 and Table 10-4.

Because this chapter is about risks, you should note that there is a denial of service risk associated with choice #3 in the preceding list. The risk is that an attacker could send a packet with a deliberately unknown option to an active multicast address, like the "all nodes" address that represents all nodes on the LAN. If the unknown option were encoded with choice #3, then every node (that is, router or end device) that received the attack packet would respond with an ICMPv6 error message to the sender. Moreover, the attacker need not use his or her own IP address, but rather the IP address of the device being attacked. This will result in an unsuspecting device being hit by numerous ICMPv6 error messages from out of the blue.

There's little you can do about this type of attack, but to limit it and contain it. Some of your devices may give you the choice to turn off the ICMPv6 error messages associated with options, ignoring whatever the option type says the device must do. Alternatively, you could configure your firewalls to drop packets containing unknown options, thereby limiting the attacker to his or her local LAN.

Table 10-4: Non-experimental IPv6 Destination Options

OPTION TYPE	IF UNRECOGNIZED	RFC	MUST SUPPORT?
Padding (1 octet)	Skip option	RFC 2460	Yes
Padding (N octets)	Skip option	RFC 2460	Yes
Tunnel Encapsulation Limit	Skip option	RFC 2473	No
Home Address	Discard packet; send ICMP if unicast	RFC 3775	No

Flagging Options that Can Change En Route

Also encoded in the value that represents each option's type is a 1-bit flag indicating whether the data associated with the option is mutable (can change) en route from the source device to the destination. For options where the data can change en route, the cryptographic protection of the IPsec Authentication Header does not apply, because it treats the option's data contents as all zeros (see RFC 2460 and RFC 4302).

This is a data-integrity risk, because the rest of the packet is allegedly from some authenticated source and an unsuspecting device would expect the same assurances on all the options included in the packet. An informed device would know about the lack of integrity and authentication of the option's data, but you shouldn't rely on your devices being informed of IPsec nuances. The real lesson here is that this is another strong argument for using IPsec's Encapsulating Security Payload instead of the Authentication Header, because the ESP protects the entire packet. See Chapter 7 for more information on the advantages of ESP over AH.

It should be noted that none of the currently defined non-experimental IPv6 Hop-by-Hop Options or Destination Options may change en route, so the AH problem is academic for the moment.

Getting Ready for 4-Gigabyte Packets

As mentioned in prior chapters, RFC 2675 defines IPv6 jumbograms, in other words packets with payloads greater than 65,535 octets in length. Jumbograms were defined initially to extend the IPv6 packet size to the range of 75,000 octets to 100,000 octets, which is where MTUs of some faster link-layer protocols are operating at present or expected to operate soon (see Table 5-2).

Representing a number that's greater than 65,535 requires at least one more bit than what is available in the IPv6 header's Payload Length field. Once the extra bit is required, however, you might as well assign a whole octet (8 bits), for data alignment reasons. Given modern computer and router architectures, a three-octet field length is still weird. The next largest convenient size for the length field is four octets. So now, to accommodate 100,000-octet packets, IPv6 has provided a mechanism for packets to contain more than 4 billion octets of payload.

With the possibility of sending (or trying to send) such huge packets comes the possibility of causing trouble with them. Fortunately, there aren't many link-layer protocols that can use jumbograms. Moreover, jumbograms themselves are not required to be supported by any IPv6 stack. It is only in the case of stacks on systems with link MTUs of at least 65,576 octets that jumbograms need be supported at all, and even in those cases jumbograms are not mandatory.

There is little written online about jumbograms, other than citations of the RFCs that discuss them. As of September 2007, implementations are probably also scarce. What you should take away from this section is that, if you have hardware that can handle MTUs of at least 65,576 octets *and* you have some reason to send jumbograms, ask your vendors what the default behavior is for their devices. The expected behavior is that nothing larger than whatever the link MTU is should be allowed to pass. Moreover, jumbograms cannot be fragmented.

Alerting Routers to Look at Packets

The other non-experimental Hop-by-Hop Option currently defined is Router Alert. This option is used, as its name suggests, to alert routers to packets that should be examined more closely. Packets without this option are processed only as far as the router needs to in order to forward them to the next hop. By using the Router Alert option, the routers perform deeper inspection of the packets. As an example, the MLD protocols (see Table 10-1) require the use of the Router Alert option.

There is a mild denial of service risk with Router Alert, because setting it without a good reason will cause a router to analyze a packet and spend CPU cycles doing so. The risk is probably trivial, however, compared to other potential denial of service attacks against routers, including simply pinging them a lot or sending a lot of SNMP queries.

Setting Limits on the Nesting of Tunnels

The Tunnel Encapsulation Limit option is an IPv6 Destination Option used to restrict the number of nested tunnels in which a packet can be encapsulated. The option's use is purely in association with tunneling as defined in RFC 2473 and the option is attached to the packet only while the packet is in the tunnel. In other words, the option is added when the packet is encapsulated for tunneling and removed when the encapsulation is removed on the other side of the tunnel.

The only security implication of the Tunnel Encapsulation Limit option is that a poorly configured tunnel may set the limit too low and cause packets that require further encapsulation en route to their ultimate destinations to be dropped. Such problems are discovered quickly and the tunnel entry points tuned, so there is little risk with the misuse or exploitation of this Destination Option. Another trivial exploit may be possible if an attacker can forcibly lower the limit amount of a packet en route in a tunnel, but before the packet reaches another tunnel, however this seems like a pretty convoluted denial of service attack.

Telling Others Where Your Home Is

The Home Address Destination Option is sent by a device using Mobile IPv6 while away from its home network. The option is used to inform other devices with which the mobile device communicates of that device's home address. As promised several times earlier in this chapter, Mobile IPv6 is covered shortly. This section serves only to complete the coverage of Table 10-4 for this part of the chapter.

What Should I Do with My Firewall Configurations?

Throughout this chapter are recommendations on what traffic to drop and what to allow through your firewalls and filtering routers. With ICMPv6 and multicast being so important to the proper functioning of IPv6, and considering the security vulnerabilities associated with some of the IPv6 advanced features, you want to make sure your firewall rules are set correctly. In addition to the standard firewall configuration steps that you're used to, you should consider the following basic preventative measures when dealing with IPv6-specific protocols, extensions, and options:

1. Drop all packets containing extension headers, Hop-by-Hop Options, or Destination Options that you are not using in the part of the network the given firewall is protecting or in networks whose traffic flows through yours.

2. Allow the appropriate multicast traffic to pass through your routers. A lot of the multicast traffic described in this chapter is link-local and, therefore, your IPv6-capable routers should automatically refuse to forward such traffic. For other necessary multicast traffic, make sure it can be routed.

3. Unless you're using Mobile IPv6, drop all packets with Routing Headers. The potential impact from the denial of service attacks these headers enable is serious enough that you shouldn't take the risk.

4. In the case of some extension headers, like the one for fragmentation, it's hard to determine whether you'll need it or not. In the case of the Fragmentation Header specifically, it should be safe to allow it to pass, provided you've made sure your routers and end devices are immune to the fragmentation exploits described earlier in this chapter.

5. For performance reasons, allow ICMPv6 Packet Too Big errors to go wherever they need to whenever possible. This error message is what makes Path MTU discovery work and lets you use your network's bandwidth to its fullest.

6. For other ICMPv6 messages that shouldn't be allowed to cross routers, ND and SEND messages, for example, make sure to have firewall rules in place to drop these packets, just in case.

7. Unless you're using the Route Renumbering capabilities of IPv6, block the related ICMPv6 messages at your firewalls. Even though IPsec is

required for any router to accept an RR command, until the implementations are more proven, it's best to not tempt fate by letting these packets roam your network.

The preceding list is for a production environment with little tolerance for network problems and down time. For more relaxed environments where you're investigating IPv6's capabilities and limitations, you can relax the rules appropriately and let, for example, your network administrators and researchers play with Type-0 Routing Headers. Select the choices you are comfortable with to maintain the appropriate proportions of overall network functionality, performance, and security.

For additional help in how to configure your firewalls, consult Chapter 6 of [Murphy], cited in "Further Reading" at the end of this chapter. IPv6 is still such a moving target that this book, published in early 2005, is already the slightest bit dated, with some obsolete RFC numbers and references to features that have since been removed. But still, it's an excellent technical (and practical) reference.

Understanding Mobile IPv6's Risks and Limitations

The functionality of Mobile IPv6 was discussed to some degree in Chapter 7, where mobility capabilities were likened to call-forwarding on steroids. Mobility is an exciting new set of capabilities for devices and Mobile IPv6's capabilities are no exception. Nevertheless, there may be concessions you need to make in the way of network performance and security to achieve mobility. As with all new capabilities, it is up to you to decide what balance of features, performance, and security is correct for your network. This section adds some details to the information from Chapter 7 on how Mobile IPv6 functions in order to describe risks and limitations associated with the technology.

Defining the Roles of Devices in Mobile IPv6

Most Mobile IPv6 functionalities involve interactions between three different kinds of devices, which are defined by RFC 3775 as the following:

1. Mobile Node (MN): An IPv6-capable device that's moving around from network to network, for example a user's laptop traveling around the world.

2. Home Agent (HA): One or more routers back at the MN's home network that, among other things, act as proxies for traffic to and from MNs so that those communicating with the MNs need not know that the MNs are mobile.

3. Correspondent Node (CN): An external device communicating with an MN, either by proxy through an HA or directly in some cases. A CN need not be capable of Mobile IPv6 functionality, but if it is, the communications can be made more optimal.

Depending on what these different types of devices are allowed (or not allowed) to do on a given network determines how efficiently Mobile IPv6 will work for you, or if it will even work at all.

Establishing the Goals of Mobile IPv6

A goal of Mobile IPv6 is that applications on MNs and CNs do not need to be aware that Mobile IPv6 communications are occurring in the network layer beneath them. It's also optional whether any part of a CN (network layer included) is aware of Mobile IPv6 at all. An assumption in designing Mobile IPv6 was that most CNs, for example application servers on the public Internet or in parts of your enterprise network that have not yet undergone IPv6 upgrade, may not be aware of Mobile IPv6 for some time (perhaps even after they become IPv6 capable). As such, the onus of Mobile IPv6 functionality was concentrated on MNs and HAs.

With CNs that are unaware of Mobile IPv6 (or that do not choose to use its features), bandwidth utilization in the vicinity of the HA, packet processing load on the HA, and latency and jitter of traffic along the MN to HA to CN path go up. These are performance constraints you may not find acceptable, especially if you're passing audio or video streams around.

Also, if a CN doesn't use all of the available Mobile IPv6 features, then the MN may have to originate packets while away from its home network that still have the MN's home address as the source in the packets. This is to trick the CN into thinking the MN is operating from its home address. Firewalls protecting the network that the MN is visiting and configured with anti-spoofing rules (meaning, the firewalls know what IP addresses are on their networks and will not let any other sources transmit out), may drop such packets. From such a firewall's point of view, the packet could not have possibly originated on the network connected to that particular interface of the firewall, so someone must be trying to pull a fast one.

Extensions, Options, and ICMPv6 Messages, Oh My!

Mobile IPv6 relies on many of the basic features of IPv6, as well as several extensions that Mobile IPv6 itself defines. How Mobile IPv6 uses each of those features is defined in this section and the following one.

Earlier parts of this chapter introduced ICMPv6 messages related to Mobile IPv6, the Mobility Header extension, and the Home Address Destination

Option without saying too much more about any of them. This section describes what those protocol features of IPv6 or ICMPv6 provide to overall Mobile IPv6 functionality and how much you need each feature to make mobility work. The features are presented in order from the absolutely necessary (for Mobile IPv6 functionality) to the possibly optional.

The Mobility Header extension (see Table 10-2) is absolutely necessary for Mobile IPv6 to function, which means it must be allowed through all firewalls between an MN, its HA(s), and optionally the CNs with which the MN communicates. Between an MN and HA, the Mobility Header is used during the MN's travels from network to network for associating addresses the MN is visiting (called "care-of addresses") with the MN's home address. Although this functionality is obviously necessary for Mobile IPv6 to work, recall that because the CN may not be capable of Mobile IPv6 functionality, the CN's role in a given communication may be no different from that of a device in a conventional (non-mobile) IPv6 communication. If, however, a CN is capable of Mobile IPv6 functionality, then by letting Mobility Headers flow to and from it, optimized communications can be established.

The Home Address Destination Option (see Table 10-4) is used by an MN when away from home to tell to an HA or CN the MN's home address. The option (and associated Destination Options Header extension in Table 10-2) must be allowed to flow at least between an MN and HA. If a CN is not capable of Mobile IPv6 functionality, then the option need not flow between the MN and that CN. Again, not involving the CN in the Mobile IPv6 protocols and exchanges will lead to degraded performance of the MN-HA-CN connection and extra work and bandwidth use in the vicinity of the HA.

The Type-2 Routing Header (see Table 10-2) is used by CNs when communicating directly with MNs. This is after a CN has accepted that an MN's care-of address is in fact associated with the same device as the home address with which the CN was originally communicating. There are a few ways the CN can come to trust that the MN's care-of and home addresses are associated with the same device, but they are outside the scope of this discussion. See RFC 3775 for a general solution and RFC 4449 for a sometimes more practical one involving static keys. The Type-2 Routing Header only need be allowed through firewalls if

1. The CN is capable of and desires to use Mobile IPv6 functionality, and,

2. Optimized routing directly between the MN and CN is required.

If it is satisfactory (or preferable when accounting for security requirements) that all communications between an MN and CN pass through the HA, then the Type-2 Routing Header does not need to be used. Note that there are bandwidth utilization costs, as well as packet processing costs on the HA, associated with electing to include the HA in all communications.

It is very important to note that the Type-2 Routing Header is distinct from the exploitable Type-0 Routing Header and firewalls are fairly safe in passing the former, but should think twice (or even thrice) before passing the latter.

The ICMPv6 messages associated with Mobile IPv6 (see Table 10-1) are the most optional parts of the feature set. The Home Agent Address Discovery Request & Reply messages are used by the MN to find one or more HAs on its home network. That way, should an HA that the MN is communicating with cease to function, the MN can possibly find an alternate HA. Some implementations could choose to hardwire an HA into each MN (perhaps for security reasons) making the preceding ICMPv6 messages optional. They could then disable those messages. Obviously, this would be an incomplete (and nonstandard) implementation of Mobile IPv6 and, should the hardwired HA not be accessible, the MN would have no way to find an alternate.

The Mobile Prefix Solicitation & Advertisement ICMPv6 messages are used by an MN to determine the network prefixes on its home network, so as to update its home address while away from home. If those prefixes are not expected to change, the messages are not required and some implementations could choose to provide a means for the user or administrator to disable it.

What Other IPv6 Features Does Mobile IPv6 Require?

In addition to the Mobile IPv6 features described in the previous sections, you'll also need to be able to send and receive encapsulated (read, tunneled) IPv6 traffic, which is not a significant technological hurdle for most IPv6-capable devices, but your firewalls will have to allow that traffic through to all the appropriate places, especially between MNs and HAs.

With the tunneling also comes the need for IPsec. Mobile IPv6's signaling protocol exchanges are required to be protected by IPsec in order to prevent spoofing and several other attacks. That means, before you can even consider rolling out Mobile IPv6, you need to role out IPsec. This dependency may make your Mobile IPv6 deployment decision crystal clear, if you've already decided against IPsec.

The final example of IPv6 features that are required by or affected by mobility is the recommended increase in the frequency of ND updates when using Mobile IPv6 so as to allow MNs to detect more quickly that they are moving. This is another potential source of traffic increases beyond what you might be willing to tolerate.

Losing Traffic While Mobile Nodes Are Moving

There is a window of time whenever an MN "moves" from one network to another, in other words changes its IP address (it actually may not have physically "moved" at all), that old traffic still on the way to the previous address will not reach the MN. The process of informing the HA and all CNs with which the MN is communicating that the MN is moving (or has moved) is called hand-off and there are multiple solutions proposed for faster hand-offs. You should be aware, however, of the risk of traffic loss and when considering whether to roll out Mobile IPv6, you should factor in whether the hand-off capabilities available to you (slow or fast) are acceptable for the amount of packet loss you can tolerate.

Regarding Accessibility of Home Agents

The accessibility of HAs is a critical factor in whether Mobile IPv6 can be made to work for your network. CNs are likely to be outside your enterprise, probably in a less restricted environment and, therefore, able to use more of IPv6's advanced features. Similarly, MNs (when traveling) will likely be in less restricted environments than your home network, at a hotel using a consumer ISP, for example. HAs will always be within your enterprise network, probably behind your security perimeter, and therefore subject to more stringent access controls. Your choices for HAs (and Mobile IPv6 in general) to work include opening your whole enterprise to Mobile IPv6 traffic, which at the current level of maturity of the technology doesn't sound prudent.

Another choice would be to establish a network prefix devoted to Mobile IPv6 somewhere on the periphery of your network, in other words a "mobility LAN." That way, the mobility LAN can be made subject to the fewest access controls, while still being able to route to all your other LANs behind the firewalls. This is very similar to how some modern VPNs work. Of course, that means your mobile laptop node may be "traveling," even when you're at your desk in the office, because you are not directly on that mobility LAN. There are performance considerations to take into account with this choice, but they are fairly straightforward for most enterprise network managers and engineers and a far better alternative to allowing Mobile IPv6 traffic all over your network unchecked.

Cracking the Books to Learn More

There are already a lot of good security features in Mobile IPv6 to counter some of the nastier threats. Rather than describe them, I focused on the remaining risks and limitations that are left after the existent security features are taken into account. You can refer to the RFCs and books cited at the end of this section to see what security mechanisms Mobile IPv6 has within it. Specifically, look at RFC 4225 to see a list of the security threats and RFC 4487 for what to consider when mixing Mobile IPv6 and firewalls.

Chapter 11 of *Migrating to IPv6* by Marc Blanchet, details for which are listed in the "Further Reading" section that follows this one, provides a description of the functionality of Mobile IPv6 that is far easier to understand than the hundreds of pages of RFCs devoted to the details. If you are serious about implementing mobility capabilities, however, you also may want to read a book or two entirely dedicated to that topic, as well as take some training classes. Two books with good reviews, though I must confess I haven't read them, are:

> *Mobile IPv6: Mobility in a Wireless Internet* by Soliman (ISBN-13: 978-0201788976), published April 2004.

> *Mobile IP Technology and Applications* by Raab & Chandra (ISBN-13: 978-1587051326), published May 2005.

The latter book is by Cisco Press, and between that and being more recent, is probably the better choice for Mobile IPv6 deployment. It's probably worth your time to check out both at the local book store or library and pick your favorite (or both).

Relevant RFCs to improve your knowledge of Mobile IPv6 are listed next. I've split the lists into standards that offer solutions and problem statements that describe what is still left to do in Mobile IPv6. When you go through the following lists, don't be daunted. See what interests you, for example sockets programming if you're a programmer porting code to Mobile IPv6, and start there. I promise that, taken in small bites, the RFCs aren't all that bad. They beat OSI documentation, set theory, and mortgage applications in my ordering of impenetrable reading.

The Mobile IPv6 standards, as of September 19, 2007, are:

- RFC 3775: Mobility Support in IPv6. June 2004.
- RFC 3776: Using IPsec to Protect Mobile IPv6 Signaling Between Mobile Nodes and Home Agents. June 2004.
- RFC 3963: Network Mobility (NEMO) Basic Support Protocol. January 2005.
- RFC 4225: Mobile IP Version 6 Route Optimization Security Design Background. December 2005.
- RFC 4283: Mobile Node Identifier Option for Mobile IPv6 (MIPv6). November 2005.
- RFC 4295: Mobile IPv6 Management Information Base. April 2006.

- RFC 4449: Securing Mobile IPv6 Route Optimization Using a Static Shared Key. June 2006.

- RFC 4555: IKEv2 Mobility and Multihoming Protocol (MOBIKE). June 2006.

- RFC 4584: Extension to Sockets API for Mobile IPv6. July 2006.

- RFC 4621: Design of the IKEv2 Mobility and Multihoming (MOBIKE) Protocol. August 2006.

- RFC 4651: A Taxonomy and Analysis of Enhancements to Mobile IPv6 Route Optimization. February 2007.

- RFC 4866: Enhanced Route Optimization for Mobile IPv6. May 2007.

- RFC 4877: Mobile IPv6 Operation with IKEv2 and the Revised IPsec Architecture. April 2007. (Updates RFC 3776)

Note that RFC 4877 updates RFC 3776, the secure signaling RFC for Mobile IPv6. Also note the reference to NEMO, which allows whole networks to be mobile. This is useful, for example, for collecting devices on a mobile platform. I won't cover it here, but you may want to give the RFC a read if the network mobility is something you have to deal with in your daily work. There are also several more NEMO-related RFCs that I did not include, because the list was already long enough.

Because Mobile IPv6 is so new, not everything about it is figured out yet. The following "problem statement" RFCs discuss what work is left to do. While you're welcome to throw in your two cents with the IETF regarding solutions, the RFCs are mentioned here primarily to point out the greatest areas of risk regarding what parts of Mobile IPv6 are not firmed up, yet. The list of problem statements is as follows:

- RFC 4487: Mobile IPv6 and Firewalls: Problem Statement. May 2006.

- RFC 4640: Problem Statement for Bootstrapping Mobile IPv6 (MIPv6). September 2006.

- RFC 4882: IP Address Location Privacy and Mobile IPv6: Problem Statement. May 2007.

- RFC 4977: Problem Statement: Dual Stack Mobility. August 2007.

Because your first implementations of IPv6 are likely to be dual-stack, you should definitely review RFC 4977. Mobility in IPv6 differs from the IPv4 version, so you need to see how they interoperate. Also, the firewall-related RFC mentioned earlier (RFC 4487) should be on your required reading list.

Further Reading

This book, in relation to all the material available on IPv6 capabilities, risks, and limitations, only touches on the subject enough to enable you to start making decisions about deployment. Whole other books could be written about the details of these things and, in fact, several have. Two excellent (and recent) sources are:

> *Migrating to IPv6* by Marc Blanchet (ISBN: 0-471-49892-0), published in 2006.

> *IPv6 Network Administration* by Murphy & Malone (ISBN: 0-596-00934-8), published in March 2005.

In addition to books, and considering IPv6's volatility, the most recent information can be found at websites like:

> `http://www.networksorcery.com/`

> `http://www.faqs.org/rfcs/rfc-obsolete.html`

The first website listed is an excellent source for RFC information, as well as detailed descriptions of the protocols and their options. The second website is a handy reference for obsolete RFCs, which Network Sorcery also addresses, but in a more cumbersome manner.

Testing Your Knowledge

The following questions should help you recall the key lessons conveyed in this chapter. The answers are in Appendix A.

1. What are the three risks associated with an IPv6 transition that are not common to most other enterprise technology upgrades?

2. What is a shortcoming of SEND that may limit its deployment? Hint: It has to do with the addresses it uses.

3. Where else should you focus your functionality, performance, and security concerns while undertaking your IPv6 upgrade, besides all the network-layer protocol changes brought about by IPv6?

4. What do non-mobile systems need to know about Mobile IPv6 in order to communicate with mobile systems?

Easing Your Transition

CHAPTER 11

Knowing What Assets You Have

Production is not the application of
tools to materials, but logic to work.

— **Peter F. Drucker**

According to the U.S. Census Bureau (http://www.census.gov/), the United States' first census was taken by U.S. marshals on horseback in 1790 and counted 3.9 million inhabitants. Today's U.S. population is a little over 300 million and the Bureau employs 12,000 people regularly in nearly 20 offices nationwide. The number of people working for the Bureau expands dramatically when the census is taken every 10 years. Census 2000 employed 860,000 temporary census workers or about 0.3 percent of the U.S. population at the time. As you can see, it's not a trivial effort to count large collections of people or things. The asset inventory you need to perform to facilitate your IPv6 upgrade is a lot like the censuses, and the difference between the early populations of Internet pioneers and today's modern enterprise networks is also similar to the nascent United States and the country that it is today. The break you get that the Census Bureau hasn't been able to fully utilize yet is that you can employ automated tools to count your assets. This chapter introduces you to those tools and describes how you can use them to make your inventory work easier.

What You'll Learn

This chapter focuses on the asset inventory work you will need to perform as part of your IPv6 transition. The emphasis is on using automated asset inventory and management tools to make your work easier. In tying your inventory work to automated tools, this chapter expands on the information and recommendations of Chapter 6, "Defining the Transition Preparation Steps." One of the first sections summarizes the relevant points of that chapter to get you up to speed quickly if you don't recall them, or haven't read that chapter yet. Chapter 6 also discusses capabilities inventories, which are as important to your IPv6 transition as are asset inventories. This chapter doesn't discuss capabilities much, because discovery and analysis of your capabilities are difficult to automate with general-purpose tools and are better left to the verification suites you built based on use cases in Chapter 6.

The chapter continues by discussing how to deploy an asset discovery solution, including the benefits of using automated tools and how to use the different types of tools together. The chapter then discusses how to integrate asset discovery tools with asset management ones and the importance of doing so. Having established that asset management tools are something you should consider, if you aren't using them already, the chapter describes the types of asset management tools and how to populate them with data from asset inventory tools and other sources.

For both asset discovery and management tools, there are sections in this chapter that highlight specific tools on the market today that have been vetted by myself and others to a degree sufficient that you should feel comfortable to assess them for your own environment. The chapter concludes with a discussion of what you need to think about if no commercial or open-source tools suit you and you want to create your own tools.

Combining Inventory with Discovery

This chapter uses the terms "inventory" and "discovery" interchangeably when discussing the processes of counting your existing assets, finding new assets, or determining that existing assets you once had have been retired. Performing an inventory implies counting things that you know you have, but whose quantities and locations you may not know. Discovery means finding new things, often with the intent to place them in your inventory. Many automated asset inventory tools call themselves discovery tools, because they do more than count. They also find. Rather than getting caught up in all those semantics, I've chosen to use the lingua franca of the asset discovery community and rely on the context around the use of each term to distinguish whether I mean you're counting existing things or discovering (and counting) new ones.

Summarizing Chapter 6, "Defining the Transition Preparation Steps"

This section is a summary of the relevant parts of Chapter 6, which establishes the assumptions and goals for your asset inventory, and outlines some basic processes. In this chapter, those processes are filled out with pragmatic means of execution, centered on the use of automated asset inventory and management tools. In addition to the material in this section and the rest of the chapter, you should refer to Chapter 6 if you have any questions about the details behind its assumptions or goals. Also, refer to the checklist in Chapter 6, because it is a concise, but comprehensive, summary of what you need to perform thorough asset and capabilities inventories. As mentioned at the beginning of this chapter, I won't spend much time on your capabilities inventory in this chapter, because discovering capabilities is much more specific to each enterprise than discovering assets, and automated tools are not as prevalent.

Remembering the Goals of Your Inventory Work

Among the most important aspects of your asset inventory is to have clear goals. The goals outlined early on in Chapter 6 are briefly as follows:

1. Validate that your hardware and software assets are what you believe them to be and what they are documented as.

2. Discover any assets of which you are unaware.

3. Eliminate any assets from your documentation that you find are no longer present in your network.

The tools and the recommendations for the use of those tools discussed in this chapter are designed to address these goals.

Having an Inventory Strategy

After figuring out what you need to get done, you have to figure out how to do it. Chapter 6 recommends a network-centric inventory to go with your network-centric IPv6 transition. I prefer the network surveying approach described in that chapter, which is very similar to surveying areas of land. An alternative analogy is a photographic one, which also has the concepts of data collection, storage, and manipulation. You can imagine your discovery tools as cameras that collect inventory data. Your asset management tools are the albums that you can populate from your cameras, either readily or with difficulty, depending on the tools. You can then manipulate the pictures in the album, labeling them with all kinds of ancillary information.

This chapter shows how to apply these strategies to your network using the tools and other recommendations discussed in the following sections.

Getting Sufficient Network Coverage

Where you inventory from is as important as what you seek to inventory. As Chapter 6 describes, your network is a physical entity, but formed of numerous logical networks, often segregated by access control policies and firewalls. You should inventory your assets from at least one place in each of those logical networks, because each logical network sees a different perspective of your whole enterprise, based on routing and firewall rules. Whenever possible, selecting two or even three places within each logical network, with each place having an orthogonal perspective to the others (for example, being in different parts of the country or world), provides the best coverage.

Saving Your Results

Once you've gathered your inventory data, you have to organize and save that data, because the purpose of the data is not just to be collected, but to be used as a reference. In the context of this book, the data support your IPv6 transition and should contain the information necessary for you to make transition decisions at the asset level; in other words, whether you need to upgrade or replace an asset, leave it as is, or retire it with no replacement.

Chapter 6 defines what information you need to store and defines the storage facility as a Configuration Management Database (CMDB). Another name for a CMDB is an asset management system or tool. Whatever their name is, these tools are discussed in more detail in this chapter, including how to populate them and maintain them.

Keeping Your Inventory Current

As challenging as collecting comprehensive inventory data for your entire enterprise is, it is almost as challenging to keep that data up to date. Chapter 6 correctly states that your inventory will never be 100-percent correct, no more than a picture of a crowded city street is correct a few seconds after the picture is taken. The best you can do is to keep your inventory "recent," in other words, keep it correct as of last week, last month, or last quarter, depending on your specific needs for accuracy.

The use of automated tools, discussed in this chapter, lets you do the one thing that gives your inventory the greatest chance of being correct, which is to accelerate your inventory processes so that inventories can be performed more frequently. This chapter also discusses the need to be able to import readily, and ideally automatically, your inventory results into your CMDB, thereby reducing translation errors and human error on input, while also accelerating the asset inventory cycle.

Deploying a Discovery Solution

For an undertaking as large and complex as an enterprise asset inventory, you are going to need help from technology, specifically the automated discovery tools described in later sections of this chapter. The sections that immediately follow describe what features to expect from tools designed to facilitate your asset inventory and how those tools can be deployed to serve you best.

As already mentioned and like with any enterprise-scale technology, you need a deployment strategy or process. Chapter 6 sets the groundwork for you to define a process that works for you, including distribution of your inventory work across sites and organizational entities, as well as phased in time.

If you have not defined a strategy to use your discovery tools most effectively, it's likely the tools' vendors have developed their own strategies, even if those strategies are only implied by how you are instructed by the vendors to use the tools. If you are relying on a tool's recommended use strategy, rather than developing your own asset inventory process, make sure you understand the tool's underlying strategy and agree with its principles and assumptions.

Benefiting from Automated Discovery Tools

The three things that leap to mind when thinking about using automated asset discovery tools to facilitate your inventory are:

1. Speed of data collection

2. Repeatability of the collection process

3. Accuracy of results

Automated discovery tools can quickly find what's actually on your network and, if there's a question about the tools' results, then the tools can be run again in short order to validate those results. Though it's true no automated tool can find everything on your network, they are far more likely to find the most things, compared to any manual process.

As mentioned earlier, manual discovery on the enterprise scale is out of the question. Even at the site or department level, things have a tendency to get lost from the inventory (see "Going Fishing for Real" in Chapter 6). Automated tools honestly report what they see and my experience is that they find more assets that you were unaware of than they miss assets that you were already managing.

As far as those latter assets are concerned, if you know enough about an asset to be managing it, then the fact that it wasn't found in a particular discovery exercise is not that important. You could argue that, if some known asset weren't found, then there probably were unknown assets that were also missed. Though this is a true statement, the response that I would offer is to look at all the assets that were found that you didn't know about, and there will be such assets, especially the first few times you look. Such findings are more important than the handful of known assets and proportional number of unknown assets that might be missed.

The net result of using automated discovery tools is that your knowledge of your network increases every time you use them. Moreover, asset inventory is a cyclic process, and anything you can do to improve an iteration of the cycle benefits the whole process.

Listing the Asset Types Your Tools Need to Find

When selecting asset inventory tools, make sure the tools you pick can find all the things in the following list that you need found, plus any others specific to your enterprise that I have not listed.

- Routers, firewalls, and other network-layer forwarding devices, and the connectivity among them

- Switches, bridges, and other link-layer devices and their connectivity, including virtual (VLAN) connectivity

- Connectivity entering or exiting the network segments you control, be it routed or switched

- Support systems, like Intrusion Detection Systems (IDSs), web and other proxies, VPN concentrators, domain controllers, DNS and DHCP servers, and so on

- Servers for things like web, database, e-mail, and custom applications

- Workstations, laptops, PDAs, cell phones, and so on, and their operating system or firmware versions

- Client applications like web browsers, e-mail clients, word processors, office automation, databases, and home-grown applications

- TCP/IP listeners in general, for services already available online, but for which the tool vendor has not yet implemented specific functionality

If you are using multiple tools, each tool does not need to handle every type of asset just listed. Make sure, however, that the combination of all the tools you're using covers the appropriate part of the preceding list and whatever additional asset types you have.

Defining the Types of Automated Discovery Tools

There are two general classes of automated asset discovery tools. I'll call them local-discovery tools and enterprise-discovery tools. Sometimes the two classes are referred to as short-range and long-range tools, respectively, but this is somewhat inaccurate. The "range" of a given tool, measured as the network-layer distance from the segment on which the tool is deployed to the segments being inventoried, is usually not a limiting factor.

A local-discovery (or "short-range") tool may only work against 256 devices at a time, for example, but those devices could be located halfway around the world, provided there is routing to get the tool's network traffic there and back and not too many access controls restricting that traffic. With that said, some features of local-discovery tools are range limited, specifically those features that operate at the link layer using protocols like ARP. Most local-discovery tools, however, have plenty of "long-range" features to make them useful at a distance (which is why hackers like them, too). What typically limits local-discovery tools is how many devices they can inventory at once or how long that inventory takes to be performed.

An enterprise-discovery tool, on the other hand, has the ability to inventory the largest of enterprise networks very quickly. The per-device information of such inventories, however, is fairly shallow. Such tools' main purpose is to give you a broad understanding of the devices on your network, not to drill down into every device. This is based on the assumption that many times simply knowing that a given device or network segment that you didn't know about before is out there is enough for you to incorporate it into your inventory and investigate further or have it disconnected if it's not supposed to be there.

Using Local-Discovery Tools by Themselves

As mentioned earlier, local-discovery tools provide a wealth of information for your asset inventory. Most provide lists of active IP addresses, TCP, UDP, link-layer, and other services running on devices, operating system and application manufacturer information and version numbers, and more. Local-discovery tools are also very good at detecting unknown devices transmitting on a link, provided you place the tool on a switch port that can see all of the link's traffic, which is a minimal requirement. These tools can also search for devices that are not transmitting to see if there have been any unauthorized network connections. It would be a stealthy device indeed that could completely elude such tools for any extended period, if the tools are deployed properly

Because I've recommended distributing your asset inventory work to the site or department level, you might assume that local-discovery tools would be sufficient to meet your asset inventory needs. At such a level of granularity, in most cases even the largest network segments that any component of your distributed inventory would encompass could be addressed by a handful of instances of local-discovery tools. In many cases, one instance might be enough. Though this may be true in a theoretical sense, it makes very poor business sense.

With limited resources, you can't realistically deploy local-discovery tools into every nook and cranny of your network. Ignoring the cost of the tools for the moment (because you could negotiate a favorable enterprise license with the vendor or simply use free open-source tools), the staff required to run the tools and interpret the results would still make the effort prohibitively expensive. Few CIOs have the money to spend to deploy such an inventory strategy properly.

Augmenting Local Tools with Enterprise Tools

Referring to the network surveying model discussed earlier, if you liken asset inventory to surveying a newly found continent, you do not start the survey by deploying hundreds of surveyors to every corner of that continent in the hopes that some will find something interesting to survey. Though it's true that Lewis and Clark did that, it was a long time ago and they weren't on a CIO's clock. If you have the capability (satellite reconnaissance, for example), you first get a broad view of the continent and then deploy your surveyors to the places in which you are interested. Such places may be population centers for census purposes or to start trade or political negotiations, or they may be mineral deposits for mining. The common thread is that you should first endeavor to find out where all these things are at a superficial level, so you can direct your detailed surveying efforts into those areas more efficiently.

In asset inventory, the theory is no different, especially because one of your key goals is to find unknown devices and network segments. You need an enterprise-discovery tool for that, because you may not even know in some cases that a LAN is out there, for example, so you can't go and deploy a local-discovery tool on it.

Enterprise-discovery tools have their limitations, beyond the limited depth in the per-device information they return. Some of these tools are limited by firewalls or they have no direct link-layer-based discovery mechanisms, because in most cases they are an appreciable distance from the network segments being inventoried. The purpose of these tools, however, is not to find out the exact details of every asset in your network, but rather to find every asset (or as many as possible) and let you decide where to focus your more thorough tools.

Creating a Known Baseline from Which to Inventory

Whether you use local or enterprise tools, even the most sophisticated discovery tools need some initial information to get started. Where to start your inventory is dependent on what knowledge you have already. Whatever it is, start with that and consider it your baseline. This may include spreadsheets, asset databases, or even simple handwritten or printed lists.

Many asset discovery tools can take a minimum of information and build on that to find other things. An authorized SNMP community string (or SNMPv3 credentials) and the IP address of a core router may be all that's needed for a tool to find most of the address blocks in your network. From there, the tool can proceed to find other routers and end devices, and so forth.

Once you've established the first baseline, which in some cases may be the output of your first asset inventory exercise rather than its input, you should place that under configuration control in an asset management product like those discussed later in this chapter, or in general terms, a CMDB. In addition to business continuity reasons (because these data are valuable and should be protected from disaster), placing the data in a CMDB will allow you to manage your assets in a more controlled manner.

The information you put under configuration control becomes your "known" list of assets. Anything that isn't in that list and that's found by a discovery process needs to be identified, cataloged, and either put in the CMDB or removed from the network. Those last two sentences, in a nutshell, define your goals for asset management.

Knowing from Where to Look

In addition to covering each of your logical networks adequately, as described in Chapter 6, when determining where to inventory from, make sure you have sufficient network access. Even if you are connected to a given logical network, the IP address assigned to you may not have sufficient access, for example. That means you may have to go to your Network Operations Center (NOC) and use one of the privileged addresses in the NOC's network segments, so your discovery tools can have the same access rights as the tools that manage those discovered assets.

Setting the Bounds of What You Are Inventorying

Figuring out what you have on your network is one of the toughest network management problems around. Sometimes, so is figuring out what on that network actually belongs to you and what doesn't. By establishing a perimeter, usually after you've defined and documented your first baseline, you can decide what is yours and what isn't. In some cases, collections of your assets may be connected to the network segment from which you are inventorying via segments that don't belong to you. You should be careful to leave those networks untouched in your inventory exercises and only use them for transit.

An important property of your network's perimeter is that it may not be one contiguous boundary line separating your assets from those belonging to other organizations. In the preceding paragraph about transit networks, your perimeter encompasses at least two sets of devices. One set is composed of the devices on the network segment where your discovery tools are deployed. The other set is on the other side of the transit network. Think of the two network segments as the contiguous 48 United States and Alaska. Though the two are geographically separated, there is only one national perimeter composed of the disjoint physical boundaries of those two areas.

Being Careful in Your Discovery Activities

No matter how benign, all asset discovery tools generate some amount of network traffic. The traffic could be anything from simple pings and traceroutes all the way to cleverly crafted packets meant to tease out anomalous behavior in order to identify specific devices or applications. The side effects of some of the latter traffic can be unpleasant or even damaging to software, stored data, or equipment, especially if those side effects come as a surprise to the owners of the assets being inventoried.

As has already been recommended, you should start your automated discovery efforts by establishing a baseline. When performing the first baseline discovery activities, don't turn on every option on the tools that you are using. You're not an international spy trying to get every scrap of information before the enemy detects you and starts shooting. Use a staged approach. That way, when you find a shaky device that barely withstands a basic ping packet, you know to be careful with that device when you turn on other features of your tools to find out more device details. If you have enough information about such an asset already, it may even be best simply to avoid that asset during your heavy-duty discovery exercises.

Treating Your Inventory Work Like Other Transition Activities

With side effects from asset discovery traffic in mind, even if those effects are minor or unlikely, you may find it best to perform your automated inventory activities within maintenance windows. Depending on your network's mission and the invasiveness of your tools, your inventory activities may require the same preparation and cleanup as other transition activities. Plan accordingly, so users are not affected, especially by the network load that some inventory tools can cause. All the other rules regarding transition activities should apply in these cases, too, like keeping monitoring organizations in the loop, communicating intent and results to users, and so on.

Dealing with Whiners

The term "whiner" is a technical term in automated asset discovery. Coined by Bill Cheswick or Hal Burch, the term describes a person who sees your asset inventory traffic and complains to you (if you're lucky) or your managers (if you're less lucky) regarding your "attack" on his or her assets. These people are one of the main reasons you want your asset inventory activities approved and well-known by the powers that be beforehand, and approved in writing, if possible (see the Jack Ryan reference near the end of Chapter 6).

As a real-world example, I once performed an asset inventory at a client's site using my company's discovery tool. Because the tool's IP address was in every packet, a user on the network tracked down the device and phoned the room in which the device was located. I picked up the phone and was promptly told that what I was doing was illegal and that I would be reported to network security. The person whom I was reported to was fortunately the same person who hired me to do the inventory. Good thing we had a signed contract. Enough said.

Humor aside, many people who see your asset inventory traffic and fear an attack against the enterprise are acting with the best interests of the enterprise in mind. They should be commended for their observation, informed to whatever level you deem appropriate regarding what is taking place on the network, and comforted that all is well. If there's ever a real attack that your MIS/IT team or its tools misses, you'll be happy to have these people as an extra set of eyes looking out for trouble.

Integrating Your Distributed Results

You've read that distribution is among the best means to realizing a successful and efficient inventory. For example, letting your enterprise's individual departments take care of inventorying their own assets should lead to more accurate results, because the people in those departments use those assets every day and know them better than some distant CIO's office does. A downside of this approach is that people who want to hide some of their assets, for whatever reasons, can do so more easily. Because these are networked assets I'm talking about, you can offset this risk somewhat by augmenting your distributed inventory with a more centralized verification function (enabled by enterprise-discovery tools).

While it is best to distribute your inventory data collection work from an efficiency and completeness point of view, a comprehensive CMDB containing all of your enterprise's information is equally important. This means that the tools doing the inventory work must be able to export their results in a manner readily importable by either more-centralized discovery tools or ultimately by asset management tools. I'll cover the workings of such exporting and importing shortly. Here, I'm just defining the requirement.

Discovering IPv6 Assets from the IPv4 Side

Because this is a book about IPv6, you should look into discovery tools that can find IPv6 assets. Those assets that use IPv6 only, and not IPv4, can be hard to find. Moreover, there are few, if any, IPv6-capable discovery tools at this time (September 2007). You could decide to build your own tools, as is discussed more near the end of the chapter, possibly employing the EUI-64-based methods mentioned elsewhere in this book. I've already established that brute force search of IPv6 address space for devices is impossible at present and for the foreseeable future, due to the number of IPv6 addresses associated with even a single network prefix. Given that limitation, aside from the EUI-64-based methods, you're going to have to be pretty clever on the IPv6 side. Recall, however, that there's still the option of looking from the IPv4 side.

As has been mentioned several times in this book, IPv4 isn't going anywhere for some time, and any device running IPv6 will also likely be running IPv4, so that it can communicate with the parts of your network and the external Internet that haven't undergone IPv6 upgrade yet. Though finding the IPv4 side of an IPv6-capable device (that you don't know to be IPv6 capable at that moment) is as straightforward as automated asset discovery ever gets, determining if that device has IPv6 capabilities, however, is another matter.

If you're using IPv4-only discovery tools, the best you can hope for regarding discovering IPv6 capabilities from the IPv4 side is that the given asset is running SNMP and that you have a MIB browser or similar tool with which to look up some IPv6 OIDs to see if the associated features are in use. You can also use this method to find unintentional IPv6 adopters. See "Discovering IPv6 in Your Pre-Transition Network" in Chapter 4 for details. Short of such an SNMP-based solution, your only other alternative is to find IPv6-capable discovery tools.

Finding the Right Tools for Your Inventory Work

When choosing automated discovery tools, there are some features that you simply must have in order for automation to ease your inventory work, rather than just moving the difficulty from counting assets to some other aspect of the process. A key feature you should look for is that the data collected by a given tool you're evaluating is exportable from that tool. Some tools use proprietary database schemas or file formats that make the tool's way the only way to view, search, and manipulate the data. Few discovery tools scale to the enterprise level *and* have good asset management features, so you want to get the data out of the discovery tool with a minimum of fuss and into an asset management tool.

Your basic technology choices for automated asset discovery regarding the network layer are either traceroute and ping or SNMP-based tools. The latter set includes HP's OpenView and IBM's Tivoli, which are more asset management tools than discovery tools, so they are covered in the asset management sections later in this chapter. At other layers of the network stack, both local and enterprise discovery tools use TCP, UDP, ARP, and a host of proprietary protocols geared to specific operating system and device vendors. Make sure the discovery features of the tools you are assessing cover the types of assets you have.

When selecting local-discovery tools, make sure they can handle local networks of the size that you wish to inventory. The tools in the sections that follow purport to work with at least 1,000 devices, some with many more. Even though all local tools are limited in the sizes of the networks they can handle, unless you're running tiny segments in parts of your network, it's probably not economical to consider tools that top out at 256 devices, unless they have some special discovery feature that you really need.

Assessing Emerging IPv6 Discovery Tools

Ask the vendors of the tools described in the following sections, along with any additional vendors that you use (and check the open source community), regarding what they are doing about IPv6 asset discovery. Be clear that you're interested in asset discovery and not management. IPv6 assets are about as easy to manage in a CMDB as IPv4, and there isn't going to be anything like a billion-fold increase in the number of assets that require management when IPv6 rolls out. On the other hand, the increase in address space size that comes with IPv6 upgrade makes discovery much harder, especially of assets that you are unaware of on your network.

If you find a vendor or open source project for an IPv6 discovery tool, ask how they inventory the IPv6 address spaces. There are no perfect solutions, but the answer to this question will tell you how much they've thought about the problem and how cleverly they've solved it. For local-discovery tools, you can rely on IPv6's own features to perform much of asset discovery. You can use ND, plus the variety of link-local multicast addresses that apply to every host and router, as well as other groupings of devices. For enterprise-discovery tools, the jury is still out on the best way to check everywhere for unknown devices. Follow what the asset discovery vendors are doing, however, because this is a problem they will eventually have to face. The solution may be to use local-discovery tools more than enterprise tools in IPv6 environments, but that still leaves the issue of integrating all that data into a comprehensive CMDB.

What Discovery Tools Are Out There?

There are many local-discovery tools, some enterprise-discovery tools, and some other tools that can be counted into either class. This section lists a sampling of all these kinds of discovery tools, in alphabetical order, to give you a taste of what's available. If you find none of the tools listed here to your liking, a few moments with your favorite search engine will turn up many more. No matter what you find, it's safe to say they will fall into the categories loosely defined by the tools listed here.

Lumeta's IPsonar

IPsonar is an enterprise-discovery tool for collecting, analyzing, and reporting on your entire network. The tool strives to find as many devices as possible, both those known by you and the unknown devices. Although IPsonar provides a fair amount of information at an enterprise level, for a comprehensive asset inventory it is best to integrate its results with local-discovery tools. Those tools can then drill down on the network segments where information is required that IPsonar does not provide, for example detailed information about applications running on your devices. Fortunately, IPsonar knows its place in the asset inventory food chain and has convenient data export mechanisms to feed those other tools.

Other important features of IPsonar include a minimal need for input information (meaning you can start with nearly a blank slate regarding what you know about your network), lightweight discovery consisting of run-of-the-mill traffic with no special payloads or options that can cause devices to react badly, and the ability to scale to huge networks. Downsides include limited information per device, which means you'll need another tool, specifically a local-discovery tool in the vernacular of this book, to dig out details for IPv6 transition. IPsonar can be used, however, to scope the size of your pre-transition network for transition planning.

IPsonar has a sister product, MapViewer, which allows analysis of the data collected by IPsonar by having the user interact with a network map that can clearly represent hundreds of thousands of devices. MapViewer includes a powerful querying capability for asking questions like, "Where are all my Windows-based web servers that are running on unmanaged network segments?" Because MapViewer doesn't have natural-language processing, questions like the preceding are asked in the form of check boxes, radio buttons, and drop-down menus.

You can find information about IPsonar at `http://www.lumeta.com/ipsonar`. Also, much like a journalist reporting on his or her network or newspaper, I must admit for the sake of fairness that I was employed as Lumeta's Chief Architect for many years and developed the first few versions of MapViewer. Of course, my taking credit for the current product is like the Wright brothers taking credit for the Concorde. That credit belongs to the development and product management teams that turned prototype into product.

Nmap

Nmap is an open source local-discovery tool with some enterprise-discovery features. It's also the tool that many network managers think of when they hear the term network discovery. Nmap is not just a tool, but a framework for a bunch of tools. It's the proverbial kitchen sink of tools. It's safe to say that, if you can think of an asset discovery (or vulnerability assessment) feature, Nmap probably has it.

From personal experience, I can say that Nmap is powerful, and as such, has its risks. As they say, with great power comes great responsibility, and unfortunately not everyone who runs Nmap (or any other discovery tool) is fully qualified to do so. I was in several customer meetings while at Lumeta where we faced intense pushback on our tool because the customer didn't want us to do to their network what Nmap did. Of course, in the same line of thinking as "guns don't kill people, people kill people," Nmap didn't do anything on its own.

I've used Nmap and it's as safe or dangerous as any other tool, depending what options you set. If you use it correctly, Nmap can provide you with a lot of information at very little cost, excluding the cost of paying someone to run it and interpret the results. You can probably kill someone with a paperclip, but that doesn't make paperclips inherently dangerous. The key is training and the lesson is either to get your people trained, or contract out to people who are trained to inventory a network properly and safely.

You can find Nmap at `http://insecure.org/nmap/`, which also wins it the award for most succinct URL.

SolarWinds' LANsurveyor

LANsurveyor is a commercial local-discovery tool. I must admit that I haven't used the tool personally, but LANsurveyor probably has many of the asset inventory features of Nmap. You'll have to check that out personally, but Nmap defines the standard for local-discovery tools, and any commercial tool competing with that "free" one needs to measure up as being better in some way to offset the price difference. Moreover, after you've been in the asset discovery business for a while, you eventually implement everything that's possible, because the protocols haven't really changed in 20 years (until IPv6) and every network professional knows what data you can collect.

LANsurveyor has a nice user interface that graphically lays out your network's devices in a Visio-style format network engineers implicitly understand, unlike IPsonar's more abstract layout that's necessary to represent devices more densely on screen and that takes network engineers a little time to comprehend. LANsurveyor's layout allows straightforward analysis and reporting against the inventory data that the tool collects, which is very detailed by virtue of the inventory tool being near the devices being inventoried. The display looks like it is limited to a few hundred devices before it gets too cluttered.

You can find information about LANsurveyor at `http://www.solarwinds.com/products/LANsurveyor/index.aspx`. The LANsurveyor "enterprise bundle" includes 1,000 of what the vendor calls Responder Clients, which presumably are installed on your devices for better inventory results. Windows, Macs, and Linux are supported for the clients. Of course, those clients won't help you on the devices you aren't aware you have.

The price at the site for the enterprise bundle, (quoted on September 22, 2007) is about $17,000 for three licenses, which look like they can each handle three big LANs, say of 1,000 devices. Because most enterprise networks I've dealt with are minimally 25,000 devices and the average enterprise network has at least 100,000 devices, a full LANsurveyor deployment could run you well into the mid six figures. That's about the price point for enterprise-wide deployment of any of these discovery tools, except for Nmap, and none of those figures includes the cost of people to use the tools and interpret the results. The trade-off decision you have to make is whether you want to run and integrate the results of hundreds of copies of a tool at the LAN level (possibly more than 1,000 copies for million-device networks like some in the DoD and larger private-sector corporations), or one tool at the WAN level and a couple of dozen tools at the LAN level.

Xprobe

Xprobe is an open source local-discovery tool that can also be used at the enterprise level, due to its light traffic load. It's kind of a one-trick pony, but what's great about this tool is that it can be used for a quick inventory of several important device attributes on an enterprise scale.

By using cleverly crafted (but harmless) ICMP, UDP, and other packets, and noting the responses from each of your devices' IPv4 stacks, Xprobe can give you ballpark guesses at the types of operating system (or router software) your devices are running. Its results are grouped into broad categories like Windows 95–based (including Windows 98 and ME), Windows NT–based (including Windows 2000 and XP), Linux, FreeBSD, Solaris, Cisco, and so on. Some version information is available, but nothing like what a local-discovery tool with access to Active Directory, for example, can provide.

Xprobe is a little dated and IPv4 stack specific, due to its reliance on peculiarities of IP stack implementations from vendor to vendor. There doesn't appear to be any development of IPv6 capabilities, which would require the same painstaking analysis of numerous IPv6 stack implementations like the Xprobe developers performed on IPv4 stacks. This is not too serious a drawback, however, because you should know by now that the IPv4 stack isn't going anywhere soon.

You can learn more about Xprobe at `http://www.sans.org/resources/idfaq/xprobe.php`. Note again that, like Nmap, this is an open source tool, so you'll need somebody skilled enough to compile and run it. Downloads are available at `http://sourceforge.net/project/showfiles.php?group_id=30984`.

Other Tools

If you're interested in lots of little tools for specific jobs, maybe you'll find some favorites at `http://www.slac.stanford.edu/xorg/nmtf/nmtf-tools.html`. There are literally hundreds of tools there for all kinds of specific jobs, all in the realm of network monitoring, though some are security related, some are quality of service related, and some monitor services for availability. There are a few discovery tools in the bunch. In any case, it's a good place for a network administrator to look for tools.

Managing Your Discovered Assets

Recalling the photographic analogy mentioned earlier in the chapter to describe automated asset inventory, the asset management tools described in the sections that follow represent the albums that store the pictures. Though some asset discovery tools have limited storage, analysis, and viewing capabilities (like some modern cameras do), to get the most out of your inventory data, you need to organize that data. Moreover, you want to manage the data with an asset management tool. Large lists of assets with no particular ordering or organization are of little value, even if they are technically complete. You want to be able to search against such asset lists to find specific assets or sets of assets, and you want comprehensive and user-friendly management functions to add, delete, and change assets in ways external to your discovery processes.

You also want the tracking of inter-asset dependencies to be part of a tool's feature set, meaning that if a software asset is installed on a hardware asset and that hardware asset is decommissioned, then that instance of the software asset may need to be decommissioned, as well. These are all things that asset management tools do that pure asset discovery tools do not.

Distinguishing Asset Management Tool Types

For the rest of this chapter, I'll divide asset management tools into two distinct types. There is the type of asset management tool that counts assets, tracks inventory, implements search and analysis capabilities of the data it manages, and is generally passive in its relationship with the assets. Then there's the type of asset management tool that does all of the above *and* actively manages (or is used to manage) the inventoried assets.

On the plus side, active asset management tools, sometimes called "Operations Support Systems," especially if they're managing large quantities of assets, have a higher likelihood of being kept up to date with inventory data, because the tools are used in the daily management of your network and its assets. If you're using such tools, and you probably are, the data contained in them makes an excellent baseline from which to start your IPv6 transition work.

On the downside, using active asset management tools requires a bit more care than using passive ones, especially when it comes to the bulk importation of asset inventory data from discovery tools. This is because active management tools can take that imported inventory data and act on it, or the user working with the tool can do so, because most tools are not allowed to operate autonomously. An error in a read-only CMDB typically leads to nothing more than network operations (or IPv6 transition) planning errors. An active tool acting on erroneous data that decides not to manage something (or to start managing something that isn't yours) can lead to outages and other problems in your network.

Feeding Discovery Results to Management Tools

As implied in the previous section, ideally you would like to take the results of your automated asset inventory and feed them into an asset management tool. Depending on the type of tools you use, and your particular preferences, you may choose to clean up and organize that data prior to importation (or as part of the importation process). As an alternative, you may decide to import the raw inventory data and then use the asset management tool to clean up the data. The latter choice might be the better one if your asset management tools have custom functions for manipulating network and software asset information, especially in bulk, and don't just treat them like raw records in a database.

As for the other side of the equation, in order to import the asset data from your discovery tools, those tools have to be able to export the data in a usable format. Many discovery tools support export of Comma-Separated Values (CSV) files and some also support XML, which is typically more structured than CSV data. A third alternative is direct access of the discovery tool by the management tool using web services or some other API. When selecting asset discovery and management tools, make sure they have import and export functions and at least one import or export data format in common.

Extracting Asset Data from Support Systems

In addition to actively probing your network with asset discovery tools and importing their results into asset management tools, you might be able to import asset data from support systems, like IDSs and other tools that collect network traffic as part of their functionality. Such tools typically report on anomalous behavior, as defined by you to them, so anything that turns up could be doubly important. In other words, an IDS might detect traffic from a previously unknown device, perhaps one that was just installed in the network and not incorporated into the CMDB yet. If the IDS detects the asset, that asset may also be in some sort of violation of security policy, or have contracted a virus. Both of these conditions could arise from a faulty installation. In this scenario, you can simultaneously add the device to your CMDB and perhaps determine what problems it's having that set off the IDS. The preceding is a bit fanciful, but you get the idea. The point is to look for asset data in places other than your discovery tools' databases.

What Asset Management Tools Are Out There?

I must confess to being nowhere near as much of an expert on specific asset management tools as I am on discovery tools, but I do know what I need asset management tools to do, especially in an IPv6 context. As such, this section and those that follow, highlighting specific tools, should be viewed more as jumping off points for researching the tools yourself.

What I can assure you of for each of the tools highlighted is that I've looked them over at a level sufficient to be comfortable that I would call the vendors in for demos, and so on, if I were in the market for such tools. Their stories (at least as far as web pages and Internet chatter are concerned) seem solid, including their IPv6 stories. As with the asset discovery tools, the management tools are presented alphabetically in the sections that follow this one.

It's important to note that some of these asset management tools can populate and manage DHCP servers. With the security issues surrounding ND and the limitations of SEND (both discussed in the preceding chapter), DHCP looks like a good candidate for implementing auto-configuration in your IPv6 networks. Remember to ask how a given asset management tool works in an IPv6 environment and whether it can interface to a server running DHCPv6, which is the IPv6 version of DHCP.

BlueCat Networks' Proteus

Proteus is an IP Address Management (IPAM) tool that is IPv6 ready and supports import and export of asset data (like from discovery tools) via web-based services. Proteus is able to construct DHCP configurations, but it is unclear from the vendor's marketing material whether the tool can push those configurations to DHCP servers. My guess is that it can, but you should verify that, if this tool interests you.

You can find information about Proteus and BlueCat Networks at `http://www.bluecatnetworks.com/`. As of May 2007, Proteus is listed on the GSA schedule under contract number GS-35F-0415T. Note that this is a Canadian company, which may impact whether you can use the products in certain classified or sensitive environments in the U.S. government.

BT INS' IPControl

IPControl is another IPAM tool similar to BlueCat Networks' Proteus and with similar claims of IPv6 support and smooth DHCP integration. The tool received an excellent review from Network Testing Labs, an independent technology research and product evaluation organization.

You can find information about IPControl at `http://www.ins.com/software/products.aspx?id=685`. You can also find a link to the Network Testing Labs review at this site.

Internet Associates' IPal

Internet Associates builds an IPAM tool named IPal. IPal supports IPv4, IPv6, and Autonomous System Number (ASN) management. ASNs are the numbers associated with an enterprise's routing communities, in other words a short form of expressing everything that routes to or through an enterprise.

I have not used IPal personally, but I have seen it demonstrated, and I've heard good things from colleagues in the IPv6 community. This is one that you should at least test drive and decide yourself. You can find information about IPal at `http://www.internetassociatesllc.com/`.

The Big Boys

When it comes to asset management, HP's OpenView and IBM's Tivoli are the big kids on the block. They are active management tools (Operations Support Systems, really), and to keep your network running at its best you are incented to keep them up to date. The last time I assessed them, they had some basic network discovery capabilities, but not enough for what I would consider comprehensive coverage of the known and unknown parts of your network. That's why they're in the asset management category, though they are a lot more than just that. If you aren't already using one (or both) of these tools in your enterprise, you can find details at `http://www.openview.hp.com/` and `http://www.ibm.com/software/tivoli/`. If you are using them, contact your vendor representative and ask them what they can do for you for managing IPv6 addresses and devices, especially in the area of importing discovery results.

Growing Your Own Tools

Nobody knows your needs better than you do and, if your enterprise has the skills, capital, and time to develop its own asset discovery and management tools, perhaps you should consider doing so. Before starting down that path, however, weigh the development costs against the cost of buying tools that don't fit 100 percent, but that are "good enough." Also, before starting from scratch, look into extending the tools found at places like the SLAC site listed in the "Other Tools" section under the asset discovery tools catalog presented earlier. Many of those tools are open source and maybe you can modify one of them to get what you need without starting a major development effort.

As for asset management tools, at an enterprise scale these are far more difficult to create and get functioning correctly. In writing this chapter, I searched for open-source asset management tools and found none worthy of managing a large enterprise with mission-critical networks. That should be fair warning that even the people who like developing software for no compensation, except the satisfaction of a job well done and well received, are steering clear of asset management tools.

You may be thinking that making up for the present gap in IPv6-capable asset discovery and management tools is a good reason to roll your own tools. Be aware, however, that gap is closing faster than you think and software projects of the scale you would be looking at take a while to plan, execute, and verify, just like IPv6 transitions. You may be better off waiting for someone else to build or update their tools.

Testing Your Knowledge

The following questions cover the use of automated tools to ease your asset inventory work. Answers are in Appendix A.

1. What are the two general classes of automated asset discovery tools?

2. What should you consider before creating your own asset discovery or management tools?

3. In addition to making sure you have sufficient coverage of all of your logical networks when deploying automated inventory tools, what else do you need to consider when choosing where to deploy such tools?

4. Other than from automated asset inventory tools, where else can you look for information with which to populate your asset management tools?

CHAPTER 12

Selecting an Enterprise Transition Strategy

Of course, some people do go both ways.
— **The Scarecrow from** *The Wizard of Oz*

This chapter is about deploying a technology that requires components in at least two different places before much value can be gotten out of the technology in either place. As you might expect, neither place wants to deploy the technology until the other place is far enough along in its deployment so that the first place's costs can be quickly recouped. Of course I'm talking about the early days of railroading. There was track to be laid and engines, boxcars, cabooses, and so on to be built. In addition, stations and depots were required to get people and cargo on and off the trains. Without the tracks the stations and depots weren't much use. Similarly, though the trains technically could load and unload passengers elsewhere besides stations, the depots served as necessary processing areas for cattle, grain, minerals, and a host of other items. The railroads' components were built because each side was motivated and believed that it would profit from the other. Each side also knew that every component had to be built before anybody saw any value. This chapter is about IPv6 and not railroads, but very similar problems are described that require cooperation, motivation, and trust in order to get IPv6 deployed not only in your network backbone, but throughout your whole enterprise.

What You'll Learn

This chapter looks at the IPv6 transition strategy from another perspective. The chapter begins by categorizing IPv6 transition as a chicken-and-egg problem between those people who run your enterprise's backbone network and those who run the edge networks that use the backbone. The motivations required to break the stalemate preventing either group from moving first and starting their IPv6 transition are also described.

You've read about depth-first and breadth-first approaches to transition in Chapter 8, "Defining the Transition Execution Steps," and this chapter talks a little more about the depth-first approach. You also read about the network-centric view of your transition in Chapter 6, "Defining the Transition Preparation Steps," and this chapter expands on that theme to crystallize a backbone-first transition strategy. This is the strategy promoted by the OMB mandate and what most of this book covers.

To play devil's advocate and offer an equally viable alternative means of IPv6 transition, an edges-first strategy to complement the backbone-first one is introduced in this chapter. The edges-first strategy involves your edge networks deploying IPv6-capable systems before your backbone transition is completed (or perhaps before it even starts). The reasons for choosing this transition strategy are described in the chapter. In Chapter 13, "Using Pilot Programs to Facilitate Your IPv6 Transition," you will read about a specific activity closely related to the edges-first transition strategy, and that is the use of pilot projects to gain knowledge about IPv6 in your enterprise.

The chapter concludes with the observation that, whether or not you are held to the OMB mandate, you are probably using both strategies to one degree or another in your IPv6 transition.

Choosing Between the Chicken and the Egg

An IPv6 transition in any enterprise network, including yours, is a chicken-and-egg problem. The general view of IPv6 in the enterprise networking community is that it's likely to be pervasive eventually, but for now there's no strong incentive to deploy it. There is also some risk that IPv6 will fizzle out and that any transition work up until when it fizzles will have been wasted (see GOSIP as an example of such wasted work in Chapter 5). When you have a technology that straddles the fence squarely in the middle between strategically critical and currently unnecessary, like IPv6 does, a lot is said about deployment, but nobody is eager to take the first steps.

To undertake all the IPv6 transition work that this book has been describing so far, as with any other resource-intensive endeavor, your enterprise requires some form of motivation. Without motivation, your people only have the feeling that maybe they should be deploying IPv6, but they have no business case to take to their bosses to get the necessary equipment, staff, time, and other resources required to perform the transition work. Moreover, your enterprise's MIS/IT department and the other departments that it serves, lacking any motivating direction, would likely spend a lot of time arguing who among them should deploy IPv6 first, before anybody actually got around to constructing a budget or resource estimates, never mind actually deploying the technology.

For the U.S. federal government, the motivation for IPv6 transition obviously exists, in the form of the OMB June 2008 mandate. A motivating direction, specifically to deploy IPv6 on the network backbones first, is included in the mandate. This chapter ignores the direction given by the OMB mandate and presumes the mandate simply requires IPv6 transition. Omitting the fact that OMB told you to start in the network backbone, the chapter presents other reasons for starting there. It also gives reasons why it may be a good idea to start your IPv6 transition from the network's edges. This devil's advocate type argument is presented so that those unaffected by the OMB mandate, those not held to it as strictly, or those who have the resources to experiment with IPv6 in more than just their backbone network, can decide what makes the most sense for them.

Defining the Sides of the Deployment Stalemate

For the sake of clarity in the rest of this chapter, I'll re-use the simplified example from Chapter 4, "Choosing When to Make the Transition and How," of an enterprise organizational structure which has a central MIS/IT department that runs the network backbone and that backbone's presence on local sites (see Figure 4-1). This MIS/IT department is responsible for providing capabilities or services to the network segments of other departments, like Sales, Marketing, R&D, HR & Finance, and so on. The network segments of those other departments are collectively called "edge networks" in this chapter. Moreover, those edge networks are presumed to be run by staff in those other departments, not the MIS/IT department. That last assumption externalizes the arguments of where and how to deploy IPv6 and makes them interdepartmental, instead of having them be less-visible discussions within MIS/IT. That externalization makes the discussions easier to analyze here.

Understanding What's Behind MIS/IT's Lack of Urgency

A key attribute of the MIS/IT department is that it is typically stretched thin, both in staffing and in capital. That implicitly makes time a precious resource, as well. This makes MIS/IT hesitant to investigate, never mind deploy and maintain, any technology with little or no user demand (at least no demand from those users that matter), and IPv6 falls into that category for many enterprises right now.

Even if OMB has mandated that a given enterprise deploy IPv6 (and recall that I'm ignoring the backbone-first part of the mandate), that doesn't necessarily mean that MIS/IT should be the department to perform the transition, at least not the first phases of it. There's plenty that can be done without the backbone having to support IPv6, especially if MIS/IT assumes that the edge networks can deploy their own IPv6 over IPv4 tunneling. That will make the backbone traffic remain IPv4-only, which MIS/IT's people can argue makes the transition mandate irrelevant to them.

With that said, you shouldn't presume that the people on the MIS/IT staff are unaware of IPv6 and its likely future as the replacement for IPv4. Many of the MIS/IT people have surely heard of IPv6 and some may be quite expert in it. Ignorance is not what's preventing them from deploying IPv6. Being busy is, along with nobody telling them that they have to do it, which would make them busier.

If an enterprise is progressive and especially if its core business is related to the Internet or IP networking in general, its R&D department may be clamoring for IPv6 to be deployed in the enterprise backbone, partly because that technology will surely be required "soon" and partly because the technology is the next cool thing. That push from R&D (a customer of MIS/IT's) meets part of the motivational need to get a transition started, but MIS/IT still is not going to drop everything (or anything, for that matter) to deploy IPv6 simply based on being asked by R&D (or anyone else) to do it.

R&D also has to help construct a business case that MIS/IT can take to its managers to get the necessary funding. It has been my experience that, though R&D often has strong arguments for investigating a technology, they rarely have strong enough arguments for enterprise-wide deployment. In other words, deploying the technology for experimentation won't make the enterprise any more money and it won't save on any expenses. So, although R&D's heart is in the right place and MIS/IT would love to help, nothing is likely to happen.

An additional factor in all this is that most R&D groups that know enough about IPv6 to understand its eventual role in modern internetworking also have enough knowledge to deploy it themselves, at least in their own edge networks. Whether that's against enterprise policy is a different matter. If it isn't, then MIS/IT will be happy to let R&D conduct its experiments, provided those experiments can be isolated from any production network segments satisfactorily. This way everyone's happy and MIS/IT can focus on the work that meets the immediate mission goals or more popular strategic initiatives.

Seeing the Problem from the Edges' Point of View

As mentioned earlier, the edge networks support the departments in which they are deployed. Those departments are focused on their business-specific responsibilities within the enterprise, in other words Sales, Marketing, HR & Finance, and so on. They are not charged with rolling out new types of network infrastructure for the good of the company, out of their own budgets and for no apparent reason. They may decide to deploy new technologies internally, if there's motivation to do so, but IPv6 offers few departments that motivation, at present.

An example of what would motivate a department to deploy a technology on its own is if Marketing decided to get a custom feed from one of the news or financial content providers. Marketing may see the need for the information such feeds provide as enough of a driver that, if MIS/IT doesn't want to handle getting and maintaining the feed, Marketing is willing to build a case to get the right people and funding to do it themselves.

Aside from the OMB mandate (again, ignore its backbone-first directive), IPv6 offers few motivations for deployment to Marketing or anyone else, at this time. The departments that own the edge networks could further argue that the mandate clearly applies to MIS/IT, because starting the transition at the enterprise network's edges and then having MIS/IT build up interdepartmental and external connectivity afterwards is like the tail wagging the dog.

Were I managing one of these departments, my likely opinion would be that the technology is interesting or exciting, but I'll wait until MIS/IT brings it to my door (because that means the enterprise as a whole thinks the technology's time has come) and then I'll deploy it locally. That's no different from waiting to buy a DSL router until DSL service is actually available in your area.

Getting the IPv6 Transition Rolling

As you can see from the preceding sections, without some driving force to motivate either the potential providers of IPv6 capabilities to an enterprise network (MIS/IT) or the consumers of those services (the edge networks, generally speaking), neither group is incented to make the first move toward a transition. I'll assume that you're interested enough in getting IPv6 deployed that you would like to find some way to get the ball rolling, first by deciding which side of the technological stalemate to motivate. In order to decide whom to motivate, you need to know the arguments for backbone-first versus edges-first transition and see which strategy makes the most sense for your enterprise.

The remainder of this chapter describes the benefits and downsides of deploying IPv6 from the inside out or the outside in, which is another way to look at backbone-first versus edges-first transitions. I also discuss the typical motivations that might incent one side or the other to start deploying IPv6, at which point the other side will have fewer reasons to offer resistance and possibly start deploying, too.

Revisiting the Backbone-First Transition

The bulk of this book so far has focused on starting your IPv6 transition in your network backbone and upgrading edge networks to IPv6 later. During those later transitions, the presence of an IPv6-capable backbone provides both IPv6 connectivity to the edge networks in your enterprise and incentive to the owners of those edge networks to start their transitions. This is one way to attempt to solve the chicken-and-egg problem of where to deploy IPv6 first. The next few sections delve into the benefits of backbone-first IPv6 transition that may motivate your enterprise to consider that strategy.

Understanding the U.S. Government's Position

The IPv6 deployment chicken-and-egg dilemma was surely one of the motivators behind the OMB's mandate that all U.S. federal network backbones be upgraded to support IPv6 traffic. Dictating such policies and in such dramatically large scales is what governments do, and that's not necessarily a bad thing. Sometimes a government simply has to step up and commit the nation to something like IPv6, because the short-term benefits of the technology may be minimal or non-existent, or there may even be short-term detriments, despite the fact that a transition is the right thing in the long term. In other words, the government sometimes has to mandate things that make no immediate business sense as a hedge against future needs or to drive the country in a certain direction, even though the path is not one that those who are being driven would like to take.

By forcing a backbone-first transition, the government is making its agencies endure the short-term pain in order to be in a stronger position later. One side effect that I've been predicting for years is that by requiring the agencies to undertake IPv6 deployment, those deployments will eventually influence the agencies' contractors to deploy IPv6, as well. Earlier in this book, I mentioned that Lockheed Martin recently announced that it was upgrading one of its larger networks to IPv6. A few days later, on September 25, 2007, as I was writing this chapter, Verizon Business made a similar announcement that it was deploying IPv6 on its public IP network over the next 18 months (see `http://money.cnn.com/news/newsfeeds/articles/prnewswire/NYTU057250` `92007-1.htm`). Because there is no visible commercial driver for IPv6 deployment in the United States, and the much more rapid overseas deployment hasn't motivated anybody in the U.S. to adopt IPv6 any faster, it appears that OMB's plan is working.

Starting Your Transition with the Network Backbone

Depending on which business sector you're in and what influence you wield personally, upgrading your network backbone to IPv6 first may be the way to go. If you're the enterprise's CIO and you've got IPv6 "religion," then you may mandate a roll-out of the technology enterprise-wide, as OMB did for the U.S. government. For such a pervasive goal coming from so high up within the enterprise, the backbone is the right place to start an IPv6 transition, mostly because you've got the clout to make it happen.

Your justifications (correct ones, by the way), could include a strategic vision of how things will eventually be, a desire to get the transition going before you have to rush to play catch-up, or the relatively low cost of starting slowly now, before there's a rush. If you recall the mad rush to get every user and every piece of information online that was the Internet boom of the mid-'90s, you may not want to go through that whirlwind of activity again. Deploying IPv6 at a leisurely pace is a good alternative. Also note that starting early and proceeding slowly is the favored strategy recommended in Chapter 4, "Choosing When to Make the Transition and How."

Putting the Transition Work and Costs Where They Hurt the Least

OMB has decided that IPv6 is strategically necessary for the United States' future as a technology leader and is making the federal agencies deploy it within their network backbones. You'll note however, as has been mentioned elsewhere in this book, that there is no mandate pertaining to the agencies' edge networks. Such a mandate would interrupt the core businesses of government (such as providing services to its people, defending the country, collecting taxes, and so on) far more than the current mandate does.

Like OMB, you also don't want to put the burden of experimenting with something as new, uncertain, and scarcely available as IPv6 on every department of your organization until your MIS/IT department has figured out how to deploy IPv6 best and that knowledge has been made available as a common resource throughout your enterprise. In addition to wanting to spare the owners of the edge networks the pain of learning how to deploy IPv6, you want to minimize the duplicate costs that would come about from every department starting from square one, climbing the transition learning curve, and solving the same problems many times over (and in a related vein, solving those problems in all kinds of different and incompatible ways).

Although the MIS/IT department still has to justify its costs, it's not as driven to be profitable as some other departments are, in other words it's a known cost center. Moreover, the likelihood of duplication of effort (and cost) while learning the tricks and pitfalls of IPv6 deployment is reduced greatly if MIS/IT is the only department charged with the first phases of making your IPv6 transition a reality.

Building It So They Will Come

Another reason you may want to deploy IPv6 on your backbone first, even with no current user demand, is that you understand the technology's chicken-and-egg dilemma and feel it's your MIS/IT department's responsibility to have IPv6 available for everyone to use, even though nobody's asking for it right now. Like Edison building out the power grid or Bell providing telephone service to everyone, you would be offering something that's currently a boutique service for a few select early adopters, but with the expectation that the technology will become a commodity before you know it. That won't just benefit your users. It will also make your enterprise more competitive when IPv6 is more widely adopted, as is already happening in leaps and bounds in Eastern Asia and (somewhat less so) in Europe.

Appreciating the Motivator That Is Ubiquitous IPv6

It's impossible to underestimate how much the ubiquitous availability of IPv6, which comes with the upgrade of your network backbone, will accelerate adoption in your enterprise. One of the greatest motivators for the adoption of any new technology is the ease of that adoption. If a user has to jump through all kinds of hoops in order to get IPv6 running, especially because there isn't any real application for the technology, then the user will quickly become dissuaded, even if he or she is the most ardent IPv6 enthusiast or the first one of the early adopters in line.

Conversely, if that user has been even peripherally interested in playing with IPv6, and if adoption involves little more than plugging a cable into a wall socket (and possibly configuring a couple of simple parameters in a GUI), then he or she will likely give the technology a try. There might not be a lot of things to do with the technology, other than to watch the Kame turtle dance at `http://www.kame.net` or to look for others online who have also adopted IPv6. This, however, is a lot like how things were on the early public Internet, and by having the connectivity in place, that user will be ready to check out new things as they come along. That's a strong motivation for entrepreneurs to develop and offer services and applications for the user to try out, especially if the user is willing to spend money to do so. Remember, that's how Amazon, eBay, and Google, to name but a few staggering successes, started.

What's Next, After the Backbone Transition?

The preceding section is more applicable to the eventual consumer adoption of IPv6. Whether it be on-demand personalized pay-per-view movies offered by cable companies and others, new Peer-2-Peer (P2P) gaming applications easily built once IPv6 eliminates Network Address Translation (NAT), or something nobody's even thought of yet (or at least disclosed), IPv6 adoption in the consumer realm will be driven by people trying to make a buck with services and applications based on the unique abilities of IPv6 that go beyond those of IPv4.

Returning to the present-day reality that you care about, the vendors of business applications would likely consider it unnecessary (and possibly even economically irresponsible) to port their software to IPv6 when there's a perfectly good captive audience of business users already locked into the applications on IPv4. These users will continue to be locked in for the foreseeable future, so any self-respecting application development manager would almost certainly nix any IPv6 version at this juncture. Some might view this as short-sighted, because the amount of time it will take to port any reasonably complex application to IPv6 (and test that application thoroughly) could arguably result in the application's release coincident with demand growing in the government sector for just that type of application with IPv6 capabilities.

One company that seems to be in agreement with the latter line of thought is Microsoft, which is committed to supporting IPv6 in its operating systems, database products, and office automation suites (see `http://www.usipv6.com/6sense/2005/may/07.htm`), probably in part due to its business ties with China and other countries in Eastern Asia and Europe. Other than in the case of Microsoft, however, which is going out on an admittedly short limb by throwing its hat in the IPv6 ring this soon, it's hard to imagine a business applications vendor seeing any reason to offer an IPv6 version at this time. This is where R&D and the tinkerers come in and how technology progresses when there's no clear or immediate financial driver.

Using R&D to Drive Application Transition

R&D programmers, along with tinkering developers (of which I count myself as one) in production software organizations, are notorious for adding functionality to programs purely in the name of research, to investigate potential new uses (or markets) for the programs, or to meet a self-imposed challenge that they can do it. By taking some application that's running just fine on IPv4 and porting it to IPv6 for no other reason than "because it's there," these people incent end users to point their IPv6-capable browsers, for example, at those applications and start adoption on the client side without the users realizing they're doing so.

The next chapter expands on the roles of R&D and the so-called tinkerers by investigating the use of pilot projects to hone your IPv6 skills prior to and as part of your IPv6 transition.

Predicting the Next OMB Mandate

Based on the logical progression described earlier, I presume that once the federal network backbone transitions are far enough along, OMB will next mandate the upgrading of applications to IPv6. The R&D and other tinkerers are a strong force to contend with, but even they cannot port all the applications that are needed on IPv6 in any reasonable amount of time. Paralleling how the public Internet (and eventually business intranets) evolved, connectivity is necessary, but not sufficient, for IPv6 to catch on and stick around. Surely, the next people in OMB's sights will be the application developers.

Examining the Edges-First Transition Strategy

The backbone-first transition strategy covered in the preceding half of this chapter, as well as extensively in the rest of this book, is decidedly the way to go if your enterprise answers to OMB or you are the CIO and have concluded that IPv6 is something that you need to start deploying. What if, however, the OMB mandate doesn't apply to you (or you have a temporary waiver) and there aren't that many IPv6 believers in your enterprise, especially in MIS/IT? There still may be other departments that foresee the technology's inevitable future and that have the budget, staff, and authority to take action. These departments may want to get started with their transitions now.

Alternatively, some people in your enterprise may want to do research on IPv6 and its various features, or its performance or security properties. There may even be the rare case where some departments actually have a real need for IPv6 capabilities. As such, an IPv6 transition may start as a grass roots movement in your enterprise.

If IPv6 is something that your enterprise chooses not to back at a strategic level for the moment, or doesn't want to commit to rolling out onto the entire network backbone at once, then you can still deploy the technology locally to the edge networks. This will provide experience with the technology, including experience in deploying it that will prove valuable to your enterprise as IPv6 becomes more prevalent worldwide.

The rest of this chapter covers the reasons to choose deploying IPv6 in your edge networks first (or in combination with a backbone deployment) and tunneling to get connectivity both externally and possibly intra-enterprise, as well, until the backbone catches up. If you are locked into the OMB mandate or you're fully committed to deploying IPv6 in the network backbone first, then you may want to skip to the next chapter.

When Else Is the Edges-First Strategy a Better One?

Suppose that you do have sufficient interest and support at a strategic enough level within your enterprise to make a backbone-first IPv6 transition possible. You may still want to consider starting your transition in the edge networks. A backbone-first transition is an enormous and long-term undertaking. You may have departments that want or need IPv6 capabilities now and waiting for the backbone upgrade to be sufficiently complete to provide those departments what they need may be unacceptable. Even if there's nobody beating down your door for IPv6 capabilities, there are still reasons that may make starting at the edges more attractive. These reasons are discussed in the next few sections.

Forgoing Boiling the Oceans Until You Know How

Your network backbone has some awesome responsibilities. For one thing, it binds all your edge networks together and, in many cases, to the outside world. Even with all this book's talk of careful preparation, using maintenance windows, and having reversion plans for cases of unforeseen events during transition activities, there are still risks associated with deploying IPv6, especially at the backbone scale. Chapter 4 asserts that, in projects of the magnitude of an IPv6 transition, it's safe to remember the mantra "planning then doing beats planning when doing." The reality is that, no matter how much planning you do beforehand when deploying something as new and unproven as IPv6, you will be modifying those plans during the transition as unexpected complications manifest themselves.

All the churning of your enterprise backbone that comes from your IPv6 transition activities will almost certainly lead to at least one or two unforeseen outages, no matter how careful you are. If your organization is very sensitive to outages or the risk of them, then it may be better to start with local transitions on edge networks where people can learn about the technology and save deploying to the backbone for when you have more foresight to potential problems.

Embracing the Depth-First Transition Approach

Chapter 8, "Defining the Transition Execution Steps," described a depth-first transition approach that promotes performing a complete IPv6 transition on a portion of your network that is considerably smaller than the entire backbone, an edge network, for example, in the parlance of this chapter. The argument in favor of the depth-first approach is that the hard parts of an IPv6 transition come later in the technology's deployment and not in the earlier steps. Refer to Chapter 8 for details of the depth-first approach.

The edges-first transition strategy described in the current chapter goes hand-in-hand with the depth-first approach described in Chapter 8. Instead of executing one massive transition of your network backbone, you are performing many little transitions, each of which proceeds from start to finish far sooner. In the first few months after starting that set of transitions enterprise wide, you'll have exercised most of your transition processes, found many of the potential problems, and modified your plans for future transitions accordingly.

Even with the edges-first strategy and depth-first approach, some IPv6 transition steps might not be exercised until your network's backbone also undergoes some amount of transition. Specifically, the deployment of ISP-assigned IPv6 addresses to your edge networks might not occur until your backbone gets external IPv6 connectivity and your edge networks start using the backbone to interconnect as well as to reach the outside IPv6 world without tunneling. Until then, the backbone merely routes IPv4-tunneled IPv6 traffic between your IPv6-capable edge networks, as well as to and from IPv6-capable external relay devices (connecting your IPv6-capable networks to the IPv6 Internet, for example) via IPv4-only ISPs. That means it might be a while before you face the problems associated with ISP-assigned IPv6 addresses and multi-homing (discussed in depth in Chapter 7). In case you're wondering, the IPv6 addresses that you will use until you get ISP-assigned addresses are described shortly.

Another downside of the depth-first approach is that IPv6-capable applications may not be available when you're ready for them. Whatever vendors are rolling out IPv6 applications, they're likely doing so with OMB's timeline in mind. That means the vendors have until June 2008 before anyone will be complaining about the software not being available, and realistically, they probably have longer than that. This means that your IPv6-capable edge networks may have to continue using IPv4-only applications, thereby providing less confidence as to whether the edge network's upgrade was successful. The good news is that, when the IPv6-capable applications are available, you won't have to deploy IPv6 in the edge networks. You'll only have to upgrade or replace the applications on an edge network that is already IPv6 capable.

Enabling Adoption without Ubiquitous IPv6

With all due respect to the earlier section in this chapter, you don't need the ubiquitous availability of native IPv6 that a full-blown backbone upgrade provides to start spurring adoption of the new technology. Ubiquitous availability enables easy adoption, but for IPv6 there are other means to ease that adoption, as well.

AT&T deployed the World Wide Web within the company in the mid-'90s starting with only a handful of servers at one or two sites. The people running the web servers communicated their presence via e-mail, symposiums, and face-to-face word of mouth. The company had clearly decided that the Web was the wave of the future, but wasn't ready to start committing its MIS/IT resources to deploying web servers everywhere. Even without the commitment of the MIS/IT department, the adoption of the Web within AT&T reflected the technology's external adoption statistics, which were phenomenal.

You could argue that, because HTTP (the underlying protocol of the Web) is at the application-layer and that TCP/IP was already prevalent in AT&T (and the Internet), comparing HTTP's adoption to IPv6's is unrealistic. For native IPv6 deployments, I would agree. For IPv6 in general, for example using tunnels, I'll argue that you don't need backbone-first deployment in order to spur adoption. As is described in Chapter 7, and is re-emphasized in the following sections, setting up 6to4-based external IPv6 connectivity requires about the same level of effort and is about as difficult as deploying a web server.

Assigning Addresses Before Backbone Transition

Many of the different types of IPv6 addresses are described in Chapter 7, including a set of three types that do not require connectivity to an IPv6-capable ISP in order to be used by your enterprise for assignment to devices. The addresses available to your edges-first transition come solely from this set until your network backbone acquires external IPv6 connectivity and makes that connectivity available to the rest of your enterprise. The potential uses of these types of addresses during your transition are described in the next few sections. For more information about the address types themselves, along with any special quirks or limitations, see Chapter 7 or the cited RFCs and Internet Drafts.

Assigning Provider-Independent (PI) Addresses

Provider-Independent (PI) addresses are assigned directly by the Regional Internet Registries (RIRs) and not tied to any ISP. Though these addresses are meant to be globally routable by any IPv6-capable ISP, recall that in choosing the edges-first transition strategy you assumed that you won't have connectivity to any such ISPs until your network backbone undergoes some level of transition. Therefore, you can use PI addresses locally within an edge network and for communications with other IPv6-capable edge networks immediately adjacent to that first one.

When your IPv6 traffic eventually has to cross one or more IPv4-only network segments en route to another IPv6-capable segment, as it must do when crossing your network backbone before the backbone's IPv6 transition is sufficiently far along, one choice that you have is to tunnel that traffic. Another choice you have is to deploy your own IPv6 connectivity. Because such deployment undermines the value of your network backbone, I'll assume here that it's not a smart business solution for you. There may be cases where the need for immediate IPv6 connectivity makes it logical for an edge network to get its own, but that is dependent on the situation and something you must analyze within that context.

In tunneling PI addresses, you are responsible for deploying a tunnel endpoint locally and working with the remote entities with which you wish to communicate to get tunnel endpoints in place on their local networks, too. This is true both when a remote entity is another IPv6-capable edge network within your enterprise, as well as when that entity is some specific IPv6-capable network external to the enterprise. You cannot connect to random IPv6-capable devices on the Internet using these kinds of tunnels like you can with 6to4-address based tunnels, which are discussed in the next section.

Using 6to4 Addresses to Provide External Connectivity

6to4 addresses are part of a transition-enabling encapsulation scheme defined in RFC 3056. The network prefixes for 6to4 addresses are based on public IPv4 addresses already assigned to your enterprise. Traffic using 6to4 addresses can be encapsulated in IPv4 packets and tunneled outside of your enterprise using various relay routers. Such routers are deployed by your edge networks or the external networks with which you wish to communicate. Moreover, there are publicly available relay routers for access to the Internet's IPv6 side and other IPv6-capable enterprises with which you do not have a tunneling relationship, at present.

As suggested in the preceding section, until IPv6 is more widely adopted, I would consider 6to4 addresses for a given situation instead of PI addresses, given that 6to4 tunnels are far easier to deploy and you don't need a tunneling relationship ahead of time with every entity with which you might wish to communicate.

Using Unique Local Addresses (ULAs) within Your Enterprise

There are two forms of this type of IPv6 address. One form is defined by RFC 4193 where the addresses come from network prefixes randomly generated by you in a specific range. The other form is fairly new and is also based on random network prefixes, but the prefixes are centrally assigned to completely eliminate the already trivial chance of a collision that's possible with the first form of ULAs. See `http://www.ietf.org/internet-drafts/draft-ietf-ipv6-ula-central-02.txt`, which expires on December 21, 2007, for details.

Unlike the other two types of addresses described in the preceding sections, ULAs are not meant to be routable to anywhere outside of your enterprise.

These addresses are solely for use within the logical confines of your enterprise's global network and any business partners with whom you wish to internetwork via tunnels or dedicated lines. ULAs are a lot like PI addresses. The one key distinction is that, if you had external connectivity via an IPv6-capable ISP, the PI addresses could be routed, whereas the ULAs cannot at this time.

There are hints that a fee-based structure might eventually evolve where ISPs would route the centrally assigned ULAs for paying customers, thereby making ULAs essentially the same as PI addresses and also completely wiping out the reason why ULAs were first conceived, which was to reduce global routing tables sizes. Whether this bizarre market ever comes to be is unknown, but you can be pretty sure it won't spring up while you're executing your IPv6 transition.

My advice is to use ULAs for the devices and network segments in your enterprise that will *never* need external connectivity. I emphasize *never*, because you must recall that, unlike RFC 1918 addresses in IPv4, ULAs can't get external access via NAT (until someone decides that they can, which I give less than 5 years to occur). Use 6to4 addresses for external connectivity until your backbone transition is far enough along, and then use PI addresses. Finally, use ISP-assigned addresses only after their multi-homing issues become more resolved.

Renumbering Devices When the Backbone Is Ready

Eventually your network backbone will complete its IPv6 upgrade, or enough of that upgrade to be usable by at least some edge networks. When you're ready to "go native" (as the popular saying has become) with IPv6 from your backbone, you'll need to replace any 6to4 addresses with PI addresses or ISP-assigned ones. The ULAs can stay as they are, because they were always meant only to be routed locally within the enterprise. You can, however, eliminate the tunnels used to route ULAs from one part of your enterprise to another, because the backbone can now handle the addresses natively. That doesn't involve renumbering the devices using the ULAs, however.

Eliminating the Problems of Disparate Network Prefix Sizes

An invaluable property of almost every IPv6 address, which IPv4 addresses don't share, is the uniform layout. For the time being, IPv6 splits almost all unicast addresses cleanly down the middle into separate 64-bit network prefixes and interface IDs (see RFC 4291). I say "for the time being," because the same RFC also says that those interface IDs are required to be constructed in the EUI-64 format discussed elsewhere in this book. You know that's not the actual practice, given all the other addressing schemes I've discussed that are in use or proposed.

You can safely assume that the 50/50 split between an IPv6 address's network prefix and interface ID will not change soon or without a fight, because it has become pretty ensconced in the auto-configuration standards. Knowing that, the renumbering of your edge networks as native IPv6 addresses and connectivity for them become available isn't a big deal from the point of view of the actual address values. Without the Class A, B, C, and so on, or CIDR formats of IPv4, you never have to worry about fitting ten pounds of interfaces into a two-pound LAN. In other words, renumbering a CIDR from a Class B to a Class C, for example, and having to figure out where to put all the devices you originally numbered above '.254' becomes a thing of the past.

Moreover, because there are 48 significant bits in the private ULA and semi-private 6to4 network prefixes, which is the same size as what your ISPs would minimally provide, you can be assured that you won't fall into the trap that many IPv4 networks fell into when they took their '/16' private networks and went to get public addresses for them, only to be assigned a '/24,' for example. That's one of the things that led to the popularity of NAT, because it was easier to deploy NAT to mate the two disparately sized address ranges than it was to renumber the large private address block to fit into the much smaller public one.

Deploying the New Network Prefixes

Starting with the simple deployments first, any PI addresses that you were using prior to the completion of the backbone transition can stay exactly as they were once the backbone's transition is complete. You presumably have the necessary external connectivity to route these addresses over your backbone to places outside of your enterprise, and that's all you need to do, other than eliminate the tunnels through the formerly IPv4-only backbone that the PI addresses were using.

Similarly, the ULAs don't change when your backbone's transition is complete, as noted in a previous section. You simply need to tear down their tunnels and route them natively on the backbone, like the PI addresses.

That leaves the 6to4 addresses and the devices using them. To completely go native, you need to renumber these devices. There are several renumbering methods available to you. The choice of which methods to use is a strategic decision, because this will not be your last renumbering, especially if you're using ISP-assigned addresses. Manual renumbering is always a choice and, because the technique and its pros and cons are fairly straightforward, I won't say more about it.

Of your more-automated choices, the one that the RFCs might have you use is the Router Renumbering (RR) protocol of RFC 2894. You may not be ready or willing to use that protocol, however. See Chapter 10, "Factoring IPv6-Specific Risks and Limitations into Your Plans," for the reasons why. Instead of RR (and the associated auto-configuration protocols), you could use DHCPv6. You wouldn't be alone in this decision, because Cisco and Microsoft seem to be leaning toward DHCPv6 in their official recommendations, probably because of all the security issues surrounding auto-configuration (see `http://www.arnnet.com.au/index.php/id;2121632322;fp;4194304;fpid;1;pf;1`).

The better DHCPv6 servers should let you renumber network prefixes without having to edit every individual IP address record in the server configuration files. Even if they don't, or you aren't using the best servers, perhaps your DHCPv6 servers allow you to import their configurations into your favorite text editor, facilitating global substitutions. Be careful, however, because global cuts and pastes can make changes that aren't intuitive and you need to review the changes before committing them to your live DHCPv6 servers. IP Address Management (IPAM) tools, like the ones discussed in Chapter 11, should also be able to allow you to edit your configurations readily and push DHCPv6 configuration files to your servers. These tools had marginal value in IPv4, but with IPv6 they are a necessity.

For other tips on network renumbering, see RFC 4192, which also covers renumbering from the point of view of DNS and BGP.

Combining the Two Transition Strategies

It's unlikely any enterprise will focus solely on the transition of its network backbone and perform no transition work on the edge networks. The opposite case is equally unlikely. Your transition will be at different stages of completion at each site and network segment from the first day you start. Within a few weeks or months, there will be parts of the backbone that have deployed IPv6 fully and other parts that haven't even started yet. Surely before the backbone upgrade is complete, the porting of applications to IPv6 will have started. Some applications may be fully IPv6-capable before the backbone upgrade completes, whereas other applications won't be fully functional until after the backbone work is done. In other words, your transition strategy will be a combination of the backbone-first and edges-first strategies described earlier in this chapter.

Testing Your Knowledge

The following questions are meant for you to remember the key points of each of the IPv6 transition strategies discussed in this chapter. The answers are in Appendix A.

1. Why does this chapter categorize your IPv6 transition as a chicken-and-egg problem?

2. What are the two types of IPv6 transition strategies and how are they different?

3. Which IPv6 transition strategy would you likely use in an organization that's clearly committed to IPv6 and has the staff and funding to deploy IPv6 at an enterprise scale right now?

4. Which IPv6 transition strategy is a better choice if you want to reap the rewards of the depth-first transition approach described in Chapter 8?

5. Why can IPv6 be adopted fairly easily by newcomers to the technology even before it is made ubiquitous within an enterprise by the transition of the network backbone?

CHAPTER 13

Using Pilot Programs to Facilitate Your IPv6 Transition

Research is what I'm doing when
I don't know what I'm doing.
— Wernher von Braun

I'm a big fan of learning by doing. You can read all of the books on a topic, but until you actually attempt to do what you've read about, you really can't grasp the details enough to consider yourself knowledgeable. When it comes to technologically leading-edge topics like an IPv6 transition, organizations need to learn new things, sometimes things that nobody has tried before. I believe that the best way possible to learn those new things is by going out and trying to do them.

What You'll Learn

This chapter describes pilot projects, a form of research used to vet capabilities for your enterprise before committing to full-scale deployment of those capabilities. You'll learn to identify what is required to set up and execute a successful pilot, including setting up the pilot's goals appropriately to its scale and the number of resources that can be allocated to it. You'll learn what you need to measure (and sometimes not measure) in a pilot project and you'll learn to prepare for the pilot's failure. Given that it is a research project, a pilot can fail, and you need to be prepared to handle that case.

After learning about pilots in general, the chapter drills down on software pilots and their particular idiosyncrasies, concluding by relating the story of a real-life software pilot that applied the principles this chapter recommends.

Creating a Successful IPv6 Pilot

This section describes what is required to identify, plan, execute, and (most importantly) learn from, a successful IPv6 pilot. For the purposes of this chapter, a pilot is considered any relatively small short-term project devised to determine the applicability or viability of new assets, capabilities, or configurations to your enterprise. The new assets, capabilities, or configurations may be new to just your enterprise, or to the technical community at large, like IPv6.

Identifying a Project or Need

The first step toward having a successful IPv6 pilot is to identify a project or a need that must be fulfilled. By focusing on a real-life problem your enterprise is facing, versus just some research experiment or personal curiosity, you are motivated to complete the project not just for your own personal satisfaction, but also to solve the enterprise's problems, which can benefit you, as well.

Defining Your Pilot's Goals Before Starting

All projects, whether they are pilots or your full-blown IPv6 transition, should have clearly defined goals with which to determine whether the given project was successful when all is said and done. It is important to define your pilot's goals before you begin. Without predefined goals, it's hard to know when you are finished and as hard to know which way to go, should you have to change direction during the pilot's execution. Sometimes a project requires end goals and intermediate goals as well, for example if the project is of a long duration.

For pilots that have significant or multiple goals, or that have a greater than average amount of risk associated with them, a staged approach with intermediate goals and associated decision points may be applicable. Instead of working to all the goals at once, working to intermediate goals that let you decide whether to continue the pilot can save time and money, especially in the case where it becomes clear that the ultimate goals are unachievable or impractical.

You don't want your IPv6 pilot to be overly trivial, because that will cause it not to be taken seriously either by your management or the people who could benefit from its outcomes. Specifically, if the pilot's eventual results conflict with what people think the results should have been, arguments that the pilot was not realistic enough, for example, could be raised, nullifying or minimalizing your results and possibly causing all that pilot work to have been wasted.

You also want the pilot to be tractable, meaning that it should run in a reasonably short time measured in weeks or a few months, but no longer. Otherwise, people, including yourself, may get bored waiting for results or the pilot may evolve into something distinctly different from what was originally designed.

One of the goals for your pilot must be to specify the intended results. The intended result of some pilots is new prototypical hardware or software, which can be refined and developed into production systems. Pilots are also used to vet configurations and procedures in the process of turning them into best practices.

A later section in this chapter covers preparing for the potential failure of your pilot. It is worth reminding you here, however, as you are setting your pilot's goals, that failure is a possibility and that possibility should be part of your goal setting exercise.

Differentiating Ad Hoc Versus Official Pilots

Pilots can be distinguished by whether they are officially planned, launched, and run by the enterprise or performed in the spare time of some set of staff, again most probably to solve some problem related to the enterprise. Though it's likely that only those on the enterprise's payroll are performing the pilot work, whether they are doing so as an official project for the enterprise or as a set of experiments in their spare time makes a difference.

For example, the identified need, the goals, and the timetable of an ad hoc pilot are completely at the discretion of those who are using their spare time to run it. In the case of a software pilot, on which this chapter focuses, given the minimal number of resource required to execute the pilot, those running it may not even inform anyone else of its existence until after it is complete and the results can be communicated.

Scoping the Pilot

Closely tied to your pilot's goals is its scope, or in slightly simplified terms, the resources that it requires. Your pilot must be scoped as far as the hardware and software required, and the time required for the pilot to execute from start to finish. Scoping also relates to the number of staff required and other resources.

Identifying Assets for the Pilot

Your pilot may find sufficient the existing assets (hardware, software tools, network connectivity, and so on) already available to you or it may require the procurement of new assets. Whatever assets you require, you need to identify them before the pilot starts or early on in its execution, so that the assets can be set aside for you or procured. If the pilot is an official one, then it definitely should be treated like any other project. You are investing real money and the time of real people to get the results that you desire from your pilot. Having the pilot team beg, borrow (and hopefully not steal) assets to get the job done is demoralizing and counter to the pilot's purpose.

When allocating assets to a pilot, make sure the assets in question are not necessary to your network's production services and the loss of those assets or their malfunction would not affect business. Pilots are a form of research and, as such, prone to failure more than daily production activities. Assets used for pilots should be used solely by them whenever possible. This should be obvious, but you should never run a pilot program on the same systems that your production services are using, for example. Even using the same network infrastructure can come with some serious risks, should the pilot suddenly flood the network in an accidental denial of service attack.

Mitigating Scope Creep

Other than assessing the costs in both time and materials of a pilot, scoping is meant to minimize a phenomenon called scope creep. Scope creep is common to development projects, administrative projects, and pretty much any other project of which I can think. You are not only giving more work to yourself by allowing scope creep, but you are also setting yourself up not to meet the expectations of those to whom you made promises regarding the success of your pilot.

Scope creep on the pilot resources side hurts those funding and supporting the pilot, in other words, your enterprise. If the pilot team, for example, initially asked for two computers, some software development tools, and three months to run a pilot and then doubled all those requests as the pilot lumbered on with no tangible results, the enterprise was being asked to devote resources that may turn out to go to waste. Such requests for scope creep should be honored only after the pilot team can justify the reasons for the additional resources, and comfort those providing the resources that the goals of the pilot can now be met in a satisfactory manner with those resources.

The more common use of the term scope creep hurts the pilot team, and that is the creep of the goals. The team may have promised a pilot application that can perform 1000 transactions per second of some type that is irrelevant here, as an example. For this, they received what they believed were the necessary resources to build a pilot version of just such an application. If later the providers of those resources decide that the application should be built to handle 5000 transactions per second, and that creep is not nipped in the bud, then the pilot team may have to perform some miracles. Either that or the funders will be sorely disappointed.

A worse type of scope creep is subtler and that is when the pilot application is asked midway through the project to be no longer concerned of just "pilot quality," but of a quality suitable for deployment in the enterprise's production infrastructure. Cobbling together an application to prove that a given capability can be achieved is wholly different from the productization of that same application to withstand the rigors of a production environment. Should this type of creep go unchallenged, the pilot team likely won't have the resources to get the job done, and again those paying for the pilot will be disappointed.

Monitoring the Pilot

Once you have set goals for your pilot, then it only makes sense to monitor the pilot while it is executing to see that your goals are being achieved. Chapter 5, "Creating Your Transition Plans," discusses project tracking extensively. Refer to it regarding why you should track your projects appropriately if you want them to succeed. There are a few nuances to monitoring pilots that are not part of monitoring more conventional projects. Those details are covered in the following sections.

Measuring the Right Things

Just as you must measure against your plan, you must plan to measure the right things. Your overall IPv6 transition is more of a conventional project than a typical pilot. In conventional projects you measure the amount of time consumed, funds and capital consumed, and the utilization of your staff and other resources against the plans you set before the project's start. You also measure the outputs (or deliverables) of your project to make sure they pass muster against whatever quality assurance criteria you have set up for the project. A pilot shares many of these measurable parameters, but because it is more of a research effort, defining the criteria for success or being on track can be more difficult.

Depending on the goals of your pilot, perfect versions of whatever the deliverables are, for example compelling and attractively formatted web pages, may not be important. It may be delivery rate of those web pages that you are measuring to see if the hardware running your new IPv6-capable software is able to keep up with the application. On the other hand, you may be assessing solely the functionality of the application, and performance may not be a factor during the pilot. The latter is the typical case for pilots, and performance is dealt with later after determining whether some new functionality is even possible.

Changing the Pilot Mid-Stream

The next section covers preparing for the possible failure of your pilot efforts. Before you admit defeat, however, it may be possible to change your pilot's goals or scope midstream and still come out with a limited success. A pilot is not as rigidly defined as a conventional project, like deploying IPv6-capable routers on a LAN. If your goal for the router-deployment project is to get 100 percent of the routers upgraded, then you are not finished until that goal is met. The goal may be delayed by failures or unforeseen events, but you will eventually have to get all your routers using the new protocol.

With pilots, partial success or modified success is often acceptable. If you decide that, using the transaction-system example cited earlier, you can't achieve the desired performance of 1,000 transactions per second, you have several choices for how to proceed, aside from declaring the project a failure. You can recommend the use of a faster hardware platform or the deployment of a larger quantity of the originally scoped system to meet the performance shortfall.

The lesson to take away from this section is that your pilot's goals are not as black and white as those of a conventional project. Look at the big picture of what your pilot is trying to accomplish and see if there is a meaningful compromise that still gets you most of what you want.

Assessing the Impact of Potential Failure

As with your overall IPv6 transition planning, you must assume that something in your pilot might fail. You need to assess, based on the pilot's goals, what to do if the pilot falls short of those goals by a significant amount. In some cases, the pilot may be a simple experiment to see if some esoteric capability can be implemented. In other cases it may be the verification of a critically needed capability before wide-scale deployment. Clearly, how you react to failure in each case differs.

Making Everyone Accept That the Pilot Could Fail

I feel like Dr. Phil here, but it is true that the first step in accepting failure is accepting the possibility that it could occur. A pilot is a research project. It may not be as risky as searching for life in distant parts of the universe or drilling for oil under the Arctic Ocean, but it is not a sure thing by any means. When you set the expectations of those to whom you report, remind them that this is research work and that the net result may be zero.

From a financial point of view, the net result may be less than zero because you will have spent time and money to run the pilot and may not come out with anything, except the knowledge that what you were trying to achieve is impossible. In that case, you may appease yourself by remembering the old saying that engineering is turning knowledge into money and science is turning money into knowledge. Even knowledge that something can't be done can be very useful.

Planning for the Failure Case

When you define the goals of your pilot, the overall goal can often be summarized as seeing whether you can deploy new capabilities to improve your network's services to its users, reduce costs, improve reliability, and so on. An example of a pilot that is more aggressive than one that you are likely to undertake for a while may be to determine whether you can deliver video to workstations via IPv6 multicasting for teleconferencing. The technology to make this possible certainly exists in IPv6, and there may be applications to help you. The question you're asking yourself in the pilot is whether you can use that technology and those applications in your environment successfully. The unspoken question, that should be spoken, is what to do if you need this video teleconferencing capability and IPv6 multicasting cannot provide it.

There likely are multiple satisfactory alternative solutions for your video-teleconferencing problems, including IPv6 unicasting, IPv4 multicasting or unicasting, or outsourcing to a vendor who has figured out the solution. What you decide is almost unimportant. In the context of this section, what is important is that you must decide before the pilot starts (or at least by the time you need the capabilities), because the pilot may fail.

Drilling Down on Software Pilots

Because I have a real-world example to share at the end of the chapter regarding an IPv6 software pilot, this section will pave the way to discussing the results of that pilot by describing more details about what porting software to IPv6 involves.

I'm a big fan of software pilots, because they can be among the easiest to provision and execute. Software pilots, especially ad hoc ones, have a very low barrier to entry. In other words, with a minimal number of assets (one PC or laptop in many cases) and access to the software that you are basing the pilot on, you can get some impressive results.

The key to a good software pilot is starting with good software. That's not just meant to be a glib expression. If you start with software that is well organized, modularized, and designed from the start to be extensible, a pilot based on that software to add new capabilities can be almost trivial. In some cases, like the one documented at the end of this chapter, parts of the port could be described more as rote changes to code (almost equivalent to substituting the term IPv6 for IPv4), than as "research" or prototype development. Don't get me wrong, in the example given later, there were some hard problems to solve, but they fell more in the realm of implementing esoteric corner-case features, rather than the basic core functionality of the application. Because having problems with the latter has been my more typical experience with the extension of complex software applications, the pilot in the example came as a refreshing change.

For the example described at the end of the chapter, a complex networking application was modified first to have basic IPv6 functionality and then more complex functionality with only a modest effort in both cases. This was partly because the pilot team was good at their jobs, but it was also due in no small part to the fact that the original application team had done such a fine job of isolating the low-level networking functionality from the rest of the software. I was not part of the original team, except for some very minor changes and additions.

Describing IP Addresses in Software Applications

Chapter 4, "Choosing When to Make the Transition and How," mentions a helper data structure used by software applications to pass information in from the top of the network stack to layers further down. This helper data structure is a part of the sockets interface used by application programs to communicate over TCP/IP and other network types. The IPv6 extensions for the sockets interface are described in RFC 3493 (for the basic extensions) and RFC 3542 (for the advanced extensions). The extensions to the API's socket address types are described briefly, along with the basic definitions for IPv4 sockets that have been used for years, as follows:

> `sockaddr`. The generic data structure for storing and manipulating addresses from any of the address families supported by the sockets API, including those not related to TCP/IP. The data structures defining specific socket address types described next can be thought of as extensions of this generic data structure containing additional information associated with the given address type. In object-oriented software development terminology, for example, this relationship can be described as meaning that `sockaddr` is the base class and that all the other socket address types are derived classes.

> `sockaddr_in`. The data structure for storing and manipulating Internet, in other words IPv4, addresses. This address type represents the 32-bit IPv4 addresses. It and the associated data structure have been around for a long time.

sockaddr_in6. A new data structure used solely for representing IPv6 addresses. This is the appropriate data structure for use if you know you'll be manipulating IPv6 addresses only, as you would be in an application that is IPv6 specific.

sockaddr_storage. A new data structure that can be used for storing IPv4 or IPv6 addresses, as well as any other supported socket address types. This is the data structure recommended for use by RFC 4038 for portable applications that handle both types of IP addresses. Defined in RFC 3493, the data structure's loosely defined internal format puts the onus on the software developer to make sure he or she knows which type of addresses are being manipulated with the data structure at any given time.

Although sockaddr_storage might look like your best choice for application portability, using it without also using the more rigidly defined IPv4- and IPv6-specific data structures puts more responsibility on the software developer for correctness in the data structure's use. The automated code-checking available via software build tools when more rigidly defined data structures, like sockaddr_in and sockaddr_in6, are used makes you want to consider the use of these version-specific data structures, in addition to sockaddr_storage to assure code correctness.

In my opinion, sockaddr_storage is a good data structure for carrying addresses at the higher layers of an application, especially when transporting those addresses from user interfaces to the sockets API calls for network connectivity. Prior to making those API calls, however, you might want to consider copying this information from the general-purpose sockaddr_storage into a specific data structure for the address type in question. Of course, you must factor in performance in such copy operations, because they are not free from a CPU utilization point of view.

What Else Must Change in the Application?

In addition to handling IPv6 addresses, the association of those addresses to DNS names and the use of DNS names must be updated in the applications software. This includes both forward and backward DNS lookups and specifically refers to the use of the new "AAAA" DNS record type and other DNS changes. See RFC 3596 and its references for more information about how IPv6 affected DNS.

For more complex applications, the socket APIs described in RFC 3493 and RFC 3542 have some subtle differences from their IPv4 predecessors. Besides the address structure changes described in the previous section, the raw sockets interface has changed to be less raw. An application can no longer create raw IP headers for IPv6 like the IPv4 raw sockets API allows. This means the use of additional system calls for simple networking tools like `traceroute`, which manipulate IP headers to implement their features.

A particularly important loss for some is that the construction of fragmented packets is no longer possible via raw sockets and is now solely the purview of the network layer of the stack. The stack makes its fragmentation decisions based on the MTU information available on the device's direct links and the paths to the packets' ultimate destinations. Though this makes implementation of the fragmentation attacks of Chapter 10, "Factoring IPv6-Specific Risks and Limitations into Your Plans," more difficult, it comes nowhere near eliminating them. This is especially true when using open-source operating systems where the system source code is available and customizable. What this modification to the sockets API has done is made legitimate experimentation with features like fragmentation more difficult, all in the name of minimal security fixes.

Finding Information on Porting Applications to IPv6

As mentioned in the preceding sections, RFC 3493 and RFC 3542 should help you with the transition of your applications to use the IPv6 extensions of the sockets API. In addition, RFC 4038 covers application porting aspects at a strategic level. As noted in Chapter 4, RFC 4038 is a little naïve regarding the modularity of software, but it offers a lot of good advice nonetheless.

Looking at a Real-Life Pilot and Its Results

Now that you understand what is required for a successful pilot, let's take a look at a real-life example. The results described in this section are from a pilot project to port a fairly complex networking application to IPv6. The porting path chosen was the one where an IPv6-capable version was created at the cost of eliminating the IPv4 capabilities of that version. In other words, all the IPv4 low-level functionality was replaced by IPv6 functionality. This is different from the case where IPv6 functionality is added, but the IPv4 functionality remains.

Assessing the Pilot's Applicability to the Organization

This particular pilot was undertaken to experiment with technology affecting the long-term needs of the organization, in other words, the ability to use the application on IPv6-capable networks. The pilot's failure would have had no short-term consequences on the organization.

The long-term effects of the pilot's failure, measured in terms of two to five years from when the pilot was started, had a potential to damage the organization. The level of damage was never assessed, because it was fairly certain that the project would not fail. There were some technological hurdles related to an application of this type on an IPv6 network, but these hurdles were no different for our organization from any other. Therefore, we were on a level playing field with competitors and could at least match whatever they had to offer.

Setting the Pilot's Goals

The real-life pilot documented here was an ad hoc project. Therefore, the time of the people working on the project was limited by their other official duties in the organization. In order to show value, because the pilot was being run as a "skunk works" operation, the results had to be demonstrable and the amount of work to achieve those results had to be minimal.

The pilot was composed of three distinct phases, patterned after the original U.S. program for a manned mission to the Moon. The phases were appropriately named Mercury, Gemini, and Apollo and their missions were the same as those of their namesakes. Mercury was to prove that some basic capability could be achieved. In the case of the space program, that meant putting an astronaut into space, and little more. For our IPv6 pilot, the goal was to show that basic application functionality that worked with IPv4 could be made to work with IPv6. There was nothing fancy about Mercury, because its main goal was to show whether Gemini and Apollo should be attempted at all.

Gemini's goals, in the case of the U.S. space program, were to develop and hone the skills necessary for reaching the Moon. Our goals for Gemini were to implement at least one instance of every type of functionality that the IPv4 version of the application had. Apollo's goals, both for NASA and for our pilot, were to assemble all the components developed in Gemini into a system that could achieve the ultimate mission.

Ironically, another IPv6 project drew some of its terminology from the U.S. space program. Moonv6, a project led by the North American v6 Task Force (NAv6TF) and still ongoing at this time, was named so due to the participants determining that the need for deployment of IPv6 throughout the United States should be deemed as significant as the need to reach the Moon was in the space race. I was unaware of Moonv6 when the names of the phases of our program were created, and the coincidence stems from my sharing the opinion of that project's participants. See `http://www.moonv6.org/` for information about Moonv6.

Simplifying Development to Reduce Complexity

In the spirit of the recommendations given earlier in this chapter, the goals of this particular pilot were set high enough to be visible, while the work required to achieve those goals was made as minimal as possible. This thinking led to the creation of a separate IPv6-only pilot version of the original IPv4 application, which is one of the porting strategies described in RFC 4038. It is not the preferred porting strategy for long-term production software development, but for pilot software to prove functionality, it is satisfactory. Moreover, predecessor applications in the IPv6 domain had already legitimized this strategy, for example `ping6` and `telnet6`, which are completely independent of their IPv4 counterparts.

Because reducing complexity also saves time, and because this was an ad hoc pilot being done during the off hours of the staff, saving time while not compromising functionality toward the goals of the pilot was considered more important than academically superior software.

How Did the Pilot Turn Out?

All three phases, Mercury, Gemini and Apollo, were resounding successes as pilot projects. The application achieved all of the functionality specified for it in the goals of the pilot and became the basis for the IPv6 Internet Mapping Project (I6MP). As of June 1, 2006, I6MP has been scanning the IPv6 Internet daily like its big brother, the Internet Mapping Project (IMP), has been doing for the IPv4 Internet for a decade. For details regarding each project, see `http://www.lumeta.com/internetmapping`.

By the way, NASA did a pretty good job too. Astronauts made it to the Moon, despite what some people believe. I know. I saw it on TV.

Testing Your Knowledge

The following questions call out the distinctions between pilots and more conventional projects. The answers are in Appendix A.

1. What is the purpose of a pilot project?

2. What is the value of an ad hoc pilot project?

3. What must you (and those too whom you report) accept about a pilot that is far less acceptable in conventional projects?

Managing After Transition

CHAPTER 14

Understanding That Your Network Isn't New

One faces the future with one's past.
— **Pearl S. Buck**

Congratulations. I'll assume that because you've reached this section of the book, you've managed to finish at least your first IPv6 transition. You might have thought that with all the hype when you started this process, you would have a brand-new shiny network by the time it was all finished. Looking around your data center, you'll probably notice some boxes that are less dusty than others. Much of the equipment, however, especially if you had been upgrading it fairly regularly before you made this transition, probably looks a lot like it did before the transition began. The point of this chapter is to remind you that, even though you've learned a lot about all the new things you have to do and to look out for with IPv6, the old things that you've been doing and looking out for are still there.

What You'll Learn

This chapter serves as a refresher or reminder of security and other issues that you should consider during and after your IPv6 transition. Specifically, because other chapters covered IPv6 issues, this chapter covers the issues that were applicable to your pre-transition network and are still applicable to your post-transition network. To keep an IPv6 flavor to things, methods for performing those maintenance functions using the benefits of IPv6 are also discussed.

Welcoming IPv6 into Network Operations

A better heading for this section might have been *"Shoving* IPv6 into Network Operations." Like a nervous teenager at a high-school prom, IPv6 has been milling about on the sidelines, perhaps due to its uncertainty whether it would be accepted if it asked Network Operations to dance. Finally, the gym coach and the drama teacher have stepped in to push the two together to show that neither is as scary as it seems from afar.

As I'm writing this, the scuttle-butt in the U.S. federal agencies that I deal with is that the people who have been funding transition studies and fact-finding exercises, and, yes, even IPv6 pilots like those recommended in the previous chapter, are getting tired of hearing that a) IPv6 is complex, and, b) there's still a lot to learn about it. The growing consensus is that it's time for action.

The moves by Lockheed Martin and Verizon Business to adopt IPv6 into their networks, mentioned in the preceding chapters, are commendable steps in the right direction, even if the two companies don't complete their transitions by the time that the mandate comes due (which doesn't apply to them, anyway). Perhaps now that someone has shuffled to the middle of the dance floor, others will join in, if only to show that they are just as brave and cool as Lockheed and Verizon. Moreover, now that IPv6 seems to be gaining acceptance with more well-known firms, rather than just the early adopters that have been on the bandwagon since Bill Clinton's first term, everyone can move on to talking about how to operate an IPv6 network, rather than just how to turn an IPv4 network into one.

To be fair, there are a few fairly large and complex IPv6 networks out there, but they are in the minority compared to all those networks that are mandated to change. The remaining chapters of this book address those organizations that have completed a significant IPv6 deployment within their networks. The chapters also act as a preview for those who have not completed a transition yet, so that they can see what needs to be done when they get there. The final chapters are meant both to recommend how to factor IPv6 into your daily operations of a production network and to remind you of some things that you should remember to continue to do, even though the network has undergone some significant changes and upgrades. Because this is not a book on network operations, per se, I'm not going to cover every detail of that complex job. Instead, I'll touch on examples from areas within network operations with which I am most familiar with the intent to spur you to consider what IPv6 means to your operational requirements and processes.

Teaching Your New Network Some Old Tricks

Now that you've completed a significant IPv6 transition, most likely of your network backbone if you're driven by OMB's mandate, you have some new network management tasks in your to-do list. These tasks include the unique aspects of IPv6 address management (like the hurdles of multi-homing), the maintenance of perhaps more tunnels than there are in the Swiss Alps, and keeping the IPv6-capable and the IPv4-only network segments appropriately isolated. That last topic and some of the others associated with managing a network with heterogeneous IPv4 and IPv6 capabilities are covered in the next chapter.

Besides all the new chores, you also have to continue to do those old mundane network-management jobs after the transition that you had to do before the transition. Those jobs include backups of data and configurations, periodic system maintenance like application, operating system, and firmware upgrades and patches, planning for expansion, and deployment of new capabilities. The good news is that, while you still have those pre-transition chores to deal with in your post-transition network, you also have some IPv6 features and benefits that can be brought to bear to ease those chores, even the chores that are not specifically IPv6 related.

Incorporating Multicast into Network Maintenance

Multicast never became as popular in IPv4 as its creators might have liked. In IPv6, with the elimination of broadcast addresses, multicast is a must. With tongue in cheek, perhaps I might venture to suggest that broadcast was eliminated in IPv6 to give multicast a better shot at success.

The auto-configuration protocols like Neighbor Discovery (ND), Secure ND (SEND), and Router Renumbering (RR) already use multicast. It would make sense, as applications are ported to IPv6, that they take advantage of multicast for their functionality, as well. Such functionality need not be limited to what many people typically associate with multicast, in other words the delivery of audio and video streams.

There are many system and network maintenance jobs where multicast fits very well. Your network and its devices are still subject to vulnerability analysis, patching, and all the other security practices that come with modern network management. With your network's IPv6 transition complete, those patching exercises now include fixes for broken IPv6 features such as the recent Type 0 Routing Header vulnerabilities from Spring 2007. Vendors could define new multicast "channels" devoted to the distribution of upgrades and particularly patches to applications.

Imagine Microsoft and others enabling you to deploy patches from a few central servers within your enterprise via multicast. That alone could save a lot of bandwidth on patch Tuesdays. Of course, such mechanisms would need to be appropriately secured, both for data integrity purposes and to authenticate the source of the patch stream as being a trusted one. For proprietary content, vendors could even choose to encrypt the multicast patch streams, though this has been of little concern in the past for unicast streams.

A final suggestion I have is to employ multicast in backup procedures. Instead of shipping tapes or other media to multiple locations for safekeeping, all you would need to do is ship the packets. The backup would take about as long as backing up to a single place, but you would have two or more copies. I don't claim this to be an original or particularly brilliant idea, but I haven't seen it in any enterprise product to date, so I'll throw it out here for someone to try.

Addressing Some of the Old Security Risks

As you defined and executed your IPv6 transition and accounted for all the security vulnerabilities and limitations unique to IPv6, especially those highlighted in Chapter 10, you hopefully also continued to look at and mitigate the risks that your pre-transition IPv4 network had. As you continue to assess your network's security, as discussed more in Chapter 16, "Maintaining Eternal Vigilance," you should rely on your experiences from a career of managing such TCP/IP networks to tell you what security-relevant issues to continue to look for in addition to whatever the latest greatest new capabilities and their associated vulnerabilities and limitations are.

Handling the Application Flaws That Are Still Present

As stated in this book several times, the network layer took the brunt of your IPv6 transition changes, with the IP and ICMP protocols being switched out wholesale. Any security flaws related to the network layer were eliminated with the protocols that contained those flaws. Of course, all new flaws were surely brought in (and I've also said that IPv4 really hasn't gone anywhere, so the old flaws really aren't gone), but that's another matter. Minor changes occurred in the surrounding transport and link layers, but nothing that sets off any immediate alarms as being particularly security relevant.

Other than at the network layer, the application layer (and the nearby sockets layer) was most affected, and many of the old security problems in both vendor and open-source applications are probably still there. They're just being attacked by IPv6 now, instead of (just) IPv4.

The previous chapter highlighted some of the changes to the sockets API, along with citing references to the RFCs documenting those changes. No RFC, however, is going to tell you how your applications needed to change. For applications whose transition you've patterned after the pilot project from the previous chapter, you may have simply switched IPv4 API calls to IPv6 calls. In that case, it is quite possible that any flaws in the application remained after the transition. If an application was susceptible to a buffer overflow attack, for instance, that vulnerability is likely still in the IPv6 version.

If you were aware of the flaws in an application, you may have chosen the time of IPv6 transition as being appropriate for fixing those flaws, because you already had the application open on the table, so to speak. For the flaws that you were not aware of, but rightfully (based on years of experience) suspected existed, you need to apply the same due diligence that you did when your network was purely IPv4 and you have to protect yourself against such undiscovered flaws. That means relying on your vendors (or your in-house development teams for home-grown applications) to keep you informed of security problems in their software. Moreover, by using a unique IPv6 feature, you can reduce the risks of those as-yet undiscovered problems a little bit more.

Hiding Potentially Flawed Devices in the Address Space

One of the themes of this chapter is that you can use new technology to solve old problems. In the case of that which you cannot fix or secure, you can hide it from attackers to prevent its vulnerabilities from being exploited.

Much coverage has been given to the size of the IPv6 address space, both in this book and elsewhere. One of the key capabilities that this large address space gives you is the ability to hide your devices from some forms of attacks. Chapter 7 covered several addressing schemes, some of which were useful for hiding devices and others that were not very useful at all.

So as not to repeat too much here, you should review Chapter 7, "Identifying Common Transition Preparation Tasks," to see if you can use some of the addressing schemes to make some of your devices less visible, and therefore less vulnerable. Though it is difficult to hide servers that host applications, because client workstations need to find the servers at well-known places, hiding the client workstations may prove useful. This can still be of great value, because workstations (especially laptops) are typically more difficult to secure (and keep secure), than servers, which are under stricter MIS/IT controls.

Assessing IPv6's Denial of Service Risks

There are several new candidates for denial of service attacks in IPv6 that were not present in IPv4 or that were not as important. The newly possible denial of service attacks are not only bandwidth consumption related, where so much traffic is put out by an attacker that bandwidth is denied to legitimate users. There are also attacks that are enabled by the use of some of IPv6's sophisticated protocols against your systems, for example the use of ND to trick a device into sending packets to the wrong device (possibly to be sniffed) or just to send those packets to nowhere in order to disrupt network traffic.

Using IPsec to Curb Certain Denial of Service Attacks

As IPsec is deployed, the denial of service vulnerabilities related to the misuse of features like ND should become less frequent over time as devices become able to authenticate to each other better. IPsec can point to the purported guilty party, allowing you to narrow the investigation brought on by the attack to see if that person was the one doing the attacking or if their credentials had been compromised. In the process of such investigations, it is worthwhile to remember that authenticated devices just like insider users can be as guilty as unauthenticated devices or anonymous users. Do not assume that just because you have IPsec in place that everybody using it is playing by the rules.

Adopting Flow Labels as they Become Better Defined

RFC 3697 specifies minimum requirements for the use of flow labels, but also admits that detailed requirements for how flow labels should be used in specific cases are out of the RFC's scope. Regrettably, no visible standards work has been done on flow labels since RFC 3697 (which was published in March 2004), which either means that anyone working on flows is coming up with their own private schemes or that nobody's working on flows, at all. Flows are a natural fit for the streaming audio and video that's getting more popular on the Internet (and in business intranets) every day, so as IPv6 becomes more prevalent, hopefully flows will come into more standard use.

Growing Your Network with IPv6 in Mind

It should be obvious that, even with your first IPv6 transition complete, your network will continue to change and grow. Moreover, when you've finally deployed IPv6 everywhere, and someday when IPv4 is perhaps a distant memory, your network will continue to be dynamic. Two things to consider with that growth are how IPv6 affects bandwidth and what it means to deploy new capabilities on a heterogeneous network that uses both IPv4 and IPv6.

Learning What Performance Means with IPv6

When it comes to increasing network capacity as your user population or application bandwidth requirements grow, after the transition you'll need to determine how IPv6 uses bandwidth differently from IPv4. There have been and will continue to be lively debates across the whole spectrum of whether IPv6 consumes more, less, or the same bandwidth as IPv4. These arguments will gel into performance figures as time goes by, because you will have the empirical data to indicate the true situation. Once you (and the Internet community and the enterprise networking community) have solid numbers, you can return band-width management to the world of engineering from the world of speculation, where IPv6 bandwidth management is currently residing in pre- and intra-transition times.

What this means to you is that, as you use IPv6 in your post-transition net-work, take the necessary performance measurements and compare them to the IPv4 numbers for similar scenarios. In other words, match apples to apples and make sure that you're looking at the same types of physical networks, user loads, application types, and so on, when comparing IPv4 and IPv6 perfor-mance numbers. If you're not chartered or staffed for that kind of data collec-tion and analysis, retain someone who is or refer to credible reports as others measure and document the performance differences between the two protocol versions.

Deploying New Capabilities

In addition to increases in capacity, the other way a network grows is by adding new capabilities or functions. Such growth is most often done via the deployment of new applications. After you have executed an IPv6 transition, new applications need to be specified and vetted based on whether they will be deployed on IPv6-capable network segments, IPv4-only segments, or both. The next chapter covers the testing required of such applications, as well as other topics associated with running heterogeneous IPv4/IPv6 networks.

Testing Your Knowledge

The following questions are meant to reinforce the pre-transition items you should still be thinking about in your post-transition network, and the IPv6 mechanisms that can help you do so. The answers are in Appendix A.

1. What held back the adoption of multicast in IPv4? Why is multicast more likely to catch on in IPv6?

2. Which IPv6 addressing scheme is good for hiding devices? Which schemes are not so good?

3. What common network management functions still need to be per-formed on your post-transition network?

CHAPTER 15

Managing IPv4 and IPv6 on the Same Network

Coming together is a beginning.
Keeping together is progress.
Working together is success.
— Henry Ford

Nobody wants more work on their plate. I can't sit here and tell you that adding IPv6 to your network will reduce your workload. I do think, however, that it will not increase your load as much as you might think. An IPv6 transition, from the point of view of ongoing maintenance, is really not much different from the enterprise-wide deployment of a new application. The initial period after transition will have its share of rough edges and you will probably put in some overtime cleaning them up. How's that different from the rollout of a new e-mail environment or timecard system, however? As things settle, you'll get change requests and enhancement requests and there will be daily mainte-nance, which should only require a minimum of resources above your IPv4 maintenance. Again, this is typical, as are the inevitable security hiccups that pop up now and then. No, IPv6 will not make your life easier. The hope is, how-ever, that the capabilities it adds will exceed the additional workload and that's the basis for all the MIS/IT (and business) decisions that you make every day.

What You'll Learn

This chapter introduces some concepts for managing your newly IPv6-capable and your pre-transition IPv4-only networks together. Note that the IPv6-capable networks are also still running IPv4. The chapter first explains why heterogeneous networks can work together and then discusses how to think of such networks as combinations of independent entities (where possible), rather than as one big heterogeneous infrastructure.

The chapter points out where you can manage all of your networks, regardless of the IP protocol in use, as one entity. It also points out the places where you should keep the protocols separated and think of the networks as separate entities, too. That chapter concludes with some tips on how to factor the different protocols in your network into application specification and selection.

Mixing Protocol Families on Networks

You can think of the cable that delivers your data-network's "content" to your computer much like the cable that delivers television programs to your home. In the case of wireless data networks, either old-fashioned broadcast TV or new-fangled satellite TV also make good analogies. The specific attribute I'm comparing here is that both the data-networking and television transmission media can deliver multiple "channels" to your devices.

TV sets receive a spectrum of frequencies with each frequency carrying its own signal. Data-networking devices distinguish the content of their feeds partly based on the types of protocols in use in the network stack. The commonality is that, although the raw feeds look like a jumble of different signals (or protocols), the structure imposed on the feeds by television or networking standards makes the combination of dissimilar elements fully comprehendible to the end devices. In other words, you can have multiple protocols running on the same LANs in your network simultaneously with bandwidth consumption being the only potential indication to the individual elements that other elements are there.

If you attach a packet sniffer to any typical data network, you will find several protocols simultaneously in use at any given layer of the stack. Some of the protocols cooperate with each other, like ARP and IP, whereas others are ignorant of each other, like IP and IPX. As a reminder, IPX is Novell's competitor to IP. IPX dates back to the 1980s, just like IP does, but is now a rare sight on modern "purely" TCP/IP networks. You can still find IPX running, however, if you know where to look.

Many networked printers support IPX and are delivered with it enabled. Because these printers are typically almost ready to go out of the box, the people who set them up rarely clean up the configurations to turn IPX off. Though there may be no other IPX devices on the network, such printers still send out periodic IPX transmissions in the hopes that somebody will answer, much like castaways throwing notes in the ocean. Other than consuming bandwidth, this does no harm because purely IP devices don't even realize that IPX traffic is on the wire.

The preceding discussion is meant to show that disparate protocols can reside on the same LAN segments without interfering with each other. This is the case with IPv4 and IPv6. In this chapter, I discuss when the two protocols should interact and when they shouldn't.

Managing Your IPv4 and IPv6 Communities as One

A concept you learn in mathematics and engineering is superposition. Superposition is, in one basic definition, the overlaying of things onto the same space in a way that the effects or properties of those things are cumulative and independent from each other. An example of superposition is the placement of several items on a grocer's scale. Each item weighs a certain amount and together they have a total weight that the scale measures and displays. The weights of all the items on the scale are independent of each other and removing any one or more items reduces the total weight by that of the removed items and has no other effect.

Superposition allows you to take complex problems and decompose them into individually manageable ones. You then solve those simpler problems and add up the solutions for the total answer. This is the fundamental methodology you should use in running your heterogeneous IPv4/IPv6 network.

Describing Dual-Stack Systems Using Superposition

Superposition comes into play when discussing devices that implement dual IP stacks. Eventually all of your devices will support both stack types, just like all TVs will eventually support HDTV as well as the older low-definition signals. Both older versions (IPv4 and low-definition TV signals) may fade away some day, but that's too far in the future to consider seriously in this book.

Each stack in a dual-stack system can be thought of as a distinct element that forms part of the overall stack. Though it's true that tunneling and translation relays make dual-stacks more intermingled than the two types of TV signals, you can still decompose the dual-stack into IPv4 and IPv6 components and define their interactions very precisely to achieve a more manageable concept.

I've found that managing dual-stack systems often amounts to managing the IPv4 side or the IPv6 side as needed with only a cursory thought required to determine how changes on one side affect the other. Again, tunneling and relaying are exceptions.

Keeping Track of All Those Different Addresses

One of the network management duties you have is caring for all of the IP addresses in use. This is a duty that your two distinct families of IP addresses share and one that has aspects that are managed independently of the address family. Chapter 11, "Knowing What Assets You Have," introduced IP Address Management (IPAM) tools and recommended their use for managing IPv6 addresses. You can read the arguments for the use of the tools in that chapter. I'll repeat that recommendation here and extend it to include the management of all IP addresses in your network using a common system. This doesn't necessarily mean using the exact same tool or instance of a tool to manage all the addresses of both protocol versions. It does mean, however, that you should be using an overall process, methodology, or whatever you're comfortable calling it, to take care of the entirety of your address spaces.

Providing ISP Connectivity to Both Communities

Now that you've completed an IPv6 transition, some of your ISP connections may be providing native IPv6, as well as IPv4 connectivity. Other ISPs may be providing IPv4 with IPv6 tunnels. There may also be some pure IPv4-only ISPs left, as well, but that is unlikely given that you can construct your own IPv6 tunnels through IPv4 with any ISP.

External connectivity via ISPs to your LANs can be viewed using the superposition concept introduced earlier. Assume you have a building containing both IPv4-only and IPv6-capable LANs. Further assume that all of the LANs have external connectivity, in other words that a path exists from each LAN to at least one of your external ISP connections. If the building is a smaller one, then all of those LANs may route externally through the same ISP and that ISP is, therefore, an IPv6-capable one. The big-picture view of the whole building is that an IPv4 packet arriving at your ISP connection from the outside (for example, from the Internet) can reach any IPv4-capable device in the building, ignoring access control rules for the moment. A similar case exists for IPv6 packets arriving from the outside and their ability to reach any IPv6-capable device. Moreover, some of those IPv4- and IPv6-capable devices may be one and the same.

By using superposition, you can create and manage the perception that you are really providing external connectivity to two distinct networks, which may just happen to be getting their connectivity from the same ISP. It's a slightly different case if all of your external IPv6 connectivity comes from one ISP, while that same ISP is only part of your connectivity solution for that building for IPv4. In that case, some of the external IPv4 packets you receive enter over a different physical connection from your IPv6 packets, while other IPv4 packets share the IPv6 connection. This still boils down to the same general case, depending how you define your connectivity perimeter (which is different from your security perimeter), because those two connections are like two rivers and all such rivers meet up in some Internet ocean somewhere and the packets can intermingle.

What I have yet to discuss are firewalls and deliberately limiting the connectivity between LANs. You may not want (and shortly I'll argue that you do not want) your IPv4-only and IPv6-capable LANs to communicate freely with each other or all of one protocol's packets to pass indiscriminately through the network segments of the other protocol. There may be a clear electrical path between the IPv4 stack of a device on an IPv4-only LAN in a given building and a similar IPv4 stack on a device in one of the building's IPv6-capable LANs. That connection may require a hop or two through the Internet, but it's still a connection. Though this may be true, you still may not want those devices to communicate and that's the purpose of firewalls and access control in general, which I discuss next.

Separating IPv4 and IPv6 Communities as Needed

The preceding sections endorse the theory that much of the management of your communities of IPv6-capable and IPv4-only LANs can and probably should be merged. That doesn't mean, however, that all of your LANs should necessarily communicate with each other. Although IPv4 is likely to be prevalent everywhere for some time, the best example of where IPv6 should not be permitted on a partially heterogeneous enterprise network is on a LAN that has yet to undergo IPv6 transition.

Imagine a simple LAN composed of a collection of end systems all connected via link-layer switches and served by two routers that are also connected to those switches. Assume that each router is fully IPv6 capable (whatever that means, but I think you get the point) and that the other LANs that the routers serve are equally so. It's possible to further imagine a case where you might want to use the IPv4-only LAN connecting the two IPv6-capable routers to pass IPv6 traffic from one set of IPv6-capable LANs to the other set. The link-layer switches and cables almost certainly are compatible and, for the purposes of the example, you can assume that there is sufficient spare bandwidth.

With all that factored in, it might still be a bad idea to transit IPv6 over an IPv4-only network. The reasoning for this is that, even if the routers, switches, and the network media are IPv6 capable, the end systems on that IPv4-only LAN that might see the IPv6 traffic may not react to it well. With modern switched networks this is less of a concern in normal operations, because switches limit the traffic that an end device sees to only what is destined for that device (or broadcast traffic, which still exists at the link layer even in IPv6).

There are, however, ports and configuration options on many switches to allow the "old-fashioned" link-layer broadcasting of all traffic to some or all devices on that LAN. Though rarely used in production environments, except for getting traffic to network monitoring systems, such promiscuous distribution of Ethernet frames exposes IPv4-only systems (or systems with unintentionally enabled IPv6 stacks) to attacks like those described in Chapter 3, "The Current IPv6 Landscape."

Defining and Enforcing Community Perimeters

The perimeters of your IPv6-capable and IPv4-only communities are defined by your firewalls and filtering routers. This concept is especially important, because your firewalls define what can cross from one LAN to another. Underneath IP, in other words at the link and physical layers, the network doesn't care that one LAN is IPv6-capable and another is IPv4-only. The odds are that they are all electrically connected and it's up to your network-layer routing and access controls to limit traffic between your LANs as you see fit.

Using Network Topology to Define Security Policy

Your network is like an office building where people are allowed into the general spaces, but most are not given full run of the building. If someone doesn't have business being in a particular section, then they are barred from entering it. The best buildings are laid out in such a manner that it is easy for people to get to where they need to be and it only encumbers those that are disallowed from entering limited-access areas. Your network should be constructed the same way and that's the purpose of firewalls.

I'm using the term firewalls to cover a general category of filtering devices. That includes classic dedicated firewalls, routers with access control lists, and anything else that has the ability to forward network-layer traffic along with the ability to decide based on some set of parameters (in other words, a security policy) whether specific traffic should be forwarded.

The IPv6 addressing format with its constant prefix assigned by your ISP, subnet numbers in the subnet-ID field, and an interface ID for everything on a given subnet, can lead to more organized firewall rules than the haphazard collection of different IPv4 address space layouts connected together in most modern enterprises based on legacy assignments. Chapter 7, "Identifying Common Transition Preparation Tasks," discussed the hierarchical use of the typically 16-bit subnet-ID field in IPv6 addresses (see Figure 7-5). This same hierarchy can be used to manage access controls in your network via your firewalls. This hierarchical concept is carried over from IPv4 access control management and is nothing new.

Also used in IPv4 management, but less so due to the limited sizes of the address spaces assigned to most enterprises, is a flat access-control scheme that simply uses the subnet IDs as tags into a security database. If you choose to lay out part of your network as a set of flat subnets, then you can associate sets of subnets into access-control groups, where a particular group might contain subnets 1, 4, 12, 36, and 108, for example, and another group contains 2, 5, 7, 11, 13, and 17. Although this is useful from a security point of view, it can make route aggregation challenging.

Remembering the Importance of Path MTU

You'll recall that, unlike with IPv4, only source devices can fragment packets in IPv6. For a source device to use your IPv6 network's available bandwidth most effectively, it needs to know the minimum MTU between itself and any destination device with which it wishes to communicate. Each destination might have a different minimum MTU, so the source device needs to track those values for every destination device. Those values are determined by source devices using Path MTU discovery, which involves sending ICMP messages.

There is a real dilemma here, because some sites explicitly forbid ICMP due to attacks that can be launched based on it. Other sites will only allow "pings" through, in other words, ICMP Echo Request messages. For optimal operation of IPv6 networks, the ICMP Packet Too Big message also must be allowed to traverse the network as unhindered as possible. If it isn't and a source device's local-link MTU is larger than some of the MTUs throughout the rest (or outside) of your network, then packets from that source may be silently dropped.

Making a Case for Proxied Path MTU Discovery

An idea that I have not seen discussed, but which seems like it has a germ of sense in it, is proxied Path MTU Discovery. This is similar to the concept of Proxy ARP, where a given router responds with its MAC address as the link-layer address for devices that are behind the router, but which want to appear like they are on the local link for whatever reason.

In the case of proxied Path MTU Discovery, a given router acts as the minimum MTU representative for a collection of LANs behind it. When a packet arrives at that router destined for one of the proxied LANs, if the packet's size is greater than the MTU of that destination LAN (or any LAN between the proxy and the destination), the proxying router issues an ICMP Packet Too Big error message to the source device on behalf of the given proxied LAN.

To implement proxied Path MTU Discovery, the proxy needs to perform Path MTU Discovery to the destinations that lie behind the proxy. Presumably, the proxy has the authorization and access to do so and that way, ICMP messages can be contained (or firewalled) by the proxy to the more trusted segments behind it.

Factoring Protocols into Application Acquisition

Application selection is the place where you cross the boundaries of your two IP-version communities most frequently. Applications are the point in the stack where everything below them requires a distinct IPv4 or IPv6 flavor. On the other hand, exposing those flavors to the layer above the applications, for example to the users, is completely at the discretion of the application developers. It can be quite easy to hide protocol-specific details anywhere in an application, except possibly for initial configuration, or configuration changes should the network be reorganized.

Initial configuration and re-configuration of applications are infrequent events, however, and the events may not even affect the application users, only the administrators making the changes. Therefore, some users are surely totally ignorant of which IP protocols are in use by their applications. This, by the way, is another benefit of the network stack.

Chapter 14, "Understanding That Your Network Isn't New," mentioned that applications must be chosen based on whether they are to be deployed on IPv6-capable or IPv4-only network segments. Part of that selection process includes performing any additional testing for applications going to IPv6-capable environments. The process may also include testing the resilience of IPv4-only applications deployed on IPv6-capable LANs, because there will be IPv6 traffic on the LAN and the application should be unaffected by it.

Testing Your Knowledge

Some of the core ideas I would like you to take away from this chapter are reviewed via the questions that follow. The answers are in Appendix A.

1. What property that has been discussed elsewhere in this book allows heterogeneous protocols to exist in the same network?

2. When should you strive to think of your network as a single entity and when should you look at it as separate IPv6-capable and IPv4-only entities?

3. What IPv6 traffic should you seriously consider being allowed throughout as much of your network as possible? (Hint: There is no IPv4 equivalent.)

Maintaining Eternal Vigilance

*He is most free from danger, who,
even when safe, is on his guard.*

— Publilius Syrus

Well, this is it. You've completed your IPv6 transition, or at least your first one, and we're about to part ways. You're now running a heterogeneous network where both protocols are equals and IPv6 is no longer like that weird new kid in school. You can now settle back into your daily network maintenance life, at least until the next transition comes along.

What You'll Learn

The progression of chapters in this last part of the book focus on your network from its transitory state just after your first IPv6 transition completes through the steady state when you're finally feeling comfortable running the network again. This final chapter talks about tracking your network's configuration and traffic with audit and logging tools. The chapter also discusses keeping your configurations up to date based on what you learn about IPv6 and your needs for it as time goes on and you get more used to running an IPv6 network.

Logging What You Can't Control

The preceding chapter primarily covered access control, which in data-networking terms means the prevention of unauthorized people, systems, or programs from being able to send or receive traffic to or from some portion of your network and its assets. This chapter covers the third "A" in the old security triple-A mnemonic of Authentication, Access Control, and Audit; in other words, Audit.

In data security circles, the terms auditing and logging are often used interchangeably, often due to convention in a particular domain. For example, the government sector often uses the term audit, whereas the commercial sector prefers the term logging. This book is intended more for the government sector than the commercial sector, but the tools I'm about to discuss are created by the commercial sector primarily. As such, I'll use the term logging. In this chapter, logging means the recording of information pertaining to events at about the time that the events transpire. Examples of logging in the data-networking domain include tracking the types of traffic that pass into, out of, and through the LANs, routers, firewalls, and other assets in your network.

Like the triple-A mnemonic, there's another old expression in the security business, which says that whenever you cannot implement access controls on a resource that is not meant to be generally available, you should log the accesses to that resource. Of course, even for resources that you have access controls for, you often log the accesses to verify that the right people have the right access.

An example of this latter case comes from your firewalls. Though you have firewalls for access control, you often still want to have logging of the traffic that passes (or is denied passage) through those firewalls. This is not only to validate that policies are correct (and that the firewalls are working), but also to provide proof if some form of legal or other action needs to be taken against an intruder.

Keeping Watch on IPv6 Just Like You Did with IPv4

It should come as no surprise to you that IPv6-related events should be logged just like their IPv4 counterparts. A multi-billion-dollar industry centered around logging and log-analysis systems came into existence as TCP/IP technology was deployed in corporate intranets and became critically related to the success of the enterprise overall. These systems are designed to log, track, audit, and snoop in general on all kinds of network traffic. They are descendants of systems associated with other types of networking, and intra-system logging before that, when computer centers consisted of one or two large systems with dozens or hundreds of connected terminals. Like those UUCP,

LU6.2, NCP, and OAYPNHO (Other Acronyms You've Probably Never Heard Of) logging tools evolved for TCP/IP, what's out there now needs to evolve into IPv6 logging systems.

Reviewing Advanced Logging and Analysis Products

As an MIS/IT professional, you've surely heard of the various types of advanced logging, log-analysis, and audit tools available for the modern data-networking environment. It still might be worthwhile for you to review quickly what these tools do and how they fit together, so I'll summarize them here.

Logging and auditing have gone from simple data collection to the analysis of that data against profiles to determine whether security relevant events are occurring in your network. Intrusion Detection Systems (IDSs) and Intrusion Protection Systems (IPSs) are specialized auditing systems that detect anomalous activity and alert a system's user or a network or security administrator. Whereas IDSs, in a purist sense, are passive logging and analysis systems, IPSs go further and actually deny access if conditions warrant, thus making them more like firewalls.

Literally hundreds or thousands of log-generating systems are deployed within a typical enterprise in the form of routers, web servers, firewalls, print spoolers, and even electronic door locks, motion detectors, and all kinds of other systems. It's safe to say that almost any piece of electronic data-processing equipment (or anything with a serial port or Ethernet jack) can generate logs. When it was just computers generating logs in the early days of MIS/IT, the amount of work to analyze those logs was daunting enough. With all the logging information being generated nowadays, a solution to merge those logs and correlate the information in them into a holistic image is more necessary than ever.

Security Information Management (SIM) systems put a layer above IDS and IPS systems to correlate the logs of multiple systems (typically very many systems) to find security-relevant events or trends across the entire enterprise. Given all the devices on your networks that generate log messages, you need something like a SIM to track them all or you might as well turn the logs off because nobody else will read them.

Adapting Advanced Logging Tools to IPv6

The preceding stable of advanced logging and analysis tools has been around for several years. The evolutionary path started with IDSs (preceded by tools called audit-trail analysis tools from companies like AT&T and Haystack), to IPSs, and finally to SIM systems. One of the next logical steps in the evolution of these tools is to add IPv6 capabilities to them.

The primary capability that needs to be added to these tools to make them IPv6 capable is the ability to understand IPv6 addresses. Because the logs these tools are collecting and analyzing consist of application-specific information for the most part, only the method of identifying which device a log pertains to has changed with IPv6. The other components have stayed the same for the most part. For example, consider a log message like the following one:

```
2007-10-12 08:27:03 192.168.0.2 karl logged in
```

The only change to this log for an IPv6 version of whatever generated it might be the address of the device, for example:

```
2007-10-12 08:27:03 2001:480:4:15:12::401 karl logged in
```

Of course I'm over-simplifying things a bit, but the point is that the key thing a log analysis tool needs to know is the format of the data it is analyzing.

The other thing the logging tools need to be able to do is actually collect the data. For the tools discussed, this doesn't necessarily mean being able to acquire and communicate using an IPv6 address, because a given tool often-times simply collects everything coming down the wire promiscuously. Technically, if the device isn't going to transmit anything, it doesn't need to have an address at all.

Of course, these devices do enter into two-way conversations, and therefore need an IP address, because they have to be accessible so that network and security managers can view their collected data and analyses. That access doesn't have to be over IPv4, however. A tool vendor could develop IPv6 logging and analysis functionality while maintaining an IPv4-based interface for access by the tool's users.

Surveying the IPv6-Capable Advanced Logging Tools

As the OMB mandate draws near, many of the popular advanced logging and audit tools are still lacking in IPv6 features. Table 16-1 is based on my personal use of certain tools or on the claims of vendor websites regarding IPv6 capabilities. This is by no means a comprehensive list, but the top ones that I or others have used or that are well-known names in the industry.

I encourage a mindset of *caveat emptor* (let the buyer beware) when assessing the website claims reflected in Table 16-1. I find such claims to be "overly optimistic" in many cases, having been written by marketing people to draw in customers. In other words, if a product is described as being fully IPv6 capable, then you're probably safe in assuming that it has some set of functionality that could be viewed as complete and useful, for example collecting and parsing IPv6 packets. That does not mean that any kind of security analysis is necessarily performed on those packets. Vendors tend to proudly exclaim their capabilities, especially if the capabilities are in demand. Simple claims like "Supports IPv6" usually imply the barest of functionalities. I know of one vendor who used that very claim, because the product *would not break* on an IPv6-capable network, but the product did nothing IPv6 related.

Partially capable products listed in Table 16-1 should be viewed as anything between fully IPv6-capable with some minor, but necessary, features still missing, to having just enough IPv6 functionality to be able to check off a "we do IPv6" check box for a customer requiring it. Some of the products rated as partially capable earned the rating by virtue of at least one of the vendor's products having IPv6 capabilities, even though the given IDS, IPS, or SIM product does not. That indicates that the vendor is cognizant of IPv6 and may be on the path to implementing it across all their products.

Of course, you should contact the vendors if their claims entice you and not take my word on their products' quality.

Table 16-1: Security Tools Available for IPv6

TOOL	TYPE	IPV4	IPV6	NOTES
Tcpdump	Sniffer	Yes	Yes	Basic raw dumps.
Ethereal	Sniffer	Yes	Yes	Nice GUI, but still a raw dump.
Snort	IDS	Yes	Partial	Website says v3.0 will support. Current version is 2.8 and only supports IPv6 packet decoding.
ISS RealSecure	IDS	Yes	Yes	Website claim.
ISS Proventia	IPS	Yes	Yes	Website claim.
Enterasys Dragon	IDS/IPS	Yes	No	Router products support IPv6.
Check Point IPS-1 (formerly NFR)	IPS	Yes	Partial	Website says it detects tunneled attacks, but certification page lists only FireWall-1 and VPN-1 products as certified (March 2007).
ArcSight ESM	SIM	Yes	No	Network Configuration Manager product supports IPv6.
Intellitactics	SIM	Yes	Partial	Pilot completed 7/16/2007.
netForensics OSP	SIM	Yes	No	Government-focused website doesn't even acknowledge existence of IPv6.

The first three tools on Table 16-1 (tcpdump, Ethereal, and Snort) are open-source and IPv6 capable, which if you find yourself in need you can deploy to manage your IPv6 networks until more enterprise-scale tools are available. Such tools are not in the same league as the IPv4-only tools listed in the table and somebody needs to get on the ball and get IPv6 tools out there.

Given the lack of enterprise-scale tools, it is understandable to see why a network management group is hesitant to deploy IPv6 when the security tools that they are used to in IPv4 are not available yet. Other network management tools and security tools that you want to have for IPv6 networks, as you do for IPv4, include virus detection, personal firewalls, spam and other e-mail filters, spyware detectors, and World Wide Web protection.

For open-source tools to fill the gap until more products become available, an excellent web page for learning the status of all kinds of IPv6 tools is at http://www.deepspace6.net/docs/ipv6_status_page_apps.html. About 75% down the web page's lists you'll find security-related tools including auditing tools like nmap and packet sniffers like Ethereal and tcpdump. There are other tools, as well, that address the needs mentioned earlier in this section.

Perhaps many or all of the usual suspects for IDS, IPS, and SIM products are wrapping up their IPv6 development and planning to announce products closer to the OMB mandate deadline. If they want to get into the procurement cycle early enough, however, those announcements should be coming pretty soon.

Choosing How to Protect Systems You Can't Watch

This chapter has asserted that there are assets and events for which you cannot provide access controls. For those things you should at least log access. What about the things for which you can't provide logging? This class of assets and events can be separated into two groups, which are the things you know and that you can't do anything about in terms of logging, and the things of which you are unaware. Former Defense Secretary Donald Rumsfeld's speech on "known unknowns" and "unknown unknowns" comes to mind here.

Because, by definition, you cannot control access to these devices, applications, or whatever the assets are, and you cannot log the accesses that are taking place, the lesson to take away is that there has to be some minimal level of access control and logging network-wide from which such systems can reap some protection. This is known as your security perimeter, and it is that area which has general access controls to limit "who goes there" to trusted users, programs, and systems. While insider threat is a very real thing, at least if there is an exploit of some vulnerability from within your security perimeter, you can review the logs to see who was there at the time to reduce the list of suspects.

Reviewing Configurations Periodically

The logs and other network instrumentation data that you collect and analyze with the tools described in the first part of this chapter provide you with information on how better to configure your network in general. You then need to use that information in a well-defined way to improve your network's overall security profile, as well as the network's performance and functionality. As you learn to manage your IPv6 capabilities better, configuration choices you made when you were not as informed may be shown to have been overly cautious and therefore you can relax those choices to obtain possible performance improvements or reductions in complexity of network management. On the other side of the coin, you may learn things that tell you that your IPv6 network management needs to be tightened, for example because of some new security risk that makes a certain configuration not as secure as you would like it to be.

To facilitate configuration changes in either direction, whether that's the relaxing of restrictions or their tightening, you need a process to go along with the inputs described earlier. The next section suggests that, if you didn't have one when you started reading this book, you should have one by now.

Using Transition-Planning Processes for Daily Tasks

The demand for network transitions never ends, whether the transition at hand is an IPv6 transition or some other type. Your network is always changing as the effects of user requests, technological progress, and organizational changes are applied. You need to plan the activities to bring about such changes and monitor the activities' execution, just like you did for the activities associated with your original IPv6 transition. After all, your IPv6 transition is just a well advertised one, but the processes shown in this book are applicable to all the others, as well.

Ironically, your network backbone's IPv6 transition was probably not only the first, but also the most complex IPv6 transition to undertake. Sometimes, however, the fact that the first steps are the hardest is just par for the course for what you're trying to accomplish. To mix metaphors, you needed some initial critical mass in order to get the ball rolling with an IPv6 transition, and as discussed in Chapter 12, "Selecting an Enterprise Transition Strategy," your backbone was a good place to start. The good news is that subsequent IPv6 transitions, such as deployment of IPv6-capable applications, will have the benefit of hindsight as to how the backbone transition went.

Keeping Current on IPv6 Security Problems and Fixes

In addition to discovering vulnerabilities and other information concerning your network's security configuration via personal experience, you have available to you many vendor-neutral and vendor-specific security groups, response teams, and other organizations dedicated to the discovery and dissemination of information about computer security in general and IPv6 in particular. You've probably been tracking the security message boards, blogs, and mailing lists for IPv4, along with similar avenues of information related to operating system security and the security of all kinds of applications. Just like you kept track of that security information, you especially need to keep track of IPv6 security information.

Because IPv6 is newer (at least to the operations world) than most other technologies with potential security impact, there will likely be more frequent security issues with IPv6, at least for the first few years during and after the transition. When such issues do show up, there's also more of a chance that they will be significant, at least compared to IPv4 networking issues. This is because, with some exceptions, IPv4's security problems have mostly been rung out. Most new problems in IPv4 are associated with new application protocols that use IPv4 in different ways from before. I'll venture that there's little in the way of new security vulnerabilities left to be found in core IPv4.

You can find IPv6 security advisories and other information via the same alert and response groups as IPv4 and other advisories are found. A short list of the computer security alert and response centers you should be aware of includes:

CERT (`http://www.cert.org/`). Carnegie Mellon's CERT, which is not an acronym for anything, was the first computer security incident response team, formed in reaction to the Morris Worm of November 1988.

FIRST (`http://www.first.org/`). The Forum of Incident Response and Security Teams (FIRST) is a coalition of individual response teams from around the world with each one specializing in a given constituent community and that community's problems. FIRST's membership list, which includes many of the other members on this list, is at `http://www.first.org/members/teams/index.html`.

DOD-CERT (`http://www.cert.mil/`). This team covers all of DoD. There are also individual teams for the military branches.

NIST (`http://csrc.nist.gov/index.html`). The Computer Security Resource Center at the National Institute of Standards and Technology (NIST) maintains ties with other such groups, some of which are listed at `http://csrc.nist.gov/csrc/advisories.html`. In addition, a national vulnerability database is also maintained at `http://nvd.nist.gov/`.

US-CERT (`http://www.us-cert.gov/`). The United States Computer Emergency Readiness Team (US-CERT) is run by the Department of Homeland Security for the U.S. government.

In addition to the vendor-neutral security forums mentioned here, you should also track the security announcements from your various product vendors. Many vendors maintain their own alert and incident response teams, as well.

Testing Your Knowledge

Here are your final questions for this book. I hope you enjoyed the content and the format. As always, the answers are in Appendix A.

1. If you can't control access to a particular set of assets or LAN, what should you strive to do, at a minimum?

2. Why should you review your network configurations, especially your IPv6 configurations, regularly?

Answers to the Testing Your Knowledge Questions

Chapter 1: What Is IPv6?

1. What are three advantages of IPv6 over IPv4?

   The three most significant advantages to IPv6 over IPv4 are:

   1. The increased address-space size to eliminate the risk of exhaustion.

   2. More efficient routing via the use of fixed IP header sizes for the vast majority of traffic and more efficiently organized routing hierarchies.

   3. Auto-configuration to reduce the effort of deploying network infrastructure and end hosts like workstations.

   Other acceptable answers are: the elimination of the need for NAT, and the enablement of true P2P applications, though those are both closely tied to the increased address space size.

2. What is the biggest hurdle in the U.S. facing those planning an IPv6 transition?

   The biggest hurdle is the installed base of IPv4 systems. Countries like China with no significant installed base are finding it much easier to deploy IPv6. Closely related to this hurdle is the dependence on the Internet and TCP/IP networks in general that the U.S. has for defense, finance, and other critical infrastructure.

3. Extra Credit: What was the dominant networking protocol prior to IP?

   The Network Control Protocol (NCP) preceded TCP/IP. NCP's short-comings led to the development of TCP/IP, but the former survived on the Internet until the end of 1982 and longer in private networks, especially in the U.S. federal government. See `http://www.isoc.org/internet/history/brief.shtml` for a brief history of the Internet by those who were there.

4. Extra Credit: If the current IP protocol is version 4 and you're making the transition to version 6, what happened to version 5?

   Version 5 in the IP header was assigned to an experimental streaming protocol known as ST. Later versions were called ST-II (for version 2) and ST2+. Designed to provide guarantees on real-time service for data streams, ST was documented in September 1979 by IEN 119 and updated by RFC 1190 and RFC 1819. ST and its descendants never caught on as the state of the art moved toward different techniques for streaming data. Because version number 5 had been used, the protocol you're upgrading to is version 6. Note that versions 7, 8, and 9 are also already reserved (see `http://www.networksorcery.com/enp/protocol/ip.htm`). They are experimental siblings of IPv6, and you're not likely ever to see an implementation of them. If you're interested in how IPv6 beat out these other candidates, RFC 1710 (the first to use 6 as the version number in the IP header) and RFC 1752 are a good read.

Chapter 2: Demystifying IPv6

1. Why do IPv4 packet headers require both an Internet Header Length (IHL) and Total Length field?

   Because the IPv4 header is not of a fixed size, a single length field is insufficient. The IHL field indicates the size of the header, and the Total Length field indicates the size of the whole packet.

2. If the Payload Length of an IPv6 packet is only 16-bits, how can the maximum packet size be larger?

   Though it's true the IPv4 Total Length and IPv6 Payload Length fields are the same size, the latter does not include the (fixed) IPv6 header size. That allows the maximum IPv6 payload to be 20 bytes bigger than the IPv4 payload. Note that this does not take into account IPv6 "jumbograms," which utilize an extension header (see RFC 2675) to allow packet payloads up to 4GB (that is, there are 32-bits of length information instead of the usual 16). The extension was not devised to send

4GB packets around the network. Instead, it was defined for links whose MTUs exceed 64KB, as some are starting to do. Therefore, you should expect that any packets using the jumbogram extension will be much closer in size to the lower limit of 64KB than the 4GB upper limit.

3. What's the difference, according to the RFCs, between Time to Live (TTL) in IPv4 and Hop Limit in IPv6? What's the practical difference?

Both fields specify a maximum lifetime for a packet after which it must be discarded, if it has not reached its destination. This typically serves to prevent packets that get stuck in routing loops from living forever and clogging the network. The IPv4 TTL is defined in units of time with 1-second granularity. A router must decrement the TTL by the number of seconds between when the packet arrived at the router and when it was ready to leave. A router cannot decrement the TTL by less than 1, even if it took less than a second to process the packet. A modern router (and probably many around at the dawn of IPv4), can forward a packet in less than a second, usually in a few milliseconds. This reduces the TTL to being a hop counter. With that in mind, the IPv6 Hop Limit changes the temporal definition to a purely hop-based one.

4. List three reasons why the Header Checksum wasn't incorporated in the IPv6 header, even though it's in the IPv4 header.

   1. The link-layer protocols below IP usually have their own checksumming, making the IP one redundant.

   2. Those protocols above IP that require checksums, like TCP and UDP, already have them, which makes the IP checksum redundant and wasteful for protocols where some number of errors is tolerable (for example, streaming audio and video).

   3. Considering the preceding two reasons, the checksum was eliminated to improve router performance, because IP checksums have to be recomputed at each hop.

5. Write the IPv6 address 2001:0000:0000:2379:01a0:0000:0000:7480 in its most compact form.

`2001::2379:1a0:0:0:7480` or `2001:0:0:2379:1a0::7480`. The former one is preferred, because the network portion (upper 64-bits) is a broad identification of your network that will appear in many places. Abbreviation will be helpful with that. The blocks of zeros in the interface ID are less likely to occur, especially given EUI-64 and other addressing schemes discussed later in this book. Note that both blocks of zeros cannot be abbreviated simultaneously, because this creates an ambiguity regarding the placement of the '`2379:1a0`' portion. Also, the '`1a0:0000:0000`' portion cannot be abbreviated as '`1a::`,' because only contiguous 16-bit sequences of zeros can be abbreviated using '`::`'.

6. Extra Credit (read, Useless Trivia): How many IPv6 addresses fit on the head of a pin? Assume the pin is made of iron (it's an old pin), the head is 1mm in diameter, 0.5mm in thickness, and has one address per atom. Hint: you'll probably need Avogadro's number.

As the hint suggests, you'll need Avogadro's number, which is $6.02x10^{23}$ and equals the number of atoms or molecules in a "mole" of something. You'll also need to know the volume of a mole of iron (the element "Fe"), which is 7090 cubic millimeters (mm^3). That can be found in online periodic tables (for example, `http://www.webelements.com/`) and means that $7090mm^3$ of iron has $6.02x10^{23}$ atoms. That's a spherical ball of iron a little less than an inch in diameter. The pinhead you have is a cylinder 1mm across and 0.5mm in height, making its volume $0.393mm^3$. By dividing the pinhead's volume by the sphere's and multiplying by Avogadro's number, you get $3.33x10^{19}$ atoms of iron (or IPv6 addresses). Though this is a huge number, it can be represented using the space of just two of the minimal '/64' allocations ARIN provides its smallest customers. Hopefully, this gives some sort of perspective to the vast spaces IPv6 provides for practically unlimited network growth if care is taken to manage the allocations and people don't get sloppy.

Chapter 3: The Current IPv6 Landscape

1. What is the true goal of the U.S. federal OMB mandate?

   Because I can't read the minds of those at OMB who wrote the mandate, I can't be 100% certain of this answer. My opinion is that OMB wrote the mandate to encourage IPv6 adoption by causing deployment of IPv6 in the federal government's networks with as little effort as possible while still having meaningful results. That amounts to the deployment of IPv6 in the network backbones only, for now. I also feel that the OMB mandate was meant to cause a trickle down effect as the agencies required to deploy IPv6 turned to their vendors and forced them to deploy it, as well.

2. Considering that hacking is at best borderline illegal (and at worst a felony), why do you need to know what the IPv6 hackers are doing?

   You need to know what the hackers, IPv6 and otherwise, are doing in order to defend against them. For the same reasons that the police put officers undercover in drug rings, gambling rackets, and so on, you would do well to have some of your staff attend the occasional hacker conference and surf the Internet from time to time searching for hacking tools.

Chapter 4: Choosing When to Make the Transition and How

1. What are the three main IPv6 transition mechanisms?

   Native IPv6 (meaning no IPv4 involved), dual-stack with both IPv6 and IPv4 available to applications, and tunneling to allow IPv6 to pass through an otherwise IPv4-only network or vice versa.

2. What is the most important set of things to migrate to IPv6: network infrastructure, applications, capabilities, or users?

   Your network's capabilities are the most important things to migrate to IPv6, because they are what your network represents to its users and give your network value.

3. You've decided to start your IPv6 transition now and proceed slowly. Magically, you've come up with a total estimate of 21 months to get the job done. What's a good back-of-the-envelope estimate for how long it will take you to upgrade "quickly" to IPv6, by planning everything first and then executing all the plans at a more rapid pace? Include the planning and pre-transition preparation work in the estimate, not just the network changes.

   Based on the simplistic example in this chapter, it is assumed the 21 months of the "slow" transition represent planning, preparation, and execution happening in parallel, with 1/3 of your total resources devoted to each. In other words, 7 staff-months each of planning, preparation, and execution. Assuming the amount of work does not change by serializing the three components and having 100% of your resources devoted to one component, it will take 7 calendar months for each phase, with the execution starting 14 months after project launch and everything finishing in the same 21 months as the slow approach. This assumes that your resources are 100% interchangeable between the components (which you know is unrealistic if you ask any project manager or network engineer). The point of the example is to drive home that your IPv6 transition is not going to go any faster if you force it and you're likely to make some potentially expensive mistakes. Taking a page from agile software development, you're far better off migrating your network in small batches with mini-transitions composed of smaller and more manageable planning, preparation, and execution components.

4. When using IPv4-mapped IPv6 addresses, what additional mechanism(s) do you need to complete a communications path between an IPv4-only application and an IPv6-only server?

You need several things to establish a round-trip communications path between an IPv4 client and an IPv6 server using IPv4-mapped addresses. For traffic leaving the client, somewhere on the way to the server you need to convert the IPv4 packets into IPv6 packets. If the server is not using an IPv4-mapped address, then you have to have a way of providing the IPv4 client with an IPv4 destination address for the server that can be put in the IPv4 packets the client sends. For the return trip, there has to be a converter to turn the IPv6 packets the server emits into IPv4 packets with source addresses somehow pointing back to the IPv6 server. The preceding assumes that all the proper routing is in place for the different flavors of addresses to get to the right systems. For a more comprehensive solution, see RFC 2767.

5. What is the minimum MTU for IPv6 links and how did it change from the IPv4 one?

The minimum MTU (which defines the largest packet that can be sent with a guarantee that it won't be fragmented) is 1280 octets, where octets nowadays are equivalent to 8-bit bytes. The IPv4 minimum MTU is 576 octets. IPv6 raised the minimum MTU (requiring bigger packets to be guaranteed no fragmentation) based on a generation's worth of improvements in network hardware and to reduce the need for fragmentation.

6. Silly Trivia: What were the round-trip times of the successful IP over carrier pigeon implementation in April 2001?

The times varied from 3,211 to 6,389 seconds. In other words, 53.5 minutes to 1 hour 46.5 minutes. This is another proof that not all research leads to useful applications. See `http://www.blug.linux.no/rfc1149/writeup .html` for the whole story.

Chapter 5: Creating Your Transition Plans

1. What are the three corners of the project triangle?

The project triangle's three corners represent the required quality of the work being performed, the amount of time required to do the work, and the amount of resources required. The lesson taught by the project triangle concept is that, once you've specified any two corners, the third corner is automatically decided. For example, if you have three engineers and a week to do the work, the maximum possible quality of the final results is a fixed value.

2. What are the interfaces between various transition plans called and why are they important?

The interfaces between transition plans are called dependencies. Dependencies are what you expect other parts of your enterprise, vendors, or other external organizations to provide in order for you to achieve a successful IPv6 transition. An example of a dependency is having vendors provide IPv6-capable hardware and applications in time to meet your transition deadlines.

3. List some of the things you need before you can start your transition planning (or at least before you can finish it).

   There is a long checklist in the chapter, but some of the key things that you will need for your transition planning include a) the set of capabilities or services currently offered by your organization that must continue to be offered after the transition is complete, and b) the list of resources you can draw from to affect the transition.

4. What factors do you have to take into account when scheduling people's time on the transition plan?

   Among other things mentioned in the chapter, you need to account for how long it will take a given person (or in general terms, a person with a given level of experience and skill) to perform the required work. You also need to factor in people's time allotted to other projects and their personal time, by making allowances for sick leave and vacation.

5. Why are project baseline schedules important?

   Project baselines are important so that you can track your project's progress against your initial estimates and assumptions. If you find the project deviating from the baseline plan, you need to determine why it is doing so and how to correct it.

6. Where can you find help for your transition planning?

   There are many individual organizations that can help you. In general terms, your two biggest sources of help are OMB (the organization forcing you to undergo IPv6 transition) and professional consulting and network management firms that are making a business of IPv6 transitions.

7. Extra Credit: What makes the IPv6 transition different from Ada, C2-by-92, and GOSIP?

   The biggest difference between IPv6 transition and any of those others is that there is already a large number of people and organizations outside of the United States that are adopting IPv6. Very few adopted any of those other standards, at least in any broad sense and certainly not commercially, in other words outside of the government.

8. Silly Trivia: What happens January 19th, 2038? At what time (to the second, please)?

This date refers to the UNIX operating system's equivalent of the Y2K problem. The current clocks in UNIX will wrap around to January 1, 1970 on this date. In the U.S. Eastern time zone, the wrap-around will occur at 3:14:07 in the morning. Though this date is still over 30 years away, and UNIX is expected to have handled the problem long before then, you can be sure there will be a handful of systems that will be affected by it. Remember that in 1969 nobody thought much about Y2K, which was just as far away then as 2038 is now and plenty of 1960s software was around for January 1, 2000.

Chapter 6: Defining the Transition Preparation Steps

1. What are the four goals of your IPv6 transition for it to be considered a success?

   1. Keeping your transition costs minimal.

   2. Retaining all the required pre-transition capabilities.

   3. Optimizing the network configuration wherever possible.

   4. Documenting the post-transition configuration.

2. In the context of this book, what's the difference between an asset inventory and a capabilities assessment?

   Asset inventories count your network assets (routers, servers, workstations) and software assets. Capabilities assessments catalog the services your network provides for its users, ranging from simple e-mail to the ability to trade stocks or perform air traffic control.

3. What are the three goals of your asset inventory and capabilities assessment efforts?

   1. Validate your assets and their capabilities as reflected in your CMDB or other existing asset inventory documents.

   2. Discover any assets of which you were unaware and that were not in your CMDB and add them to it.

   3. Eliminate any assets from your CMDB that you find are no longer present in your network. Also eliminate any reference to their capabilities.

4. What are two required attributes for each asset in an inventory?

   You need to be able to uniquely identify each asset and to find it physically in your network, for example to repair or replace it.

5. What do you want to associate with every software asset?

   The hardware asset on which it is installed.

6. How many logical networks are typically in a physical one?

   Four: the inside, outside, DMZ, and management.

7. How can you make an asset IPv6 capable?

   You can upgrade it or replace it. You can also eliminate it, provided you can consolidate its required capabilities into another asset which itself is IPv6 capable.

8. What capabilities must an asset have to be fully remotely manageable in IPv6 terms, in other words if all IPv4 access was turned off?

   The asset must be able to be remotely managed using the IPv6 protocol and its IPv6 capabilities must be remotely manageable.

9. Silly Trivia: Who is Jack Ryan and why is he important to IPv6?

   Tom Clancy's fictional CIA character from books like *The Hunt for Red October*, *Red Storm Rising*, *The Cardinal of the Kremlin*, and of course, *Clear and Present Danger*. As of July 23, 2007 a Google search yielding 107 responses shows that Jack Ryan has nothing to do with IPv6.

Chapter 7: Identifying Common Transition Preparation Tasks

1. What are AfriNIC, APNIC, ARIN, LACNIC, and RIPE? What do the abbreviations mean?

   These are the five current Regional Internet Registries (RIRs). They are the regional authorities for IPv6 address allocations and assignments. The abbreviations stand for:

   AfriNIC: African Network Information Centre

   APNIC: Asia Pacific Network Information Centre

   ARIN: American Registry for Internet Numbers

   LACNIC: Latin American and Caribbean Internet Addresses Registry

   RIPE: Réseaux IP Européens (French for European IP Networks)

2. What properties do IPv6 addresses have, particularly in how the addresses are acquired, that IPv4 addresses do not? What do you need to be aware of, as an enterprise customer, based on those properties?

   IPv6 addresses are much more closely tied to the ISPs from which you get them. The IPv6 addresses from a given ISP are not likely to be routable through other ISPs, because an ISP's job is to aggregate all the addresses they are allocated from the RIRs and present them to the global routing infrastructure as one collective set. This means, if you change ISPs, you may have to renumber all your internal assets as well as externally facing ones. Such renumbering can be difficult or easy, depending on how much of IPv6's auto-configuration functionality you have implemented. Moreover, as an enterprise customer who will want to use multiple ISPs for redundancy, the difficulties in multi-homing IPv6 that comes from the ISP-centric addressing hierarchy is something you have to be very careful about when engaging ISPs.

3. In what sizes should ISPs assign IPv6 address spaces to their customers, given the recommendations of the RIRs?

    Most RIRs recommend their ISPs assign spaces in sizes of '/48' for sites with multiple subnets and '/64' if there will be only one subnet at the site. ARIN adds the recommendation to use '/56' spaces for smaller sites.

4. Can you get IPv6 addresses directly from an RIR?

    Yes, provided you meet the special conditions the RIR sets, which varies with each RIR. ARIN, for example, may assign you IPv6 addresses directly if you qualify for IPv4 addresses under ARIN's IPv4 assignment policy. You may also get IPv6 addresses directly for infra-structure deemed critical to the operation of the Internet or for your internal-only use.

5. Can you use 6to4 with dynamically allocated (for example, via DHCP) IPv4 addresses?

    Yes. According to RFC 3056, there is nothing wrong with using DHCP-allocated addresses to construct network prefixes for 6to4 IPv6 addresses. However, should you lose the IPv4 address via a DHCP license expiration, then the IPv6 address block is no longer usable, either.

6. If IPv6 addresses are so plentiful, why do you need a numbering plan?

    A numbering plan doesn't just document how much of a resource you are using and when you might need to get more. In IPv6, that's the plan's least important function. You need the numbering plan to know how IPv6 subnets are distributed throughout your enterprise so as to organize them for better intra-enterprise routing, to manage deploy-ment of new subnets, and to find assets for troubleshooting purposes. Finally, you need to document how each subnet generates its interface IDs, so as to avoid conflicts between devices on the same LAN.

7. If you are setting up three IPv6 LANs, the first requiring 30 single-interface devices, the second requiring 900, and the third requiring

8,200, what size network prefixes would you provision (including the subnet portion) and how many addresses would be set aside for each LAN for growth based on those provisioned sizes?

All subnets in IPv6 address spaces (at least the ones currently allocated by the RIRs) use 64 bits per LAN. That means each of the three LANs you're setting up uses the same size subnet (that is, a '/64') and each have the same number of addresses available for devices (that is, essentially an infinite amount). Isn't that easier than deploying IPv4 LANs?

8. What are the three drivers for how you should implement sub-netting in your enterprise's sites?

   Your enterprise network should be sub-netted based on its physical topology, the differences in security profiles between subnets, and the mission-criticality of each subnet.

9. In defining your hierarchical sub-netting, what should you take into account when determining the levels of the hierarchy and their sizes? What may have Hierarchy (C) in Figure 7-5 failed to take into account?

   To reduce wasted space, look to define each level of your subnet hierarchies so that its size comes as close to a power of two as possible without going over. At the same time, make sure to give each level enough room for growth based on projections of at least five years. Network renumbering (which is what you're facing as the enterprise grows if you don't get your hierarchies right) should be no more frequent than every five years, barring unusual circumstances like a corporate merger or major reorganization. Sometimes you'll get lucky and your growth estimates will be covered by the power-of-two "waste" you are forced to accept. Other times you may have to allocate even more bits to a level just to cover potential growth and as insurance against renumbering. The "Floor" field in Hierarchy (C) of Figure 7-5 doesn't seem to account for subnets in the basements of buildings, although it's possible basements are encoded in the field. This could be done by defining the "Floor" field as a signed number, which limits the field shown to representing a ground floor (represented by a zero), up to seven stories above ground and up to eight levels of basements. There are several alternate (but less straightforward) formats, but the lesson you should take away from this is to account for things like basements when defining hierarchies based on the physical locations of subnets. Another lesson is to keep the field definitions simple enough that they can be understood by visual inspection without always having to refer to the numbering plan.

10. What are EUI-64-based interface IDs and what do you need to consider before using them?

   An EUI-64-based interface ID is generated in a simple well-documented way from the MAC address of a device. Such an interface ID has the security vulnerability of exposing your device's MAC address (which includes the identity of its manufacturer) to a wide audience that can include those looking to harm your network and who shouldn't be getting such information. EUI-64-based interface IDs are also far more predictable than random ones, which is a weakness if you wish to keep your devices safe from brute-force searches by worms or casual hackers attempting to attack your network.

11. What is arguably the most important question you should ask your potential IPv6 ISPs that you would take for granted with IPv4?

    When looking to engage ISPs to provide external connectivity to your network, make sure to ask how they plan to handle multi-homing. In IPv4, addresses and connectivity have little to do with each other and, for the most part, any ISP can route any particular set of addresses within their RIR's region. With IPv6, the addresses are much more tightly coupled to the ISPs, and determining how multiple ISPs will provide continued external connectivity of all your addresses, in the event one ISP goes offline, is something you should figure out before committing to any ISP.

12. Extra Credit (or, Irrelevant Trivia): It would take 64 coin tosses to produce a random IPv6 interface ID. If you had a six-sided die, how many tosses of that would it take?

    Each toss of a six-sided die produces a little more than 2.5 bits of randomness, which you can determine by taking the base-2 logarithm of the number 6 or `log2(6)`. To find out how many throws it takes to get 64-bits of randomness, divide 64 by `log2(6)` and you'll get a little more than 24.75. Therefore, it requires 25 tosses of the die. See why it's better in software?

13. Truly Irrelevant Trivia: Which RIR covers Antarctica?

    Per `http://www.arin.net/community/countries.html`, as of July 29, 2007, ARIN is the RIR covering Antarctica. RIPE may also be correct, because there are LIRs served by RIPE that service Antarctica, per `http://www.ripe.net/membership/indices/AQ.html`.

Chapter 8: Defining the Transition Execution Steps

1. When deciding the factors for when you have to revert to a prior normal state, whose views should you listen to, what do you need to establish, and when do you need put the factors in place?

The overarching view regarding the usability of the network belongs to its user community. No matter how much you want a given set of transition activities to succeed, if the network can't be restored to being usable by the end of the maintenance window, then the activities must be reverted. The criteria for reversion, specifically the "revert times" within the maintenance window when particular reversion activities must start, need to be defined in a way that the reversion activities can complete within the remaining time of the maintenance window. The revert times must be defined *before* any transition activities start, so that they can be determined objectively.

2. In the context of this chapter, what does the "normal state" of your network mean?

The normal state of a network is one where the users have available to them all the capabilities that they need and expect from the network. There are typically two normal states, the one prior to a set of IPv6 transition activities starting and the one after all the activities in a maintenance window complete successfully. Normal state pertains to the users' perception, meaning that if a set of transition activities added capabilities that are only partly functional, but invisible to and not adversely affecting the user population, then the network can be said to be in a normal state.

3. What qualities should you look for when determining the locations where you'll be executing your first IPv6 transition activities?

You should find locations that are not critical to the redundancies in your network. For example, you should pick locations that, if you take them offline to execute transition activities (or if they go offline as a result of a failure during those activities), the remaining locations in your enterprise still have redundant connectivity to the network.

4. What are the advantages to executing a "depth-first" transition at some of your sites?

A depth-first transition exercises the whole IPv6 transition process from start to finish, including the upgrading of network equipment to being IPv6 capable, the provisioning of IPv6 addresses and external connectivity, and in some cases, the configuration of advanced IPv6 capabilities like IPsec. By performing a depth-first transition on a few of your less-critical locations, or those that are already mostly IPv6 capable, you can work the bugs out of your whole transition process. This approach is the opposite of a breadth-first transition where you first upgrade all the network equipment in your entire enterprise, then provision IPv6 addresses and connectivity enterprise-wide, and then configure advanced features. The breadth-first approach leaves the discovery of many of the more difficult IPv6 problems until very close to your overall transition deadlines.

5. What methodology advocated previously in this book is also good for identifying dependencies between IPv6 transition activities?

   The decomposing of your activities into smaller sets of steps and seeing what those steps depend on can help isolate dependencies that might be difficult to find or hidden by the complexity of the larger set of activities.

6. What must any group of transition activities assigned to a maintenance window achieve when, regardless of whether they complete successfully, the maintenance window ends?

   A group of transition activities must restore the network to a normal state before the maintenance window ends, either by successful completion of the activities or reversion to a prior normal state.

Chapter 9: Defining the Transition Verification Steps

1. What are the downsides of too much testing or too little testing?

   Testing too much can be a waste of resources, while testing too little may leave the network with undiscovered flaws. It's hard to detect that you've tested too much and you usually steer away from doing so due to resource limitations. Testing too little, especially if it's far too little, is usually detected by your users.

2. What is the primary component of a successful verification phase?

   Testable requirements are the foundation of high-quality tests and a successful verification phase, where success is defined not only as passing all your verification test cases, but also having a correctly functioning network.

3. Are there any transition activities that can occur outside of maintenance windows? If so, what are they?

   Transition activities that don't affect the availability of the network's capabilities to its users can be performed outside of maintenance windows. This includes many types of verification activities, as well as the software development activities to upgrade in-house applications to IPv6.

4. Name some of the testing concepts and paradigms that can provide you with a more successful transition verification phase.

   Execution and verification separation, black-box, white-box, and grey-box testing, regression tests, and automated test suites all can improve the results of your verification phase and make the verification work easier, as well. You can re-read the appropriate sections of this chapter to familiarize yourself with each of them.

Chapter 10: Factoring IPv6-specific Risks and Limitations into Your Plans

1. What are the three risks associated with an IPv6 transition that are not common to most other enterprise technology upgrades?

   IPv6 transition is affected by the fact that there is little available online in the way of practical experience or "lessons learned," in contrast with the typical wealth of information available for other new technologies undergoing adoption by enterprises. The implementation of IPv6 also caused a lot of changes to hardware and software and many systems may not function per the RFCs, at first. Also, there are also many new networking concepts and designs being floated and tested with IPv6. Some will catch on and be useful. Others will be cast aside due to performance or security issues.

2. What is a shortcoming of SEND that may limit its deployment? Hint: It has to do with the addresses it uses.

   SEND is presently limited to using Cryptographically Generated Addresses (CGAs). Though CGAs have some very nice properties (randomness being one of them), SEND's inability to support manually configured or EUI-64 addresses may seriously hinder its adoption.

3. Where else should you focus your functionality, performance, and security concerns while undertaking your IPv6 upgrade, besides all the network-layer protocol changes brought about by IPv6?

   Implementing IPv6 necessitated changes throughout the TCP/IP stack. When validating systems that have been upgraded to be IPv6 capable, make sure the "old" TCP, UDP, SNMP, and so on features still work, as well. There are so many interdependencies in the typical modern network stack, that few things can be changed without having a broader effect on functionality.

4. What do non-mobile systems need to know about Mobile IPv6 in order to communicate with mobile systems?

   Non-mobile IPv6 systems don't need to know anything about Mobile IPv6 in order to communicate with mobile systems. The Mobile IPv6 features are defined so that a Mobile Node (MN) can communicate with any other IPv6-capable system and that latter system can remain unaware that Mobile IPv6 communications are even taking place. Of course, as stated in the chapter, if all systems involved in the communication at hand are able to use Mobile IPv6 features, then routing can be optimized to eliminate the Home Agent (HA) from the loop. Depending on how far from home an MN is traveling, this could be a far more efficient means of sending packets from one device to another.

Chapter 11: Knowing What Assets You Have

1. What are the two general classes of automated asset discovery tools?

    By my definition in this chapter, the two classes of automated asset discovery tools are called local discovery and enterprise discovery. Local-discovery tools provide detailed information about small networks, but do not scale well to enterprises. Enterprise-discovery tools are scalable to the largest of networks, but are limited in the data that they collect about each device on the network. The two classes of tools work best exchanging data between each other to improve the results of both.

2. What should you consider before creating your own asset discovery or management tools?

    As with all "build versus buy" decisions, you need to consider whether the costs of developing and maintaining your own tools are sufficiently offset by the gap you are filling by creating custom tools specific to your environment. You also have to consider the technical expertise required to build good discovery tools and the amount of complexity associated with developing enterprise-scale management tools.

3. In addition to making sure you have sufficient coverage of all of your logical networks when deploying automated inventory tools, what else do you need to consider when choosing where to deploy such tools?

    You need to make sure that the exact places from which you are performing those automated inventories, for example the IP addresses you're using, have the required access to allow you to traverse the parts of the network that you need to, and that they allow you to access your network's devices as required to get detailed information about those devices.

4. Other than from automated asset inventory tools, where else can you look for information with which to populate your asset management tools?

    Support systems, like IDSs and network flow analyzers, which sniff network traffic as part of their jobs and keep logs of the IP addresses they've seen, can be a useful source of asset information.

Chapter 12: Selecting an Enterprise Transition Strategy

1. Why does this chapter categorize your IPv6 transition as a chicken-and-egg problem?

Your IPv6 transition falls into the chicken-and-egg problem category because the transition's two primary participants, the MIS/IT department running the enterprise's network backbone and the various other departments running edge networks served by that backbone, are each waiting for the other to start deploying IPv6. Each side is waiting, because until the other side expresses a need or starts deploying IPv6 itself, there is little reason for the first side to do so.

2. What are the two types of IPv6 transition strategies and how are they different?

The two IPv6 transition strategies defined in this chapter are the backbone-first strategy and the edges-first strategy. The backbone-first strategy reflects the OMB mandate and emphasizes the transition of the network backbone first. The edges-first strategy is the opposite of the OMB mandate and emphasizes the transition of the edge networks served by the backbone first.

3. Which IPv6 transition strategy would you likely use in an organization that's clearly committed to IPv6 and has the staff and funding to deploy IPv6 at an enterprise scale right now?

You would likely choose the backbone-first transition strategy in this case, because that strategy requires a significant level of commitment from your enterprise. The strategy's end result, ubiquitous IPv6 connectivity throughout the enterprise, is an excellent motivator for the edge networks to start transition themselves.

4. Which IPv6 transition strategy is a better choice if you want to reap the rewards of the depth-first transition approach described in Chapter 8?

The edges-first transition strategy embraces the depth-first approach. Because there are many relatively small edge networks and only one large backbone, transition activities taking place in the edge networks are more likely to exercise your full transition process from start to finish sooner, and educate you as to where your transition plans need to be modified for the later transitions of other edge networks and the backbone.

5. Why can IPv6 be adopted fairly easily by newcomers to the technology even before it is made ubiquitous within an enterprise by the transition of the network backbone?

Although IPv6 is rarely available in its native form from every (or any) Ethernet jack that serves up network connectivity in an enterprise at present, tunneling of the IPv6 protocol through an IPv4-only backbone, especially using 6to4 addresses and encapsulation, is straightforward for those with a modicum of TCP/IP networking knowledge. The bar is set pretty low, for anyone with access to an Internet-routable IPv4 address, to get tunneled IPv6 connectivity and start playing with the technology. Playing with a technology and testing the portability of applications to it, for example, is one of the first steps in technology adoption.

Chapter 13: Using Pilot Programs to Facilitate Your IPv6 Transition

1. What is the purpose of a pilot project?

   Pilot projects are used to assess the applicability or viability of new assets, capabilities, or configurations to your enterprise. A pilot allows you to build something on a smaller scale than what the potential solution's eventual deployment would be, should it prove feasible. The smaller version is meant to take less time to build and require fewer resources, while still enabling you to determine whether what you are piloting can address the problems that you're trying to solve.

2. What is the value of an ad hoc pilot project?

   An ad hoc pilot is one that is not officially sanctioned by the enterprise. This allows the pilot team to run the project on the team's own terms, which is usually accomplished by the team working off hours or in their spare time to develop and run the pilot. Sometimes called a skunk-works operation, after the famous Lockheed Martin organization, an ad hoc pilot circumvents typical enterprise bureaucracy in order to tackle a challenging technical problem that is germane (and perhaps even critical) to the enterprise's success.

3. What must you (and those too whom you report) accept about a pilot that is far less acceptable in conventional projects?

   Everyone associated with a pilot project must realize that the pilot may fail to reach the goals set for it. This doesn't just include goals in terms of timely execution or staying within budget, for example. It also includes the fundamental goal for which the pilot was created. In other words, pilots are a form of research and one of the acceptable outcomes of a research endeavor is that it could fail.

Chapter 14: Understanding That Your Network Isn't New

1. What held back the adoption of multicast in IPv4? Why is multicast more likely to catch on in IPv6?

There are several possible reasons that multicast didn't catch on in IPv4, including complexity of configuration. One IPv4 feature that certainly doesn't promote multicast adoption is broadcast addresses. These IPv4 addresses allow the transmission of a packet of network-layer traffic to every host on a LAN. Broadcast addresses were eliminated in IPv6, leaving multicast the only way to send a packet to more than one device simultaneously.

2. Which IPv6 addressing scheme is good for hiding devices? Which schemes are not so good?

IPv6 addressing based on randomly generated interface IDs is the best scheme for hiding devices in a LAN. When augmented with periodic renumbering, preferably in an automated fashion, devices numbered in this manner are essentially impossible to find by anyone not able to sniff the LAN, for example worms launched from afar. Unsatisfactory addressing schemes for hiding devices include static numbering, of course, and to a lesser extent EUI-64. See Chapter 7 for more information on all of these addressing schemes. Also note that hiding in the address space does little to prevent attacks from worms and such that use application-layer data (like address books) to propagate.

3. What common network management functions still need to be performed on your post-transition network?

There are many network management functions that are not related to the type of network or the protocols in use and, therefore, must be performed on all networks. Some such functions listed in this chapter include the backing up of data and configuration information, vulnerability analysis and patching, software and hardware upgrades, expansion planning, and the deployment of new capabilities.

Chapter 15: Managing IPv4 and IPv6 on the Same Network

1. What property that has been discussed elsewhere in this book allows heterogeneous protocols to exist in the same network?

Though not strictly required for heterogeneous protocols to exist on the same wire, the concept of the network stack facilitates separating protocols into pairs with a sender in one stack being associated with a receiver in another stack at the same layer.

2. When should you strive to think of your network as a single entity and when should you look at it as separate IPv6-capable and IPv4-only entities?

This is kind of a trick question, because the answer is that it depends. This chapter recommends managing your network's IPv6 and IPv4 addresses and ISP connectivity together, while keeping the actual traffic separated partly for host-security concerns. Your answers in practice may differ here, though I don't think you'll ever go as far as to have two distinct management organizations with responsibilities divided up along IP protocol version lines. Neither will you unify the management of the IPv6 nor IPv4 parts of your network down to the level that many have unified their management of hardware where routers, workstations, laptops, PDAs, and so on are in a single asset inventory system and every asset is essentially equal in the inventory's eyes.

3. What IPv6 traffic should you seriously consider being allowed throughout as much of your network as possible? Hint: There is no IPv4 equivalent.

    The ICMP Packet Too Big message, which is the foundation of Path MTU discovery, must be allowed to flow through your network for you to use your network bandwidth the most efficiently.

Chapter 16: Maintaining Eternal Vigilance

1. If you can't control access to a particular set of assets or LAN, what should you strive to do, at a minimum?

    If you can't control access to something, then you should at least try to log the access that takes place. This applies to individual assets, sets of assets, LANs, or any other objects that are not meant to be available to everyone equally and without restriction. Such logs can help you detect intrusions in your systems and may also help in establishing a case for instituting access controls where they don't exist now.

2. Why should you review your network configurations, especially your IPv6 configurations, regularly?

    IPv6 is still somewhat of an unknown, especially in operational environments. When security is important, unknown issues are often addressed conservatively, which can lead to overkill in deploying security technologies, policies, and procedures. As you get more comfortable with your IPv6 network, you may be able to relax controls that were too strict initially. Conversely, because IPv6 is so new, there will likely be a steady flow of security advisories about it for a while. You should check your networks for compliance with those advisories more frequently.

Index